THE PROMISE OF THE SUNFLOWERS

THE PROMISE OF THE SUNFLOWERS

The Life of an
Innocent and adventurous boy
Growing up in
WWII Europe

Franz Elmer's
Life story given to and written by

DIANE GRAY

ISBN-10: 1511450665
ISBN-13: 9781511450669
Library of Congress Control Number: 2015904809
CreateSpace Independent Publishing Platform
North Charleston, South Carolina

TABLE OF CONTENTS

I dedicate this book to my Mother and all the Mothers whose husbands had to go to war and leave them to raise and provide for their children under unimaginable circumstances (death, destruction and starvation). After seventy years it still brings tears to my eyes just to think of all that my Mother went through to bring my sister and me to a safer place and a good life.

Franz Elmer

LIST OF PEOPLE

MOTHER'S SIDE
Nikolaus Hoger, 9/21/1878, Stanišić, Yugoslavia
Theresia Eberhard Hoger, 04/05/1892, Stanišić.
Anna Hoger Rauh, circa 1903, Stanišić.
Elisabeth Hoger Elmer, 8/14/1913, Stanišić
Adam Hoger, 11/17/1919, Stanišić.

FATHER'S SIDE
Stefan Elmer, DOB unknown
Paternal Grandmother, unknown
Stefan Elmer, 08/07/1907, Sombor, Yugoslavia
Manci Elmer married Peter Merkel, children Jani and Dori Merkel

FRANZ' IMMEDIATE FAMILY
Father Stefan Elmer, 08/07/1907, Sombor, Yugoslavia
Mother Elisabeth Hoger Elmer, 8/14/1913, Stanišić
Franz Elmer 8/31/1932, Sombor,
Catharina (Kati) Elmer Eisenreich 9/05/1938, Sombor

SOMBOR, YUGOSLAVIA COMPANIONS
Jani Merkel, cousin (a little older, shorter)
Various friends and relatives
Yellow Nanny – former landlord (Mrs. Jelloneni)

STANIŠIĆ, YUGOSLAVIA COMPANIONS
Anton Haut – ornery friend, next door
Adam Sujer, 4 or 5 houses down, across the street
Stefan Baier, down the street, lived with grandparents
Tony Baumgartner, last house on the street, a few houses past
Anton Haut

FRANZ' ESCAPE GROUP
Franz, his mother, Elisabeth, and sister, Kati.
Anton (Tony) Baumgartner, sister Berbl, Aunt Lissi,
Lissi's mother, Eva.
Sep – their Yugoslavian guide to escape
from Yugoslavia to Hungary,
woman Sep brought along.
Hans, a German POW from Pfaffenhofen,
joined them in Hungary.

INTRODUCTION

THIS BOOK IS not a political commentary, but is an account of one remarkable and resourceful boy and his family surviving WWII in Europe. This is a picture of what happened to the farmers, shopkeepers and families as they battled the lack of many things due to economy and war. They knew little of Hitler and nothing about sufferings and deaths of the Jews (and other "undesirables") in concentration camps.

I first met Franz Elmer in the 1980s when he worked for us in our machine shop for a few years. An amazingly creative and accurate Tool and Die maker, he was tall and thin, with memorable deep dimples. He touched us with his gentleness and kindness.

I had no idea how writing this would influence my life. I came to love Franz's family – people I never met. I chose to write it in third person, from Franz' point of view. All mistakes are mine alone.

Thank you, Crossroads Writers, especially Carolyn Steele and Steve Amos! I discovered this group after I was well into my writing and wish I'd found them earlier!

I had much to learn of WWII! Along the way, I studied PTSD, was amazed at how many concentration camps and work camps there were. Very little of my research shows up directly. I focused on one special young boy/man and his journey to survival.

Diane Gray

PART ONE

CHILDHOOD OF PREPARATION

1

Late July, 1938 – Franz turns six years old on August 31st
Stanišić, Yugoslavia

WITH DEEP CONCENTRATION, Franz sawed down another stalk
with his pocketknife and laid it down to form more flooring. Now he had enough room to lay down with Opa's sheep dog,
August. If someone else came in, they could sit up. His dimples
deepened as he looked around. He'd made a good Sunflower
Hideout in Oma's flower garden. It felt warm and safe, and the
word 'war' would never be spoken here.

Franz leaned back and watched the waving of the sunflowers
overhead. August's tail wagged swiftly as he sat close beside him.

"Franz! Where are you?" Uncle Adam's voice called from the
house.

"I'm here! Come inside my hidden room," he shouted.

After some rustling of stalks, Adam pushed his way into view.
"Well, this is a fine place you've made." He folded his long, slim
legs and sat beside Franz.

"Are you excited about the harvest tomorrow? Do you know
what's going to happen?"

"Yes!" Franz pulled a fallen flower closer to their faces, "I've
never been here at harvest before. I'll bet it's fun. Last time I
came Opa showed me the black part of the head needed to
be brown and dry looking, like this. He said he plants acres of

sunflowers north of here to sell the seeds. A lot of neighbors will come tomorrow to harvest them. Opa sells them to the mill and somehow they become cooking oil." He looked up at Uncle Adam and grinned.

"You have been listening to Opa! I enjoyed it when I was your age," Adam said. "We always have a big party when the men get together for any harvest and the women cook and talk. If you manage to stay awake, you'll hear some good stories."

August yipped for attention, making Franz and Uncle Adam laugh.

"The reason I called for you is because everyone has work for you. It's getting busy out there."

Franz helped feed the chickens, geese, hogs, and cow. Then he gathered eggs and took them to the kitchen, where Mama and Oma worked on a list of things to do to prepare for the harvest.

"When will Vati be here, Mama?"

Mama's brown eyes twinkled. "Sometime this morning. Then day after tomorrow you and I will return to Sombor with him. Are you about ready to go back home?"

"No!"

His mother laughed. "I think Opa would be glad to keep you to help around here, but your father misses us."

"Don't limit this to Opa." Oma tapped her pencil on the table. "I'd have no trouble keeping you busy." Sometimes Oma's dark eyes and thin lips made her serious face look stern, but Franz heard only love in her voice.

Mama gently patted her rounded belly. "This baby girl or boy wants to be born in Sombor and I miss my husband."

She stood up, put her hands on the small of her back and stretched. "I think I need to move around a bit. Franz, come outside and we'll sweep the sidewalk and courtyard." She brushed Franz's light brown hair off his forehead and planted a kiss there.

She wandered outside with a broom and began to sweep the yellow brick sidewalk along the dirt street.

"It's so far I can't see where it stops." Franz stood in the middle of the street and looked east and west. "When can I walk to the end of it by myself?"

"Not today," she listened as she swept, but stopped and leaned on the broom handle. "What do you see?"

Franz looked around and shrugged his shoulders. "Tall walls all the way," he said in a singsong voice. "And every house has a big gate for wagons and a little one for people." Franz thought a moment. "But the wall stops to show the end of each house and then the wall starts again!" His mother laughed at the description.

"When I was a little girl growing up here I thought the end of the houses were faces."

Franz glanced from house to house at a pattern. He laughed. "They're watching us! The windows look like eyes!"

His mother chuckled and finished sweeping. She opened the small gate to return to the yard. Franz liked its familiar thunk as it closed.

A few minutes later, Franz turned at the sound of squeaking as the double gates swung open. Familiar horses pulled the wagon inside the yard. With a big smile on his face, Franz' father hopped down for hugs of welcome.

"I'm so glad you're here today, Stefan!" Mama said as they clasped hands.

"Sombor's only home with you both there. Peter and Manci say Jani's not the same without you," he chucked Franz's chin. "He hasn't been in as much mischief without his cousin's help!"

Picking up her broom again, Mama stepped back and waved them off with a smile, "Go, follow your son," she said, "he's been very eager to show you—everything! Let him help put the wagon in the back and the horses in their pasture."

The afternoon passed swiftly, and after the evening meal was finished and dishes washed and put away, the adults sat around the dining table, each sipping from a glass of wine. Franz got out one of his favorite things, grandfather's big book of the world, and stretched on the floor. Knowing exactly where to find it, he turned to the map of America and held it up to his grandfather. "Opa, tell us about when you went to America."

Opa's deep-set eyes twinkled. "You sure you want to hear it again? Elisabeth, perhaps your son will be an adventurous one like your father, eh?" With a forefinger, he stroked his neat, brown mustache. "Yes, I did—two times. The first time I was seventeen years old, in 1895." Seeing he had everyone's rapt attention, he continued. "With the help of an agent recruiting workers, I took a two-day train trip to North Germany, caught a ship from Hamburg, and seven miserable weeks later reached America. What an adventure! We came in through Ellis Island, in New York harbor. Franz, look at the picture in the book." He waited while Franz turned to the familiar page and studied it.

"I went to Chicago, worked fourteen to sixteen hours a day building railroad cars and lived in a boarding house run by German people and made friends. Letters from family helped me when homesickness got too much. I stayed the full five years I'd agreed to, because I had such a hunger for land of my own."

Franz sat up now, crossed his legs and leaned forward. "You went another time!"

"Several years later we wanted more farm land for crops, so even though it meant leaving my first wife and our baby, your Aunt Anna, several years later I went to St. Louis and worked on the Mississippi River. We cut chunks of ice, loaded them on the wagon and delivered ice blocks to homes."

"Did you see any Indians?" Franz asked.

Opa chuckled and shook his head. "America is full of people from many countries. I met Germans, Swedes, Irish, English—but no Indians."

"What about your lost wallet?" Franz's dimples deepened with anticipation, since he'd heard part of the story before.

"Oh, you want me to tell on myself again, do you?" He settled back in his chair, his long legs crossed at the ankle. "I went from St. Louis to New York, a very big city, to catch the ship back to Europe. A few weeks earlier I learned my wife had died and I was sure eager to get home to my little Anna. I carried all the money I'd earned those five years, bought the ticket and walked around the corner."

"After so much time in America I finally held my passage home. I set my wallet on a window sill while I checked the date and time of departure and the spelling of my name. Satisfied, I left and whistled as I strolled down the street. Had I forgotten something? I patted my pocket to feel my wallet. It was gone! I retraced my steps, but saw an empty window sill."

He shook his head, took a sip of wine and continued. "I frantically asked people around the area, but no one knew anything. I stood there trying to think what to do and an older gentleman came up to me and pointed out a ruddy-faced man standing in another ticket line. He told me he was the thief."

"Quietly, I moved closer to the line and asked the man politely if he had the wallet. He said no, but he looked very nervous and wouldn't look me in the eye. And I knew. I'm pretty big, and I just grabbed the guy by the front of his shirt, picked him up and shoved him against the wall and asked again if he had my wallet. I guess I scared him enough because he said yes and reached into his shirt and gave it back to me. Then he ran away."

The clock chimed just then. "So, enough stories for one night." He stood up and yawned. "Tomorrow is a busy day, so we'd all better get some sleep."

Everyone woke early in anticipation of the activities of the day. Breakfast finished, mother and grandmother began preparations for the neighbors who would drift in for an afternoon meal.

Daily chores completed, Franz and his father hopped in the wagon with other workers to the large field a couple of miles out of town. The fields were beautiful with the bright yellows and browns and greens.

"Notice how the flowers bow over the rows instead of each other?" Uncle Adam said as he walked up to Franz. "We plant the rows north to south so it's easier to cut off the heads as we walk down the path. One of your jobs is to run the baskets back to the wagon when they get filled and return for more."

Franz noticed the men didn't need instructions, but quickly whacked off the flowers from their stems, tossed them into various containers, and reached for another head. All morning, he gathered dropped blossoms and ran errands. As the hours passed, the field lost its beauty and the wagon filled with an ungainly pile.

He grew tired and thirsty, despite frequent drinks of water. Finally, it was time to leave for home and he hopped on the wagon with Vati.

As the men came back to finish the harvest and celebrate, Franz joined them when they headed to the well and brought up buckets of water to wash hands and splash over their faces, necks and arms. The ladle passed from one man to another as they drank cool, clean water.

Franz dashed along black and white square tiles running the full length of the porch, where tables were set up to display the afternoon meal. The courtyard on his left was busy with returning workers. On his right, five doors opened to the house—the living room (which peeked between walled fencing to the street), kitchen/dining room, pantry and cellar along with an unused kitchen at the far end of the house. This became Franz' bedroom when they visited and where Mama stood with her arms loaded.

"Mama! Mama!"

She set a stack of plates on the table and turned to see Franz. His hands had been scrubbed and his face somewhat cleaned, but everything else carried evidence of the day's adventures. "Phew! I smell dirt, hogs, cattle" she sniffed robustly, "and wet dog!" Franz laughed with delight.

"This morning I showed Vati the new piglets and calves! Then we helped with the harvest and I get to help knock out seeds tonight!"

His father joined them and shared a smile with Mama.

"Come on," Franz motioned to Vati, "let's check out the food!"

They turned and walked along the table and lifted one lid after another to enjoy sights and aromas of corned beef with cabbage, two different Schnitzels, several soups—one that included *Jaegerschnitzel*, pickled carrots, potato salads and Franz's favorite dumplings. A smaller table was filled with desserts. "I'll eat everything but pickled carrots," he said with a wrinkled nose.

"You can have everything else. I think I'll just go the Black Forest Cherry Cake," Vati said with a wink.

Hungry workers formed a line, grabbed a plate and helped themselves to food. Conversation dwindled as they ate. After a leisurely meal, women cleaned away the dishes while men and boys began threshing. Sunflower heads were held up and hit with a stick until all the seeds fell out onto the tarp. Thwak! Thwak! Each man found his own rhythm to hit and shake seeds and all of their motions together made a sort of music. The seedless heads were tossed aside and another dry flower briskly picked up.

Franz sat by his father as he worked. "Why aren't my seeds coming out?"

"I think you hit them more on the side, and it works better to hit them on the back." His father showed him how. With a satisfied smile, Franz successfully tried it again.

Discussion about crops, markets and livestock continued, and wine passed around. Voices of the men and the rhythmic sound of their work began to blend into a pleasant hum. Franz found it difficult to remain awake. He stopped for a time and rested against his father's side.

Old songs and new were sung by various men until they all joined in. As Franz's eyes closed, he smiled in deep contentment.

"I think you've forgotten Germany's economy before Hitler!" Franz woke up with a start when he heard Herr Peitz's loud, angry voice. "I'm not the only one who remembers the turnip winter, when food itself was scarce. While the entire world struggled with the depression, Hitler eliminated unemployment and put people back to work building roads and bridges and government buildings." His face turned deep red as he spoke loudly. "Hitler took control and fixed things. He's what Germany needs."

"I agree it's better economically," Herr Kalanj said slowly, his palms up and facing Herr Peitz. "I'm not sure taking the Rhineland and Sudenland are justified. But this movement is growing. For example— *Anschluss*? Granted, Austria cheered when annexed. I guess my true fear is about what's next."

Franz looked around at the circle of men. Some nodded their heads, some shook them. Most of them looked at the ground as they listened.

"Good Germans support the mother country! We needed to reoccupy the Rhineland, after all—it belonged to Germany before the Great War, and we were humiliated to lose it." Herr Peitz shouted and shook his finger in Herr Kalanj's direction. "As for the Sudenland—three million Germans live there; speak German, live as Germans. It's past time they be taken."

"I'm a proud German and challenge anyone to say other-wise." Herr Kalanj's voice rose to match his opponent, "I won't apologize for expecting my Fatherland to uphold high standards. Perhaps *Lebensraum* is needed as Germany grows and needs land to expand so I won't argue about those two areas even though the Sudenland was a part of Czechoslovakia.

"But is it in Germany's best interest to let Hitler have unlim-ited power?" Herr Kalanj appealed to the larger group. "I sus-pect Dur Fuher is like a dog that snuck into the coop, killed his first chickens and received rewards from doing so. But can he be stopped? Who's next? Poland? France?" He looked around again, "Afghanistan?"

Franz understood all too well what happened to a dog that killed chickens. But he didn't understand any of this.

"You're either blind or stupid—he just wants to make Germany strong and to build a secure and prosperous country!" Herr Peitz stood, and planted his feet apart, his hands fisted.

"You can't really believe that's all he wants?" Herr Kalanj's eyebrows pulled together, his words shouted precisely. "Who or what can limit his desires and ambitions? *Kristallnacht* couldn't have happened without Hitler's orders. How can you justify attacks and damage of this magnitude? It just spreads fear to some and power to others within Germany. And it ultimately could lead to destroying the country from within."

Men squirmed in uncomfortable silence.

"We weren't there for *Kristallnacht*, but from all reports, I agree it was bad. The Nazis overreacted when that Jewish teenager killed Ernst Von Rath." His voice lowered, some of the anger left.

"Overreact! That's what you call the Nazis' slaughter of Jews, their store windows destroyed, synagogues burned!" Herr Kalanj shouted back as he stepped closer to Herr Peitz.

"Sit down, both of you." Opa's deep voice ordered. "We're neighbors. Can we have a discussion and not come to physical blows over this?" Both Herr Peitz and Herr Kalanj sat back and nodded, but they didn't look happy.

Herr Terzin, one of the older men, raised his hand. "Since the Jewish situation has been brought up, I'll tell you another thing I find worrisome. I got a letter from my nephew, Helmut. He's a priest in Berlin. He wrote the kindergarten children now recite:

'Fold your hands, bow your head
And think of Adolf Hitler,
Who gives us work and gives us bread
And takes away all our troubles.'

"Think about those words, what they really say." He looked at his friends, and gave them a moment before he continued, "Helmut is concerned for all of us if the church is replaced by Hitler. The possibility is terrifying. Hitler's against Jews now. Will Christians be next?" Smaller discussions erupted amongst them.

Franz squirmed as the men spoke. It was nothing new to hear voices shout over differences of opinions, but this anger frightened him.

With relief, he saw Opa stand up.

He stretched his cramped muscles as he stood. "Gentlemen, it's late. Don't forget we're Yugoslavian Germans and friends here. These things are important, and alarming, but we can't solve anything tonight." He gestured to the small mountain of seeds. "Thank you all for your help. The only chore left is to scoop them into burlap bags and we're done." After the bags were full and thrown into two wagons, the men sat and smoked and finished the wine. Discussion returned to local matters, of farming and health. Finally, their neighbors left.

Since His father would take them home very early in the morning, Oma and Opa said their good-byes. The family got ready for bed without speaking.

Franz felt a hand on his shoulder. He opened his eyes but saw mostly darkness. His mother whispered "Time to get up, in five minutes we leave for home." He listened to Vati hitch the horses to the wagon, put his clothes on and crawled up into the wagon and sat between Mama and Vati. The lighter sky on the horizon announced the rising sun.

Oma came out, dressed in her nightgown and robe. She handed up a paper bag loaded with food. Franz smiled as he scooted it between his feet. "Oma always thinks we'll starve before we get home," he whispered to Mama as the wagon moved through the gate.

"I'm so glad we came for the harvest," Mama said. "It's always been my favorite time of the year. When I grew up here, I remember winters so bitter cold with ice on the ground for weeks, people got sick and the days were long. Then cheerful sunflowers pushed their way up to stand tall, strong and beautiful. We'd forget about the harsh winter." She laughed gently and looked at the fresh hay in the back of the wagon. "Franz, you might as well rest on the way home because Jani is sure to come over early."

Vati clicked the reins as Franz hopped over the seat. They rode in silence while Franz wondered if his dog, Max, had missed him. He had lots to tell his cousin, Jani. He wiggled to get more comfortable in the hay.

"My life has always been about family and work," he heard Vati say later, "I've ignored Yugoslavia's battles between the Partisans and Chetniks because I think it'll run its course.

"This Hitler situation worries me. He's suddenly come out of nowhere and become too powerful."

Franz listened, but neither of his parents said any more.

2

November 1938 to early 1940 – six and seven years old.
Sombor, Yugoslavia

"MAMA! MAMA!" FRANZ pointed to the other side of the street. "It's Yellow Nanny!" They crossed the street to greet their former landlady, a short, stocky Yugoslav.

"Hello, Mrs. Jelloneni," Mama said in Yugoslavian. "I'm so glad to see you." With smiles the women hugged. "How are you doing?"

"Good, but I miss this boy since you don't live in my rent house now," Mrs. Jelloneni replied as she smiled at Franz. "I'm glad I'm still your 'Yellow Nanny.'" She turned back to Franz' mother, "Actually, I've just left a cousin who lives nearby. I seem to keep busy all the time. Well, how is your new baby?" she leaned forward and pulled the blanket down for a peek.

"This is our little Catharina, Kati for short. We're on our way to our butcher shop. I've rested enough and time to get back to work. It's too much for Stefan to work in back with the meat and dealing with customers at the same time. Besides, he's ready to show off his daughter."

Mrs. Jelloneni smiled at Franz. "What do you think of this fine baby sister?"

"Well, Mama says she is really pretty and when she gets older, she'll look better."

With a laugh that shook her ample body, Mrs. Jelloneni patted Franz on his cheek. "I see you're not too shy now to talk! Remember when you used to get groceries with me? And who prompted you to announce you were Deutsch in the German shops and Yugoslav or Hungarian in their own stores?"

"You did!" he giggled. "I liked to go with you. They gave me candy or a piece of sausage!" He stood tall, put his hand to his chest and in his loudest voice announced, "Icb bin Deutsch!" They smiled in shared pleasure as he reenacted their memory.

"Remember how concerned I was because he wouldn't talk in front of people?" Mama chuckled and shook her head. "I even took him to the doctor to see if there was something wrong. I happened to mention that at home, Franz could speak our native German, and Yugoslavian, since we live here, surrounded by the language. Many of our customers are Yugoslavian. I grew up in Stanisic, near the Hungarian border and Franz is around that a lot, also. After examining him, the doctor said 'I think he's just not sure which language to use, and when he uses a mixture no one can understand him unless they speak all three languages. Watch and see if I'm not right.' I couldn't believe I'd paid a doctor to figure that out!"

"We had fun, didn't we?" Mrs. Jelloneni leaned closer to Franz. "How do you like living in this neighborhood?"

"It's nice to be close to cousins, especially Jani. And it's a short walk to school."

Mrs. Jelloneni nodded her head, "I'm glad the move worked out you."

"How is your family?" Franz' mother asked.

"My son still travels a lot, but he rarely brings special goodies when he returns," she winked at Franz. "Mirko misses you and your enjoyment of fine sweets."

"He always brought the best candy!" Franz replied.

She hesitated a moment then turned back to his mother. "Mirko learns many things as he travels. Some is good news, some is not. Elisabeth, do you know what is happening in Germany? We hear there's a compulsory two-year military service there. Are they building up to expand the war?"

"I don't know," Mama replied. Though citizens of Yugoslavia, the ethnic Germans were a close-knit community, and they still retained strong loyalty to Germany. "We hear young men take more pride in Germany now than they have since the Great War. Also, they have work and can earn a living. Our men discuss politics, but I don't think they really know what's happening. Stefan says Russia may be a problem to all Europe and there is talk of war everywhere. But we probably don't know any more than you do. What does Mirko say?"

"Oh, that son of mine may be an important man in the Communist Party, but he doesn't tell his mother anything."

Franz felt his mother's gaze. He fidgeted when talk turned to war, and wanted to continue their walk. "I guess we'd better go," she said and the women agreed to see each other more and parted. Franz led the way to Vati's shop.

Many customers, who had become friends, came into the shop. It surprised Franz how much people fussed over Kati. His parents smiled with pride. Franz looked more closely. Truly, he loved his baby sister, but all she did was sleep and eat and cry.

Late that night Franz crawled out of bed to go the outhouse. The brightness of the moon made it easy for him to follow the pathway. He walked past his parents seated on the porch swing and overheard his mother say "After we left Mrs. Jelloneni, I couldn't quite stop wondering about it. What do you think?"

Franz heard soft squeaks as his father pushed the porch swing slightly. "I don't know what's going to happen. If it comes to war against Communists, I think we'll have to support the Chetnik's resistance. But the bigger problem might be Jews being punished just for being Jews. They're not allowed to travel, go to school or sell to non-Jews."

Franz hurried to the outhouse and on his way back listened again to the soft, deep voice of his father. "We're Yugoslavian Catholics of German decent. Where does that put us?"

Franz watched his mother rest her head on Vati's shoulder. "I hope all this is just gossip and greatly exaggerated." She sounded hopeful but sad at the same time.

Franz continued to his room, lay down, and pulled up a blanket. His parents sounded worried now. Sometime later he fell into an uneasy sleep.

After school the next day, Franz and Jani kicked their soccer ball as they zigzagged up the street. Herr Berger's house sat on a large corner lot protected by a beautiful yellow wall facing each street. "Augg! You got me!" yelled Jani as he kicked the ball and shot it toward Franz. Over the wall it went. Both boys stood in shocked silence a moment, then looked at each other. "We're in trouble now." Jani said.

Franz nodded. "He hates kids. What'll we do?"

"No way we can get over the wall." Jani stated.

"We have to get it back." Franz sighed. "Let's go knock on the door and ask."

So both boys mustered up their courage, walked through the gate up to the house and knocked.

Herr Berger opened the door with a fierce frown on his face. "Yes?" he snapped.

"I'm sorry, sir, but our soccer ball is over your fence. Could we please have it back?" Jani asked.

"Humpf," he muttered, "You need to keep your things where they belong. You'll learn by losing your ball." He shook his index finger in the boys' faces. "Next time be more careful!" With a grunt, he slammed the door.

Not surprised, the boys slowly trudged home.

"It's still early. Maybe we earn some money for another ball. Want to collect some old steel, or search for chicken eggs in culverts on the streets?" Franz suggested. "Or get leeches?"

"Let's collect leeches, it's faster," Jani said. They'd earned money doing this before. The pharmacies in town used leeches to help sick people. They could sell any leeches they found.

With the solution to their problem of a lost soccer ball, they ran home for a glass jar and small box of salt. They went to their favorite damp culvert and bent over as they entered and let their eyes adjust to the dim light. Soon they could readily see the 'worms' with suckers on each end. The boys plucked various shades of brown and black leeches off the sides and floor of the culvert, and dropped them into the container.

"The jar's full!" Franz announced a half hour later. Out in the sunlight the boys could see the leeches attached to their arms, legs and some on their clothes. "Time for the leech dance!"

Jumping and flapping their arms, they tried to shake them off, with little success. Instead of plucking them off and leaving sores, they sprinkled a bit of salt on the area so the leeches would fall.

"Wouldn't you know it, we've got extra leeches and no girls to tease," Franz said with disappointment.

"Let's go sell them now while they're fresh," Jani said. "Since I'm older I'll keep the money at my house."

"As long as we get a new ball, I don't care." They hurried off to the pharmacy before it closed and made their sale.

During supper, Franz told about Herr Berger and the commandeered ball, "He's just plain old mean!"

Vati put his fork down and leaned toward his son. "You know how Herr Berger is. What else would you expect after kicking the ball into his yard?"

"Nothing, I guess," Franz mumbled. "But we didn't mean to!"

"What will you do now? Besides complain?" he prompted with a teasing glint in his eyes.

"We'll have to buy a new ball. Jani and I already filled a big jar full of leeches and sold enough to pay for most of it," Franz explained. "But he could have let us get our ball back," he persisted. His parents changed the subject and discussed the day ahead. Franz thought it looked like rain, so perhaps he and Jani could fill another jar tomorrow.

The next day after school they returned to hunt leeches, but found few. Resentment grew as they passed Herr Berger's house.

"Wow! Thanks to last night's rain, we have these wonderful mud puddles," Jani stopped and knelt by the side of the road. They both grinned with mischief.

"It would be a shame to waste them, wouldn't it?" Franz looked up the street one way, then the other. "I don't see anyone, do you?

"We need to keep our clothes clean," they each grabbed two muddy handfuls.

"I think a wavy design would look good here. What do you think?" Franz walked over to the nearest part of the wall. Again, they looked around and saw no one.

"This looks beautiful, doesn't it?" Jani said while he smeared on a glob and raked his fingers through over it to spread uneven lines on the surface. They made mostly designs, but also drew a dog and a house.

"We'd better go before someone comes." They wiped their hands on a nearby bush and skipped home.

As they strolled close to Jani's home, they had to pass their grandmother's house next door.

"Oh, no!" Franz said when they saw Oma Elmer with a whip in her hand. The fun was over and fear moved into their hearts. Franz recognized her 'mean' look and glanced at Jani, who looked as scared as he felt.

"You boys know better than to vandalize a neighbor's yard," she screamed, her cold, blue eyes narrowed in anger, then her short, stout legs narrowed the distance, and she grabbed the nearest boy, which happened to be Jani.

Franz ran to the back of the yard, jumped the fence and went home. He said nothing to his mother.

He looked up as the door opened and saw Vati. He was not smiling. "Did you tell your mother what you and Jani did on the way home from school?"

His sense of safety disappeared. Mama usually doled out punishments, and he knew what to expect. Both parents looked at him until he confessed.

"Uncle Peter told me about it and we've agreed our sons will clean Herr Berger's wall until no traces of mud remain. And that means cleaner than it was before." Vati shook his head and spoke to Mama, "It really looks bad."

Franz and Jani spent Sunday afternoon with buckets of water and brushes and rags and cleaned the fence to the satisfaction of their fathers and Herr Berger, who stood and watched.

"How did Grandmother find out about it? Who saw us?" Jani whispered.

"Maybe a bird flew over and told her?"

———

The next week, Franz caught up with Jani, Alfons and Claus on the walk to school. A first year student, he found it interesting to listen to the third year boys as they traveled a half mile to school.

"China is way east," Jani said with authority. "We'll find it on the map when we get to school. Japan is an island even farther east. It would be stupid for little Japan to attack big China!"

"But it's what the newspaper said. I read it twice," Claus replied.

"What difference does it make?" Alfons asked. "We don't live in either place."

"You guys are always talking about wars," Franz complained.

"You're just too little to understand," Alfons said. "I think it would be exciting to be in the army. I'd like to march in a uniform and shoot at enemies. I'll bet I'd be good at it."

He pulled out his finger, lifted it and aimed it at some people in the distance. "Pow! Pow!" Then he aimed at Jani. "Let's play war later."

"We all know I always win," Jani taunted cheerfully. "And Franz will be on my side because he's fast."

They arrived at school so war was put off for another time.

Later that day, Franz looked at the clock. Two more hours of class. Why couldn't he sit near a friend so they could both enjoy class more? Herr Schmidt gave homework to read both Yugoslav and German stories. He liked this class, but grew restless.

At last, eight hours of school came to a close. A short game of war erupted before he arrived home, changed his clothes and sat at the table doing his homework while Mama ironed. Today he read out loud and when he made a mistake, Mama gently slapped him on the neck so he would look back and read it correctly.

After the noon meal on Saturday he and Jani went to the park. In its center stood an ornate pavilion and outdoor cafe with white chairs and tables. In the evenings waiters dressed in formal tuxedos and a live band played requested songs. But during the daytime families came and visited with friends. It was much more informal.

Leaves crunched as he and Jani raced beneath the tall trees. A gentle breeze and warm sun brought many people out today. The boys explored walkways looking for something to do. As they dashed past a trash container, Jani spied a partially opened can. It intrigued Franz. Jani started to put it back.

"What can we do with it?" The lid had not been opened all the way and could be pried up. Looking around for an idea, Franz checked his pockets and found a nail and a long piece of twine.

It took but a moment for Jani to find a rock and two taps to make a nice hole on the top edge of the lid. "Let's tie this string to the hole." he suggested.

Jani went to some bushes and scooped some handfuls of dirt to partly fill the can. Then, the boys thought it needed to have water and found plenty at a nearby fountain. Now what?

Franz spied a small, stout tree with a strong horizontal limb leaned over a path and since Franz was the best climber of trees, Jani gave him the can with the lid pressed down. The twine measured about seven or eight feet long and soon Franz found the perfect place. He wedged the can upside-down between some branches. He draped the twine through leaves so it hung down about five feet from the ground.

The boys went to a nearby bench and watched for the play they hoped would happen. Parents followed as one boy and two girls walked along. The boy saw the mysterious twine. With a curious tug, he pulled on it. Suddenly the lid opened and mud plopped on the boy, and his sisters as well. Their eyes blinked and mouths opened to gasp air, until the girls began to squeal. Everyone looked at them to see what happened. The littlest girl tried to get the mud off her cheek, but just smeared it. Then she stared at her dirty hand. Embarrassed, the parents scolded the mud-covered children as people all around clucked their tongues or smiled. Franz and Jani turned their heads away as they giggled.

"That boy sure looked surprised!" Jani said.

"And the girls, too! We'll have to do that again!" Franz' dimples deepened. In excess of energy they shadow boxed as they left the park.

"What are you doing tomorrow?" Jani asked.

"I'm going to earn some spending money by setting bowling pins."

The next day he finished setting the last pins, got paid, and walked around the carnival which would be in town for a few days. He marveled at everything and didn't want to spend money without thinking about it first. He liked to watch people play games at different booths.

A stranger walked up and talked to him about the nearby bean bag booth. "Think you could win?" he asked. He wasn't one of Franz's uncles but looked a lot like them.

"Maybe, but if I spend my money, it will be for something I can eat." Franz answered.

"You look like you could use some candy from the table over there," the man said. "If I buy a bag, will you share it with me?"

Franz, used to a friendly community, walked around with him and ate candy.

"Well, I'm kind of tired of walking," the man said. "I think I'll go to see a movie. Do you want to go?"

It sounded like fun. "Thank you. I don't see picture shows much." After buying the tickets and sodas they sat down and enjoyed the refreshments. Soon the lights dimmed and the movie started.

The action captured Franz's attention until he felt a hand move around on his lap. The hair on the back of his neck stood up, but he froze as he struggled to understand. It happened again. This time he leaped from his seat, dashed from the theater and raced all the way home.

He thought about telling someone, but whom? Mama or Vati would ask a lot of questions. Jani might think it was funny or he might think it was his own fault. He didn't know what he'd done wrong, but felt ashamed and embarrassed. One busy day moved into another and he pushed his first real secret into the back of his mind, where secrets belonged.

"See the beautiful leaves, Kati?" Franz held up a colorful maple tree leaf and handed it to one-year-old Kati. Her tiny hand cheerfully squeezed the prize. "Come on, walk with me." He offered his finger for Kati to hold. She walked unsteadily on the rough ground; her slightly curly, blond hair caught the sunshine. She had dark lashed blue eyes but didn't have deep dimples like Franz'.

Vati's pigeons circled above the house. "If I could fly, I'd go around and around." He squatted down and pointed up to the pigeon. "Can you say 'pigeon'?"

She laughed and clapped her hands.

He moved away from Katie and held one arm horizontal to provide a perch. When a pigeon fluttered close to him, Franz turned his head from the rapid wind of the wings until he felt the gray-black claws rest on his arm. He looked over to Kati to be sure she wasn't frightened. She didn't like the birds, but she must have been far enough away because she laughed. After putting the bird on a nearby fence, he studied the sky again and saw more birds circled now. His favorites were the short-faced Tumbling Pigeons. Their instinct to wildly tumble from the sky as if shot never ceased to fascinate him and he loved to see them trained to do it for show.

"Hello!" Father came around the house to the back yard. He picked up Katie and held her high in the air and brought her down quickly many times, to the sound of her joyous belly laugh. After a few minutes of play, they took Kati inside to Mama.

Franz and his father went to the attic to care for the twenty or so pigeons. Most were hens, a few juveniles and one cock. About ten feet back from the gable, Vati had attached a screen wall to keep the pigeons in a limited space at the end of the attic. This area could be entered by a screen door. Inside the birds' room, toward the gable and against the wall, nests had been built from scraps of old wood, sometimes three or four high depending on the number of pigeons at the time. The birds entered and exited through a hole right under the gable supports. Father and son both checked the nests and replaced hay where needed. Franz poured fresh water into three heavy bowls and food into the other three. As they worked, occasionally a bird would fly in, strut around, find its preferred place to nest, and focus one red-orange eye on them.

"Are we shoveling the droppings tonight?" Franz inquired.

"No, let's do it after the competition," Stefan said. "We'll dump them in the garden then."

"Vati, where is Spotted Brown? His home over there is empty." Franz pointed to the west side of the attic. "We need to take him on the tumbling competition tomorrow!"

"Yes, Franz, we will. I put the best birds in the traveling cage so they would eat as much as possible tonight. We want them to rest and be energetic when they're released to the sky, don't we?" In mock seriousness, Vati asked, "Whose birds will go the highest and tumble down the fastest?"

Full of confidence, Franz yelled, "Ours!"

Early the next morning father and son again fed and watered the Tumbling Pigeons. "I think Spotted Brown will make them win!" Franz announced. Mama and Kati stood at the wagon and waved good-bye.

Noise of many contestants and their good natured bragging filled the air. "Remember, Vati, you said I could get Spotted Brown from his cage," Franz reminded his father seriously. With a twinkle of his blue eyes, Stefan nodded his head. "You'd better get over there and talk to him."

Finally it was their turn. Franz reached into the cage and gently cupped Spotted Brown in his hands, and gave him to his father. Franz stood back, opened the cage for the other birds to fly also and watched Vati expertly toss Spotted Brown in the air while the others swirled around him. Franz' favorite flew high and higher than the others; his circles looped wider in the beautiful blue sky. Franz shouted, "Now!" With a smile, his father pursed his lips to use the specific whistle they'd used in training to call them back. With a burst of admiration they watched all the birds backward somersault over and over as they came down, but Franz's eyes remained focused on Spotted Brown. "He tumbled eleven times! Aren't they beautiful?" Franz shouted. Vati ruffled his son's hair and beamed.

The judges used score pads to record the estimated flying heights and number of circling tumbles the birds completed. With great pride Franz returned Spotted Brown to his cage and gave him some dried corn and checked his water. Within minutes all the birds were caged and another contestant was showing his flock.

As morning passed, the birds all began to look alike to Franz and he no longer watched attentively. After noon the contestants gathered and winners were announced. Franz didn't make any effort to stand still, but fairly bounced with excitement. His exuberance was contagious and many cheered for Spotted Brown.

"First place to Stefan Elmer's flock with its lead bird, Spotted Brown!" the judge announced.

"I knew he could do it, Vati! Spotted Brown is happy we won! See?" And indeed, the bird did seem to be doing more than the usual amount of strutting in the cage. Franz reached in with one finger and softly stroked his feathers. "He winked at me!" he shouted.

On the way home, silence settled on father and son. Franz didn't mind. He leaned back on the side of the cage and gazed at the clouds in the sky. Most were white, but off in the distance some were dark. He tried to puzzle where the rain might fall.

"Franz, I've made some changes," his father hesitated. "I've closed the butcher shop. You've probably heard talk about it not bringing in enough money." Franz nodded and waited. "I'm going to work for Swartz' Grocery. I'll deliver supplies to the smaller stores in surrounding areas. Sometimes I'll be gone for a couple of days, maybe even a week." Franz looked at his father's face to see if this was bad news or good news or something in between. Vati was relaxed as he explained it, so Franz just smiled a bit.

"Can I go with you on some trips?" he asked.

"Yes, when you don't have school or chores. You can be a good company to me, actually." Franz leaned closer as his father's strong arm hugged him. The easy silence again returned.

Weeks passed and a new year began. 1940 was a very cold winter and January and February drifted by quietly. In March, Franz did go with his father. They hitched the horses to the wagon loaded with boxes and bags of food to deliver. Franz wore the coat his grandmother made with lambs' wool inside. It was long enough to keep even his legs warm. A matching hat covered his head and the back of his neck. His mother wrapped his feet in newspapers and pulled large wool socks over the papers. He wiggled his over-sized feet into large wooden shoes filled with straw and his feet stayed relatively warm. Father dressed similarly. Mama's knitted wool scarves shielded their faces. Nothing could be seen of them but blue eyes squinted against the whistling wind.

For the first few miles, Franz and Stefan, each in their own cocoon against the cold, enjoyed the clip-clop of the horses' feet and the wagon's rhythm. "The wind sounds lonely, doesn't it, Vati! I mean the way it rushes past everything like it's hurrying to be somewhere. Almost like it's crying."

Stefan's chuckle was muffled by his scarf and snatched away by the wind. "You do have a robust imagination, son! But when I stop and listen, it does sound like that."

Today only two villages needed delivery, so they would be home before dark. Even though Franz kept busy asking questions, he observed many interesting things around them. "When will we get there?" he asked. "I'm not cold but I sure am tired of sitting."

"The first store we're delivering to functions as the area town hall. We'll stay a while and get out of our heavy coats. It's primarily Yugoslavs; I don't think I've ever seen a fellow German here. They have a radio and discuss everything they hear, and," Stefan said with a tilt of his lips, "plenty of what they think." Father and son carried the boxes and bags up steps onto the porch and with help of many hands the parcels moved swiftly inside without leaving the door open for long. The warmth of the room felt good as they shed themselves of bulky outer clothes. As soon as the owner verified the items and reckoned the accounts, Stefan received his cash. He removed the strap of the leather pouch from around his neck and put the money inside, then hung it on his neck again and slid the pouch inside his shirt. Work finished, Stefan joined the men seated around a wood-burning stove, accepted a beer and smoked and visited.

"We just heard on the radio that Britain is rationing meat. Last year butter, bacon and sugar were rationed and now it's meat. I wonder how long they can fight the Axis."

Franz looked around the store, perfectly understanding everything spoken in Yugoslav.

As the man relayed the latest news to Stefan, another man offered, "British armed merchant ships are in the North Sea. Germany announced she will treat them as warships. We're talking about what they'll do now."

A short, stocky redhead shook his head and held up his fist. "I'm more interested in what Prince Paul Karadjordjevic will do for Yugoslavia. We'll be better off allied with Germany and Italy against the Communists, but our Prince seems to be doing nothing. We're not strong enough to stand alone."

"Maybe he's just prudent." Another argued. "If we jump on any side, it could be disastrous for us. I think he wants what will be best for Yugoslavia. We have no friendly neighbors other than Greece, right?" He looked around for affirmative response. "We are one of the few countries in Europe that remained a monarchy after The Great War. Chetniks may be renegades, but they do support Prince Paul and are staunchly anti-Communist but not pro-Nazi. Let's see what they can do."

Scratching his bearded chin, another man spoke up. "But aren't the Chetniks awfully militant against Communism? I don't see the CPY being a great danger to us, do you? Is the Communist Party of Yugoslavia so powerful?" he asked skeptically.

"We don't see it here because we're a land-holding people and we think about farming and handing down a legacy to our children. Belgrade University has three times more Communists than they had in 1937. Young people listen to Josip Broz, or Tito, as he's calling himself. If the CPY continues to grow, Prince Paul may never get enough support to return."

As always, the discussion revolved around war in one way or another. Used to it now, Franz no longer felt as alarmed. While the men continued to debate, he looked at some toys. Mostly he figured out how he could make them himself instead of spending money.

His father stood, and Franz knew they were ready to leave as soon as they replaced their warm clothing. The horses hitched again, Franz sat in his spot on the wagon. "This next delivery will be quicker, son. It's a bigger store in a small village and we won't stay long." Two hours later they finished the delivery and headed for home. Tucked into his coat, hat and scarf, Franz leaned on his father and fell asleep.

The next week passed with many tests at school and Franz' homework increased.

On Thursday his father left early for a two day trip.

"This trip will be easy and profitable," he predicted.

3

1940, Franz is seven years old.
Sombor and Stanišić, Yugoslavia

V ATI's TRIP WENT as planned the first day. Most customers were businesslike, and accepted the delivery, paid him without haggling over the price and he was on his way. A few felt compelled to question every charge and insist it should cost less. It took all Stefan's patience to remain polite but firm while showing the previous orders. Others had become friends and he enjoyed a few minutes visiting with them. His last stop was one of his favorites.

"If you can get us some more cough elixir, I'd appreciate it," Hermann Schultz said. His face looked serious but the twinkle in his eyes exposed his humor. "The ladies swear by it for curing whatever ails them. Sometimes I'm sure they really know what they smell, but I don't question them. I just take their payment."

Both men chuckled and Stefan wrote it on the order pad. "How is your delivery business working out for you?" Hermann asked.

Stefan opened his palms to face up. "Pretty good most weeks. I'm building up the route." He handed the next order to Hermann, who put on reading glasses and read down the printed items and signed for it. Out of the cash box he counted money due. Stefan put the receipts away and carefully tucked the leather pouch back into his shirt. The bag bulged more than usual. Elisabeth had her eye on fabric to make matching dresses for herself and Kati. He anticipated her smile of pleasure.

Whistling a cheerful tune, he urged the horses and empty wagon toward home. He would be later than Elisabeth expected. Usually he left well before sundown, but the long day reflected a good profit. The forest closed around him while he leaned back for a restful ride and listened to an owl's soft lament.

Though he wished to be home quickly, he knew the horses couldn't see obstacles or holes in the dimness of the forest and it would be safer to let them walk slowly. As the trees thinned he and the horses would see better and could increase their speed. He closed his eyes a moment and listened to the sounds of the woods. Cleared land was around the bend of the road.

"Halt!" he heard in Yugoslavian. He sat up quickly, and looked ahead. Four men seated on horses blocked the road. Each held a gun and aimed a flashlight at him. His heart pounded painfully.

He gripped the reins tightly and sat very still, except for his eyes, as he searched for a plan of escape. Stefan studied each of the men, but bundled as they were against the cold, there was little to recognize. He sat quietly and waited for their next move.

One of them rode his horse around the wagon and cursed at its emptiness. As he came back to Stefan, he stopped. "Get down!"

Stefan loosened the reins and tied them to the post. "I have nothing, as you see. I'm just on my way home to my family." He tried to stay calm and hoped they would do the same. If he remained in the wagon he could leave quickly if the opportunity appeared. To run on foot wouldn't be nearly as fast as the horses pulling the wagon.

One of the other men moved closer. "What's your name and where is home?"

Stefan hesitated. He could think of no advantage in not answering. He cleared his throat, "I'm Stefan Elmer, from Sombor."

Suddenly the man's posture relaxed and his eyes smiled. "I thought I recognized your voice, Stefan. I'm Edward Maksimovic. We went to school together as boys. Do you remember me?" He pulled his scarf down to expose a rugged face with a familiar nose broken so many times it had no original shape.

A relieved sigh escaped Stefan as he also removed the scarf from his face. "Yes, I do. As I recall you always lead us into mischief and most often talked the teachers out of trouble when caught. And that happened often. It's been a long time since I've seen you." How odd to sit and reminisce with guns pointed at him.

"Perhaps people don't change? Can I talk myself out of trouble here?" Edward smiled, "I would love to visit and catch up with the years, but I think we'll say farewell and not remember we met today. Are we in agreement?"

"Very much," Stefan replied. Each of the men moved beside Edward. Their guns were lowered. "Thank you." He said simply as he took the reins in hand and told the horses to move. As the wagon rolled past, he turned and waved at his childhood friend. "I look forward to meeting for a brew at a better time."

As he continued toward his family and home, he fervently thanked God. Also, he felt relieved to still have possession of his pouch. That evening he told his family of the adventure, and his sense of relief when he saw his friend, Edward.

"Wow! Were you scared, Vati?" Franz's eyes widened with fascination, "What would have happened if he'd not been an old schoolmate of yours?"

"Fortunately, I did know him long ago, so it worked out."

Mama's hand slipped into Vati's and they squeezed one another.

The year before, Italy invaded and annexed Albania, which spread more unrest and speculation. Czechoslovakia had already disappeared, swallowed up by the Axis. By summer, they saw more members of the Royal Yugoslavian Army around town. Sombor, about 45 to 50 miles from the Hungarian border, was always in dispute between Hungary and Yugoslavia. Franz and his friends found the uniforms fascinating and learned from the older veterans that they wore the same style used in the Great War. At first, shyness prevented them from really staring at the soldiers, but they quickly got used to army presence. Every night at ten o'clock a bugle sounded and the soldiers had to be back in the barracks but during the day and early evening they patrolled the city when they weren't busy with exercises and classes at their base.

Seated on a bench in the city park, the soldiers could be observed and studied. Franz and his friends grew quite familiar with the grey uniforms and sturdy brown leather boots. The tunics buttoned on the right side and had red collar flashes. One of the older boys, Ivan, sat by a soldier and initiated a conversation. Franz and his friends gathered around. "I'm near the age to join the army," Ivan began with a slight exaggeration due to being only fourteen, "maybe I'll be in a uniform soon."

The soldier smiled and leaned forward, "The girls really like uniforms," he confided, "It's easy to get acquainted." The younger boys wrinkled their noses; it didn't sound too brave to them. "But they are designed for service as well as appearance." He gave the boys a friendly smile. "Do you know what the red is here, on my shoulder strap piping?" Various boys shook their heads. "It's my arm-of-service color. It shows I'm an infantryman. Members of the artillery arm wear black."

Franz's curiosity gave him courage to step forward. "Why are your trousers shaped big at your hips?"

"These are called Jodhpur style trousers. Part of it is the military look. It's more comfortable when we're riding the horses.

— 33 —

Also, wide hipped pants allow us to move quickly in all positions. Like if I crawl on my belly through the mud, I can move my legs easily or to jump or twist around. Lots of flexibility. The heavy cloth will be durable in the field."

"Why does it fit tightly from knee to ankle?"

"Well, suppose I climb over fences or through dense under-brush in the woods, I won't get hung up on something, but will be able to move quickly and quietly." Each of the boys could see himself bravely creep up to surprise the enemy.

Pointing to the grey fabric over his trousers that covered the lower part of his leg, another asked "What is this?"

"This is called a puttee and as you see, it covers the leg from ankle to knee. We take a long, narrow strip of cloth and wind it tightly and spirally round the leg. This gives both support and protection."

"Do you keep your bullets here?' the youngest of the admirers asked, his hand on a brown leather receptacle which hung by his waist on a matching belt. It looked to be about ten inches wide and five inches tall in the middle, less on the ends.

"It's called an ammo pouch, and yes, I keep my ammunition in here." He picked up his helmet and stood to leave. "Do any of you want to try this on?" Every boy raised his hand. The soldier handed it to the nearest boy, who happened to be next to Franz. Then Jani tried it on and passed it back to Franz. It felt heavy and uncomfortable and muffled sound a little. Franz rocked his head from side to side and giggled at how it banged against his boy-sized head.

"It's actually called a French Adrian helmet," the soldier continued, "and can mean a big difference in life and death if we get shot at."

Before he passed it on, Franz studied the emblem on the front of the helmet. "It's a two-headed eagle, isn't it?"

"Yes, the Yugoslav coat of arms. See the crown above? For King Peter."

"My older brother is a Chetnik, but he doesn't have a uniform as good as these." One boy said wistfully.

"Well, you tell your brother if he's a royalist Chetnik guerrilla, he should join us. We're fighting for the Yugoslav Monarchy also. They should help us fight the communist Partisans and the murderous Ustashi. If the Royal Army and Chetniks stopped fighting each other, we'd be a strong force." He playfully punched at the boy's arm.

"Have you been shot at?" A blond boy about sixteen years old touched the rifle beside the soldier. Wide eyed listeners leaned in for the answer.

"No, but we're just getting ready for when and if Yugoslavia is attacked. I'm supposed to keep this Yugoslav 7.9 mm M1924 with me when I'm in uniform." By now the helmet had been passed around and the owner reached for it and put it under his arm. "This will all be over before you boys start to shave," he predicted. "It's time I left. Perhaps I'll see you around another time."

Inspired, the boys' hands magically became guns and they snuck through the fallen leaves in the park and spied on unsuspecting visitors. They listened in on conversations as though they contained important clues to enemy activity. But even their imaginations couldn't find anything of interest or subversive about discussions on weather and family matters or plans for the evening. Within minutes each of them drifted toward their own homes.

A few weeks later Franz woke up as usual at ten o'clock by the musical sounds of the Yugoslav Army's curfew bugle. He fell back into a light sleep, when the excited sound of Max barking woke him again. His father got up and opened the door a crack. Franz peeked out the window. When Vati opened the door, they heard a whispered "Please, we don't mean to bring you trouble, but the patrol is out there, searching for us because it's after curfew. If you don't give us away, we'll return to barracks soon. Please call off your dog."

By now, they could see what happened. When the two soldiers jumped over their front wall into the garden area, they didn't see the open water well and barely missed a long fall into the deep hole. The frightened young men sat up and scooted away from Max, who continued to bark aggressively. "Call him off!" they begged again. Vati stood next to the massive German Shepherd. Max sat down and exchanged threats of imminent attack for an equally frightful low, steady growl.

"We visited with some pretty girls and forgot the time," the other man explained very quietly, but with a quiver in his voice.

Vati nodded his head, "Max, you did your job. You're a good dog." He squatted down and stroked Max's head. They didn't see the young men leave. Vati returned to the house and peeked into Franz's window. "Good night, son," he said gently. The rest of the night passed uneventfully.

With the beginning of November, Mama made plans to ride the train the eleven miles to Stanisic. Vati would take them to the depot before he continued with some deliveries. She missed her mother and father, but also wanted to see her younger brother, Adam. Franz adored his single uncle and Kati should know him better. And with the war building up, she just knew she had to go now.

Ordinarily they didn't use the train, but went by wagon, because it took about an hour to walk from the house to the train. Vati made sure they arrived at the station early so Franz could explore a bit. He and Elisabeth sat with Kati on one of the benches to wait for the 8:20 to come through and pick up passengers and let off others. Franz walked along a train and studied the cranks and gears and rods; he found the ordered logic of the steam engine fascinating. A few members of the train crew worked outside. One man took three bags of mail and hoisted them one at a time to be shipped to their destinations. Franz glanced up the track to the front of the train. The conductor stood on his toes and reached up high to give the engineer some papers. Franz studied the large clock which hung outside the station. Two minutes until 8:20. The conductor began the familiar chant, "All aboard!" He mentioned other destinations, but when Franz heard him say Stanisic, he hurried to the platform and joined his parents and sister.

With good-byes to his father, they quickly climbed aboard and settled in seats. Too excited to sit, Franz raised on his knees to better see outside. He listened to the first hisses as the steam power began to turn the wheels. Then they began to move faster to the sound of the puff, puff and wheezing steam flowed above the moving train and the wheels below. Face pressed against the window, he enjoyed the flat terrain as they headed north. His father had explained to him this whole area became excellent farm land because sediments from the Danube and Theis had enriched the ground for thousands of years. From time to time, the engineer pulled the whistle to announce their arrival as they either passed through or stopped at a village.

It didn't take long for Kati to become restless, and she reached out to her brother. Franz pulled her to his lap and pointed to cows, people, small villages and farms. Kati loved the game and settled back to enjoy the trip. Mama relaxed against her seat and rested her eyes.

At last they saw the familiar sign identifying Stanisic in bold letters. As soon as they stopped and stepped down to the platform, they took their bags off to one side to wait for their ride. With a glad cry, Franz pointed out his Uncle Adam and ran to him. Adam resembled his own father, Nikolaus; they were tall, lean and muscular with straight noses and square chins. He had deep-set eyes like his mother and father, and thick brown hair. He grinned as Franz weaved around a few people to reach him. After hugs and greetings and collected luggage, they climbed in the wagon and headed to the farm.

"Elisabeth, you picked a good time to come, I can sure use Franz's help with the vineyard." Adam said with enthusiasm as he encouraged the horses to trot.

"I think you and his grandfather will turn him into a farmer!" she laughed. "But he appears very willing. Am I right, Franz?" she teased.

Franz glanced out of the corner of his eye at Uncle Adam as he nodded. He wished to be like his favorite uncle. Within a short time they arrived at the wagon gate and drove into the yard. Franz never felt like a visitor here, but as if he returned to his second home. Franz jumped down. Before seeing his grandparents, Franz dashed over the long porch on the house, past the pantry and to the unused kitchen behind. He dropped his suitcase in the room and went to the kitchen to join his family. The rest of the day he spent following his patient grandfather around, peppering him with questions and observations.

The next morning, eager for the new day, Franz jumped out of bed before Adam had a chance to wake him. Oma cooked up a hearty breakfast, which they ate quickly, then headed almost five miles north to the vineyard. Adam and Franz rode along and talked about many things, or at other times enjoyed a companionable silence. They slowly rolled past a rippling field of wheat ready for harvest, and fallow fields waiting to be brought to life the next season. The steady clip clop of the horses' hooves beat a peaceful rhythm. "How far is Hungary from here?" Franz suddenly asked

"Only seven to ten miles from Stanisic, so it's not far. In about three minutes I'll show you what's happening ahead. The Yugoslav Army is building anti-tank trenches up here." Sure enough, in a short time Franz noticed the changes. Adam stopped the wagon and hopped down, and Franz jumped from his side. They walked closer. The deep concrete trench sides slopped down at forty-five degree angles.

"Wow!" said Franz. "That's a long way down!

"It's about ten feet deep, so don't fall in. Also, the concrete would hurt as you go!" He ruffled Franz's hair. "But if we're attacked by anyone, tanks will stall here and not be able to continue to Stanisic."

"Who would want to attack us?" Franz asked.

"Apparently no one wants us, but our location is desirable — I heard someone say we're good for going through on the way to someplace else. We're not that far from Germany, we're accessible along the Adriatic Sea and the eastern Mediterranean as well. Some think it could be a good route to Libya and other African countries." Adam shrugged one shoulder. "So precautions are taken and we hope they're never needed."

Franz pointed to a distant place on the trench. "What's down there? Is it a little house or something?" He shaded his eyes with one hand.

"It's a bunker and they put one in every quarter mile or so. Later, if needed, there will be cannons installed."

Franz studied his uncle and wondered at the troubled expression on his uncle's face. He seemed to shake something off and smiled, but it didn't really reach his eyes.

"Let's go get some grapes!"

They climbed back in the wagon and soon arrived at the field. The men harvesting the grapes were almost finished, so some helped Adam and Franz transfer the grapes to their wagon. In ten minutes the wagon headed home.

Adam pulled the wagon past the kitchen garden and stopped by the wine cellar below the pantry. Franz hopped down and followed him through the door and down the steps.

As they strolled back to the courtyard near the wagon, Franz looked up. "Uncle Adam," he began hesitantly and very seriously, "will you have to go into the army?"

Adam stopped and ran one hand through his hair as he gathered his thoughts. "Which army would that be?" he asked sadly.

"I can't see fighting against German family and friends. And Yugoslavia is busy fighting within. The Royal Yugoslav Army has some strength, but the Partisans and Chetniks fight each other and the Army, and off to the side the Ustasa regime is volatile. The number of people in the Yugoslavian Communist Party has doubled since last year. None of them appear to be strong enough to make a difference and no two groups work together. So I don't know. I'm almost twenty-one, but the only place I want to be is right here in peace."

Franz nodded, glad to be given a true answer.

"Ah, well," he said as he put his hand on Franz's shoulder, "the things we worry about don't often happen, do they?" his expression relaxed as he replied. "Right now we've wine to make!"

"I'm glad I get your help to press the juice from the grapes," Adam said as he grabbed the three-legged press frame and placed it on a flat area of the courtyard. "We start from the bottom and assemble it. Help me pick up that round, shallow metal tray and set it on the frame."

Franz studied the tray. About six inches deep, the raised lip encircled the top edge until it came to a drain spout. At the tray's center stood a coarse-threaded three-inch diameter shaft about three feet high. When that was in place, they lifted up a two and a half foot barrel made of wooden laths and lowered it to the metal tray. The laths were connected to each other with about 3/16 inch spacing between them.

Franz anticipated the next part of the process and dragged over a bench so he could reach the top.

As they worked in silence, they filled buckets with grapes and poured them into the barrel. The threaded shaft stood in the center, several inches above the top rim. At a nod from Adam, Franz lifted one part of the wooden plate and helped slide it above and over the turn screw and lowered it to rest on the grapes. Finally, they topped it off with a big threaded nut which had two long handles opposite each other. As they walked around the barrel rotating the handle, the flat top moved down with the screw mechanism to squeeze the juice out through the laths and down to the metal tray. Franz could turn it slowly for a while, but the lower it turned the more strength it took.

"Let me finish it off, Franz. I'm lots bigger."

With a nod of agreement, Franz relinquished his hold and hopped down to crouch beside one the three legs below the press. He watched the juice as it squeezed between the laths, flowed down to the trough and dripped into one of the special, clean buckets, like a miniature creek.

Franz announced when an empty bucket should replace the almost-full one. Adam lifted the juice and carried it to the cellar door. By then Franz had already slid the empty bucket under the pouring juice. When the juice stopped dripping, they both lifted off the top of the press and lowered the barrel. Franz used a tool similar to a hoe to scrape and pull the fragrant pulp out. It would be used to feed the hogs.

Franz dashed to the water well and grabbed the ladle for a taste of the grape juice. "Needs more sugar!" he announced cheerfully.

Mama stepped from the kitchen door, "Time to eat!" Franz returned the ladle and they washed up before joining the others.

Days flowed by with the routine of the farm. Each morning Franz helped feed the hogs, chickens and their lone milk cow. Sometimes he helped the women dig up the few remaining vegetables in the garden, and prepared for planting next spring. Busy days and relaxed evenings provided time to converse, read or play dominos.

Kati, Oma and Franz about 1940

One evening as the weather began to feel chilly; Franz sat with Uncle Adam on the front porch steps. Grasshoppers were singing their end of summer song, and the shadows stretched over the yard. Franz looked sideways at his uncle. All afternoon Adam seemed preoccupied and spoke sparingly. Occasionally he tipped his head back and closed his eyes, but not in a tired way. Franz glanced at him. Could he be doing something to annoy Adam? Sometimes his grandfather told him he'd asked enough questions and suggested they could work faster without chatter. But Franz watched himself and he also became very quiet. Adam hadn't noticed.

After the evening meal, the women washed the dishes. They all gathered around the kitchen table for mince pie and coffee.

"Did you get the mail, Adam?" Grandmother asked as she poured his cup.

"Yes," he answered tersely, then inhaled deeply. "There wasn't much, but I did get my notice. I'm to be inducted into the Royal Yugoslavian Army. I'm supposed to report next week."

Grandmother set the coffeepot down and sank to her chair. The only noise in the room was the ticking of the clock. Franz looked from Uncle Adam to Grandmother and Grandfather, then to his mother. And not a word was spoken.

4

Winter 1940 to Spring 1941 - eight years old.
Stanišić and Sombor

ELISABETH FINALLY ASKED the question. "What will you do, Adam?"

"I don't know. I've prayed more this afternoon than I have in a long time." He picked up his fork. "Right now I think I'll eat some of this delicious pie."

Everyone but Franz followed his example. Kati, oblivious to the emotion charged room, continued to play with her stuffed kitty. Franz glanced at his grandparents. Opa appeared stern and bowed his head. Oma didn't seem to notice the tears running down her own cheeks as she got up and continued pouring coffee. His mother's hands clenched into fists on the table.

"Well, you have a few days to decide." Elisabeth leaned toward her younger brother. "We haven't discussed the possibility much, but we knew it might happen. I don't know what you should do, but just remember you're always welcome in Augsburg at Anna's."

With a frown and shake of his head, he observed his family. "Then I'll be a cowardly deserter in Yugoslavia and won't be able to come home for a long time," he paused, contemplating the situation.

"If I stay I'll be in an army heading toward disaster. Even if we have a strong army there's the problem of being at war with

Germany. I can't shoot at friends and family there. No matter what I do, it will be wrong." He looked around, hoping someone would tell him a good solution to this problem.

"As Elisabeth said, there are a few days before anything must be done." Opa's voice was gruff with emotion.

The domino game lay opened but no one mustered interest in playing. And then it was time to retire for the night.

Franz jumped out of bed very early the following morning, dressed, and ran to the kitchen. With relief, he saw Uncle Adam. He hadn't left in the night.

"Have you finished milking?" he asked. At Adam's negative shake of the head, Franz followed him out to the back barn where the cow waited. Even more than usual, he tried to be such a big help that Adam couldn't do without him. They bottled the milk and put it in the cool pantry. Most days Franz would alternate between Uncle Adam and grandfather and help whoever was doing the more interesting job, but now he needed to stay right with Uncle Adam. After they washed the milk bucket, fed the horses, chickens and hogs, it was time to have their own breakfast. With little discussion around the table, they ate quickly.

"I'll replace the rotten boards on the barn this morning." Adam walked to the door but turned around quickly as he remembered he needed a pencil to mark down measurements. He tripped over Franz, who was as close as a shadow, but managed to keep them both on their feet. He forced a smile, otherwise he'd unfairly snap at his nephew.

Pencil in hand, they gathered the tools they needed and spent the morning prying off the boards to be replaced, then measured, marked, cut and nailed the new ones. Franz tried to be quiet for a while but felt abandoned by the serious mood that covered Uncle Adam. Efforts to cheer him up by talking and telling stories didn't seem to help either.

When finished, they began to till under the leftover stems and stubs from last season's kitchen garden until it was finely ground soil for next spring. Franz was tired and relieved when they returned to the house and cleaned up for the noon meal.

As he entered the kitchen with Adam, he noticed his mother and grandmother watching them, and then they looked to each other. Kati cried out from the bedroom. "Franz," Mama said "come help me get your sister out of the crib since she's through with her nap."

After they left the room, Adam sat down and rolled his eyes. "What's up with Franz?" he asked with bewilderment.

Theresia sat down beside her only son. "Think! After last night's announcement, Franz is afraid you'll suddenly disappear if he doesn't stay right with you. You've always loved him in a special way and he adores you."

"Whew", he slumped in his chair. "I am so sorry. All I've been thinking about is myself. I just didn't realize what it might mean to him. What should I do now?"

She pulled out a chair, sat down and placed one of her work-roughened hands on his. "Do you plan to just suddenly be gone?" She let the question hang in the air. "If not, talk to him. Let him know you'll say goodbye when you leave. He's mature enough to understand, even if he doesn't like it." She stood and put her hands on the sides of his face. "You're very loved by all of us." She straightened her apron went to stir the soup.

Franz carried Kati in and put her in the high chair as the women carried the food. Grandfather sat down at the head of the table. While they enjoyed delicious vegetable soup and bread, Kati entertained them. Many of her words were very clear, others created guessing games for them all. As usual, she played and flirted, her blond curls bouncing. Over and over, between spoonfuls of soup, Franz bent down below the top of the table and quickly raised his head to say "peek-a-boo!" Kati's deep belly laugh brought chuckles all around.

As they finished, Adam cleared his throat. "I just want you to know I'm thinking I might go to Germany and stay with Anna for a while. They can get me on at the brewery, I think. Either way, if I go there, or go to the Yugoslav Army," he focused directly at Franz, "I'll let you know beforehand what my plans are, both where and when I leave."

Franz simply nodded; he couldn't say anything past the lump in his throat.

"Fair enough," Nikolaus gazed around the table at his wife, daughter, son and grandson, and last of all, to Kati. "Let's copy Kati and enjoy what we have right now. Today is a good day but we can throw it away with fretting."

Nothing had changed, but they all went back to work in a lighter mood.

Later in the afternoon Franz went out the gate to the street and kicked a rock around. It wasn't as good as a ball, but he found it entertaining. The boy next door, Anton Haut, came out a few minutes later carrying a couple of sticks a bit similar to hockey sticks. They'd spent time together a few times when Franz visited, but didn't know each other well.

"Want to come play Land Hockey with us?" he asked.

"Sure," Franz tipped his head to one side and lifted a shoulder. "But I don't know how."

"Aw, it's easy. Come on, we'll teach you." Franz followed him up the dirt street to the 'T' intersection where there was a vacant lot. He noticed four other boys there, each with a stick that appeared as though they'd whittled their own.

"We thought you decided not to come, Anton," one of the boys said "But we've been warming up the ball."

The boys eyed Franz, trying to figure out who he was. Anton simply said "This is Franz, the Hoger's grandson. He's going to play with us." They all nodded diffidently.

Gesturing at the others, Anton Haut said, "This is Adam Sujer, that's Stefan Baier, and Tony Baumgartner."

After friendly nods, Tony began to dig another hole off to the side.

"See those holes?" Anton spoke to Franz as he pointed around in a circle about seven feet in diameter and every foot or so there was a hole. The mound of dirt beside each gave the appearance of a gopher village. Franz turned his head as he counted around the circle. Four holes. Five boys. They all gathered in the center of the circle at another hole like the others, about three inches deep. Adam dropped a ball in the hole and they all gathered around. "We'll just show you this first time."

Each boy put his stick on the ball in the center hole. Anton gave Franz one of his sticks to use. Franz put his with the others and waited to see what happened next.

Tony Baumgartner, built like a solid tree, yelled "Go!" and he and all the other boys ran to the wider circle and each put his stick over a separate hole. Franz stood in the center trying to figure out what to do. There was not another hole for him. "You're 'it'!" they all yelled together.

Anton turned to Franz. "You and I chase the ball and until one of our sticks touches it, and the race is on. Whoever controls the ball back to the middle hole wins. I'm the one to race you since I'm throwing the ball." Anton picked up the ball from the center hole and threw it down the street.

Not waiting for confirmation of Franz' understanding, Anton took off like a shot. Franz didn't hesitate, but started pumping his legs as fast as possible. He managed to get around Anton, encouraged by the shouts of the other boys who followed. He gave a burst of speed when he saw Anton out of the corner of his eye. Smack! Franz' stick touched the ball. The boys all yelled. "Take the ball back to the center!!! Run!" Franz picked up his speed, but Anton controlled the ball and got there first, neatly getting it in the designated hole.

All six boys again put their sticks together and at the "Go!" command they ran to get a hole. This time Franz knew not to think, just run to one of the holes. Without an outer hole, Stefan, a short, stocky boy with determined eyes, became "it" and then Franz became Anton's successor to throw the ball down the street for the race to be on again. As they played the game over and over, Franz quickly became a skilled player.

His mother and grandmother put aside their sewing when he got home, eager to hear about his new friends and Land Hockey. Adam was off with Opa.

With no immediate chores to do, an idea popped into Franz' mind. He rushed to the unused kitchen in back, now his bedroom. He always kept a box of treasures and junk in the corner. He dug through and sure enough, he'd remembered correctly. He had started a slingshot on a previous visit. If he finished it, he could give it to Uncle Adam.

From the box he picked up a branch from the Dogwood tree that towered in the back pasture. He sighed with contentment; he held a perfect frame. It was somewhere between a 'Y' and a 'U' shape and all three parts were the same thickness, but the handle longer. Last time, he'd used his pocket knife to scrape the bark from the Y-shaped part so he had the real work already completed. It had been in the box long enough to dry out and harden and was ready to complete. He grinned in anticipation. It wouldn't take much effort now to turn it into a real slingshot.

Grandfather had given him some leather for the pocket and a few red rubber bands to use for the sling itself. He sorted through them to find one wide enough, but not too wide and cut it into two long strips. But first, he had to use his pocket knife to cut a slit in the top of each 'Y' of the branch. That completed, he tied a knot in one end of the first rubber band, then pulled the rubber to thin it out and pushed it into the slot on the right side of the 'Y' and pulled it tight to the to the outside. Then he tied a second knot inside the same slot, anchoring it firmly. The other rubber band he tied to the left side in the same way. How big to make the leather pocket? It needed to be big enough to hold a rock sufficient to hunt a rabbit.

The porch bricks made a good surface to use his faithful pocketknife to cut the leather to size. Then a hole was needed in each side to attach the rubber bands. After a bit of thought about the right length of the bands, he tied each to the leather pocket. Franz smiled with satisfaction at its strength. He held it up, turned it for inspection. Both tops of the 'Y' firmly gripped the tethered ends. It was a fine slingshot. Maybe he would give it to Uncle Adam after mass at Immaculate Heart of Mary tomorrow.

He put it under his pillow. He had to wait for the right moment.

As he came out of his room he saw his grandfather and Uncle Adam by the water well. He hopped down from the porch and skipped toward them. As he got closer, Nikolaus nodded his head at something Adam said.

"Hi, Opa," he suddenly felt shy with their serious expressions.

"I want to talk to you," Uncle Adam began, "let's sit over by the flower bed." He took Franz by the hand and Grandfather headed to the hog pen. As soon as they sat on the brick border, Adam leaned forward and put his elbows on his knees. "I just told My Dad and now I'll tell you. I decided to go to Augsburg."

Franz felt like he'd had his wind knocked out and couldn't reply.

"I'll pack tonight and leave tomorrow after mass. The border is open now so I can take a train through Hungary and change trains to go to Augsburg." They sat in silence for a few heartbeats, and then Adam continued, "Any questions?"

"When will I see you again?" he asked in a small voice.

"I don't know, but I will write and Anna will also. I'll send letters to you in Sombor. So, to answer your question, I just don't know. So much depends on how long the war lasts and how far it spreads. I don't want to go. But I'll either be in the Yugoslavian Army or I must go somewhere else. My greatest comfort is my family. No matter where we are, our blood tie is consistent and permanent. For example, you and your father are not together right now, are you?"

"No, he's in Sombor," Franz replied in confusion at the sudden change in subject.

"But you love him and miss him and he loves and misses you, right?" He watched Franz nod. "You're tied together by being family. And you and I are tied together in the same way. We're related and no matter how far apart we are for however long, we'll still hold each other in our hearts. Then when we see each other, it's as if we've never been separated. I'm not much with words, but this is the best I can explain it."

Franz nodded in understanding. "Just a minute," he said, "I'll be right back." Leaving a puzzled Adam, he ran to his room and got the slingshot and returned. He held it behind his back. "I made this for you," he said as he handed it to Adam. "I planned to give it to you tomorrow, but this is a good time."

Adam was speechless as he took it. He blinked back tears when he smiled at Franz again. "Thank you," he said as he hugged the boy, "I'll treasure it always."

Knowing they said all that needed to be said, they went to the house and Adam told his mother and sister of his decision.

It gave Franz pleasure to listen to Grandfather and Uncle Adam scrutinize and discuss the merits of the slingshot. The next morning was filled with silences and a few sighs as they dressed for Mass. After they ate the noon meal, Franz accompanied grandfather as he took Adam to the station.

Adam bought his ticket and they walked to the platform. "You be sure you write soon, son. You know how restless your mother will be if she has to wait too long." The slight curve of his lips acknowledged it wouldn't be just the mother checking the mail frequently.

The conductor rang the bell and called "All Aboard!" Opa and Franz didn't head back to the wagon, but stood till the train chugged its way out of the station. The important blasts of the whistle left a lonely sound in its wake.

They stood there, wordless. At sixty-two years of age, Opa stood tall with his hands in his pockets as he watched his only son leaving to an uncertain future. At a movement from Franz, he glanced down and put his hand on his only grandson's shoulder. Together they shared a brief period to mourn this unwelcome change in their lives.

The next few days they kept busy around the farm. Mama and Franz eagerly planned to celebrate Christmas at home in Sombor. The day they packed to leave, a letter came from Augsburg.

> *Dear Family,*
>
> *The winter weather has arrived but we're prepared for it. We've all had slight colds, but Adam seemed to miss the worst of it and didn't slow down as the rest of us did. Perhaps working at the brewery is healthy. It will be a quiet Christmas this year since none of the family is planning to travel.*
>
> *I've been doing a lot of sewing lately and actually earning money this way. It's fortunate to be able to make a profit doing what I enjoy.*
>
> *I hope you are all well. We miss you.*
>
> *Anna*

Oma read it aloud, then after they all relaxed from the tension of wondering if Adam made it to Anna's home, she read it again.

"The boy has a job and is in Anna's home." Opa lit a cigarette and took a deep drag. "For now, he's better off there," he said with equal parts relief and concern.

Elisabeth hugged her mother, then Franz. "Anna knew we'd all be unsettled until we heard from her." She gave a wobbly smile through her tears. "It may not be logical, but I hated to go back down to Sombor without knowing Adam is there. Now I'm completely ready to leave today and take my children home."

The train ride home was uneventful; its sole purpose to take them back to Stefan.

When they got home, Max ran circles around them as he wagged his tail exuberantly and for several days stayed very close to Franz or Kati. Christmas came quietly and the new year as well.

His father continued to travel throughout the week delivering groceries to outlying areas. Though he kept busy, stores were ordering only the minimum needed. The present income became insufficient for them to continue and Franz heard his parents discuss different options. In the meantime, they were especially vigilant over using everything as long as possible.

On Palm Sunday, April 6, with unusually serious expressions, Aunt Manci and Uncle Peter and Jani came to their house. Franz sat on the floor playing with Kati. While his parents and aunt found seats, Uncle Peter stood.

"We heard on the radio early this morning Belgrade has been bombed by over 500 German and Italian air-raid sorties. Ground troops are entering. Many have been killed and many taken prisoners!"

"Did they say if the Yugoslav Army is doing anything?" Stefan raised his eyebrows in skepticism.

"No. No surprise there." Peter muttered. "Usually I think Belgrade is a long way from here, but now I'm thinking it's only about 100 miles away."

Franz and Jani stared at each other. This wasn't one of their playtime war games.

5

Spring 1941, Sombor - eight years old
Sombor, Yugoslavia

"Do you see any soldiers?" Jani asked as they walked home from school the seventeenth of April. In silence, Franz and Jani meandered for a couple of blocks, looking in every direction. Since the bombing of Belgrade eleven days earlier, people scanned the sky frequently as the number and variety of planes increased. People were tense and the army's presence helped.

"That's odd," Franz ventured. "I wonder where they are. At the Yugoslav installation?"

They quickly decided to check it out. They each dropped their books off at home, changed clothes, let their mothers know where they were going, and met at a nearby corner to run to the military base a mile away. After wiggling the locked gate, they shouted greetings, but didn't see or hear anyone. Not so much as a vehicle moved. Puzzled, they went home.

Thursday, April twenty-fourth two German Stukas circled above Sombor. "It's a really small plane," Franz said, squinting into the sky.

"It's shaped like a fish. A little bit like a fish, anyway." Jani observed.

Spellbound, they watched in silence. Suddenly one of the bombers turned into a near-vertical dive accompanied by fierce whistling and dropped one bomb over the Yugoslavian military installation. The pilot jerked the aircraft out of the dive just after the release. Black smoke billowed upward and filled the sky. Even though frightened by the drop of the bomb, the boys admired how precisely the pilot dived, released the bomb and retreated. They heard the explosion, but also felt it in the rumble beneath their feet.

Immediately, they heard the screaming siren of the other Stuka as it dived and released a second bomb and they knew the army wouldn't be back. Were more bombers coming?

Franz felt the start of panic bubble up and breathed heavily through his mouth as if he'd been running. His cousin looked pale and still. They turned to run toward their homes.

"They're like evil hummingbirds!" Franz shouted as he turned off to his street. People were outside their homes, looking off at the sky. Mothers called their children, who were already on their way home.

"Mama!" Franz yelled as ran up to see her standing on the porch, "We saw planes drop bombs over the army's compound!" He skidded to a stop as his mother wrapped her arms around him. He rested against her until his heart slowed to a more normal beat and they walked inside together.

"I heard the explosions." Mama sounded near tears. "I've been worrying and wondering where you were." She rested her chin on his tousled hair.

At the sound of Franz' voice, Katie turned from the window where she stood on the davenport.

"Ran!" Kati called and held out her hands.

Both Franz and Mama laughed with nervous relief as Franz swooped over to Kati, picked her up and swung her around. Kati gurgled with glee. Just seeing her happy face made him feel better.

"I want you to stay close to home for a while until things settle down again," his mother cautioned.

After being at home for another four days, Franz skipped down the street with several dinara in one hand and Mama's list of things to pick up at the store in the other. He had enough money to buy a piece of candy for himself. After he gave Mr. Majoros Mama's list of black thread, white thread and three yards of muslin fabric, Franz stepped over to the glassed bins and studied the available candy. First, he thought of getting a chocolate bon-bon, but that would be gone quickly. Maybe he'd pick a couple of gummi frogs or Werther candies, which would last longer.

"I'll take a couple of gummi frogs," he finally said. He could eat slowly, first the legs, then part of the body and work himself up to the head.

"I've got your mother's things here," Mr. Majoros eyes twinkled as he added Franz' treat to the total. "Are you going to the parade?"

Franz' dimples deepened as he grinned. "What parade?"

"Because the Yugoslavian Army has left Sombor, the Hungarian Army is celebrating tonight with a parade downtown, right up the main street. Our two-year-old army loves to march and display their handsome uniforms." Mr. Majoros stroked his thin, brown mustache. "We Hungarians are particularly looking forward to the festivity, but everyone will enjoy it."

"I'll tell my mother about it, so maybe we'll see you later." With a wave, he ran home to tell Mama. He really wanted to see it.

"After the past few weeks, I think a that sounds wonderful." Mama smiled at the news. "It will be good to see friends and neighbors!"

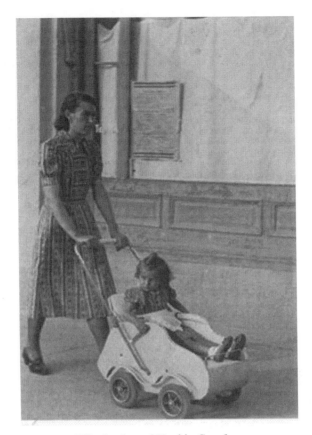

Elisabeth and Kati in Sombor

Mama pushed Kati in her baby carriage. "We'll follow you, Franz," she said.

The sidewalk curved around the corner to match the rounded corner of his yellow brick school. He wanted to be in the middle so he could see them come and when they left. Young trees grew along the street. He found a spot where they would have room, and Kati's stroller could be on the front row. They were early, so stayed in their place and visited with people around them. Franz looked across the street. Downstairs were shops selling just about everything—clothes, ladies' hats, shoes, hardware, a drugstore, and offices for various business. Franz looked at the upstairs apartments, most of the windows were open, and people leaned on their sills to get a good view. At the end of the street, he could see the Serbian Orthodox Church, the landmark used for directions.

"I hear a band coming!" Franz moved into the street to see the beginning of the parade. "Here they come!" Instruments played cheerful songs with a solid beat as the band marched past. "The soldiers are next!" he announced to Mama.

The soldiers marched in perfectly straight lines. Franz tried to copy them as their knee-high black boots moved in synchronized steps. Then he listened to Hungarians shout while he returned to Mama and Kati. "Why are they cheering and shouting welcome?" he tipped his head in confusion. "Usually we just clap and smile."

"I guess they hope this land will become part of Hungary," she said uneasily. She stood tall and looked around as if something bothered her, but Franz noticed everyone enjoyed themselves. Many shouted loud and enthusiastic encouragement to their new heroes. Mama pulled the buggy backward. "Let's go home," she said to Franz. "It's almost seven o'clock anyway."

He started to protest, but something about his mother's expression changed his mind and he turned away and followed her through the crowd.

Just as Franz, Mama and Kati arrived at their front gate, four individual shots rang out from four different directions. Suddenly many cracks came from all directions.

Mama locked the gate behind them. Franz snatched Kati from the buggy and they crawled to the front door. Mama reached up to open the door and let the German shepherd, Max, come inside, where he paced and occasionally whimpered. Franz stroked the dog's back. "Max is trying to figure out how to protect us!" he whispered.

"Oh, I want your father here now!" Mama, frightened and exasperated, pulled both children close to her and hugged them. Vati had a long route and wouldn't be home from this delivery for a couple more days.

Franz listened to the terrifying sound of snipers shooting in spurts from rooftops all around the city. "Some of them sound really close, don't they?" Franz' voice soft as he curled close to his mother. "Can they shoot through the walls?"

"It's unlikely. Houses are built here to withstand harsh winters; the brick walls are two to two and a half feet thick. We just have to stay below the windows."

As she finished speaking, they heard a loud scream followed by shouts. Max twitched his nose and growled. Kati flung herself on top of her protector. "Mat, Mat" She hugged his neck.

"It's Max. Say Max," Mama corrected absently.

Kati's little hand pointed as she shook her head. "Mat!" she repeated playfully. Mama and Franz gave her wobbly smiles.

"It's getting dark out now. Let's stay here on the floor, try to sleep and see what tomorrow brings."

The next morning they continued to hear guns, rockets, and sudden cries of alarm or injury. "When I go rabbit hunting with Opa, we see the grass move in a pattern and we shoot." Franz said. "Is this the same?"

"Hmmm, maybe so. I've noticed the shots aren't aimed to or from any one direction," she hesitated. "My heart beats faster when I hear shooting, but hearing people scream in pain is the worst."

Conversation slowed to a trickle, except for Kati's chatter. Franz helped Mama keep his baby sister safely entertained on the floor. Katie repeatedly tried to climb on the sofa to look at the world outside her window, and then wailed loudly when denied her favored view. Finally, Kati fell asleep in her mother's arms.

Restless after hours of inactivity, Franz stretched. "I should feed the pigeons," he said.

"No," Mama shook her head, "The pigeons can fend for themselves. It's safer for you and Kati and me to stay together here on the floor than walking around where we might draw attention."

He nodded reluctant agreement and the day dragged on slowly as they entertained Kati, ate and Franz did practice reading. They stayed out of sight from the windows. By night time he welcomed sleep.

The second night they slept fitfully, waking often to the sound of shots. When a series of many shots rang out, Mama and Franz sat in the dark and marveled at Kati's sound sleep. "I know your father wouldn't be able to do anything right now, but I wish he could be here! Maybe tomorrow."

"Who is doing all this shooting?" Franz punched his pillow."

"I don't know. Just close your eyes, Franz. It will probably be back to normal tomorrow."

Franz pretended to be asleep and Max rested his head near Kati, so he would respond if she stirred. The shepherd looked over at Mama in reassurance. "I need sleep as much as they do," she whispered to the dog, "Thank you, Max."

Franz fell asleep, knowing that the shepherd watched over them.

Before dawn Mama got up and brought food from the pantry and pencils and paper and Kati's favorite toys and book. The shooting continued sporadically throughout the morning and afternoon. Franz wondered about the night ahead. They had plenty of food in the cabinets and icebox. He hated not being able to use the outhouse, but they had a chamber pot and bucket in the bedroom and kept a board laid over the bucket so the smell wasn't so bad.

Restless and insatiably curious to see what happened, Franz fidgeted. "I wonder what Jani and the other guys are doing right now." He hated the annoying whine in his own voice but wanted to go see things for himself. With a deep sigh, he lay down beside Kati. "You're too little to understand about staying down." Time passed while he drew pictures for her, traced her hands and helped her sing songs and read to her.

With darkness, they fixed their temporary bedding for another night. "Why are they shooting?" Franz asked again.

His mother shrugged. "It's a puzzle to me. It's not the Axis. They would just get it done and not be like cats pouncing on and toying with mice for so long. The Hungarian Army started marching before it began and the Chetnik insurgents hate the Hungarians so maybe it's the Chetniks. And maybe not. From here we don't even know who the targets are. They may be after the Hungarian Army, or Yugoslavians, I really don't know, so try to get some sleep."

Intermittent sounds of war lasted three long, tedious days and nights; time without school, no games played with friends, or money-making projects. Kati did fine whenever Franz played with her, but if he stopped, she wanted to climb up and look out the window. He loved his little sister, but found the time boring. The afternoon of the third day they heard just occasional sounds of shots, and during the night, none.

Early Monday they raced to answer a knock on the door. Uncle Peter and Jani, come with news. "Things seem to be quiet now so we wanted to see if you need any help."

"Come in," Mama opened the door wider, "I'm so glad to see you. We don't know what's happening."

"I know Chetnik insurgents opened fire on the Hungarian Army and their supporters, and all hell opened up. Several people who watched the parade were shot as well as a lot of soldiers. Now the Army is hunting Chetniks, who seem to have become invisible." Peter looked out the window. "I think it's safe to get out a little bit now. Officials announced school won't resume since it's so close to the end of the year anyway. Things are just too volatile now."

Mama sagged with relief. Franz perked up at the news. A little disappointed not to finish third grade as scheduled, but excited about an early summer break.

"Do you want to go downtown with us now?" Uncle Peter asked.

"No, I think we'll continue to stay here another day or so." She glanced down to see Franz's look of disappointment, "Do you want to go?" she asked.

"Yes!" Franz nodded his head rapidly. With a chuckle, Uncle Peter ushered the boys to the door. As they walked, Jani told Franz the stories he heard.

Franz looked at their school as they rounded the corner. It looked the way it always did, but as they turned to the next street, they saw many broken windows and streets littered with both merchandise and debris. Muttering shopkeepers busied themselves restoring order. Uncle Peter stopped to speak to a friend who owned the clothing store.

"*Szervusztok,*" they all turned at the greeting from two Hungarian infantrymen. The men nodded, and the soldiers shook their heads in sympathy. "The Chetniks consider us enemies, but to harm innocent citizens is unfathomable!" The one who spoke gazed up the street. "Did you see where the shots came from? Do you know Chetniks who live here?"

Filled with anger, a couple of men pointed out the homes and businesses of the guilty. Immediately the soldiers aimed their machine guns and shot up all the roof tiles and the attics. Franz stared at the flying pieces from the buildings. Franz and Jani instinctively pulled closer to Uncle Peter. The townsmen wore varied expressions. The angriest looked vindicated. Others, like

Uncle Peter, showed little expression, but Peter put his hands on his son and nephew as a show of protection. The soldiers nodded their heads and sauntered up the street. Sombor merchants resumed gathering anything useful and filled a nearby wagon with broken parts of buildings, windows and merchandise destroyed by looters.

"Do you want to look around?" Uncle Peter asked unnecessarily. "You can go up Skolska Street but stay away from the other part of town."

"Thank you!" Franz called out as they quickly escaped being put to work. From the distance, it looked like something was wrong with the Serbian Orthodox Church, so they slowly headed in that direction. They walked around trash swept into piles, and people as they worked.

They arrived at the Church to see how much damage it received. From the outside, they viewed the steeple with its gaping hole.

"The corner is completely gone!" Franz yelled. They ran around the back to the other side of the oval building and looked up at the white walls trimmed with pink. "This side hasn't been touched at all."

On the front, one tall brown window shutter hung askew.

"Let's go inside," Jani shouted as they moved. "It's quiet in here," he added as they stepped inside the door. Franz and Jani walked up the curving steps into the tower. Muffled sounds from outside seemed to bounce off the walls, but only a strange quiet accompanied them on the stairway. As they climbed higher, they stepped on increasing amounts of debris from the damage above. Once up there, they just stood still. Churches were to be held in honor, not destroyed. The floor of the tower lay hidden under jumbled glass, wood, bricks and tiles. Sunshine covered everything as it streamed through the huge hole in the outer wall.

"Franz," Jani whispered, "look!" he pointed to the darker side of the room.

Both boys walked slowly nearer a Yugoslavian Priest lying on his back, his face covered with blood. A closer look and it became obvious he'd been hit in the eye by a bullet. Both eyes remained open but the right one held a pool of dried blood and no visible iris. He still clutched a powerful rifle in his hand.

"The priest was a Chetnik," Franz said softly. His heart thumped so hard he could feel it in his ears.

Jani's face paled as he backed farther away. "Is he alive?"

Franz saw more death at his grandparents' farm in Stanisic then Jani did in the big city of Sombor. But not like this. He stared at a person, a priest and not an animal. Timidly he touched the priest's cold face. "No," he whispered as he stood up and joined Jani. "We'd better go tell someone."

They went down the steps much faster than they'd gone up. A group of five men gathered in front of the church, so the boys quickly told them about the priest. Their sense of adventure was replaced by the need to be home.

When Franz opened the door, he saw his father seated on the chair with a sleeping Kati in his arms. Mama stirred supper but turned with a smile. Vati put Kati down and came to the door to eagerly welcome his son.

Vati laid his arm over Franz's shoulder. "The roads weren't open till this morning." He looked Franz over carefully as if to reassure himself his son remained unharmed. "Your mother said you were a big help to her. How are you doing?" He asked simply.

Franz' mind raced and for a second he didn't know where to start. He took a deep breath and raised his arms high and wide. "Jani and I found a dead priest!" he shouted. With such a stark announcement he seemed to collapse.

Surprise flooded Vati's face. "I hadn't heard about this!"

Mama put her spoon down and walked over to Franz, "What did you say?"

"We looked around town and wondered about the stained glass in the churches. Jani heard about damage to the Serbian Orthodox Church's steeple and we wanted to see it. Then we climbed the steps to look inside the tower." He took another deep breath and continued, "That's when we found him. The priest I mean. He still held one of the Chetnik rifles. They shot his eye out. When I touched his cold cheek I felt death." His eyes darted from mother to father. "He was covered in blood! So we ran downstairs and found men coming into the church and told them." He talked fast, fueled by adrenaline.

Both Vati and Mama were speechless as they absorbed this news. Mama guided him to a nearby chair where he collapsed rather than sat down.

"Well, I don't know what to say, son." Vati stepped back, brushed his fingers through his hair, and slumped. "I guess you've grown up a lot this week," he added.

While they ate, Vati listened to Franz tell all about the long, boring days and frightening sound of various kinds of explosions during the days and nights. "It sounded like a lot of crazy people were everywhere." Franz summed it up.

After they ate, Vati paced their kitchen, unable to relax. "Time to get out of the house!" he announced at last. "Let's go by and get Manci, Peter and Jani and go to the park or Holy Trinity Square, if you'd rather."

"The park sounds lovely," Mama quickly agreed with the plan and put Kati in her stroller. Manci's eagerness to be around people matched Mama's and they chatted as they walked. The two couples followed their sons, Franz and Jani, to join their neighbors.

Jani spied other boys from their school as he spoke. "Come on!"

After initial greetings, everyone seemed to talk at once. Fear of food shortages brought looters to Alfon's uncle's grocery store. Otto told of a toy shop vandalized just out of meanness.

"Did you hear about Karl?" Otto asked.

Franz shook his head.

"He sat down to eat with his family at the dinner table when a bullet came through the window and shattered his elbow. My mother said his mother cried so hard she couldn't get the words out, and the doctor had to amputate his arm to save his life!"

"Amputate?" Franz furrowed his brow, "What does 'amputate' mean?"

"The doctor had to cut it off. He won't be able to do a lot of things. But his mother said he'll still be able to write with his right hand."

Franz felt sort of sick for Karl. He looked at his arms. What would it be like to not have one of them? "Karl loves sports, and hunting and reading. How will he be able to do those things? Well, reading would be good, but how could he do the other things?" Franz asked, but there were no answers.

Hungarian soldiers roamed in the park, ready to enforce a new curfew. People began to go home.

As Franz moved to join his parents and Kati, he saw a pretty woman, wearing a blue dress, carrying a basket of flowers. She strolled up to one of the soldiers on the edge of a woodland area. Franz saw her friendly smile as she lifted a rose and held it toward the soldier. She must be one of the girls who liked uniforms, or maybe she knew the man. Then Franz recognized her as Herr Bauer's daughter, who had joined the Chetniks. He started to turn his face away when he heard gunfire. The soldier fell, blood quickly flowing from his neck. The girl dropped the flowers she'd held, and Franz saw a gun still in her hand. She ran into the dense woods while several soldiers surrounded their fallen comrade. Others ran after the woman, yelling *"Abbahagy! Abbahagy!"*

and blew shrill whistles. Franz didn't know why, but hoped the woman got away.

The park emptied quickly and quietly.

During the night Franz woke up many times both by the sounds of shots, and by nightmares about the dead priest and seeing the soldier fall after the Chetnik girl shot him. At one point Mama slipped into his room and sat beside the bed. She stroked his blond hair back and murmured gentle reassurances. He tossed about in bed, but having his dad home made it easier to fall asleep again. The next morning as he dressed, he pushed aside the memories and forced his mind to think of possible activities for the day.

Vati stood in the outside doorway, his head turned to hear something, his eyes squinted. Franz came to a full stop and listened as well. Off in the distance he heard unfamiliar banging sounds, followed by loud protests. His father closed the door. "I think today will be a good time to stay inside and do projects around here."

"Why? I thought I'd see my friends!" A sense of injustice welled up in him for a moment, "Why?"

"Franz, the Hungarians won't put up with the Chetniks' continuing attacks. Today they will establish who's in power." He flipped his thumb toward town, "I'm guessing those sounds are doors being busted in, houses searched and Chetniks found."

With an effort at normalcy, he ruffled Franz' hair. "I think it would be a good time to shovel out the pigeon droppings after we feed them. We can do an especially good job and not just the quick ones you've been doing." He words came as a smile, not a rebuke.

Mama declared a day to do housework, which left Franz free to work alongside his father.

"We may not need to stay so close to home for long." Vati told Franz.

As they entered the attic, the pigeons flitted from one place to another, their hackles up and crying "Oorhh! Oorhh!".

"Wow, it's their cry of alarm," Franz's eyes widened at the pigeons' reactions. "They don't like all the shooting this week either!"

"Just talk to them, son. They'll respond to our voices and steady movements."

"Sorry we've not been up here for a few days," Franz spoke soothingly as he went about his chores, "I'm giving you fresh water and food now." When finished, he scooped one of them onto his hands and stroked him slowly. The bird's orange eyes watched him as he spoke softly and all the pigeons relaxed. Franz and his father smiled at each as Franz calmed the birds.

Vati shoveled the heavily littered floor until no droppings remained. They put supplies away, closed the screen door and Vati carried the droppings bucket as they went down the stairs. They emptied it in the garden area, and Franz and Vati cleaned up.

Random shots still filled the air, but doing work at home made things seem more normal. On the living room floor later in the night, Mama and Vati recounted favorite family stories as they all huddled together before going to bed.

In the morning Franz lay and listened. He heard only birds outside, and dogs barked in the distance. But no shooting. After he dressed, he went to the kitchen for breakfast and then fed Max. A few hours later Vati told his family to stay at home. "I'll find out what's happening." In two hours he returned.

"They've filled the jail with Chetniks. The ones who didn't get caught have probably left." Late in the afternoon they listened to the sound of many rifle shots. After about ten minutes, an uneasy quiet returned.

Vati left again and when he returned he brought news. "They blindfolded and executed them. The Hungarians are patrolling heavily right now, so perhaps the worst is over."

6

1941 – Franz is 9 years old in August.
Sombor and Stanišić, Yugoslavia

VATI'S PREDICTION HAD been correct. With a tenuous peace and confidence, Sombor began to rebuild the damage caused by the Chetniks and Hungarians.

Whump! Bang! "Jani?" Franz stood on the wagon's tongue and peered over the edge of the trash wagon. "Where are you?"

"I think I'm under the door," Jani coughed. "When I stepped on some bricks, I slipped and something fell on me."

"Uh-huh, it fell." He grinned, leaned over and knocked on the door. "Are you home?"

"You're not funny," the door shifted an inch. "It's too heavy. Can you lift it?"

Franz tried, but without a handle it couldn't be budged. "Just a minute," Franz searched for an idea. "I see a pole under the top of the door. Maybe I can pry it up." He scooted along the top of the wagon side, held on to the side with one hand and reached down with the other. "I can't reach it." He shook his head and stretched a little more "I don't want to fall in on top of you! And I need both hands to lift. Maybe I should run for help."

"No! I can't breathe under here. Try again!"

Franz stepped onto the front wheel on the side of the wagon. "I'll try to bend over farther and use both hands." The wooden edge bit into his stomach, but as he leaned to lift the pry bar but not fall in, his stomach muscles tightened to give protection. "I've got it in my hands. Can you push at the same time?"

With Jani's agreement, they counted "One, two, three, lift!" The corner tipped up. Franz' face turned red with exertion and as soon as Jani scrambled out, he dropped the pole.

They both jumped to the ground and sat down, "And we didn't even find steel in there!" Jani wailed as they rested. ." They chose this refuse wagon because there were no other people around to compete for the old steel pieces to sell.

"Let's go back and hang around the stores again. We can always run errands or help the merchants. They're a long way before the shops are fixed up to be as good as before the parade." Franz crossed his feet and rested his elbows on his bare knees. "I have to buy lumber to build a handcart or wagon. It'll be easier to earn money if I deliver more than my arms can carry."

"What do you plan to buy?"

"Just things," Franz said. He wanted to tell Jani, but it would embarrass his parents. Vati lost two more customers last week when they joined the Hungarian Army. No, he'd better not say anything, but he could earn money. During the next week, he earned money every day. Franz wiggled under the bed and pulled the savings jar out. Clink. Clink. The sound of coins as they dropped thru the hole in the lid gave him satisfaction. But would it be enough to help? He shoved it back under his bed.

"Eight, nine, ten! I'm coming to find you!" Otto shouted as he stepped out from behind the tree. His head turned from one side to another. "Where are you?" Sometimes a helpful answer would come, but most often he had to dash around the park in search of his friends.

Franz hid in a holly bush behind a statue of a long ago hero. The least movement and the sharp leaves poked him. It seemed like a perfect place to hide but now he knew why no one else used this spot. Too late to move. Otto ran right past him.

"I found Claus!" Otto shouted. Franz tried to look over his shoulder but couldn't see where Claus had been. Off in the distance Otto's voice coaxed them to answer. "Alfons? Franz? Jani? Where are you?"

By now he hated the bush and its needle-sharp leaves. Otto's voice came from the other side of the park. He could be the last one found and win or he could get out of the prickly bush now. After what seemed like an hour, he heard Jani's voice.

"Franz! Otto found all of us, so come out wherever you are!"

"I'm over here!" he wiggled toward freedom and ignored new scratches on his face and hands and legs. "I win!"

The other boys gathered around him. "You look like you had a fight with a cat!" Alfons said. Franz laughed along with them. "It's getting late – I need to go home." They agreed to meet the next day after their chores were done at home.

Franz didn't have to tell his parents where he'd been. One look and his mother tipped his chin up and studied his face. "Did you destroy the bushes?" she asked with a smile. After he shook his head, she handed him a towel to take to the pump. "Go clean up. Dinner's just about ready."

"Schnitzel! My favorite!" Encouraged by the aroma, he hurried, did a very quick wash and returned to eat.

"You're dirty!" pronounced Kati as she pointed at the streaks of dried blood on Franz's face and arms.

"No, Kati," he said. "These scratches are the price I paid to win hide-and-seek in the park."

Unimpressed, she frowned at him. "You're dirty!" she repeated as Elisabeth placed a plate of food on her tray and they all enjoyed her specialty of schnitzel. When they'd finished their meal, Elisabeth gathered the dirty plates from the table.

Stefan took a sip of wine, pushed his chair back and cleared his throat. "Franz, we've decided you and Kati will go with your mother to stay in Stanisic with your grandparents."

"You mean we'll go for a visit?"

"No," he looked at Elisabeth as they shared wordless communication. "No, to live there. I'll stay with Aunt Manci and continue to work from here. Weekends I'll come up to Stanisic."

"But why can't we all stay here?"

"War has changed everything. We simply can't pay the rent here. This is temporary until things get better." He picked up his wine glass and sipped again.

"Wait! I have something to show you." Franz dashed to his bedroom and pulled out the money jar and carried it back to the kitchen. "Here, I've been saving. Will this help?"

Franz looked from Mama to Vati. "See how full it is?"

"Yes, we appreciate the offer of your savings," Vati swallowed and blinked his eyes, "but it's not enough. I'm sorry."

Elisabeth stood, "Vati will come on weekends. Oma and Opa are eager for us to come, and with Adam gone, you'll be of big help."

"Do you have any questions?"

Franz clamped his mouth shut and looked at the floor. He wanted to demand to know how he would see his friends and plead to stay with Vati at the home of Aunt Manci, Uncle Peter, Jani and Dori.

"Rans! Rans!" Kati called him to take her out of her chair. How could he stay without Mama and Kati? He walked over to take the tray off Kati's chair and lift her down.

"How soon will we move?" he asked softly.

Again, his parents looked to each other first. "Within the week." Elisabeth said. "It won't be easier to leave in two weeks or a month."

"What about Max? Will he go with us?"

"No," Stefan said, "remember the last time we took him with us? He chased the livestock and ate chickens. I'm afraid he wouldn't be welcome. He'll stay with me at Manci's."

As Franz climbed into bed that night, his thoughts chased around in circles. Eventually, sleep came. By morning, things didn't look so bad. He loved the farm and his grandparents. Adam wouldn't be there, but maybe he'd come from Augsburg for a visit. Opa needed help to take care of the animals. Also, he'd see his friend, Anton, next door.

Most of all, the decision had been made by Mama and Vati and he couldn't change it.

The next few days they sorted through their belongings. Franz helped pack dishes, took care of Kati and ran errands. His own things were easy. Mama never kept anything he'd outgrown, so they would take almost all of his clothes. His treasures were few and fit in one box. The pigeons were given to a friend who wanted to enlarge his flock.

"Franz's last day in Sombor arrived, at least until he moved back someday.

Franz looked around at the now-bare bedroom walls, the empty shelves. Tomorrow they would strip down the bed and pack it in the wagon. He looked out the window. Had it only been a few months since the Yugoslavian solders jumped over the fence because of their curfew?

"Max?" he called and the German Shepherd appeared at the screen, tail wagging. "Good night. I'll miss you." Franz snuggled under his blanket and fell into a restless sleep.

"Help! Help!" Franz screamed. He was back inside the Serbian Orthodox Church's steeple where the priest with one eye sat up and reached out for help. On the other side of the tower, a Hungarian soldier moaned and pressed his neck, blood flowed between his fingers. Franz' heart beat rapidly; his feet tried to move but were caught in a rope. The priest and soldier moved closer to him – panicked, he tried harder to run.

"Franz! Franz!" his eyes opened to darkness, Vati beside him. He'd been brought back to his bedroom. "You've had another nightmare, you're safe." He repeated the words as he held Franz close to him.

"Oh!" Franz sagged against Vati. His breathing settled as his heartbeat lowered. "They were there. The priest wanted my help! Then the Hungarian! I saw so much blood and I couldn't get away!" As Stefan patted his back, the image faded and he put his head back on the pillow and drifted into a dreamless sleep with his father's gentle voice in the background.

"Why did you plant so many potatoes? We'll never eat them all." Franz tossed another potato into the wheelbarrow. He looked over his shoulder at Oma. He didn't appreciate the twinkle in her eyes.

"Franz, five us live here, on weekends, six. We have company often. How many do you think we cook every week?"

He picked up a stick, smoothed out some of the dirt and began to scratch the numbers to add. Opa had a hearty appetite and he ate two, so it took six every day. Eight on weekends. His eyes widened as he added and multiplied. "Almost fifty every week for only one meal!" He dug another from the ground and tossed it with the others. "I guess it's a good thing we have both summer and winter harvests."

Oma laughed and dusted her hands on her apron. "Let's push the wheelbarrow before it gets too heavy."

"I'll do it," Franz straightened his back manfully and picked up the handles. Slightly wobbly, he pushed it through the pasture gate, past the wine cellar and water well. He turned left and tipped the load to the ground. He and Oma scattered them on the high, dry ground behind a short brick wall. "How long do we leave them here to dry?"

"If it stays nice like this, just a week."

Opa, Adam and Oma 1940

"This is so peaceful. I could almost believe there is no war anywhere in the world." Mama said as she pushed the porch swing with one foot. She leaned her head back and let a warm breeze surround her. Even Kati watched as the sun sank gracefully behind the trees, long shards of red light filtered through the leaves.

"A rabbit!" Franz pointed to the garden "he's looking at us."

"Want to take the salt shaker and sprinkle salt on its tail?" Opa asked. Mama and Oma chuckled.

"I fell for your trick a long time ago, but I know better now!" Franz laughed. "It must have been funny to watch me chase rabbits every evening because I never got close enough to get the salt on its tail!"

"You always kept us entertained, you know."

"What day is it?" Franz asked suddenly.

"Friday," Opa lit his cigarette. "And yes, your father will be here this evening or in the morning."

As the sky darkened, fireflies came out. "Come on, Kati, let's catch them!" Franz held up a glass jar and took Kati's little hand in his own. "See the fireflies? See the lights?"

"Lights! Lights!" Kati took off in pursuit of one, then another. Just as they tired of their game, they heard the sound of a horse and wagon.

Franz almost flew to the gate to swing it open so Vati could drive through. He released the horse from the wagon and took him to the pasture behind his own bedroom. When finished, he joined the adults and Kati on the porch.

"Jani sent this to you. He said you earned most of the money for it," Stefan tossed the soccer ball to Franz. "They all miss you, but he's eager to come here for another visit. He really enjoyed last time."

Franz tossed the ball in the air and caught it. In Sombor, he'd play soccer with his friends. He sighed, and looked over to Anton's house. Now he lived in Stanisic and would have a game with new friends.

His father and grandfather stepped up to the porch and sat down. "How is the political situation now?" Opa asked.

"I don't know if this is significant or temporary, but theYugoslav Partisans strongest leader is a guy named Tito." Stefan answered. "They've become a tough guerrilla movement and now fight the Chetniks for control. Have you heard the latest along the Russian front?" Stefan continued when Nikolaus shook his head. "Germany attacked Russia a few weeks ago."

"Oh, no! None of this makes sense," he shifted in his chair, "It's been a while since I went to town for news, I have so much to do here before cold weather sets in. How bad is it?"

"Germans, Finns, Romanians, Slovaks and Hungarians gathered together for a big assault from several places. It's called Barbarossa. Apparently both sides have high mortality rates."

Franz sat down on the step. Constantly busy on the farm, he forgot the world outside. He thought of the parade, the shooting, days and nights of fear and boredom, explosions, blood and the awful missing eye. Safe on his grandparents' porch, he remembered. It couldn't happen here. Little prickles of fear danced along his skin.

"How this will affect Adam?" Oma leaned back in her rocking chair. Her chair slowly squeaked back and forth. She didn't expect or receive an answer.

"I've learned to milk the cow, Vati," The next morning Franz greeted his father in the kitchen. "Want to go with me this morning?"

"Sure, let me finish this coffee and I'll be ready."

Quite ignoring the fact his father had come here for years and always helped out, Franz led the way through the pasture gate, past the pigs and chickens to the cow barn. He picked up a clean milk bucket from the shelf. "Sometimes she won't stand still, but Opa taught me to talk to her and she usually settles down for me." This time she stood still at the sound of his voice.

"Shee. Shee." Franz began the rhythmic milking and a wild cat came at the sound of milk filling the bucket. Franz tipped up one teat, aimed at the cat and squirted before he returned to the bucket.

Franz giggled, "Cats are funny, aren't they? See how she's cleaned herself and no one told her she had to." The cat shook her whiskers and father and son looked at each other and smiled.

Gradually, the milk slowed and stopped. Franz took care of the cow, turned her into the pasture and carried the bucket to the pantry. "Want some cream for your coffee?" he offered.

"No, but your Mother and Oma both like cream in theirs, don't they?"

"Yes, and I like a little coffee in my cream!" Franz' laughed.

They scooped the cream off the top and poured the rest into milk jars, and tightened the lids. "Mama said today I should churn the cream into butter. She'll use the whey to make cottage cheese. The women usually do this chore, but they have laundry today."

"I'll help you." Stefan's eyes shinned with humor and pride. Franz felt quite mature.

"Will we move back home soon?" Franz asked.

"No." They carried the cream to the porch and poured it into the churn and began to turn the handle. "Business is still bad. Also, the Hungarian army didn't leave, so Chetniks surface from time to time. It's safer for all of you here right now." He winked and said "I can tell you're not tired of farm life. Soon you'll have school no matter where you live. This isn't so bad, is it?"

"No, but I miss you and Jani and my friends and I want to go home." Franz hesitated. Vati didn't like separation from all of them either, but he didn't complain.

"Tell me what you *do* like about life here."

"No one shoots at us," his lips tipped up in an effort to smile. "Also, it's interesting because we do everything here. Opa says we're 'self-sufficient'. He raises cows, chickens, geese and pigs for meat. The cow gives milk and butter – like now. From the garden we have potatoes, corn, onions and lots of food. Opa sells other crops to buy what we can't raise or make. Every day is different."

"I'm glad you're learning so much from your grandfather. "Franz thought his smile looked a bit sad. "You make me almost want to be a farmer as well."

Just then the kitchen door opened and Oma stuck her head out. "Stefan, would you go with Franz to get our veal for tonight? I think we'll need two pounds."

After they left the churned butter in the kitchen, Franz and Stefan walked several blocks to the butcher shop. When the bell over the door rang, Mr. Garevski came from the back. As usual, he wore a blood smeared white apron. "Hello there, Franz. What do you need today?"

"Good afternoon. Oma wants two pounds of veal today, please."

"Hello, Stefan," Mr. Garevski tipped his head in a friendly nod as he reached under the counter for his record book. "Hoger, Nikolaus . . . "his finger went down the list to Opa's name. In neat handwriting he recorded two pounds. "Tell your grandfather this I.O.U. will soon be used up."

"He told me I get to come with him in two weeks when we bring our three-month-old calf in to be butchered."

Mr. Garevski turned the book around to Opa's page. "See, I'll put the pounds in this book when we get the calf butchered. Then all year we keep track. Usually he runs out after a year or a little more."

Franz rocked back on his feet and looked up at Vati. "The veal we pick up today isn't from our calf. Opa said we have meat because our neighbors do the same at different times of the year. The meat here is always fresh and as long as we contribute a calf we can draw on those many pounds." They said good-bye to Mr. Garevski and walked home.

The weekend passed swiftly and Stefan took the wagon back to Sombor and his delivery job. And the farm work continued.

Early one morning Oma handed Franz a shovel after breakfast. "Follow me; it's time to put the potatoes to bed! They are nice and dry now." The corner section of the potato garden had been dug long ago, but each year they needed to line the five foot by six foot by five foot deep hole with fresh straw. Franz carried over many armloads and spread it along the bottom. Then he loaded dried potatoes in the wheelbarrow and brought them to the garden. On hands and knees, he and Oma distributed the straw.

"It's sort of like we're chickens putting eggs in a nest, isn't it, Oma?" Franz asked as he dropped a potato in and covered it with more straw. When they filled one thickness with potatoes, they covered it with straw and started another layer. The top required dirt spread over the whole area, which made a big mound above the ground. They placed a door on top of the dirt so they could take advantage of the occasional mild winter day, open the door and transfer potatoes to the pantry. Snow would add additional insulation.

"Franz, I'm so glad you're here to help us," Oma said. As she walked slowly back to the house, she leaned on him a bit.

"I'm glad we're here, too," he replied, and realized he meant it.

"A letter came from Adam!" Opa announced after he returned from town. They gathered on the porch where Elisabeth and Theresia shucked corn. One whacked the ends off and the other peeled the husks and silk off the ear. All labor ceased as Opa handed the letter to Elisabeth.

"Ahem," Elisabeth cleared her throat as she opened the letter.

> *Dear Family,*
>
> *I guess you are all busy this time of the year. I think of you getting ready for fall. Food from the garden is being preserved for the long winter. Soon you'll fatten the geese. The grapes are big and full of promise. I wish I were there. But it gives me pleasure to think of you all together. Franz, enjoy your farm chores in my place. I keep my slingshot in my pocket.*
>
> *I received a draft notice from the German Army. I don't know where they will put me, but always knew this might happen. I'll keep my job at the brewery until I know what to do next. Just pray for me and for the end of war for all of us. I think I'll be able to catch a military train and come home through Hungary before or after my training.*
>
> *I love you all,*
> *Adam*

Elisabeth folded the letter and put it on the table. "Well," she said simply. "At least we can hope he'll be here in the next few months."

Franz's heart felt full in his chest. Uncle Adam still kept the slingshot. He tipped his head down. He couldn't remember clearly what Uncle Adam looked like and he needed to see him again. Soon.

Franz' chores were done and he had free time. "Mama, if you don't need me now I'll see if Anton wants to do something."

"Have a good time; just don't be late for dinner."

He walked next door and found Anton in his father's shoe-maker's shop. "Tony and Adam just went to town – let's go there." Anton suggested. "Maybe we'll see the Town Crier since it's about time for him to give the news."

When a new law or ordinance passed at City Hall, or any-thing happened of concern to the area, the Town Crier spread the news. With no telephone service, he had an especially impor-tant job in the village. When the boys reached town, they saw his familiar uniform, cap and the shoulder strap around his neck with a drum in front of him. He beat a brisk marching song on his drum as he walked toward an intersection, stopped and com-pleted the tune while people assembled.

Satisfied with an audience, he called out "Hirek! Ma Mo Hirek!" the Hungarian Town Crier reached to the loop on the drum strap, pulled out the paper, unrolled it and read the news.

"Today is August 20, 1941."

"On the war front. May 1, Tito issued a pamphlet calling on the people to unite in a battle against the occupation. June 27, the Central Committee of the Communist Party of Yugoslavia appointed Tito Commander-In-Chief of all project national liberation military forces. July 1, the Comintern sent precise instructions for immediate action to defend USSR." Another drum roll. "Closer to home, Swartz's General Store has a large supply of flannel material ready to make those cold weather shirts."

"School starts September 15th this year. After the first of September enrollment begins for both public and Catholic schools." With his drum sticks, he did a rapid "Rat-a-tat-tat". "Hungarians will raise taxes – more later." Again a few beats of the drum.

Excitement mingled with dread. "School starts September 15," they repeated together the most important news. Franz knew some of his friends said the nuns were mean teachers, others said they were tough, but fair. Which would it be? This would be his first year in Catholic school and he would be in the fourth grade.

The Crier rolled the paper, returned it to the loop on his shoulder strap, beat the drum again as he continued half way down the block and repeated the news and announcements. Franz and Anton followed, skipping in circles behind the drummer as he moved to all five intersections and every block center. More children joined the parade, Georg and Jacob among them as they followed the Crier to the end of the block.

7

Late 1941, nine years old.
Stanišić, Yugoslavia

"Go!" Adam Sujer yelled. Adam, Franz, Anton, and Stefan Baier ran to the four holes that formed a large circle, each determined to put his hockey stick in one of them first. This time Franz was too late. "You're 'it'!" they all yelled together. Adam picked up the ball and threw it down the street and ran. Franz passed him and got closer to the ball, swung and missed. Adam moved in. "Got it," he shouted.

"Not yet," Franz swiftly pushed his stick behind the ball and whacked toward Home. Back and forth they ran in the dusty street. Franz kept control of the ball and guided it successfully till it dropped into the center hole.

The wind picked up, the temperature began to drop and they studied the dark clouds rolling in from the west. Probably time for one more round.

Each boy put his stick over 'home', and when Franz shouted "Go!" they ran to get an outer hole. Stefan got the hole Anton headed for. "You're it!" they yelled to Anton.

"This is our last game today." Franz grinned at Anton. "It's between you and me!"

Franz faced the street, ready to throw the ball. He glanced at Anton, who rocked from one foot to the other, slapping his stick in his hand. He glowered at everyone. When Franz jumped and gave a mighty throw, the ball zoomed up the street, Franz right behind it. The race accelerated.

Franz ran ahead and close to the ball. Suddenly, Anton stopped, turned around and stomped back to the circle with a wild look in his eyes. He swung his stick at his side in short, angry strokes, his head hunkered down.

"Uh Oh!" Franz said. He slowed down since he had no opponent. He shook his head at Anton's retreat. "I guess I win!" he shouted.

Anton stopped, turned around, and the other boys stepped away. Anton's fists gripped the stick, his eyes narrowed and he tipped his chin down a notch like an angry bull.

"The Look! He's giving you The Look!" Adam said and everyone laughed except Anton.

"Aren't you glad you taught me to play this game so good? Now I'm the best." Franz teased.

"You aren't the best! The storm is coming and I'm going home." Anton stomped off, still angry.

"He's sure mad, isn't he?" Stefan walked along with Franz, who simply smiled.

"Yeah, but he'll forget all about it tomorrow." He threw his ball in the air and caught it. "He's a lot of fun until he gets mad, but he doesn't stay that way long."

"I hope so," Stefan mumbled.

As they headed in different directions toward their homes, Franz glanced at the street that led south to the railroad. Someone walked toward him. He looked again. Why did the man look familiar? He wore the field-grey uniform of the German Army.

"Hello, stranger. Can you tell me where to find Franz Elmer?"

"I'm —," he cocked his head and looked closely at the soldier. "Uncle Adam!" he shouted as he ran to his grinning uncle. "We didn't know you were coming? How long can you stay? I'll bet Oma cries when she sees you!"

"Slow down," he raised the palms of his hands toward Franz in slow motion. "First, I didn't know ahead of time when it would work out. I'll be here two weeks. And you're probably right about Oma," he said with a wink.

"Oh, it is so good to be back here," Adam continued as he swung his bag over his shoulder. "I've missed all of you." They turned at Church Street to home. "What do you think of living here now?"

"Except for missing Vati and my friends in Sombor, I like it. School starts in a few weeks and I'll be in fourth grade at Immaculate Heart of Mary." He ran ahead a few steps as they approached the gate, and opened it to let Uncle Adam walk through first. Rain began to fall then, and they hurried into the house.

As expected, when Oma saw him, she burst into thankful tears and Mama joined her. Three-year-old Kati stayed back and eyed this man in uniform with suspicion as he answered questions from his mother and sister. Yes, Anna, Hans and their daughter Annie were fine. Annie, a young lady now, showed great talent for organizing them all. No he didn't know exactly where he would be sent. No, he hadn't met a special girl yet; later there would be time for romance. Oma shook her head at how thin he seemed but had to be satisfied since Augsburg provided a good place to work and live.

The sound of hail hitting the house drowned out conversation and they stepped out to the porch to sit and watch. It lasted about five minutes before it stopped abruptly.

"They're as big as large marbles," Franz picked up a handful.

"I want to get out of this uniform and into my own clothes," Adam stood and stretched.

"Why aren't you wearing the high boots?" Franz raised his eyebrows.

"You don't like these boots, huh?"

"Well, they won't look so good marching."

"No, I guess not. We're wearing these short boots because the need for leather is greater than its supply. They may not be as impressive, but they lace up quickly." He sat down and crossed his foot over his other knee and began unlacing his boots. "Look at the hob nails on the bottom and the steel on the toes and heels. Is this more fitting for a tough soldier?"

"Not as good as the tall, shiny black boots," Franz laughed at his own stubbornness. "Mr. Haut puts hob nails on the soles of shoes for when there's ice or snow, and sometimes Anton and I deliver them for his father. But they make it hard to sneak up on someone, don't they?"

"Elisabeth," Uncle Adam called to his sister, "Your son is not impressed by my German Army boots, and complains about the noise as well. What kind of soldier will he be?"

"I hope he never has to be any kind of soldier," She sat down by Adam, "He won't be eighteen for nine more years, and by then we'll live in peace." With a decisive nod, she smiled. "My son can use his mind and hands in work of his own choosing."

At the sound of a knock, Elisabeth turned to open the door to the Haut family from next door. Mrs. Haut held a plate full of butter cookies.

"Welcome home, Adam," Mr. Haut said. "We stopped to say hello and see how you're doing." Anton squeezed past his parents and came closer to Adam.

While the adults visited, Anton noticed the boots on the floor. He picked them up and studied the hobnails briefly, then put his hands inside and rubbed the bottom of the boots together.

"You're right, Franz, they are noisy!" Adam said.

"And they're hot," Anton brushed the soles together again. "Want to see?" He held one out to Adam. Before Franz or Adam's parents could warn Adam, he reached to touch the hot nails. Clump! Anton slapped the other shoe down hard on his hand.

"Ah, yes, it is hot." Adam shook his injured hand. "I take it you've done this before?"

Aware of all the looks of disapproval, Anton set the boots down. "Touching with a finger doesn't show how hot they are," he muttered, "but the nails on both sides of a hand do."

Obviously embarrassed, the Hauts apologized and abruptly said their good-byes. Mr. Haut pulled his son's arm in a tight grip as they left.

"I think your friend is in trouble." Uncle Adam observed with a cocky grin.

"He's in trouble a lot. He does this trick to other kids, but he's never done it in front of his parents."

<hr />

"How's Anna's health these days?" Elisabeth asked as she and Adam walked along the sidewalk.

"Some days are better than others — she seems to be having more problems with breathing and rests often. She's still cheerful and interested in everyone."

"Sometimes I wonder if she inherited something from her real mother. She died of tuberculosis and maybe somehow it caused Anna to be frail. She's smaller than I am, her hair is lighter brown and for some reason she's never been hardy .... ."

"How old was Mother when she married Father?"

"Eighteen. I don't know how she adjusted to being a child herself, then a mother with nine-year-old new daughter. I was born the next year. For me, Anna is part big sister and part mother."

"She fusses over me and any weight I've lost is due to exercise, not lack of good food. Living with Anna and Hans in Augsburg has given me a chance to know our older sister better. And their Anni is not a little girl anymore, but an interesting young lady." They walked along in silence for a while.

"How are things with Stefan's business?"

"Oh, Adam, he's discouraged right now, and so am I," she blinked back sudden tears, "with food shortages, people try not to buy any more than they need, which gives him less business and shops are closing. We have to do something, but don't know what." She stopped walking for a moment and lifted her chin slightly, "Stefan grew up in the city with all of its advantages and he has a need to know what's going on in the world around him. He's really not a farmer and doesn't want his father-in-law to make a job for him here."

"Well, there are many jobs available in Germany if he's interested. The big plants are in full production without enough people to work. Prisoners are being put to work because of the shortage."

"What kind of jobs?"

"Assembly workers are trained for their particular position, so not having experience isn't a problem. You could work, too, because women are needed as well."

"Me?" Elisabeth tried to picture what it would be like. "We hate being separated all week, every week. If we both worked, the additional income would sure help, but — what about the children?"

"I don't know. It's just something for you and Stefan to discuss, and Mamma and Dad might have some good advice. If you want me to, I'll get more information."

"Stefan comes tomorrow and we'll discuss the idea." She hugged Adam. "I'm so glad you're here, we all need you."

Franz dumped the rocks out of his pocket, placed one in his sling-shot and aimed at the edge of the sidewalk to a circle he'd drawn in the dirt. He pulled it back and the rock landed right in the middle. He looked for a better target and saw Anton run toward him. He looked frightened. As he hurried past, Franz became alarmed.

He wanted to follow, but hesitated and ran into the house instead. "Mama, Oma, something's wrong with Anton!"

Both women stopped their work and walked closer to the gate. "What do you mean?"

"He's got foam on his mouth. Like that dog! Anton looks blue."

Mama and Oma looked at each other. "Should we go over to see?" His grandmother took off her apron and draped it on a nearby chair. "I'll go."

Oma led the way, but Franz and his mother followed behind. They opened the Hauts' gate and saw Anton laying on the ground, his grandmother beside him. Anton breathed deeply, his face pale.

His grandmother smiled weakly and held up a plum. "This was in his mouth and he couldn't breathe." Her hand shook a bit as she patted Anton's head. "I got my fingernails into it and pulled it out."

By now Anton felt better and sat up.

"What happened? How did the plum get stuck there?" she asked.

"I went to the Hungarian section to play and one of the kids had some plums in his hand."

Oma stepped over to the nearby well and brought up a bucket of water and filled the ladle. She handed it to Anton and he drank slowly, but with thirst.

"He told me to close my eyes and open my mouth so I did. He pushed it in farther than he intended." He took another sip of water. "He sure looked scared when I couldn't breathe. I just wanted to get home. I knew it would be okay if I got here."

"I don't understand how you were able to run," his grandmother held up the plum and all three women looked at it. "Oh — see, there's a little dent on this half. The hail storm damaged a lot of crops, and I think this is one of them. It saved your life by letting you get just enough air to come home."

She held it up in the flat of her hand and they all stared at the misshapen plum. "I guess we'll have a special 'thank you' when we say our prayers tonight!"

Routine chores filled rest of the day and Franz enjoyed having Uncle Adam work alongside him as they fed the animals, collected eggs and milked the cow in the late afternoon. That evening Franz looked at Opa's book of the world and listened to conversations around him. Mama and Oma sewed new kurtze hosen for him to wear to school; they were not decorated with embroidery but had the usual suspenders and drop-front flap. He would be well dressed for the start the Catholic school year, but it would sure be nice to be sixteen, when he could wear long pants.

The next morning Vati came and helped with the morning chores. By late morning, Oma had started a big pot of coffee and they all gathered in the kitchen.

"How do you like living in Germany, Adam?" Vati asked as he sat in the chair next to Franz.

"Actually, I do like it. It's beautiful and everyone has work. I've finished basic training in the Army, so now I guess I'll be using it."

"Any guesses where you'll be sent?" Vati asked.

"There's a rumor our unit will go to Greece, but it might be sent elsewhere."

"Franz, please get the book of maps." Vati said, "It's easier to look at the map while we put together what we've heard." When

Franz brought the book, they turned it to the page of Europe, and spread it on the kitchen table.

"Last October Mussolini invaded Greece from Albania." His finger traced the route. "From what I understand, Italy's determined, but the Greek are a strong people. In November the Greeks threw the Italians back into Albania and a week or so later they defeated the Italian 9th army. In February Britain agreed to send forces to support Greece. Greece repelled another Italian counter-offensive in Albania." He looked up at Adam, "Does this sound somewhat accurate?"

"Yes," Adam said, "first Hungary invaded Yugoslavia, then Germany, with Italy and Bulgaria, finally got tired of Italy's gaining and losing Greece so they came in and dealt with the British and by April 22 the British withdrawal began. Now there's no real presence of Britain in Europe."

"So is the war almost over?" Franz asked.

"Probably not," Vati shook his head.

"You see," Adam explained, "this isn't really one war, but several happening at the same time all over the globe. We're just talking about what affects us most directly here."

"Franz, the Italians are like fleas on a dog — by June the Italians began to reoccupy Greece again while the Luftwaffe attacked Soviet aircraft bases. Also, Italy and Rumania declared war on USSR. So they desperately need a supply route up through Greece." They all leaned over the map.

Franz nodded his head as Uncle Adam and Vati pointed out the route.

"I heard Bor Copper in the Serbian area is at full production," Opa said. "Makes them pretty valuable, doesn't it? Greece is right next door."

"Yes, with Macedonia's chrome, zinc and lead mines, whoever holds Greece has their resources as well." Vati tapped the map for emphasis.

"Why do they need those things?" Franz asked.

"Bor has always been busy, but with the war there's an insatiable need for copper," Adam said. "Have you thought about how many radios are in use? How many airplanes, ships, ammunition and even phone lines?"

Franz and Opa looked at each other. "Lots," Franz guessed.

"Yes," Vati took up the discussion, "and copper is used in the wiring for all of them so it's vital. Copper is also mixed with zinc for shells. Chrome is needed to harden steel. Small arm shell casings are made of brass, which contains lots of copper; most bullets have a "jacket" of copper on them to keep them from fouling the gun barrel when fired."

"And lead is used in bullets," Franz said.

All four leaned their heads over the map again. They traced from Macedonia's mines, crossed over to Serbia for the copper mines and up through Yugoslavia, through Austria and then Germany. "Yugoslavia's extensive rail system is needed for transport along this route."

"What would you do if you're sent to Greece, Uncle Adam?" Franz asked.

"Maybe I'll get to stay on one of the surrounding islands and meet beautiful women." They all laughed. "But someone has to hold the line against Italy."

They all turned as Mama and Oma stepped through the doorway from the living room. "Franz, it sounds like you've had a good lesson in geography, natural resources and logic but we need our kitchen to start the noon meal."

"There are no more eggs, Mama," Franz announced. "Can I go play with my friends now?"

"Run to the pantry and get the small bucket of lye so I can stir it into this water and then you're free."

He ran for the lye and returned quickly. "Why are you putting the eggs into the water and lye?" He peered at the solution.

"Lye closes the fine pores on the egg shells to protect them so we'll have fresh eggs all winter, long after the chickens stop laying — which will be soon. I appreciate your help, and you can go now!" his mother said with a laugh.

⁂

Stefan sat beside his wife and lifted eggs from their baskets and gently put them in the solution. "Is Kati down for her nap?"

"Yes, our tired, cranky daughter really needed it!"

"I've got to leave tonight, but I like this. Just being with you, I mean." He dropped a couple of more eggs in. "I'm so tired of war. Everything is changed and I wonder if we'll ever have 'normal' life again."

"I know," Elisabeth said, "I find it scary — this is becoming real and our old lives are long ago." She wiped her hands on her apron and sat back. "Adam said Germany is desperate for workers, both men and women, and wages are good."

"I've heard that. Several people told me anyone can get a job at the munitions factory in Leipzig, but it would be a drastic move." He straightened his back. "It could also be a solution."

"The main thing I worry about is the children. Would we take them with us if we both go? Who would care for them while we worked?"

"I'm not sure it would be a healthy place for them anyway. Franz is used to a lot of freedom and it may not be possible there. Would it be better for them to stay with your parents?"

"I think they would love it. Franz is nine now, he's a big help and has friends and school starts soon. I don't want to leave him, but he'd be fine. Kati is my biggest concern. At three, she still needs me and quite frankly, I need her."

"I just don't know what to do. Manci and Peter never make me feel unwelcome, but they're crowded already. I'm just not keeping a route big enough to justify staying there." He took her hand and laced his fingers through hers. "Perhaps I could go to Germany by myself."

"I just hate our being apart so much. If we both go we could save money much faster to start over again when the war is over." She lifted his hand to her cheek. "Nothing is a completely good choice."

Nikolaus and Adam came in from working the north acres and sat down on the porch also. Oma heard their voices and joined them.

"Elisabeth and I are talking about the possibility of going to Germany to work; either both or all of us, or me alone." Stefan explained. "Nothing is decided— right now we're wondering what would be best for the children. What do you think?"

"You know we always want Franz and Kati," Nikolaus said "You're both welcome to live here as well, we'll make room. It doesn't matter what you decide about Germany, Franz and Kati have a home here." Nikolaus said.

"The children are happy, busy and we're family. It's safer here than most places." Theresia leaned over and took her daughter's hand, "I'd suggest you check things out and be sure before you take them with you."

A tear rolled down Elisabeth's cheek. "Actually, I think the children will be fine staying. I'm feeling sorry for myself if I'm not with them."

"If things were different, you could go there and check things out and return, but nothing is simple now." Adam leaned against a yellow brick porch support post. "It takes two days by train to get here and two days to return, all the checkpoints are a problem for civilians and it's simply not safe to travel as we could have a year or two ago. You'll have to live for a long while with whatever decision you make."

Stefan put his arm around his wife. "Let's take time and pray about it for the next few months. Then maybe we'll know what is best."

The squeak of the small gate as Franz and Anton came through effectively closed further discussion.

When Franz hugged his father goodbye later in the day, he noticed the adults were all a bit serious and quiet.

It seemed as if Uncle Adam hadn't been gone at all. He helped Franz with chores in the morning and worked with Opa in the afternoon until the evening meal. It left Franz free to do things with his friends, but he noticed Adam appeared restless and talked more about leaving soon.

8

1941—nine years old.
Stanišić, Yugoslavia

"ADAM, WITH YOUR help, we've finished planting," Opa leaned on his plow and looked over the field with satisfaction. "I like to plant winter wheat, it's like a bonus crop."

"When will we harvest it?" Franz asked.

"If it sprouts before freezing occurs, it'll remain dormant until the soil warms in the spring. Winter wheat needs a few weeks of cold before being able to flower so this should be just about right." Opa explained. "We'll harvest by early July."

They all looked at the sky as the sound of a screaming plane flew closer and louder.

"What kind of plane is that?" Franz asked as he shaded his eyes and stared off in the distance.

"It's a Junker Ju-88 —but it sounds odd. Something's wrong." Adam set his rake down and frowned as he watched the airplane. "See there's a bit of smoke on the bottom."

Franz thought the plane began a coughing sound.

Then the plane dipped out of direct sight as it went down beyond a line of trees and they heard a loud crash rapidly followed by a series of smaller explosions and a great cloud of smoke billowed upward. "I'd better go and see if someone can be helped."

"Yes, let's hitch the horse back to the wagon. Franz, throw the old hay in for a softer bed. Do you want us to come with you?" Opa asked.

"No," Adam said, "I think it would be best if you alert Mama and Elisabeth. If there are survivors, I'll bring them home where they can get treatment for any injuries."

"I could help you," Franz stood in front of Adam.

"True, but probably you would be of more help at home if your Oma or Mama want you to get Dr. Spreitzer or any run errands."

Franz nodded. First, he felt disappointment because he desired to see and not just be told what happened, but relief followed as memories of the Hungarian priest lying dead in the church flashed through his mind.

"We'll meet you at home," Opa said as he and Franz prepared to begin the two mile hike.

For the next hour, both Mama and Oma bustled around the kitchen to prepare food and gather first-aid items. Franz ran over to Anton's to tell him of the excitement and now both boys hung around the big gate, and waited impatiently. At last they heard and saw the wagon coming up the street. Adam sat alone on the seat. As they drew nearer, Franz saw a blue-eyed man with sandy colored hair sitting in the back and another man lying down.

The first man introduced himself, Heinz Walter, as Opa helped him get down from the wagon. "I'm not hurt," he said, "just a bit shaky, but I thank you for your arm."

Adam helped the other man scoot to the back of the wagon. They worked slowly, with little conversation.

Franz wondered how old he was. He looked far too young to be a soldier, his face smooth, his voice soft. The screen door swung shut and Opa returned to help.

"This is Karl Schmidt," Adam said, "and Karl, this is my father, Nikolaus Hoger." The men shook hands. "This is my nephew, Franz, and his friend, Anton."

"You look pretty good for a guy who just survived an airplane crash," Opa remarked. "What kind of injuries do you think you have?"

"We managed to bail out at the last minute, so didn't actually go down with the plane." He gestured beside him. "I grabbed the radio before I jumped and held it close to me. I may have broken some ribs when I landed on it. And an ankle is sprained, I think." He grinned, "The radio is fine."

Franz and Anton took the horse and wagon to the back pasture and quickly returned to the house so they wouldn't miss anything. A pot of Oma's specialty soup simmered as everyone gathered around the table. Franz held out a bowl as Mama ladled it generously, and took one to each man.

"The first thing I saw was a large shape looming over me," Heinz Walter waved one arm in an ark above his head, "Adam looked like a freaking angel when I looked up," the laughing man told his audience. "A big, dark, hairy angel with a smile on his face. Not a wing on his back or halo on his head, but a welcome sight!"

"I suspected you were dead until you opened one eye and whispered 'hello'. I almost fell over!" Adam laughed and turned to the other man. "I thought Karl had passed out until I tried to take his radio from him! No mother bear ever held more tightly to her baby cub than he did to his radio!"

"We were trained to never, never, never let our radio fall into enemy hands. While I could breathe, I'd save our means of communication." Karl laughed, but quickly winced as it became apparent any movement caused pain.

They ate in high spirits, all aware of what could have happened. After eating, Oma took old material torn into strips and wrapped Karl's ribs to keep him as rigid as possible, and propped up his foot. They used the radio to contact their commanding officer, who told them to spend the night and take the train in the morning and return to Germany. Since Adam needed to return as well, he decided to leave with Heinz and Karl.

"Good idea," Opa said. "It'll be safer for three well-armed German soldiers to travel to the train station in the Yugoslavians' area. I'll take you in the wagon so Karl won't have to walk very far."

As the evening stretched out, Karl and Heinz felt comfortable and accepted as part of the family. Filled with good food and fine wine, they leaned back and visited.

"We were told Yugoslavia is a strategic linchpin of the Balkan Corridor and as we flew from the Island of Crete back to Austria we were admiring its beauty. Then suddenly the plane failed for some reason," Heinz said. "We don't really know what happened."

He swirled the wine in his glass, and watched it go around. "We're thankful we have only minor injuries and we'll heal." He hesitated and studied Adam and Opa before he continued. "I wonder about Germany's future. Ultimately, will the war benefit Germany, or create mortal wounds?"

"Are you referring to something specific or war in general?" Adam asked.

"To be honest, I'm afraid Der *Fuhrer* has gone far beyond stretching the borders of Germany, but now seeks to be dictator of the world itself."

Total silence filled the room. Franz wondered if they'd stopped breathing.

Karl frowned and wiggled uncomfortably, "Heinz speaks too freely," he spoke quietly, in a deep growl, and the intensity of his gaze carried a warning.

"Yes, I know the penalty for criticizing Hitler is imprisonment or death," Heinz hesitated, "I see Germany being pushed and led step by step, in questionable actions."

"We conducted Blitzkrieg over Britain from September 1940 to this last May," he continued. "Did we gain anything but to expand the war? Daily, it seems, new troops leave for USSR and even Africa now. What are we fighting and dying for?"

Franz sat very still and studied the faces of the silent group. Oma, who sat beside Adam, reached over touched her son. Adam's face showed no expression, but he squeezed his mother's hand. Oma's chin quivered.

"I never understood the insanity of Yugoslav resistance groups battling each other—Mihailovic's Chetniks and Tito's Communist Partisans," Adam said. "But now I can't avoid war because it's everywhere."

"Hopefully this will be over soon and we can go back to our lives and families and return to being regular Germans," Karl said. "If you show me where I can bed down, I'm really tired now."

"I'm sorry," Heinz bowed his head, and then leaned back. He looked very tired as well. "All of you please ignore my rambling. I'm just frustrated and, as my Mother always said, the things we worry about don't happen. I'm just a simple man with a simple education. And I agree with Karl, it's time for some sleep."

Good-byes the next morning were brief and somber. Then Franz turned to hug Uncle Adam, and pressed his head to Adam's chest. "When will I see you again?"

"I don't know," Adam cleared his throat. "It's a blessing you're here with your Opa and Oma." And he was gone again.

As often happened when evening came, the adults brought out their chairs to the sidewalk. Everyone wanted to know about Adam and the downed plane. Slowly, the women congregated together in front of Oma's home, the men farther down, in front of the Hauts'. Pipe smoke circled the men's heads, wine in their glasses, as they compared farming news and, as invariably happened, talk of the war.

The women shared news of their families and of the war as it concerned people they knew. Franz had asked his mother how she knew so many people in the village so quickly. She reminded Franz she grew up in Stanisic and still had friends, but also she made new ones when she went to the village. "I knew their families as well, so this is like my big extended family," she explained.

The boys played kick-the-can in the street and the girls enjoyed jump ropes until it grew dark and cold and mothers called the children in and fathers gathered chairs as relaxed families returned home.

"Is something bothering you, Franz?" he shrugged his shoulders at his mother's question. "It can be helpful to talk about problems or questions." She resumed peeling a potato.

"Well," he gave a great sigh, "I'm kind of worried about Catholic school here. I heard the nuns are really mean and they scold all the time. Maybe the Hungarian school will be better."

Mama smiled as she took his hand. "Anton is the one who told you this, correct?" At his nod, she continued. "How often are you in trouble here at home? Or in school last year?"

"Sometimes, but not too often."

"How long does Anton go *without* being in trouble somewhere?"

"Sometimes a few days," he looked up and smiled in relief.

"You go to Immaculate Heart of Mary for a couple of months and then we'll talk about it, agree?"

It was still dark the next morning as Franz walked out the gate. They lived in the third house south of the northern most cross street in the Village. Anton lived in the fourth house. As Franz turned south, Anton came out of his gate and they began the half mile walk together. The Church sat at the center of the Village with school and the Nunnery adjacent. Despite his earlier misgivings, curiosity and eagerness filled him as he drew closer. During the eight-hour day some classes seemed to move quickly and others slowly. The priest spoke to them in the morning for a half hour and explained this period would be their religion class. By the end of the day, Franz' fears drifted away. The first day they weren't given homework, but Franz knew this would be an exception.

"Mama!" he cried as he entered the house. Oma and Mama had a plate with cookies ready for him. "The nuns were nice—they spoke German," he announced, "I thought since the Hungarians are in control they would use Hungarian, but Sister Beatrice said even 'if other things changed, God's school will not'," he stopped and took a deep breath. "We have exercises during the day, and most of the classes are interesting so I can sort of sit still. I met some new friends. You were right, Mama, this school will be fine."

After he went to his room and changed out of his school clothes, Mama called him. "Mrs. Haut died today, Franz."

"Anton's mother died!" his eyes widened in surprise.

"No, his grandmother. You know she's aged a lot this past year. Since this is Wednesday, she'll be buried on Saturday."

"Will Anton miss school?"

"Probably not," his mother said. "Mr. Haut went to pick up the coffin this morning. We're cooking a special strudel for them."

Franz walked over later with his mother and grandmother and grandfather to carry the strudel and offer condolences. A pole by the sidewalk held a black flag on its top, announcing a death in the family. Visitors clustered in groups, speaking quietly. The entrance to the living room had been draped with black fabric and as they entered, they saw the coffin placed on two chairs with flowers around it and candles added soft lights to the darkened room.

Franz hung back a moment as the others went to see Mrs. Haut in death. He wished he stayed home, or hadn't continued to this room. It was too late. Now he'd draw attention to himself. Taking a deep breath he glanced quickly at the body, then looked again. She could have been asleep, except her hair was fixed up and she wore a Sunday dress. Relief flooded him. It wasn't like the violent and bloody death of the priest. His mother looked down at him with her eyebrows raised in question and nodded at his little smile. They filed out of the room as others entered.

The rest of the evening passed in routine chores.

As Mama predicted, a subdued Anton continued to school with Franz on Thursday and Friday. Saturday morning turned cold and clear. Opa and Franz completed their regular chores and changed into their Sunday clothes. He had just enough time to go meet his father's train and walk home with him.

The train had already pulled in. Franz looked over the platform till he saw Vati walking toward him. With a big smile, he began to run.

"It's so good to see you," Vati said as he hugged Franz, "but you didn't have to dress up for me, so why do you look so clean and pressed?"

"Anton's grandmother died. The funeral is in a little while."

"Let's go," Vati handed Franz a small bag.

Franz peeked inside. "Candies! Can I have one now?" he asked as he reached in for a favorite.

"Apparently, you can," Vati chuckled. They began walking back to the farm. "How was your week? What do you think of your new school?"

"It's good. I've got a lot of friends around the neighborhood in the same school."

"What's the best thing about living here?"

"The best thing?" Franz cocked his head thoughtfully. "Maybe it's the farm work. Every day is a little different and Opa really needs my help. He teaches me things like how to read the sky for the weather. Did you know animals can tell time? If I'm late milking the cow, she gets mad." He danced around a bit and flexed his arm. "Opa calls these my farm muscles." He laughed.

"But I really like my new friends here so I have lots of favorites."

"How about Katie—what does she do for friends?"

"Oh, she goes with Mama or Oma when they go to the market and sometimes Katie visits with Mama's friends. Some of them have little girls. So Katie has friends here, too."

"Little girls need friends, too, don't they?" Vati said. "It's a nice village and I'm glad you're here." Companionable silence filled them both as they walked.

"How is Jani? What are my friends in Sombor doing?"

"Mostly school I guess. Recently he fell out of a tree onto bushes and has scratches all over and a sore arm."

Franz laughed. "Boy, I wish I'd seen that! I'll bet he's getting teased a lot."

They turned onto Church Street and saw there were more people than usual congregating at the Hauts' house. Vati had time to say hello to the rest of the family, but quickly cleaned up and changed shirts to join them.

Anton came over. "Our house is filled with relatives I don't know. And they all hug me and talk about how I've grown." He frowned. "What else would I do - shrink?" Under strict orders from both of their mothers to stay clean, the boys went to the pantry and cut off a piece of smoked pork. They sat on a nearby wall, swung their feet and ate.

A few minutes before eleven, a black carriage pulled by two horses draped in black and a driver wearing a black suit and top hat stopped in front of the Hauts' house. Six men entered and carried out the coffin. Windows on each side of the carriage were covered in black as well, so Franz couldn't see anything there. The Haut family led other mourners as they slowly walked behind the carriage to the cemetery.

Franz' mind wandered as the priest droned on in Latin. He sighed. The school required the students to attend five o'clock mass several evenings each week, and there would probably be some Latin then as well. Anton stood in front, between his mother and father. Franz smiled to himself as he watched the back of Anton's head lean to one side, then the other, both forward and back. His father put his fist on the back of his head and gave him a sharp knuckle knock. Anton stood straight and still. For a little while.

On Sunday afternoon Elisabeth and Stefan waited until they heard Franz shut the gate and head off to meet his friends. Stefan took her hand and they sat on the porch swing.

"We came to a decision last night, but we can still change our minds," he said.

"No," she shook her head, "the facts don't change. There are no jobs available for you here, and there are in Germany. And if we both go, we'll save up money much faster to start over again when things get better." She stood up and looked over the farm. "This is the best place for our children now, with or without me here. My parents love Franz and Kati so much and will keep them busy and useful as well as safe and secure."

"I asked Franz about life here when he walked me from the train. I was glad to hear that he's made friends, likes school and has plenty of love and work here. And Katie has some friends of her own, I understand."

She sat down again and leaned against Stefan. "It's going to be difficult to be separated from them now, but if we keep focused on why we're doing this, it will be easier. It's not forever." She took a deep, bracing breath, and expelled it quickly.

"Then we tell the children before I leave this afternoon? Or should we wait a couple of weeks so they don't have too much time to worry about it?"

"We can let them know you're going to Germany because they're used to your being gone every week. I think it might be good to leave before my father's Saint's Day celebration on December sixth—the many activities will make it easier for them."

Elisabeth pressed her lips together. Her head knew this was the right decision for the situation. If only her heart could be so practical . . .

———

The nights began to be very cold and days shorter, a slow drizzly rain fell for three days. Each day Franz came straight home from school, changed clothes, and did his homework at the table. Mama leaned over his shoulder often and observed. He wanted to rush through the assignments, but knew it was faster to do his best or Mama would make him do it over again. And again, until he got it right. Kati sat beside him, doing her 'homework' as well. At three years of age, she made many scribbles, then read her story aloud, or drew pictures. Somehow, her presence made it easier for him to concentrate on his own, real lessons.

By the weekend, the sky cleared and all the children in the neighborhood were eager to for adventure. Anton, Stefan, Adam and Toni filed through the gate just as Franz finished mucking the cow's pen. Anton saw him in the distance and led the way.

"A bunch of us are meeting at the old tank trenches! Want to come with us?"

"As soon as I get this stinky coat and my barn boots off and put on my regular coat." He unbuttoned as he ran. "Be right back, I'll meet you at the gate." True to his words, he quickly returned much cleaner and better smelling. They all headed a mile north out of town, several conversations going on at once.

"I saw the anti-tank trenches with my Uncle Adam when I came here before."

"Before?" Stefan asked, "Before the April bombing, you mean?"

"Yes, but I didn't live here then. Anton told me you guys come here to ride a coal hopper with wheels on the train track."

As they walked up the road over the crest of the small hill, he saw the results of the Hungarian attacks. Various sized slabs of concrete stood at angles above the ground, where last time they'd been out of sight below the surface of the grass. Franz stopped and tried to recreate in his mind how it looked just the year before. With Uncle Adam he'd looked off in the distance and seen a long, snake-like trench at forty five degree angles deep into the ground and a bunker in the distance. Now the bunker was gone—concrete chunks flipped over its top. He vaguely recalled there'd been a narrow gage track running alongside the trench and up the hill. Some of it remained.

As Franz looked around, three other boys were already by the track. Quickly, others joined them as they surrounded an old u-shaped coal hopper off to the side. He saw they'd already put the frame with wheels on the track. The bucket had handles on each end and they lifted and shoved it get it close to the wheels. With a big grin, Franz ran to join them.

The youngest of the group, Toni Baumgartner, assumed leadership of a sort. With the hopper in their hands the boys who lifted it couldn't see the wheels. "The back is too far over — move toward the trench about an inch!" Toni watched closely, "that's it, lower it down!" and it settled firmly on the wheel frame.

As soon as Anton jumped in, Franz joined him and quickly most of the others as well. Toni gave it a good shove and hopped over the side as it started to roll.

Cold wind whipped their faces and the boys shouted loudly to mimic the sound of bombs as they picked up speed on their way down the six hundred foot incline. As it slowed to a stop they all climbed out and pushed the hopper back up the hill.

"It rocked sideways on the track more than I thought it would!" Franz shouted enthusiastically.

"This time, hold your hands in the air, don't hold on to the side!" Anton said. Once more they loaded up and shoved off. Most of them successfully held their hands in the air, and stood in the hopper with their feet apart and legs tightened for balance. Whew! The ride came to the end too quickly.

Again, they pushed it up the hill.

"Lean forward! Maybe it'll go faster!" Franz said. Eager for a new twist in their sport, they quickly tried any new idea.

After an hour or so, they pushed it up the hill for the last time. "Do we want to take it off the track here, or put slabs at the end and jump out?" They all agreed to go down one last time and stop there.

Franz and Anton ran to the bottom and pushed and shoved some cement slabs over the track to stop the hopper, then raced back to the top, and jumped in.

"Franz," Anton said before they shoved off, "when we get near the bottom, be ready to jump and when we yell 'jump!' then do it. You don't want to be inside when it hits the stop—you'll lose your teeth!"

Franz nodded and off they shoved. At the shout, all eight boys scrambled out the sides and back. From his place on the grass, Franz looked quickly and saw the hopper hit with a loud whack, and it flew about ten feet in the air. Good thing he'd been warned to jump out.

"We dismantle it so the other kids don't play here," Anton explained. They all headed for home, amid a lively discussion on which trip down had been the most exciting. Franz favored the last one, where they jumped out just at the right moment. Not too early, for that would have been far too easy. Not too late, for it could have actually hurt them. It required the skill of perfect timing. And he eagerly looked forward to next time.

9

Nov/Dec 1941—nine years old
Stanišić, Yugoslavia

"WHEN WILL THEY be fat enough?" Franz carried the last of the 20 geese to Oma. He looked to see how much corn remained soaking in the barrel of water.

Oma sat on her stool, reached up to take the grayish brown goose and placed it between her knees. "We'll feed them for another week. It takes four or five weeks." She opened the goose's orange bill and put a handful of corn in its mouth and pushed it down its craw. Franz had helped her every afternoon for more than three weeks.

"We'll finish next Saturday, when you don't have school. It's time for you to learn how to clean them."

As planned, on Saturday Oma and Mama were set up on the back end of the yard to begin turning geese into food for the months ahead. Again, Franz rounded up the geese. Kati followed behind him, doing her best to help.

"Let me carry one, Franz." She reached out her hands while Franz looked around for a light weight one. Scooping up a smaller goose, he handed it to Kati. Smiling happily, she stroked its back. "I'm taking you to my Mama and Oma."

"Does the goose have a name?" Franz teased playfully.

"Yes," Kati said thoughtfully, "Her name is Supper." She grinned triumphantly when everyone laughed.

"Franz, you're about to pluck your first goose today," said Mama, "so listen to Oma and you'll learn to do it well. These soft down feathers will be added Oma's last batch to make you a larger comforter and new pillow for the long, cold nights ahead."

Oma sat down on the bench, and turned a goose to face Franz. "Down feathers are here," she gestured to the whole front, "Pull the feathers out with the grain, otherwise some will break off in the skin and we'll notice every one we bite into. Drop the down into this box. Start on the neck, go down over the belly and finish when you're past its legs."

Awkward at first, he pulled a few feathers as the goose watched him. His dimples deepened as he felt their softness.

"No, not one at a time," Oma corrected, "but grasp them like this." She showed him to bend his forefinger and squeeze several between his finger and his thumb. She nodded cheerfully at his hand. "Milking has made your fingers stronger." Before long he pulled them out quickly and smoothly. Occasionally one would poof out and float upward. Then he'd blow it, making a game of getting it into the box, or sometimes he'd blow it to Kati. She picked up the game and did her best to blow it away, but she had a hard time giggling and blowing at the same time. One by one, most of the geese were plucked.

"Vati will be here today," Franz commented. "Will we eat some of these while he's here?"

"If you want to, we will," Oma said. They handed off the goose to Mama, who twisted the head, cut it off, then clipped away the wings and claws with pruning shears, extracted the heart, liver and gizzard. All unused parts were tossed in a refuse bucket, anything the pigs would eat saved separately.

"Wow! You're fast!" Franz marveled as he watched his mother's swift, efficient movements.

"After years of practice, I guess I am," Mama agreed with a chuckle, then cocked her head. "Do you remember we told you Vati is going to Germany to work?"

"This time he'll go there instead of returning to Sombor, won't he?"

"Yes, he'll be here today and stay all week so he can spend more time with you and Kati before he leaves." She grabbed another goose and continued the process as she replied. "We've talked about me going with him and we'd both work there." She glanced at Franz. "We could earn money faster if I go, too."

"We'll move to Germany?" He blinked his eyes in surprise.

"No," she continued to work steadily, "just Vati and me because we'll work long hours to save as much as possible. You and Kati will stay here. You've got school and Opa needs help with the farm and all of you will take care of Kati."

Kati noticed Franz's confusion, stopped talking to the remaining geese and walked to him. She slipped her hand into his.

As she picked up another goose, Mama watched the children. Oma plucked the last goose. And Kati looked from one of them to the other.

"Any questions?"

"Why can't we all stay here?" he sighed dramatically and shook his head.

"Sometimes we don't get to do what we want. You know how hard Vati has tried, but jobs just aren't available. He could live here and help with the farm, but we need to earn money. When the war is over we'd still be broke. This way, we can start again." Mama kept working but blinked her eyes rapidly a few times.

"Come on, Franz, time to take off the larger feathers and wash the geese to cook them." Oma picked up a de-clawed, de-winged, beheaded one and placed it in Franz's hands. "Let's get them cleaned so we can do the fun part and cook." They finished in relative silence.

Franz watched as the women first cut geese into parts and then fried them. He placed them in round containers, each layer covered with hot lard. This went on layer by layer until all the parts were protected. As containers filled, Franz carried them to the pantry above the wine cellar where he placed it on a 10 foot x 12 inch shelf, beside the canned vegetables and fruits.

As they worked, they discussed the St. Nikolaus' day celebration the next week.

"Why do we celebrate Saint Nikolaus?" Franz asked.

"Opa was named after him, so every year we celebrate Opa on his saint's day, as do all Catholics named Nikolaus." Mama handed him another slice to put into the container and poured the lard over it. "December 6 is the celebration of St. Nikolaus, a bishop from Asia Minor who died on that day a long, long time ago. He did a lot of good deeds during his lifetime, especially for people in need. It's a good name for Opa."

Just as they finished, Franz heard the familiar sound of Vati's wagon enter the gate. He ran out the door, Kati right behind him. Vati's eyes lit up and his smile spread over his whole face as he hugged Franz and picked up Kati and swung her up to his arms. "My *lieblings!*" he said with enthusiasm as he hugged them again. The evening passed in cheerful reunion without mention of Germany. Franz took it as much needed reassurance.

The next few days turned bitterly cold as a blizzard dumped two feet of snow. They did necessary work outside and Franz didn't miss school, but they were content to stay inside doing projects and catching up with reading. Vati played games with them and read stories and tucked Kati in each night. He helped Franz with his chores, both before and after school.

Late in the afternoon, Franz milked the cow while his father mucked out the stall. When they finished, Vati sat down on a bale of hay and waved Franz over to join him. "Son, we've not talked very much about what it will be like when Mama and I go to Germany. Do you understand Mama and I, as well as Opa and Oma, have thought this through and it seems to be the best choice of bad options?"

"I guess. But you won't come home weekends, will you?"

"No, and it will be the hardest part for all of us. The train ride might take several days each way. If we're working we won't be able to leave any time we want to."

A single tear rolled down Franz' cheek.

"A man has to do whatever it takes to support his family. Eventually I want to have another butcher shop, but will take money. Money we don't have. We'll make this work by leaving you with grandparents. They love you and Kati fiercely, and they need you here as well." He sat quietly, letting Franz think about it.

"Maybe it won't take very long," Franz said softly.

"We all hope it doesn't." He put his hand on Franz' shoulder and squeezed.

Excitement for the St. Nikolaus celebration built up, even as they looked to the overcast sky for a good weather forecast. All discussions were bittersweet since Mama and Vati would leave two days before the big day.

Finally, the sun came out and the wind settled on Saturday.

"Today I want you to organize the smoke house for the new meat," Oma said, "and make sure there is a good supply of corn cobs for the fires."

She started to go back into the house when his friends came by and she overheard them ask him to go to town with them.

"What do you think, Elisabeth?" Oma asked his mother. "Can we spare him for a while?"

"You boys have been rather house-bound because of the weather. Franz, you can go as long as you get back in time for your chores."

With excited chatter, Franz, Anton, Adam and Tony escaped to play and explore.

Snowballs were made and thrown and feet turned into skis as they went up the street. In the distance they saw the Town Crier, almost unrecognizable because his uniform was covered by a long, warm coat and stout boots. He began to beat his drum and invite a small crowd to hear the news. By the time the boys arrived, the Crier reached to the loop on his drum strap, pulled out the paper and unrolled it with his customary ceremony.

"Today is December 2, 1941" he announced importantly. "Present temperatures hover around four degrees, the highest it has been for a week." He tapped his drum to change the subject. "Despite record cold temperatures and heavy rains, the Russian Front has been pushed east to Kursk earlier this month, then in the Crimea, where Simferopol and Yalta have fallen. Sources say the German Army and Hungarian Third Army's Rapid Corps continue advancement into Russia with only summer kit. Troops suffer extreme cold, reportedly minus forty degrees, without proper clothing and supplies. Engines don't start, and frostbite is a growing problem for both men and weapons. Worse, there are heavy losses in the Hungarian Second Army." Another rat-a-tat of the drum.

"Swartz's General Store has a new shipment of flour and is priced to please our local ladies."

He rolled the paper and replaced it in the drum strap, picked up his drum and did his marching tune and headed for the next place to stop and repeat the news.

The boys looked out over their snow-covered paradise and tried to reconcile the two different realities. "I heard the Crier's news, but it's more like he told a story," Adam said, "I mean, I know it's true, but it doesn't *seem* real." He hesitated. "Understand?"

Franz nodded his head. "I think I'm glad Adam is in Greece, but it's like he's just off on a vacation, not to war."

Just then a snowball hit him on the back of the head and he turned to Anton's grin of challenge. And the game began again.

After being cooped up inside for the past week, the boys thought of nothing but freedom. They returned to Toni's and built a gigantic snow fort. Other boys joined them and several hours passed with many battles won and lost before their cold feet and hands became unbearable and hunger drove them to end their game.

As he turned for home he remembered he should have left earlier. As soon as he saw his mother's stern face, he wanted to give a good explanation but there was none.

"I'm sorry I'm late," he began, "we just had so much fun I didn't think."

"Oma told you what she needed you to do. I think you owe her an apology." Franz saw the worry in her eyes. "When we're in Germany and you're here, I expect you to be of great help to Oma and Opa."

Franz looked at the ground. "I'm sorry," he mumbled again and went in search of Oma.

"You'll have to double up on your chores tomorrow, but I think you can do it, don't you?" she asked. "Opa will be home soon so you get cleaned up and set the table."

Thankful for the easy pardon, Franz hurried.

The next day he worked double fast. Vati helped him pull out the large wooden tubs used to clean the hogs and all equipment they would need. Then they moved things around in the smoke house to allow the additional meat to hang there, and kept up with the usual tasks. Usually he worked quite a bit of the time with Opa, but now on his parents' last day before they left, he and Vati enjoyed the day together. Much of the time they worked without words, other moments they talked about the celebration and their dreams for after the war when life promised freedom, prosperity and being together.

"Maybe we'll go to America, like Opa did," Franz smiled as he looked off to the future.

"We'll have wonderful things to experience," Vati said pensively.

The next morning the men did the necessary farming while Mama and Oma packed for the trip to Germany. They gathered around the table for breakfast, each tried to act as if it were a normal morning, but didn't quite succeed. Even Kati remained subdued.

The clock chimed the hour and Opa and Franz took Mama and Vati to the train station. The train came on time and they were off, waving out the window.

"Seems we get to take people to leave us, doesn't it, Franz?" Opa asked. "But we'll all get through this time just one day and then another." They climbed back into the wagon and started for home. Franz' eyes watered. It could be simply the sunshine on the bright snow. Or because he missed his parents already.

"Have you ever wondered why I have so many fields for farming?" When Franz shrugged, Opa continued, "The land is ours. The weather changes, we plant different crops, but land stays. We always have food—if one crop fails, another thrives. If one animal dies, others are available. It's security and it gives me peace to know I'll be here till I die and pass it on to my children and grandchildren. Your mother, Adam and Anna grew up here. They always know where home is, even when they move away with their own families, this is still home." He shook the reins to make the horses pull the wagon a bit faster.

"We just stay here, and after the war they'll all come back. Right?"

"Yup," Opa answered with a decided nod.

And Franz felt comforted.

St. Nikolaus Day celebration began about five in the morning when Franz and Opa started the fire and pumped well water to boil. Opa built the brick cooker years ago. Three feet high, it had a large opening below for fuel to keep the fire burning. Yesterday he'd shoveled much of the snow away from the porch and courtyard and some in the area where the hogs would be butchered.

"You have two main jobs today. First, keep water hot and available here for the slaughter and for the women to use inside. Second, keep the fire going with sufficient corn cobs." Opa said. "I don't think I told you why we have to separate the hogs and take them out one at a time, did I? If they see each other butchered, they get stressed and run around their cage and get all upset. It sets off some kind of reaction and their meat is tough and doesn't taste good at all."

"Maybe Mama ought to sing to them, they'd fall into a peaceful sleep," Franz laughed at the picture in his mind, then remembered his mother was gone.

"If you had fed the hogs last night as usual, you would never do it again before butchering. I don't know any words to describe the foul odor of the bile in the gallbladder and if the stomach had been full, it would have smelled terrible also. All the water they had instead of food helped to clean it out."

As soon as a bucket of water got to the boiling point, they poured it in one of the three large hog-sized wooden tubs. "Think you can keep the hot water coming all day?" Opa asked with a twinkle in his eyes.

"All day?" Franz looked uncertain, then smiled. "Yeah. Anton, Adam Sujer and Stefan will be here with their fathers or grandfathers. They'll help."

As the sun rose and shed light, men trickled in, each with their own leather apron.

Two six-foot chains with a handle at each end were placed in the tub of boiling water with the handles draped out over the edge of the tub After each hog was killed and placed inside, four men, two on each side of the tub, took the handles and pulled the chain back and forth, up and down to remove the its hair.

As Franz and his friends pumped water and hoisted the buckets onto the cooker, they also kept an eye on the fire and shoveled corn cobs in, as needed, for fuel. When a container came to the boiling point, they put the stick through the handle and two boys carried it to the hog tubs. They kept busy, but while they waited for water to heat, they observed everything.

After the removal of hair, the hogs were hung by their legs on a hoist in a tree. Another man took a cone shaped funnel, made of sheet metal, to scrape the remaining hair away, especially around the head and the legs. The hogs were then split down the middle, lengthwise, and gutted. Mid-morning by now, the fresh livers, pieces of the jowls and the hearts were removed from all of them and taken to the kitchen. They were fried and served along with eggs and bread so everyone would have a good hearty meal after their hard work.

When Oma announced breakfast, no one loitered, but washed up, took their filled plates and ate before it cooled.

"Well, ladies, now our real work begins," Oma, and the rest of the women stood and began to collect dirty dishes and tableware. "After we get these washed and out of our way, we'll prepare the intestines and stomach and start the sausage."

While they cleaned up after the meal, the younger children ran around throughout the kitchen and living room, played tag, hid from mothers and peeked around corners to watch them and entertained themselves in various ways.

"Elisabeth and Stefan left a couple of days ago, didn't they?" Mrs. Haut asked, her hands in dishwater.

Several heads turned in surprise and looked to Theresia for news of her daughter.

"Yes," she lifted one bowl to a high shelf, "for those who don't know, she and Stefan went to Germany to work. The children will stay here. It'll take time to find jobs and get located there, and Stefan said we should assume letters may be read so we'll have to be careful with details even then."

"Everything's changed, isn't it?" another woman said, "We have so many people to pray for now. I think every one of us has a family member active in the war."

"And we'll have lots of food put up for them when they do return and we can all celebrate!"

Just then Anton and Adam brought a pail with the intestines and stomachs from the hogs to the women. "We washed the outsides off pretty good," Adam said.

Franz and Stefan Baier carried a bucket in on a broom handle, "We've got more water heating. We'll bring it in soon," Franz said.

"Thank you, boys," chorused the women.

The intestines were dumped out on an old tarp spread on the table, and several women sat around it. "The boys did a good job of cleaning the outside, didn't they?" Oma asked. It had been cut in long, manageable pieces. Oma and Mrs. Sujor, Adam's mother, each took one, put a small clip on one end of the intestine and pushed it inside, working it along the way till the intestine turned inside-out and spread them across the table. Now the tedious and difficult work began for all the women. Similar to a quilting bee, they visited as they worked. Each took a blade and began to scrape the porous tissue clean of the inside membranes. As they worked, moving it occasionally, and turning it over, they caught up on news of their children and grandchildren. And they continued to scrape. A few recipes were traded. Kati and the other young children climbed up into their laps long enough to be bored, and then toddled off to play again. Finally satisfied, they washed the intestines in hot water and put them aside. Next, the process began with the stomachs and another bucket of hot water was brought to them.

Franz leaned to peer over Oma's shoulder. "The inside of the stomach looks like a giant sponge, doesn't it?" He watched the scraping process a few minutes, but then left to join the real action outside.

"I've got to walk around a minute to stretch my back," Oma said "I'm don't usually spend so much time in one position." She went to check on the children, then returned, picked up her blade and resumed work.

Opa and Mr. Sujer stood on opposite sides of one of the hanging carcasses and began to saw away on a thigh with sturdy butcher knives. "You boys know what this is, don't you?" Mr. Sujer asked with a cheerful whack.

"Ham!" they all shouted together. They looked down the line where teams of two worked on the other hogs for ham retrievals.

"Bacon will be cut next," Franz said. He ran to Opa, "Do you need us for a while or can we go play?"

"Go on, we've plenty of men to do this heavy work. Just don't be too long."

Tired of the cold, they tramped into the house, shed coats, mittens, hats and dirty boots. Franz got the marbles and they sat in a circle in the living room near the blue enamel stove. He stirred the coal and then added some more. As they played, Kati moved into the middle of the circle and giggled. She looked around at their frowns and giggled again. This time Franz chuckled with her as he picked her up and put her on his back.

"Watch us play from there." He reached and patted her head as her chin rested on his shoulder. The other little ones laughed and squealed as they threw themselves into the new game and piled on the other boys. "A little thing like monkeys on our backs won't slow us down!" he said, "put your shooter marbles down and let's play." One by one, they lost their passengers and played without distraction till all the marbles had been captured.

"Guess we'd better see if we're needed out there," Franz suggested after an hour passed and they were sufficiently warmed and relaxed.

"Wow! Look at all the hams and bacon!" Adam yelled as they ran to see what had been done while they were inside.

They counted six big hams and dozens of one and a half foot by three foot long slabs of bacon. Nearby, a huge pile of fat waited to be turned into lard.

The rest of the afternoon, knives constantly cut up the other meat into chunks and put the pieces through the grinder for sausage. Seasoned and again sent through the grinder for finely sized pieces, clean intestines were brought out and pulled over the nozzle. As the handle turned, meat pushed into the intestine. When about ten to twelve inches of meat filled the casing, they twisted it around to make a link. This continued until the intestines were filled. Next, the stomach casings received seasoned, coarse meat.

Franz and Anton carried a big copper kettle with water to the kitchen. As water simmered, the sausages cooked until done.

"Boys, take the Stomach Sausages to the smoke house and be sure to put the weights on to flatten them." Oma looked at the group of boys. "I think some of you call this Head Cheese—well, it's the same thing."

By evening the sausages were ready and the aroma of meat and seasonings floated outside every time the door opened. Neighbors stomped the snow off their feet, carried their pots in for soup after a hard day's work.

"Thomas, will you be ready for us to come celebrate St. Thomas Aquinas on January 28?" Opa asked.

"I think St. Thomas would be very pleased if we do," he replied. "Hmmm this is sure good! We should thank St. Nikolaus for giving us this saint day."

As neighboring families left, the house seemed to take an audible sigh and settled down.

"Tomorrow we'll do the smoking and finish preserving, but now I'm ready to go to bed early," Opa said. He slowly lit his pipe and leaned back in his chair.

Kati crawled onto to his lap, curled up and fell asleep instantly. Oma carried her into bed.

"Your brick is in the oven, Franz," Oma said when she returned. She opened the door and pulled it out, wrapped it in a towel and handed it to him. "Sleep well. You really worked hard today." She patted his cheek softly.

He took the brick and went to his room behind the pantry where there was no heater. He put the brick under his down-filled comforter and exchanged his clothes for pajamas. As he lay in bed, he thought of his mother. "Mama," he whispered, "I kept busy as you said I should, but I missed you and wanted you here."

With a slight sniff, he turned to his side and fell asleep.

10

Spring 1942, nine years old.
Stanišić.

"COME ON, IT'S the first beautiful day we've had in a long time. Come play a little Land Hockey, then do your chores." Anton coaxed even as he began to run up the street to join some others.

"You go on and if I get done in time, I'll be there." Franz hollered. For a moment regret welled up in him, but then left. "Anton just doesn't understand," Franz muttered.

How could he explain to Anton—who never thought ahead—how Opa and Oma depended on him? Even harder, there weren't words to tell how he'd come to love the farm and the land itself. He thought of the sketch Opa drew to show him how the Danube and the River Tisza ran parallel from north to south. As the Danube passed Somber, it turned left and flowed east and the two rivers joined and flowed through Romania into the Black Sea. Opa told him this area, where they lived, between the two rivers is called the Batchka. This ideal farm land had very rich, jet black soil with no rocks. Well, there would be other days for Land Hockey.

As soon as he arrived home, he changed into work clothes, cleaned out the bedding for the cow and horse, and put new straw in both stalls. Then he built up a fire on the stove to heat water so when his grandparents and Kati returned from the fields they could wash up before Oma started dinner.

"Oma and I followed Opa and his hoe," Kati explained proudly as she lathered her hands. "Oma carried the sack of kernels and I helped plant them. Did you know they'll grow into tall corn someday?"

"If they don't become weeds, I suppose they could be corn." Franz teased.

"Oma said they'll be corn," she said with finality as she gave him a stern look.

Franz and Opa shared a smile. "And if Oma said it, corn is what it'll be." Opa said as he playfully tugged at one of Kati's curls.

"Tomorrow the herders start spring roaming time." Opa said when they sat around the table. "You weren't here last year, so I think you'll find it interesting. We have five Yugoslavian hog herders who take all the hogs to the barren land west of the village every day during the week from our street and the other four north-south streets. When we hear the herders' small trumpets come from north Main Street, we open our gates and all the hogs go out and follow the whistle to his herder. They have whips to guide them the right direction, but they are seldom needed. The hogs love to run free before pigging time. They're home about four o'clock, so be sure you don't play in the street then."

They'd just finished eating when Herr Sujer, Adam's father, knocked on the door. "Evening, Nikolaus." He took off his hat as he entered. "I just stopped to see if you need help with spring planting."

"Yes, I'm hiring men to plow and harrow the east field for cabbage. Also, the manure piled up during the winter and needs to be hauled and mixed in. If you're here in the morning, I'll put you to work," Opa said. "We've just finished our meal. Would you like to sample my latest wine?"

"I believe I will." Oma poured the glasses and Franz carried them. Opa explained what he needed the next few days to prepare the land for more spring planting.

"What do you think of the news of Germany's summer offensive in Russia?" Herr Sujer asked.

Opa shook his head, and Oma and Franz moved closer to listen to news of the war. Kati played with her dolly, unconcerned with something far away.

"I don't know." Opa rolled his glass between his hands. "After they abandoned the attack on Moscow in December, and pulled out of Russia, I hoped things would scale down."

"Well, since America officially entered the war, there's no way to end hostilities soon. It's too big now. Especially since Japan bombed the Americans at Pearl Harbor, Hawaii."

"I never thought we'd see anything as big as the Great War." Opa sounded part sad and part angry. "And here we are, with war spread over the globe."

As Herr Sujer left, Franz thought of his parents. And of Uncle Adam. Were they safe? Shortly after they left for Germany, his parents sent a very brief letter telling them they were in Leipzig and employed. They sent their love.

A somber evening passed. Katie noticed their preoccupation and quietly went from one of them to another and gave hugs to them all.

The next day Franz and his friends gathered on the porch of Anton's house to watch the hogs return. Sure enough, around four they heard a rumble in the distance. Herr Haut leaned on the fence with the boys. "Though I don't raise hogs, it's interesting to watch them. On Main Street about five thousand of them will return home from their day in the country and somehow they turn on the correct street and then know which gate to enter for their own home. All they think about is a meal of corn and no one better get in their way. You'd get trampled."

At the sight of a thousand hogs turning onto Church Street, Franz' mouth opened in amazement. The thunderous sound of so many hooves, accompanied by loud squeals and snorts, drowned out any other sounds on the block. The stench of so many hogs after they wallowed in sour mud all day quite overwhelmed them. Part of the herd turned into the first gate up the street, then more split off and turned into Franz's yard. Everyone on the porch leaned over the fence as the herd continued, groups found their own pens on both sides of the street and separated themselves to enter where they belonged. Several smaller hogs turned into the gate of the fourth house to the north, Tony Baumgarten's gate. Within ten minutes, the dust settled and quiet returned to the street, but the smell remained for hours.

"Now I know why Opa told me not to be on the street at hog run time!"

"It sounds like a bird concert, doesn't it?" Franz asked as he and Anton tossed a ball around in Anton's backyard. A sparrow flew overhead and hopped under the roof tiles of Herr and Frau Weiss's house.

"She's been building her nest, but this time she didn't carry materials in her beak. Maybe we could find eggs in the nest now." Anton walked closer to the fence for a better look. "Let's get the ladder," he said, "and check it out."

Franz held the ball and studied the activity next door, then nodded in agreement.

Each boy grabbed the end of the tall ladder and leaned it against the back of the house. Quickly, Franz scrambled up the rungs and peeked inside. "I see some eggs in there!"

"Come on down, I want to see," Anton sounded impatient, so Franz grinned and changed places with him.

"I see three sparrow eggs!" Anton stepped up a bit higher and lifted the tiles up so he could retrieve the eggs from the nest. "Crack," they both froze as they heard the tile break. Anton quickly stepped downward, eggs cradled in the crook of one arm.

"What are you boys doing?" Frau Weiss, short and stout, stood with her hands on her hips. "Get your ladder and go back to your own yards." Franz, embarrassed to be caught in mischief, took one of the eggs and put it in his pocket and Anton put the others in his shirt. Each took an end of the ladder and returned it to the Hauts' yard.

A few days later Frau Weiss discovered the broken tile and complained to Anton's parents. Herr Haut gave Anton several additional projects to do as punishment. Anton tucked his anger inside. The worst job involved cleaning out the tack room behind the house. Frau Haut kept a few chickens but they had no animals, so they used the tack room for storage.

Herr Haut insisted Anton take every item outside, sweep the inside and replace them more neatly. "If it's something we use fairly often, put it on this shelf." He pointed toward the wall by the door and returned to his cobbler shop.

Franz went over just as Anton finished sweeping the room. Anton looked angrily at the various items in the yard. "This is all Frau Weiss's fault," he muttered as he grabbed the first box to take inside.

"Come on, Anton, with both of us working it won't take much time to do it right." Franz leaned over and read the name on the boxes. "These were your grandmother's so let's put them in first." Item by item, they replaced everything in orderly stacks. Two broken chairs lay on top of an old sideboard. Finally, they placed some tools, a scale, and chicken feed on the shelf.

The next day Anton saw his mother and Frau Weiss talking. Quietly he got closer, but stayed behind the side of the house, out of sight.

"I need to weigh this package to mail. Can I use your scales?" Frau Weiss asked.

"Certainly," his mother said and led the way to the storage room and showed her the scales. "Just help yourself and I'll return to hang out my clean clothes."

Anton watched his mother go around the house, and then followed Frau Weiss, who hummed as she put the package on the scales. He slammed the door shut and locked it from the outside. "Now see if you can get out of here."

Everyone went on about their daily business and forgot about Frau Weiss. Anton ran over to Franz's to brag about his revenge. He waited for someone to find the neighbor and spent the day both anticipating it with glee and dreading the reaction. A long day passed.

"Are you in trouble, yet?" Franz asked late in the afternoon when he saw Anton on the sidewalk.

"No. But it's time for my mother to feed her chickens. She'll find Frau Weiss when she goes back there."

"What are you going to do?"

"I don't know," uncertainty crept into his voice, "I figured she'd be in there an hour or two, not all day. Want to watch?"

Undecided at first, Franz nodded. "It's sort of like trying to look away from a train crash, isn't it?" He followed Anton to peek around the corner.

Sure enough, they heard some muffled banging as they came closer. Frau Haut stood by the tack room door. "Just a minute! I'll get this unlocked," she turned the lock, "but how did this happen?"

A very weary Frau Weiss tumbled out. "It was that devil son of yours!" Her voice quivered in outrage and exhaustion. "He locked me in!"

"Anton!" Frau Haut's voice rose louder than Franz had ever heard before, but soft when she soothed Frau Weiss.

"Go on home, Franz," Anton said quietly. "No sense letting anyone assume you did this with me."

"I guess you're right," he whispered hesitantly, "I'll see you tomorrow." And he beat a hasty retreat.

With slow steps Anton walked to the women. One close look at his mother's expression of embarrassment, anger and despair and Anton wished he hadn't locked the door. Why didn't he ever think before he did these things?

After a long day of planting and the evening meal finished, neighbors carried chairs and benches to the sidewalk. Men sat in one circle, the woman in another. With very little traffic, the children played on the street. Franz noticed Frau Weiss and Anton's mother sat on different sides of the circle and all the ladies looked relaxed and pleasant. Everyone knew what Anton had done, but appeared to ignore it for now.

Women compared news from family members off with the war, recipes, area news.

"Oh, I meant to feed the horses," Oma suddenly remembered a few minutes later. "I'll be right back." She went to put feed in the horses' crib and as she scooped, one horse nickered unhappily and pushed her with his head. "I know I'm a little late," Oma waved a hand, "shoo, step back!" And all too swiftly, he bit her. She scooped the usual amount of feed, but by now, her hand throbbed and bled. At the water well, she lowered the bucket and raised it up to pour cold water on the injured hand. With her right hand held above her head, she went to the kitchen and found an old but clean towel to wrap the wound.

"Theresia!" Frau Haut cried out when she saw her.

Franz saw the commotion in the women's circle and ran to see what caused the stir.

Oma sat in her chair. "Our pesky horse punished me because I fed him late." She held her hand up, "He bit me."

When she would have brushed them off and changed the subject, the others drew closer, each determined to help. Franz squeezed in and kneeled at the side of her chair.

"How bad is it?" he asked.

"It'll heal," she said firmly.

Frau Steiner, the unofficial nurse and midwife in the village, reached over to unwrap it. "Yes, it's a bad one." She rewrapped it tightly. "I think you should see Dr. Spreitzer." There were many nods of agreement among the women. "Do you have Epsom salts on hand?"

"Yes," Oma said. "It'll help with this, won't it?"

Frau Steiner nodded. "I'd suggest twice a day. And tie a sling around your neck so it can rest. Don't use it too much for a while. It'll heal slowly."

"Wrap it tightly," offered one.

No," another countered, "keep it covered loosely so air can dry it out."

"Maybe you should just not use any bandage."

"Keep it warm."

"Keep it cold."

"Well, Dr. Spreitzer can tell you what is best." Frau Steiner summed things up.

Satisfied they'd given sufficient suggestions on how to treat the bite; they all sat again and resumed other topics. With school the next morning, families began to leave.

"Franz," Oma shook his shoulder, "you need to wake up early today."

"Hmmm?" Franz lowered the downy comforter from his face. "Now?"

"Yes, you'll need to cook breakfast this morning." She gestured to the sling, "my hand hurts too much."

He nodded. "Sure," he hopped out of bed to dress as she returned to the kitchen.

"And plan to cook supper tonight. I'll tell you what to do," she added as she shut the door.

Oma must really be miserable to have him fix the meals. She always cooked, no matter what.

"I'm sorry," she said as he entered the kitchen, "I really thought I'd be fine this morning, but I guess it will take a while to heal. We've decided I should have Dr. Spreitzer take a look at it. Kati and I'll stay here today and not help Opa." Slowly she stood up from the chair. "Get out the bread, and slice some pieces off. Then go the pantry and get the stomach sausage and some eggs."

Franz grabbed a large bowl and walked along the porch to the pantry. As the door opened, he stopped and inhaled the aroma from twelve hams and six big slabs of bacon hung on hooks along the walls. They'd been cured in a salt brine for a couple of weeks before they were taken to the smoke house and then here. He glanced at the ceiling where hundreds of feet of smoked sausages hung horizontally from broom sticks on the rafters. Another sniff and hunger reminded him to get the food.

He grabbed the large knife in the pantry to cut off some stomach sausage and then added eggs to the bowl and returned to the kitchen. Oma stood at his side, and told him which skillet to put on the stove and just how to fry the summer sausage and eggs and toast the bread. Opa made coffee earlier. Kati put plates and utensils on the table.

This set the pattern for next two weeks. Franz put on the coffee, cooked breakfast before school, hurried home, did chores as usual, heated water both morning and afternoon to wash with and make the Epson salt mixture to soak Oma's hand. Then Oma talked him through every step of making the evening meal. He eagerly learned to cook potatoes several ways, vegetable soup, and even schnitzel. His favorite was satrich. The smell of ground beef cooked with onion, green pepper, tomatoes, rice, paprika and salt and pepper was enough to make him hungry even if he'd just eaten a large meal. With daylight later each day, he had time to play with his friends.

"What will we fix to eat tonight?" Franz asked the next week. "Your hand looks better, how does it feel?"

"Hungarian goulash. Yes, it's really healing fast now. I think Kati and I will go back to the fields tomorrow and I can fix supper myself," she hesitated, "but to tell the truth, I've enjoyed teaching you to cook. You're a very good student!"

"It's fun to learn how to cook all kinds of food," he grinned, "I'm glad your hand is better though."

She nodded. "Thanks to so much help from you, and the doctor's salve, it is much better. And for supper, let's start Hungarian goulash and we'll have *spaetzle* for a side dish." She gave him a sweet smile, "but first let's read a letter we received today from your mother."

"A letter! What did she say? Are they coming home?" deep dimples bracketed his smile.

"It's on the shelf with the glasses. Get it and we'll read it now." She opened the envelope and began. Kati climbed on Franz's lap and leaned back to listen.

> *Dear loved Ones,*
>
> *You're never far from our hearts or prayers. We feel both closer to you and also farther away when we hear anything from or about you. We work long hours to reach our goals.*
>
> *This is such a large city and quite takes our breath away. We've almost no time to go any place but work and sleep. We've heard the population is around 700,000 so you can imagine it is very different! The largest cotton mill on this continent is here as well as many other places of employment. And there are so many automobiles! The noise is both fascinating and incredibly annoying. I do long for the quiet of horses hooves at home!*

I read this quote recently: "I come to Leipzig, the place where one can see the whole world in miniature." Stop and imagine the possibilities, Lieblings.

Apparently everything is here– music, art and Leipzig University is only one of many fine schools. Perhaps Franz will go to the university someday!

Leipzig Opera House is very famous, as is St. Thomas Church and the Botanical Garden is one of the very largest in the world. It is a beautiful city. I sound like a travel guide, don't I? But it comforts me to dream of a better time when we as a family might come to visit and stroll together to share these marvelous places of beauty.

If you think you sense homesickness from me, you're right. But we're busy and well.

Till we hug again, my special Lieblings, remember how much your Mama and Vati love you. And thank you, my own dear parents, because you shower them with such affection and care.

I'll write later, but it's time for work now.

Love,

Mama/Elisabeth

Franz slumped and put his chin on Kati's head. "She didn't say when they would come home! What kind of jobs do they have?"

"Remember, before they left Adam warned us all to be careful what we write. Our letters to and from them may be read by others and it could be dangerous to give too many details. It has to be enough to know they are healthy and busy."

Franz nodded in understanding. "They miss us, too and I'm glad we got a letter."

"After the war life will get back to normal and we can tell each other all we've experienced." She stood up, "let's cook some goulash."

The next day after the last class, the principal, Sister Beatrice, spoke to all the students. "We've been asked to raise silkworms to help in the war effort. Silk is needed to make parachutes and other things as well." She paused and cleared her throat. "As you leave, one of the sisters will hand each of you a piece of paper, a little bigger than the palm of your hand. It's covered with hundreds of small black dots. These are silkworm eggs."

"Your assignment is to find a small box and some mulberry leaves. Look around your neighborhood for mulberry trees and if necessary, ask permission to take leaves off. This is the only thing they will eat. Put the paper and leaves in the box. After one or two weeks, tiny worms will hatch. They will be very small and you'll barely be able to see them, but will grow very fast and have big appetites. We'll send you home with instructions."

"My father told me we'd get these silkworm eggs today," Anton said on the walk home, "and he's already started raising them for extra income. He has boxes for the eggs and the attic ready—do you want to put your eggs with ours?"

"Sure," Franz quickly agreed, "I'll do my chores at home then meet at your house and he can tell us what we need to do."

Herr Haut stopped his work when Franz arrived at their house and they all went to the attic. "We'll put your eggs up here to start. As they grow, we'll provide them with mulberry leaves." He rocked back on his heels and gestured over the area, "see, some of mine already move around here in search of food. In a couple of weeks we'll spread papers over the whole attic and have worms from one end of the attic to the other." He smiled with satisfaction. "The Germans buy them since they need a lot of silk for parachutes and various decorations on their uniforms. I hate the war but we might as well make some money." He rubbed his hands together. "Think you boys can be my source for mulberry leaves? When the cocoons are sold, I'll pay you for each sack of leaves. Just keep track of how many you provide. As they grow they need more leaves. Yours just need a few now, Franz, but in one or two weeks when all have hatched into worms we'll need a large amount. Are you willing?"

"Yes!" they both shouted and quickly and eagerly picked up the offered sacks.

"It'll be dark soon, so we'd better go now." Franz said as the boys ran down the stairs.

The Hauts had two big mulberry trees in the back of their lot, so they started there. Franz scurried up one tree, Anton slowly climbed the other.

"This is perfect!" Franz said, "We'll earn money by having fun—climbing trees."

"Hmf," Anton answered, "you can say that because you're like a monkey. I'll just think of the money and not look down."

"This is a lot like plucking goose feathers," Franz said as he used the same motion of thumb squeezing the leaf on his bent finger. "Snap, snap, snap." Quickly he settled into a pattern and rapidly began to fill his sack.

The next days were easy, only a few of Herr Hauts' silk worms devoured leaves.

"How are our babies?" Franz asked one afternoon when he and Anton stopped at the cobbler shop.

"Come see," and Herr Haut led the way to the attic.

"Are they different?" Franz asked as he looked at the little dots.

"Get closer," Herr Haut urged.

They got on their knees and studied them. "They're not eggs anymore! I see a worm shape here!" Anton grinned.

"And if we narrow our eyes a bit we can see they wiggle." Then Franz heard a little noise. "The older ones are eating!" And sure enough, a steady static came from the pile of mulberry leaves spread over the board.

"When Uncle Adam's friends' plane crashed, I saw the parachute. It's odd to think these little hungry worms make silk to make the strong parachute!"

"Well, a great many silk worms are used." Herr Haut chuckled. "Now we need a steady delivery of many leaves, boys."

And so they did.

After school each day they filled bags for the rapidly growing worms, now out of the box and on large boards covered with leaves. The boys' job entailed spreading the freshly picked food. The sound of them munching on the leaves grew louder each day.

"All the eggs are hatched," he told Oma one afternoon. She nodded, but her attention remained focused on taking clothes off the clothesline. He wandered off. If Mama or Vati were here, they'd ask a lot of questions and would want to see. A pang of longing flooded his heart and mind. How long would they be gone?

He didn't miss them as much when he was busy, so he worked extra hard to get plenty of mulberry leaves. One afternoon he and Anton climbed an older tree in a neighbor's front yard.

"I'm going to pick a lot of the new leaves since they seem to like them the best," Franz shouted to Anton from his perch on a branch extending over the garden wall, providing shade to the sidewalk.

"I'll go down and get the bag and scoop them up." Anton said.

They worked in silence for several minutes. Crack! "Oh!" Franz shouted as he fell with the limb.

He heard voices. His eyes flew open to see a group of people above him, some kneeling, and some standing back.

"I'm okay," he said with difficulty. "I just want to go home."

"Here, let me help you," Frau Braun said. She helped him sit up, then stand.

"Thank you," Franz mumbled and he turned toward home, with Anton beside him.

Maybe I should tell Oma, Franz thought, as he went through the gate. But he just wanted his bed, so slowly walked there.

"Franz?" Oma's voice shattered his sleep. "Frau Braun came to check on you. She said your back got hit on a concrete curb when you fell. Are you in pain?"

"W-w-w- what?" Franz blinked his eyes.

Oma placed her hand on his forehead. She looked worried. "Can you tell me what happened?"

"I don't know. We c- c-c- climbed up for leaves." He closed his eyes, then with effort, opened them again. "SSSS leepy."

"Come on," Opa slid her arm under his upper back and raised him to a sitting position. "Let's get you in the living room so we can keep an eye on you better."

Days later, the silkworms turned a slight golden color and grew as big as a tomato worm. When the worms stopped eating, it got quiet in the attic, and Franz climbed the trees again, carefully, but this time to cut off many forked branches. Each worm selected a triangle in the branch and started to wrap itself in a cocoon. The cocoons were shaped like a peanut except twice as big in size. Herr Haut set aside some cocoons for the next spring, when a moth would push out and lay eggs, and the process would start again.

The cocoons were sold and Franz and Anton received their pay.

"W-W-W-What will you spend your money on?" Franz asked Anton.

There it was again – the stutter. It wasn't so bad with Anton because he ignored it, but Franz kept trying to figure out how to stop it.

"Probably a new ball," Anton said. "How about you?"

"Don't know." Franz didn't really need anything. In Sombor he'd had a lot of ways to earn money and always knew what he wanted to buy. But things were different here. He could buy candy for Kati and himself. A folding pocket knife would be really handy. Should he get something for Oma or Opa? Maybe he should save it and find other ways to earn money to use later.

Still undecided, he put it in the box under his bed.

11

End of 1942, Beginning 1943 — 10 years old
Stanišić and Budapest

OMA SNIFFLED AS she obviously fought tears. Franz wished his mother could step into the room right now. She'd know what to say. Kati sat at the table, earnestly coloring a picture to send to Uncle Adam. She always drew a sun shining in the corner of every one of her pictures. This one had Oma, Opa, Franz and herself along with a kitten. With precision, she wrote her name as befitting an accomplished four-year-old.

Oma wrapped the last of the candies and tucked them into the corner of the box. Kati added her gift and last, Franz had made something to remind Adam of the farm. He took it out of his pocket and dropped it on the top. He'd drawn an outline of a hog, and carved it with his pocketknife.

"Do you think he'll know what it is?" Franz studied it critically.

Oma leaned over to look. "Of course he will!"

"See the tail? It's a hog!" Kati helped.

"I just hope it gets to him," Oma muttered. "This is the address we're supposed to use when we put it on the train." Again, she blinked back emotion and smiled weakly at the children. "I know you think of Adam as a grown man, a soldier. But to me, he's my youngest child and only son." After another sigh, she seemed to feel better.

Everyone screamed as they sailed down the hill in the coal hopper, arms held high in the air. The hopper slowed and came to a gradual stop. "I sure wish it took longer to go down and faster to push it up!" Tony grumbled.

They flopped on the dormant grass and wordlessly looked at the drifting clouds. Adam Sujer rolled to his side, his elbow on the ground and used his hand as support for his head. "Toni, who are all the people who came to your house yesterday?"

"You remember my cousin Rolf, who's in the German army? He fought in the battle for Moscow the end of 1941, but was wounded and sent home. Some of my mother's family came to visit and they told us all about it."

"What happened?"

"He lost a leg, so he had to be pulled out and taken back to a German hospital. He said it's really bad in Russia and losing a leg probably saved his life because they lived in tents and it got down to minus thirty degrees. Also, they were short on food and weren't dressed for the frigid temperatures. He said the Russian women are in combat the same as the men and the women are the primary farmers because so many men are gone for military service. Under communism, the Russians were already starving before the war. Most of them are just bones with some skin over them. Rolf said if any Russian refused his duty to USSR, Stalin sent them to Siberia or the GULAG camps. And they die there anyway."

Speechless, the boys merely gaped at Tony. Franz looked at the ground. Adam had gone to Greece. Could he be in Russia now? No, he had to be in Greece. And he knew his parents lived and worked in Leipzig.

Sobered, but with energy restored, the boys got ready to push the hopper back up the incline. "Shall we make this the last run?" Franz asked.

"Yes, and let's do the jump-out thing!" Efficiently, they gathered to shove a big slab of concrete over the track to make a stop for the wheels. "Too bad these are so heavy—a pile of smaller rocks might be easier for us to use."

Franz and Anton looked at each other. "We could go to the brick yard north of here and bring some of their rejected ones here. I wish my grandfather still owned the brick factory and we could have all we want," Franz said. "Stefan, could you use your horse and wagon to bring the bricks here?"

"Probably. Let's push up the hopper now and I'll let you guys know after I ask my grandparents."

As colder weather came, the days grew shorter and life fell into a routine of school and chores before supper, but Franz usually had time to be with his friends. One Friday night Opa warned him he wouldn't have much free time the next day. They needed to move the privy in the back yard. Franz woke the next morning without his usual enthusiasm. His friends were free to play land hockey but he had to help with the worst job on the farm.

"Franz, we only have to dig a new hole for the outhouse every few years, not once a month! Besides, you muck out the manure from the stalls and don't complain." Opa scolded as Franz wrinkled his nose in disgust and walked slowly. "Come on—let's dig the new hole on this side of your grandmother's lilac bush. We'll move the privy back for now and as we dig, we'll carry the dirt to cover the old hole. Then we put the outhouse on this new, fresh smelling hole!"

Franz sighed. If he didn't get started, he knew what Opa would say—they could dawdle and take all day, or they could just hurry and get it done in the morning. Faster sounded better to him so he started digging where Opa pointed. Before long he felt encouraged at how deep the new hole grew while they filled the old one. By the time they finished the new outhouse hole it looked deep enough to last a long time.

That afternoon Katie sat beside a tired Franz as he did his reading assignment for homework. Katie sighed and leaned on

Franz's side. He tried to ignore her so he could get his chapter finished. She sighed again and he found it impossible to concentrate. "What's the matter with you, Kati, why aren't you playing?"

She shrugged her shoulders and looked up at Franz. "Why is your nose so big?" he put his book down and touched her nose. Tears welled up and she looked down again. "Oma," Franz raised his voice to get her attention. "Something's wrong with Kati's nose."

Oma sat down and tilted the child's head up. "What did you put in your nose, Kati?"

"A pretty green bead," she said sadly.

"Oh, Kati," Oma sounded exasperated "Franz, get my sewing needle, please."

When she had the needle in hand, Oma squeezed Kati's nose with her left hand. "We don't want to drive it up farther," and she leaned over to put the needle in Kati's nose.

Kati began to push away "No, no, I don't need it out. It doesn't hurt too much."

"Kati!" Oma said firmly, "hold still!" She turned to Franz, "hold Kati on your lap and restrain her if necessary. It has to come out before it causes more trouble."

Quick as a wink, Oma squeezed Kati's nose just below the bone bridge and poked a needle till it stuck in the bead and she pulled it out.

Kati sniffed. "I just smelled it really good and it popped inside."

Oma and Franz chuckled at her sad tale and Oma hugged her. "Well, I daresay you won't smell a bead so closely again!"

Relieved, Kati danced off to find her latest kitten. Franz shook his head and resumed his book.

As Franz and Anton walked home from school later in the week, they heard a loud explosion in mid-air east of the village.

They turned to their right and saw an airplane bouncing more than flying. It leaned one way, then another, went up, then down. "Something just fell off the plane!" Franz shouted. "See the white star in the blue circle under the wing? I think it's an American bomber!"

"They've lost control!"

Spellbound, they stood in disbelief till it fell from view accompanied by a loud series of crashes. Then a deathly quiet settled before birds resumed singing above.

"We don't have school tomorrow—let's go see it!"

"I'll get up early and really rush through my chores," Franz said. "Opa doesn't have any big project for me so it shouldn't be a problem. I wonder how far away the plane is."

Quickly they planned to pack a lunch and leave as early as possible.

The next morning Franz jumped out of bed with eagerness and hurried thru his chores. No time to talk to the animals, just feed them and milk the cow. After he returned to the kitchen to eat breakfast, Oma handed him a sandwich, some cookies and a jar of water. In high spirits, he and Anton started walking east on the Batchka.

"At least our walk will be easy along the flat land and we don't have to swim across the river!" Anton observed. The cold air felt comfortable without any wind.

"Opa guessed it's about six or seven miles away, but he said it could be farther.

"I keep thinking of Tony's news about the Russian Front and what it would be like to be starving. What is the hungriest you've ever been?" Anton asked.

Franz thought and so did Anton. "I've never really been hungry, but those days while the Hungarians and Chetniks were shooting in Sombor, we didn't cook because we stayed down close to the floor out of range of flying bullets. The food wasn't as good but we had plenty. I just sort of didn't want to eat. I'm hungry just before a meal but it's not the same. How about you?"

"Me neither. Sometimes my mother doesn't put meat on the table because one of Vati's customers can't pay for a while. But we still eat and when he gets paid, then Mama buys better food. Sometimes I get hungry enough so my stomach growls and I complain." Anton hesitated, "I've never thought about having food, because we always have something to eat."

They walked along quietly. As the sun rose directly overhead they stopped and ate their lunch and drank some of the water, then kept walking.

First they saw the nose of a plane, all broken pieces of aluminum painted muddy green and broken window pieces scattered around the area. A long strip of bare dirt showed how it plowed on the ground before coming to a halt. Ahead they saw more metal shining in the sunshine.

"Look at this," Franz held up a piece about four feet by three feet. "A picture is painted on this. It looks like an arm here, probably a woman."

They scanned the ground for anything else of interest. "I found a face!" Anton put another painted section next to the part Franz held. "She's blond and pretty."

Bored with this discovery, they continued to look around.

"Here's one of those . . . fan things," with great effort, Anton tipped one end up.

Franz laughed. "I think they call it a propeller, not a 'fan thing'." Anton shrugged and smiled sheepishly.

Gradually there were more bits of airplane parts, mostly unrecognizable.

"Look at this," Franz said as he held up a broken clock, "These words are English, I think. But it's not working; it still says 4:30 from yesterday when it crashed."

THE PROMISE OF THE SUNFLOWERS

Anton went off to the right and straight ahead. When they got close they saw parts of the inside of the plane and lots of blood on a damaged radio and blood also on seat parts and on the ground. Franz stopped and scratched his head. "Where are they?" Quietly they stood, looking as far as they could see. "There should be bodies."

"There's something over this way," Anton ran ahead toward the south and kept walking east. "Look, there's a machine gun." Anton touched it hesitantly. "Should we take it home with us?"

Franz shrugged. "No, I don't want it. What would we do with it?"

They stepped on ammunition scattered on the ground. About a quarter of a mile farther on another machine gun lay. Still, no sign of any person, living or dead.

"I've never seen anyone dead but my Oma" Anton said. When Franz didn't say anything, Anton continued. "Have you?"

His silence made Anton more curious. Franz rarely talked to his friends here about what happened in Sombor, just to say there'd been the days of shooting. But nothing about the priest or the Hungarian shot by the Chetnik girl. He didn't know why he never talked about it, but he just couldn't. His friends would think it a really great adventure but not understand the reality of it. Suddenly his memories surfaced and he remembered everything as if it just happened.

"In Sombor, Jani and I found a dead priest. He'd been shot in the eye and his other eye remained open. Not at all like your grandmother. Blood covered the priest and everywhere around him. For a long time I had nightmares. I still don't like to talk about it."

Anton, in a rare moment of sensitivity, didn't quiz Franz.

More airplane parts were strewn around and wordlessly they stopped from time to time to bend over and study them.

Then they saw a large engine. "Hmmm it fell early, maybe this is what we saw fall."

By now they walked about a mile east and a half mile south from where they found the nose.

"Let's turn to the north and cover different areas on the way back home."

When they saw a wing, they discussed possible uses for it, but its weight prohibited them from carrying it home.

Nothing of interest surfaced among the scattered parts as they headed west in the direction of Stanisic. Nothing until they found a boot, the foot still inside, a bloodied and rough ankle quite visible. Both boys felt sick. Someone had belonged to this ankle and his foot wasn't much bigger than Franz'. They continued their walk.

Several other people arrived from Stanisic to look around. Two men cut the straps off the parachutes and folded up the silk as they talked about what fine jackets their women would make from them.

The boys walked around another place with pools of blood. One of the men picked up another machine gun and took it as well. They nodded to the boys in acknowledgement but no one said anything.

Gradually they came back to the nose where they'd begun.

"Where do you think they went? Why would anyone want dead people?" Anton asked.

"Maybe a survivor came down with a parachute," Franz suggested tentatively, "and he pulled them away for rescue so their families will have something to bury. Possibly an airplane came nearby during the night."

With questions and no answers, they were ready to go back to Stanisic. It turned dark by the time they arrived home and parted at Anton's gate. Tired and in a serious mood, he joined his family. After eating a bowl of delicious soup, energy returned.

"What did you see?" Opa asked as Oma bustled Kati off to get ready for bed. Franz described everything from the pieces of a picture of a woman painted on the plane to the boot with the foot still inside. Opa said little. Just nodded his head from time to time and listened intently as he let Franz talk, and in some strange way, it made it easier.

The end of the year came and 1943 began. His parents had been gone over a year and Franz missed them every day but with chores, school, friends, Opa, Oma and Kati, the days were too busy to dwell on it.

When a thick blanket of snow covered the ground, Franz gave extra hay to the cow and horses both morning and evening. After school he met his friends in Anton's yard for a rousing battle with snowballs.

"Hey, Franz, a soldier just went into your yard." Tony shouted as he came to join the game.

With the briefest hesitation, he went home. As he opened the kitchen door, he saw Oma hug someone. Opa stood beside her with an odd expression on his face. He looked happy, but also sad.

"Franz, look who's here. It's Adam!" Franz felt shy and didn't move, but just watched.

After hugs and multiple questions, Adam sat at the kitchen table and Oma put a cup of coffee in front of him. Oma alternately talked rapidly and quietly wiped tears of happiness.

Franz tried not to stare at Adam, who appeared quieter and somehow older than before.

"If I'd known you were coming, I'd have something really special on the stove," Oma said.

"I couldn't get word to you I planned to come because I didn't know ahead. Besides, anything you cook will be a delicious treat," he tipped his head and looked around the table at each of them. "Elisabeth and I met at Anna's at the same time and we all had a good visit." Adam leaned back in his chair, long legs stretched out and his hands laced behind his head.

His lips curved in a pensive smile. "There's nothing quite like being with two older sisters to make a guy feel like he's still a kid in some ways." He winked at his mother. "I just let them fuss over me!"

Conversation flowed around the table as they ate. Before long, it felt natural and Franz enjoyed seeing Uncle Adam. Kati alone held back and looked at Uncle Adam only when he didn't look at her.

"How long will you be here?" Franz ventured when no one else asked.

"Just today and tomorrow. This isn't a vacation for me." He leaned forward, his elbows on the table. "We've received orders. Our unit is going to Russia. Since I'll come back here after the war, I've brought a couple of boxes of my things to leave here."

A pained silence filled the room at the mention of Russia. Franz stopped breathing as he remembered the news from Tony's cousin, Rolf, and pictures of frozen and hungry soldiers marched through his mind.

"Can't you stay here and just not go?" Franz asked desperately.

"Truthfully, I don't understand why we're fighting a war on both sides, especially tackling the eastern front along eighteen hundred miles. Whatever I think of the war, I can't abandon the other men in my group—they're brothers to me. My conscience wouldn't ever let me live in peace. It's not a choice for me. Also," Adam shook his head "the army does not tolerate deserters."

Not surprising, Oma's tears increased and Opa sat straight in his chair, unable to show any emotion.

Kati crossed her arms over her chest, tipped her head forward with a fierce frown on her face. "Why did you make Oma cry?"

"I'm sorry, Kati, I didn't want to, but I had to give them some bad news."

Oma got up and motioned for Franz to help her. She cut a fresh carrot cake and Franz carried a piece to everyone.

"Unfortunately, it's not the only reason I'm here."

Franz' heart began to beat rapidly. Uncle Adam looked at him when he spoke. Oma sat after she gave everyone a fork.

"I wouldn't spring this on you right away, but I must leave tomorrow afternoon. When I saw Elisabeth she asked me to complete a mission for her before I go to Russia. She and Stefan both are very, very homesick for the children."

Oma and Opa looked each other with alarm, then at Franz and Kati and back to Adam.

"Things are pretty stable now," he continued, "they make good money and save almost all of it. Elisabeth thinks Franz will adjust to and enjoy living with them in Leipzig." Without words, they all understood Kati, because of her age, would obviously be much better off in Stanisic with her grandparents.

"How soon will Franz go?" Opa asked gruffly.

Adam squirmed in his chair. "When I leave, they want me to take him with me by train to Budapest and then a military train into Germany."

"We just have one day?" Oma gasped.

Suddenly understanding came to Kati. She jumped from her chair and ran around to Adam and began to hit him with her small fists. "You can't take my Franz! You're a bad man and I want you to go!" Opa picked her up and patted her back as she burst into tears.

Franz battled with a kaleidoscope of thoughts. Opa needed him on the farm and he wanted to be here. He also had a strong desire to see his parents and explore Leipzig, but he'd have to leave Kati and Opa and Oma. He thought of his friends. A change of schools. What would happen if he insisted on staying here? He'd disappoint his mother and father.

He noticed Adam waited for his response. What could he say? Adam's kind eyes gave him comfort and strength.

"Who would do my chores? Should I stay?" Franz quietly asked Opa.

Kati wiggled down and ran to Franz and held his hand. Opa's smile held more sadness than cheer. "Mr. Sujer is always ready to work and I'll just use him more, I guess."

"As much as we love you and want you here, your mother is right—you'll probably enjoy being with them in Leipzig and Kati is too young to go. And all of you will be back here when the time is right," Oma said bravely. "In the meantime we'll still have our little Kati-bug."

As he lay in bed under his down-filled quilt, Franz thought about the days ahead. He wouldn't return for the rest of the school year because if his parents were coming back soon, they wouldn't have sent for him.

He didn't want to leave. He belonged here with his friends. And with Kati, Oma and Opa. Spring would be here soon and the farm a busy place. And he wouldn't be here!

But he missed his parents and wanted to go. He never told anyone, but sometimes he worried because he had trouble seeing their faces when he closed his eyes. They loved and wanted him there. And Leipzig would probably be interesting.

The next morning he got together with his friends for a brisk game of Land Hockey and to say goodbye. Berbl, the girl from his class in school, lived four houses up the street right where they played. Shyly, she handed him slices of sugar beets. Franz ducked his head at her sparkling eyes and gentle smile. "Goodbye, Franz," she said. "Don't forget your friends here."

Even milking the cow and feeding the animals had a feeling of finality about them. When would he do this again?

Oma packed both a large suitcase and a smaller one with his clothes and included many link sausages and a couple loaves of bread.

Oma and Kati stayed at the house. "It'll be easier on Kati not to see you get on the train," she explained as she hugged him tightly and kissed his cheek. "Remember we love you always and forever."

He blinked back tears and bent to pick up Kati. "Take good care of the new kittens, Kati-bug." Then he turned to follow Uncle Adam to the wagon, and sat between Opa and Uncle Adam as they rode to the train.

"Franz, there's something I want you to understand and remember," Adam began. "You must be very careful with what you say while you're in Germany. Just be aware the walls have ears. I'm not a Nazi and a great many Germans, even members of the army, aren't. But some Nazis are true believers and vigilant in reporting remarks detrimental to the dignity of the fatherland or the Fuher. If you ever criticize Hitler or any part of the Nazi party or even listen to someone else doing so, you could be in big trouble. Don't trust neighbors or even friends." He searched Franz's expression for reassurance. "It won't be the same as living in Stanisic."

Franz tried to swallow past a knot of fear in his throat, and settled for nodding in agreement.

The train ride was interesting, but it just took so long as they slowly chugged their way north. Finally they were in Budapest, where Adam hurried while Franz followed. He kept on eye on Adam, but looked around at this big, beautiful city as they passed street after street until they came to another place to catch the military train.

"You don't have any papers— no visa or passport. Plus, you're quite obviously a civilian," Adam teased, "you're too young to pass for an adult!" He waved at someone and began to lead Franz toward him. "But I have friends," he added.

"Hello, Heinz," he put his hand on Franz' shoulder. "This is my nephew, Franz. I need to get him on the train to Augsburg to my sister. Can you help us?"

Heinz looked around carelessly. "Am I to understand that we're doing a covert operation here?" Franz shifted from one foot to another as Heinz looked him over as if he calculated his size. "Come on, we have the perfect spot for him."

12

1943 - Ten years old; eleven in August
Augsburg and Leipzig, Germany

CAREFUL TO KEEP Uncle Adam in his peripheral vision, Franz noticed many soldiers but few families traveled. Budapest depot was very active as trains arrived and others departed. Quickly looking around, he stayed right beside Uncle Adam as they followed Heinz.

Heinz hesitated at a car and stepped up to peek inside. "This is it," he said with a smile.

"I'll take your bag, Franz, while you go up the steps," Adam instructed.

Franz looked at both sides of the aisle and saw only German soldiers. Some played card games, some slept and others were busy getting settled in seats. A few glanced at him, but resumed what they were doing.

"We have a little while before we cross into Germany, then we'll travel for hours before we arrive at Augsburg itself," Adam said, "Heinz will help us get you across without papers. There shouldn't be any problem leaving here but, at the border, the SS will be sure all passengers are checked for permits since any form of travel for pleasure is no longer permitted."

Franz nodded but his heart beat too hard to say anything. The train whistle blew and they heard the familiar "all aboard" cry to announce imminent departure. Uncle Adam's hand folded into a fist, as the train slowly began to inch out. Instinctively, Franz lowered himself in the seat and tried to melt into Adam. The whistle blew more robustly and steam poured above their car as speed picked up. Adam took a deep breath and smiled.

Franz relaxed and enjoyed the ride as the tracks below rocked the car in a soothing rhythm. The terrain changed with the miles while gray clouds covered much of the sky.

"How are you doing, kid?" Adam asked.

"Actually, I'm a bit hungry," Franz said softly.

Adam stood and walked to the back to pick up Franz' smaller bag. He opened it and took some of the sausage and bread along with a bottle of water. "Heinz," he said, "time to eat!"

The three ate enthusiastically. "It looks like we're in two different places. I look out the windows on the right and I see flat lands and farms. Then I turn my head and there are hills and trees." Franz giggled and looked from one side to the other. He noticed other men looked from one side to the other and smiled at his observation. "We're going west, aren't we?" he asked.

"Yes—sort of along the Danube, the largest river of Central Europe. We'll go a little north, but mostly west."

The miles were left behind as Franz looked out the window, determined not to miss a thing.

After a while, Heinz stood up, stretched and nodded to a few men seated around them. "The border is not far from here."

Without discussion, Heinz motioned to them and they gathered up their guns and packs.

"Franz, come over here," Adam said.

Uncertainly, he walked to the back. Heinz eyes smiled encouragement. "Sit down back in the corner and take a nap or something. Do not look out the window. If someone comes through, you just hide like a little mouse."

Franz sat in the corner, folded up his knees and put his hands around them. He lowered his head while the guns and packs were stacked around him. Very carefully he peeked out the narrow view between parts of his wall of weapons.

"Well, Adam, can you see your nephew?" Heinz asked.

"No." He sounded relaxed and pleased at how well they'd hidden Franz.

The train came to a gradual stop. Outside, loud commands overshadowed muted conversations. He heard men exit and others enter. After a while things became less noisy as soldiers waited in their seats for the trip across the border.

"Car check," he heard Adam's warning words. Franz, aware of the sound of his own breathing, put his head on his knees and tried to relax as heavy boots stepped up into the car. He peeked through his very small hole.

"We leave in five minutes," a deep voice announced. "Show your paperwork" Two SS field soldiers stood behind the railroad police official who held a list. Row by row, the official walked to the back. Every time he stopped to scrutinize paperwork and ask questions, Franz' tension grew. After what seemed a long time, Adam's turn arrived.

"Name?"

"Adam Hoger" he said, then handed over his papers.

"Are you bringing anything from Hungary?" the official's voice sounded sharp, as if he knew something.

"Well, I do have a little bit of my mother's superior sausage." Adam boasted.

Surprisingly, the man chuckled briefly. "Enjoy it, then."

He turned and joined the two SS men at the door and stepped off the car first. Franz leaned forward closer to one peephole to see them leave. It would be dangerous to move for a better view, but he listened as the SS soldiers snapped their heels together and shouted "Heil Hitler!" Then came answering sounds of movement as the men all raised their hands in the Nazi salute.

"Stay as you are for a while," Adam said when the train began to move.

With the movement of the train, he wanted to jump up immediately and not stay frozen in the same awkward position, but waited for Adam's word.

After what seemed a long time to him, they crossed the border, but Adam said to stay a few minutes longer. Finally, Heinz took some guns off Franz and welcomed him back to a seat. He was in Germany! He glanced around at the other soldiers on the car. They didn't look at him and acted as though he weren't there. It made him feel odd, usually adults smiled or said something to him. Maybe this made it possible for them to let him enter Germany but not be a part of making it happen. What they didn't really see, the SS couldn't punish.

Men pulled out cards and had a rousing game going; others closed their eyes and took naps. Franz watched one man who sat with paper and a pencil; he stopped from time to time, leaned his head back as though wearied, and then resumed writing. He looked neither young nor old. Was he writing to a wife? Did he have a son like Franz? Had he lived on a farm before the war? He looked strong, but his complexion was fair. Maybe he'd been a shopkeeper. Or . . . maybe he became a soldier by choice and not because of the war.

He tired of the game and looked out the window again. Fluffy clouds hung in blue sky and an eagle flew gracefully in the distance.

"Will we stop at Wien?" he asked after he read a sign proclaiming the next town.

"Yes," Adam answered, "but they don't check the cars after the border unless there is something suspicious, so I'm confident we'll be fine."

"Where is this, actually?" he asked.

"Austria, but it's part of Nazi Germany now. The German name is Wien, but the English name is Vienna, so you'll hear it called both. The mountain ranges around Wien are a transition between the Eastern Alps and the Carpathians. You'll be able to see some off in the distance."

Franz nodded, but continued to look out the window. A few dormant vineyards dotted the landscape, and he felt a pang of longing to see Opa. They passed through a small town and he looked forward to what lay ahead.

"You might as well take a nap now. Between Wien and the next big town, Salzburg, we'll see the Bavarian Alps. They're the most beautiful sight you'll ever see."

"I am tired, but I'm excited, too." He hesitated, "I'm hungry. Can we eat some more sausage and bread?"

"Sure," and he pulled the suitcase from under the seat.

"What's Aunt Anna like?" he asked as they ate.

"She's older but smaller than your mother or I am," Adam said, "you'll like her. She's very gentle and likes to take care of others. She and Hans have one daughter close to my age, so she won't be a playmate for you."

Later, filled with food and nothing much to do, Franz did sleep. He got up and walked along the isles. The men were friendly after riding on the same rail car for many hours. In a latrine area with a privacy partition he entertained himself by watching his urine hit the rocks below. Mostly he sat and wiggled and slept some more as the hours dragged on. Then majestic mountains came into view and each scene seemed more beautiful than the ones before. From Salzburg to Munich land became more level and more small towns appeared. The sun set as the train continued the journey.

"We're almost there, aren't we?" Franz looked out the window. He saw primarily his own reflection and the area around him, but sometimes lights in the distance signaled a city nearby.

"Yes, Augsburg Union Station is about ten minutes away." Soon they grabbed Franz' bags and disembarked. As they walked away, Franz glanced over his shoulder for the station clock and found it on the front of what looked like a small building sitting on a large two-story building. The hands pointed to midnight. Uncle Adam led him through the streets to Aunt Anna's apartment.

"Why are the streetlamps blue?" Franz asked. "Most of them aren't even on and we can't see much with them."

"You're right," Uncle Adam said. "It's because of the blackout. They don't show up as clearly as regular streetlamps."

All of a sudden, a piercing, ear-splitting alarm rang out. Franz pressed closer to Adam. "What's that?" he asked in alarm.

People flooded the street with purposeful strides, some carried crying babies, others boxes or bags of possessions. Most were dressed, but some still wore pajamas. Uncle Adam pulled him toward a basement where painted florescent arrows pointed to the entrance. They went down and sat with many other people.

"This is an air raid shelter," Adam explained. "I guess you noticed the siren?"

Franz looked up at him. Uncle Adam must not be frightened if he could joke about the shrill sound. He looked around and noticed the people in the shelter were mostly calm, except for the children who continued to cry at the painfully loud alarm.

"Augsburg hasn't been bombed, so we do this mostly for practice," explained an old man who sat beside Franz. The man must have noticed how frightening and new all this appeared to him. Fairly soon a single, solid all-clear siren sounded and they resumed the walk to Aunt Anna's place.

"I thought you might arrive tonight, so I couldn't sleep," she said as she hugged Adam and Franz. "And then the sirens went off and we went to the shelter up the street. You both look totally exhausted, so I'll wait till morning to visit with you. Are you hungry?"

Assured they didn't need to be fed, she took them to a guest room where they fell into bed and were quickly asleep.

Franz woke early and looked out the window for an outhouse but didn't see anything remotely like one. He'd never stayed in an apartment and wondered what to do. He followed the sound of voices into the kitchen. Adam, Anna and a man he didn't know sat drinking coffee.

"Hello, good morning," Anna said as she walked over to give Franz a welcome hug. "You look much better today. Did you sleep well?"

He nodded and shifted from one foot to the other.

"This is your Uncle Hans," she nodded to her husband, who lifted his cup in greeting.

Aunt Anna tilted her head as she studied Franz. "If you need to use the pot, it's the second door to the right."

Relieved she understood his problem, he hurried down the hall. They must use chamber pots inside. What did they do about the odor? He slowly opened the door and peeked inside. Well, a white thing sat in the corner, so he thought it must be what Aunt Anna meant. The top looked sort of like a seat with a hole in it. Uncertainly, he looked around again. This was the second door to the right so it must be correct. And what else could it be? It looked like maybe five gallons of water filled the bottom.

His situation didn't allow time to ponder any longer, so he sat down. When he finished, he didn't have a clue what to do next. Again, he looked all around and saw a chain hanging from a big square tank above him. It had a handle-like thing on the end.

He pulled the chain and immediately heard a very loud hissing and splashing sound. He didn't scream but he jumped away rapidly. What happened? Had he broken something? He stepped forward and peered into the white container. A big smile covered his face. Everything had gone away! New, clean water began to rise. With caution and curiosity he reached over and pulled the chain again. Whoosh! Down it went, to be refilled once more. He grinned again.

He shook his head in amazement. Anton and the other guys wouldn't believe this!

What other marvelous things would he see in Germany?

Everyone looked at him when he returned to the kitchen.

"I told them you've probably never seen an indoor toilet!" Adam said with a chuckle.

"No, I haven't!" he said, "It's like magic, isn't it?"

Aunt Anna giggled a bit and gestured to a chair by the table and put his breakfast before him. "Thank you for bringing the sausage and bread," Anna said.

Franz looked up to Adam, who winked at him.

"Since we have such a difficult time getting meat, poultry, game, eggs or oil, we have to be inventive here with our rationed goods." She hummed in enjoyment as she savored a bite of sausage. She placed another piece in her mouth, closed her eyes and enjoyed the flavor. Then she blinked tears from her eyes. "This takes me home to Stanisic. We've been rationed here for so long I'd quite forgotten how very good this is. I'm so glad mother packed this for you to bring!"

Adam cleared his voice. "Franz, I've got to go," he said. "I didn't want to leave without telling you goodbye, but I must rejoin my unit this morning."

"We'll send a telegram to your mother today," Aunt Anna said quickly. "She'll come get you as soon as she can. She's so excited!"

Franz and Adam hugged each other and Adam left. Franz felt lost until Aunt Anna found her purse and put on her coat.

"Let's get a telegram off!" And they walked downstairs and out the door. "I know it was too dark last night for you to see anything on the way to our apartment, and then you had to go to the shelter, but the post office is close to the railroad. We'll walk and you can look around."

Crowds of people were the first thing he noticed. Stanisic seemed to be a very small village compared to what he saw now. Even Sombor shrank in comparison. Here there were no massive stone walls surrounding homes, but many apartments and businesses everywhere. The rail station had dozens of train tracks and not just the four used in Stanisic. Automobiles zipped past, their growling made Franz both alert to danger and fascinated.

"Is it a little train?" Franz asked with perplexity as he pointed to a vehicle going up a street on rails.

"Oh, it's a streetcar," Aunt Anna laughed. "They're very handy for going across town or if a person can't walk far. We'll try to ride one while you're here."

"Here we are!" she said as they came toward the post office. She walked over to an old man standing behind a counter. "Good morning. We want to send a telegram." She gave him a few coins and told him what to send to the Leipzig office. "Elisabeth, Franz is ready for you to fetch him and take him home. Love, Anna."

Now finished, they took a leisurely walk back. It would sure be fun to explore Augsburg with Jani or Anton. He paid attention to everything he saw so he could tell them all about it someday. So many buildings! So many tall apartment houses! The sounds of automobiles, streetcars, and the occasional honked horns were far noisier than a spring hog run at home. He'd never heard so many people speaking at once. Mothers called out to children, children to one another, businessmen talked as they walked.

"What are those lights for?" Franz asked as he pointed to colored lights on a pole.

"Let's stop here for a moment and you watch," Aunt Anna suggested.

"When the light is red, they stop! And then they go when the light changes to green!"

"Without them, we'd have a lot of accidents and fighting. The lights are turned off with dark so we aren't so clearly marked for bombing. Headlights are darkened as well, so most people just don't drive after dark."

They finished their walk and went up to the apartment. Franz wanted to check out the 'private' room again and excused himself. Aunt Anna fixed sandwiches for the noon meal.

"Would you like to lay down for a bit?" Aunt Anna asked. "You couldn't have slept too well last night and with all the travel I suspect you're tired."

Suddenly it sounded like a good idea and Franz nodded and walked into the bedroom he'd shared with Uncle Adam the night before. Within seconds, he slept.

He awoke to sounds of cooking and muted conversation. He needed a drink, so he patted down his hair and joined Aunt Anna and Uncle Hans. He stood in the doorway as Hans obviously complained about some problems on the production line at the brewery.

"Did you have a nice rest?" Aunt Anna asked when she noticed him.

"Yes, thank you," he sniffed with appreciation, "something smells pretty good in here."

"With the policy of autarky, I'm making Eintopf," she looked over her shoulder as she stirred. "Your grandmother has no need to cook this way, so it'll be new to you."

"What is autarky? And Eintopf?"

"It's a meal of necessity. Under autarky we receive almost no imports, but use only what is available in Germany itself. Everything is because of the war, Franz. We don't import food for livestock, so our meat is of poor quality now, plus so many farmers are in the army. We take poor-quality meat and cook it slowly and add vegetables. This way we also use less cooking fuel."

"And every time she cooks this way she remembers the plentiful supply of potatoes in Stanisic! And the pantry filled with the very best quality meat," Uncle Hans added. "So she gets homesick on the first Sunday of every month, which is 'Eintopf Sunday'."

Hans sounded a bit annoyed and Franz didn't know what to say.

"I'm sorry if I sounded as if I'm complaining," she directed her words to Franz, "but you need to understand autarky while you're in Germany."

"Before I go to work, Franz," Hans said, "I have something here you might want to read. I've heard you're fascinated with America and love your Opa's stories of going there." He walked over to a bookshelf and took down a book. "This is *Winnetou* and is about an Apache Indian chief and his white friend, Old Shatterhand. Many boys love these adventures. Read it while you wait for your mother to come, if you want."

At the mention of America, Franz perked up and took the book. "Thank you," he said, "I would like to see it." He began to read while Anna did household chores and time went by as he read of the Indian's adventures with the transcontinental railroad being built there, and various quarreling tribes.

"Come on, Franz," Aunt Anna said. "Let's go for a walk. Supper will be done when we return." She opened a door in the oven and placed a scoopful of coal inside and adjusted the heat under the pot.

"Oma uses corn stalks for fueling her stove," Franz said as he watched closely. He missed Kati, Oma and Opa. He even missed the stove. That thought made him smile.

Later, he and Anna strolled leisurely around Augsburg. Franz again enjoyed seeing street lights, the constant traffic and activity around them. All afternoon he heard frequent sounds of train whistles and was pleased to go to the depot again. As he'd noticed last night, the travelers were almost all soldiers of various ranks.

"There sure are a lot of Nazi red flags around," Franz observed. "I've seen a few before, but what is the name of the black thing in the circle?"

"It's a swastika." She answered tersely. He looked up at her but she had pressed her lips together so he didn't pursue it. He thought of Heinz and of how helpful he'd been. He wondered where Adam was. A horn honked nearby and he turned his head to see what happened. Then Aunt Anna guided them back to her apartment.

His aunt's casserole tasted delicious and he helped her wash and dry the dishes when they finished. Then he curled up with *Winnetou* again. The book told of a heroic and noble chief. "If I ever go to America I hope I get to see a real Indian," he told Aunt Anna, who laughed. In bed with his eyes closed, he heard continued noise outside. In Stanisic he heard only an occasional dog barking. Soon his tired state overcame the unfamiliar sounds. His mother might arrive by train in the morning.

After breakfast the next morning, he looked out the window and read some more while Aunt Anna sewed. They heard a tap at the door and someone called out a greeting.

He saw his mother, but in a way, it wasn't his mother. She looked different somehow and he stood up hesitantly. Then she smiled. His deep dimples bracketed his answering grin.

She paused and blinked away some tears. "Oh, Franz, you've grown so much in the last year. You're taller and stronger and look even more like your father." She reached him and gave him a fierce hug. "And you have sun-bleached hair." She looked him over more carefully and cocked her head. "You look so much older now." She wiped away some tears and put her hand to his face, "I've missed you so much!"

Then she turned to Anna and both sisters giggled and embraced each other. "I'll be here today and tomorrow we must leave in the afternoon. One of the other cooks is filling in for me."

"I'm going to the market, so you and Franz enjoy a nice visit by yourselves."

His mother put her hand out to Franz. "Come, sit down and tell me all about what has happened the past year. I've been so hungry for news!"

Franz suddenly couldn't think of a thing to say.

"Well, let me make this easier. How is Kati and what is she doing?"

"Did you hear about Kati getting a bead up her nose?" She shook her head so he continued. "Her nose got big and sort of red. I held her while Oma pinched her nose and stuck a needle up to the bead and pulled it out! I sure laughed when she told us she'd smelled it and it just popped in. And she's printing her name now. She always has a kitty nearby. I think the cats like her so much they just keep making kittens to keep Kati happy."

Then he told about farm news, and how the daily pig run in the spring both fascinated him and made him stay behind the gate, when Anton took the Sparrow eggs from the Weiss' roof, and how Anton locked Mrs. Weiss in the shed. He took a deep breath and told of growing silk worms for money. She laughed and asked questions, just as she always had. When he told her about Oma getting bit by the horse and the cooking he'd learned to do, she smiled proudly.

"An American airplane exploded east of Stanisic and Anton and I walked over and saw parts scattered everywhere." He described what they'd seen and told her about the blood and missing bodies. "Then we started 1943 and Uncle Adam came to get me and here I am!"

Aunt Anna returned after the news about Oma's horse bite but she just went about her own chores and let mother and son talk and talk.

The next morning they took a couple of excursions in the area to get exercise and see the city. The sisters visited and talked of their parents, their husbands and the difficult food situation with shortages. Franz eagerly looked forward to seeing his father.

Riding the train to Leipzig, Franz' interest never waned as he looked out the window and saw big cities and thick forests. "This looks a lot like Opa's big book of the world." Finally, they arrived at the biggest city Franz had ever seen. They stepped down from the train and walked along the train shed. Franz looked up. Steel framework overhead made a series of grand arches, which were filled with glass panels the whole width and length of the walkway. Sunshine poured down upon them as if they were outside. Everywhere he saw the red flags with the swastika inside a white circle. Finally, they left the station and continued to walk in Leipzig. He found it difficult to fully concentrate on all these marvelous and strange things around him because soon he would get to see his father.

"Come, Franz," his mother encouraged. "We're going where I work. Your father lives in barracks nearby and will come for you this evening. But first, we're going to the kitchen and eat some supper. I want my friends, especially Lili and Margaret, to meet you as well," she said with a twinkle in her eyes.

Franz switched his suitcase from one hand to the other and walked a bit faster.

"Yes, thank you," he said to what must be the fifth woman to stop at the table and ask if he were glad to be in Germany with his parents. By now he knew to eat fast, between visits from his mother's friends. Out of the corner of his eye, he saw the door open again and put another forkful of pork in his mouth and chewed quickly.

"Hello, son."

He recognized the voice at once and jumped up to meet his father, whose smile covered his whole face as he greeted his son with a hearty hug. Vati took Mama's hand and they smiled in shared pleasure to have their son with them.

Franz picked up his suitcase, ready to follow his father anyplace. His mother walked with them as far as the edge of the company property and hugged them each good night. His first sight of the barracks amazed him. It stood three stories high and as wide as the pasture at home.

"I've got off for two days so I'll show you around Leipzig, and we'll spend time together. You can't stay here with me permanently, but will be with your mother. I'll come often!" Dad's eyes gazed at him with love. "There hasn't been a day pass when I didn't miss you and Kati." He blinked moisture from his eyes and opened the door to enter. They walked up to the top floor and placed the suitcase beside Dad's bed. Franz would sleep on the bunk above him.

"Come, I'll show you the indoor latrine. It's on the second floor."

He smiled at the merriment in Franz' eyes. "What do you think of indoor facilities?"

"It's much better than digging a hole for the outhouse! Also, it's like a magic trick!"

Other men filed into in the barracks and soon many were in bed, some began snoring immediately and others talked quietly as they ended the day.

"I'm too excited to sleep," Franz said, then anticipated his father's response, "but I'll lie down and be still."

The next thing he knew, sunshine filtered through the window. He sat up and realized no one else was in the room. Franz hopped out of bed, put his clothes on quickly and looked for his father on the way to the latrine downstairs.

Part Two

Devastation of War

13

1943 - Ten years old
Leipzig, Germany

FRANZ INHALED THE steamy fragrance. "It makes me think of Stanisic," he said, his eyebrows lowered in thought. He smelled it again and took a sip. "I like it."

"Hmmm," his father replied as he stood and reached to pick up bread from a nearby table. "Since we can't get real coffee grounds, we use imitation coffee made of roasted oats—kaffee-ersatz. You've spent a lot of time in Opa's fields so I guess the smell reminds you of his crops."

"It's good," Franz said, and drank the rest of it.

"Son, things are different here." Vati cleared his throat. "You can't have the freedom you've enjoyed at your grandparents' home. We must know where you are all the time."

Franz sat up straighter. When his Vati said "can't have" and "freedom" together, it didn't sound good.

"Why?" he asked in alarm. "There's no fighting here, is there?" He felt a quick fluttering in his chest. Memories of Sombor flooded his mind, and he remembered the days and nights of violence when Chetniks fought Hungarians. A picture flashed through his mind of finding the dead priest and touching him to see if he were alive. He remembered the pool of thick blood where an eye had been. Again he saw a Chetnik flower girl shoot the Hungarian soldier, whose uniform quickly leaked a red stain. Later, he and Anton searched the crashed airplane in Stanisic, and found no bodies, but lots of blood. He blinked and returned to being in Leipzig with his father.

"No place in Europe is completely safe now." His arm reached around Franz's shoulder. "We've had a few bombings, but we're too far inland to be an advantage for the Allies." He hesitated. "We may need you in a hurry and not have time to search for you. You can't let your curiosity lead you from one place to another. Not here and not now."

"But Vati, can I at least go for a walk or meet some guys to play a game? I won't go far. I know how to stay out of trouble." A bit of guilt wiggled in his mind. It last part wasn't always true.

Vati cocked his head and his lips curved a bit. "Uh huh," he said slowly. "No, not at first, but we'll see later. These rules are for your safety and our peace of mind, not to punish you.

"You'll make friends when you start school. You can walk to school—it's just a few blocks from here." Vati hesitated. "Do you understand?" He tipped his head forward, his eyebrows went down and he fell silent.

"I guess." Franz bit his lower lip and shrugged. He might not like it here.

"Come, we're not far from Market Square."

The rest of the day father and son relaxed together as they walked from one impressive building to another. At first, he enjoyed seeing their great sizes and the many differences in each building. By the time they stopped and his father used a ration stamp to buy from a small café, Franz grew bored.

"Can we go back now?" he asked when they finished eating.

"Just one more," his father said, "I think you'll like the Memorial to the Battle of Nations." They stopped at a cross-walk and turned the corner. "They built it to honor to Prussian,

Russian and Swedish armies for the defeat of Napoleon here in Leipzig more than a hundred years ago. Have you studied Napoleon?"

"Uh," Franz tried to remember what he knew. "Yeah— he was a French Emperor and stood around with his hand in his jacket." Franz laughed, "At school we argued about what he hid in there. The teacher said he tried to be Emperor of the whole world or something. There were lots of wars."

"Kind of like what is happening in Europe now," his father said. Franz noticed his Vati looked around quickly before he blinked his eyes. "Ignore what I said," Vati whispered. "Did Adam or your mother explain the dangers of criticizing anything to do with the Nazis?"

"Yes, Uncle Adam did," Franz mumbled.

"Good," his father nodded. "Now let's see a monument."

Franz halted at his first sight of the building. Built of huge, black rocks with an imposing base as high as the Cantina, but far wider, it had no decoration to soften its appearance. On top of the base, each section became narrower, until it became a tower. The Memorial to the Battle of Nations compared to nothing Franz had seen before. He tipped his head toward the top of the spire and down again. Something about it bothered him, so he stepped closer to his father.

"It kinda looks like a mean castle, doesn't it?" Franz glanced at his Vati. "People wouldn't want to live here, or smile or sing happy songs."

"Oh," his father nodded as he studied the building. "You're right. I guess because it's meant to remind us how determined those armies had to be to overcome Napoleon."

"Can we go inside?" Franz asked.

"Sure, and if you want to, we can hike up about 500 steps to the top. I've heard the view is beautiful."

After two flights of outside stairs, they opened the door and walked inside.

Franz looked around. He saw large statues of Viking-like warriors with medieval weapons, complete with armor. They bowed their heads seriously toward the floor, their helmets at their feet. He stepped close to one statue and looked up into his face. He looked so real, his face sad.

They moved toward another, much like the first but this statue held a tall pole in one hand which looked like an axe on the top. Franz looked around. Each statue showed differences but all had their heads bowed.

"When I see something like this from the past, it doesn't seem real," his father said. "It's easier to think of it as an old-time story and not people with families."

Franz nodded, content to say nothing.

"Shall we walk all the way up?"

Franz nodded again.

They walked up hundreds of steps, stopping only to look out when windows appeared. Finally they got to the top.

"Which way is Yugoslavia?" Franz asked.

His father pointed toward another window. "A pigeon would go pretty much south."

Each window showed a different view. The ones overlooking Leipzig showed the great size and beauty of the city, but Franz favored windows opened to the small area of countryside with its varied hills and trees and plowed fields. The walk down seemed very long and tiring.

"It's not long till time for supper. Let's wait for Mama at the Cantina." Vati suggested and Franz quickly agreed. They walked back to the barracks, used the latrine and washed up.

"Your school's on the way. It's closed for today, but you can see it."

The giant building intimidated Franz at first, till he saw boys his age kicking a soccer ball. He had friends in Stanisic. Surely he'd make new ones here, couldn't he?

He and Vati headed west, then south, and used a sidewalk to go under railroad tracks. They walked under the last track when a train off in the distance announced it was moving through . Tall trees, dense bushes, and flowers replaced wood and stone structures.

"Is this a forest?" he asked.

Vati looked around, nodded and chuckled. "It's a nursery where people come to buy growing things. It's about forty acres, so I guess you could call it a forest." He smiled, "But it doesn't have wild creatures living here. I like walking by here when I go to work."

As soon as the land cleared, Franz noticed three buildings ahead. Two women in white uniforms entered the middle building. "Where are those nurses going?" he asked.

"It's the first aid and emergency treatment building where Mama stays at night with other women. A few boys around your age have a large room together. You'll probably move here in a few weeks." They walked to the front of the building.

"Hey, I never saw steps like these!" Franz looked at three half-circle steps which spanned from one side of the building to the other. He hopped on the lower one, then the middle and his left leg stepped up and right leg stepped down. "I've got a short leg!" he said as he hobbled along the curve to the other end. He looked at the two entries. "Which door goes to Mama's room?"

"The door on the left is to the medical and office part and off limits for you. The door on the right leads to the second floor."

"This is the Cantina," his father said as they walked south to the next building, "We eat noon and evening meals here. Also, the air-raid shelter is in the basement."

Franz looked around and noticed arrows pointing down to a steel door. "It looks like the one in Augsburg."

Without speaking, Franz studied everything. The first floor had large windows, but the other four levels had smaller and fewer ones. He fixed in his mind what it looked like. He squinted at something on the roof of the building, shaded his eyes and pointed upward.

"What's up there?"

"An *Acht-acht–*, 88 mm anti-aircraft flack cannon with four barrels. It's automatic so when one barrel is fired, a new round of ammunition slides in—ready to go again. A soldier takes aim as best he can. With four barrels firing in fast succession, it's extremely loud. It goes as high as twenty thousand feet and will protect us against enemy attack. This Cantina is the most important building for you to remember."

"Because of the shelter," Franz said to show his Vati he understood.

"Yes, when the sirens turn on, you come here from wherever you are."

"Will you and Mama be here?"

"If you get here first, we'll be right behind you."

"Okay," he said. He really hoped he wouldn't have to go there by himself.

"Well, time to eat."

As they stepped through the door Franz saw his mother wave. She nudged a short, round woman next to her and pointed to Franz, so he smiled at her as well. Carrying trays of food, he and father joined her.

"Franz, this is one of my roommates, Lili. You met her the first night when you ate at the company kitchen."

"No, don't feel bad you don't remember me," Lili said. "So many people wanted to meet you that night. I'm on my way to work but wanted say hello. I'll see you around." With that, she smiled at all of them and left.

He sat between his parents and managed to tell Mama about the day while he looked at other people in the room. Three boys sat together at a nearby table. They looked to be close to his age.

"So, where did you hide Slim?" the smallest boy asked quietly.

Franz leaned closer to listen without being noticed.

"Where no one will find him," said one with curly, blond hair.

"You're not being fair, Karl!" The third boy's eyes squinted.

"If you can find him, then he's yours." Franz peeked at Karl as he spoke.

Silence stretched out as the two boys frowned at Karl. Then one of them laughed. "When he's found, we'll be the ones who get in trouble." And he picked up his spoon, put some peas on it and flicked them toward Karl.

Franz' dimples deepened as a pea war escalated until several mothers stopped the fun.

If they became friends, maybe they'd tell him about 'Slim'.

Franz and Mama with friends in Leipzig

The next day Franz and his father returned to another part of Old Market Square and saw the huge publishing house of Breitkopf & Hartel, many vendors and even an artist who displayed his paintings. Franz walked beside his father as they headed north to the University of Leipzig.

Suddenly he stopped at a vacant lot and cocked his head. "I saw a barrel like this near the kitchen where Mama works. What are they?"

"Never go near them, Franz. They're very dangerous. These fifty-five gallon drums are placed around the city. They contain acid. When approaching plane warnings are received, only members of the Wehrmacht are allowed to open the barrels to add another chemical, which turns into a huge fog. It's hurts to breathe, will sting your eyes, and you won't be able to see far in front of yourself." His father looked up at the sky. "Planes can't see what's below, either. By the time the acid cloud spreads, you should be in or on the way to a shelter. After a few times, you'll know what to do without thinking about it."

Franz hopped out of bed and dressed in his best youth shorts and clean shirt. Today he would enroll in the sixth grade. What if he didn't know the subjects and they think he's stupid? He didn't have a friend to talk to, either. Taking a deep breath, he hurried downstairs to meet Mama and they walked to his new school.

After Mama filled out his paperwork, she gave him a brief hug and walked away. Franz smiled with effort at the teacher beside him and followed him to the first classroom.

The teacher hadn't started yet, so he stood near a desk and looked around. Prominently hung on the front wall of the room was a huge picture of Hitler. Of more interest, he saw a bookshelf along one side wall under all the windows. He wanted to go over and see what they were, but felt too shy since he knew no one.

"Hi!" a round-faced, blue eyed boy stood beside him. "I've seen you at the Cantina—our mothers work together in the officers' kitchen. I'm Josef Wolf."

"My name's Franz. I'm from Yugoslavia." He smiled. "Does your mother live above the First Aid Station too?"

Josef nodded then took his seat when the teacher began class.

By the end of the day Franz knew several kids by name and enthusiastically joined in exercise games. Like Stanisic, school would last eight hours every day but he'd also have an extra half-day on Saturday.

"With spring, we'll go to *Jungvolk* on Saturdays," Josef told him after school. "It'll be fun."

"Tell me, who or what is Slim?" Franz said.

Josef laughed. "He's a garter snake, but we let him go. We had to find worms, slugs and caught a couple of mice. Karl' mother is terribly afraid of snakes and our mothers don't like them either. We got tired of him anyway."

Each day brought new things to learn, games to play and the beginnings of friendships.

When night fell, Franz didn't mind going to bed. Fatigue and knowing his father slept on the bed below helped him fall into a very easy slumber.

He woke early one morning after Vati went to work, but lay with his eyes closed, just content to listen to voices and footsteps from the hallway. Everyone else had left the room but two men close by who spoke quietly.

"This morning I hooked up the radio and heard German s-s-surrendered at S-stalingrad. Russia has over a hundred thousand of them captive. It was easy since they were already s-starved, frozen and ready to s-surrender." The man's voice raised in volume before he regained control. "My brother's in the S-sixth Army."

His stutter was at odds with his deep voice.

Franz knew they couldn't see him on the top bunk. He remained still and waited.

"Maybe Ernst transferred out earlier. Did the radio say where they're being taken?" The second man said in a whisper.

"No. Perhaps to work camps. Insanity led us into this big battle for S-stalingrad! For two years we've laid s-siege at Leningrad—to what results?"

Boisterous voices announced some men returning, and ended their conversation.

Franz thought of Uncle Adam. Where was he? Was he okay? He slipped out of bed, got dressed and headed to the kitchen.

He knew not to repeat any of what he heard.

As the only child in the barracks, he got to know the other men. One day after school Otto Schmidt motioned Franz to join him at his table in the kitchen. Franz brought his kaffee-erasatz and sat down. Herr Schmidt started to put a picture in his pocket, then leaned forward and laid it on the table in front of Franz.

Franz picked it up. It was a woman and she was naked. Fascinated, his mouth fell open. Franz held it closer for a better look. Completely naked. She sure wasn't shy. His eyes darted from one interesting part of her body to another until a hand snatched the photo from him.

Startled, Franz looked up as his father threw the picture to the floor, grabbed a chair, and raised it high over Herr Schmidt.

"What do you think you're doing? My boy is only ten years old! If you ever do anything like this again, I really will smash your head in!"

Franz had never seen his father so mad. Truthfully, it frightened him. The room went silent.

Herr Schmidt sat like a statue, and then looked away. "If it's such a big deal with you, I won't," he muttered.

The chair dropped to the floor. "Come on, Franz, let's go." His father stomped out. Franz followed behind.

"I'm sorry I lost my temper." He smiled a little, and sighed deeply, "You're not in trouble. Good men don't pass around pictures of naked women so they can snicker and make crude remarks about them. That woman is someone's daughter, or sister, maybe a mother."

Franz nodded and didn't mention that it had been interesting.

"And it's time to go to the Cantina and eat."

"Vati," Franz asked as they neared the First Aid Station, "where do you work? Can I see it?"

"The name of it is Hasag and they make lanterns, street lights, automobile lights and some sheet metal things. It's been a large company for years, but with the war they've expanded to making parts for the military. Now it's guarded. You can see it better from the other side of the bathing area." Once there, he pointed off in the distance. "All those buildings are a part of Hasag."

"Which one do you work in?" Franz saw a row of large, mostly red-brick buildings, some several floors high.

"You can't see the building from here, but they all look pretty much alike. Before you ask, I really don't know how my part fits into anything. I make several different sizes of tapered pipes. Not exciting, but it's good to have the paycheck."

A horrible, piercing sound jerked Franz from a deep sleep. Air raid sirens were on. He fought panic, dropped down from the bunk and took the clothes his father handed him. They both dressed quickly as the wail amplified with additional sirens announcing danger.

"Grab your pillow and blanket," his father said.

Franz saw shadow people in the faint light of the moon as everyone moved toward shelter. "Will Mama be there?" Franz asked as he hurried alongside his father.

His voice was lost in the terrifying screams of the siren.

14

1943 – ten years old
Leipzig, Germany

B OMBARDED BY THE constant sirens' wail, Franz couldn't think. He just held fast to his father's strong, work-roughened hand and clutched his pillow as they hurried in the dark. Finally, they came to the nursery so he knew they were close to the shelter. Bare tree limbs jerked around in the wind like enemies' arms ready to reach down and grab him and every bush hid danger.

A fog moved in and rapidly grew thicker. He held on to Vati even tighter and blinked his eyes. Acid must have been added to the big drums. Finally, they got to the Cantina basement and filed into the room past the steel doors. Mama stood by the wall, waiting for them.

And the sirens continued without a break.

Franz huddled between his parents on a nearby bench, took a deep breath and sagged against his father. He felt safer. Dim, yellowish light bulbs hung in various places on the wall, making people look sick and foreign, even Vati and Mama. Mama's brown eyes and Vati's blue ones had little color.

A wiggling Josef sat across the room with a woman who had the same round face framed by big ears as he did—she must be his mother. Farther back in the crowd Karl, from the Cantina, stood with a lone woman also, but the third boy, the smallest one, had both parents with him. Everyone looked as frightened as he felt. Somehow, it made it easier.

Every seat on the steel benches and tables quickly became occupied, and latecomers sank to the floor to lean on a wall. Franz looked over his shoulder and saw an older girl standing still, not looking at anyone or anything. Tears streamed down her cheeks, otherwise she showed no expression, except one hand twisted and untwisted a strand of long, blond hair.

A tiny baby wailed constantly, and a little girl younger than Kati cried for her dolly while both their mothers tried to comfort them. An old lady rocked and moaned. Franz didn't even bother trying to talk to Mama or Vati because of the noise inside and the ever-constant alarms from outside.

With so many people shoved together, the shelter's warmth felt good at first, but rapidly became hot and stifling. Franz took the blanket off his shoulders, removed his coat and pushed the pillow over one ear. The shelter might be built of steel but nothing could shut out the sound of sirens, the rooftop *Acht-acht* shooting, bombs whistling in the distance or intermittent explosions. People got as comfortable as possible and settled in to wait. Franz tried to relax, but he tensed every time the cannon shot and when it didn't, he tensed for the next one. He needed to pee and noticed a blanket hanging over a corner area. He wanted to use it, but wouldn't leave the safety of being between Mama and Vati.

Hours later, the booming stopped and eventually a single siren screamed.

"It's the 'all clear' signal," his father said. The door opened, and many people stood up and flexed stiff limbs. The soft light of early morning filtered from the open door into the room.

As Franz went up the steps and outside, he looked up and smiled at Mama and Vati.

"I hear a bird singing. Where did they hide?"

"I don't know," Vati looked around. "My guess is they found a window ledge or some bridges to gather under."

Franz glanced around and saw the girl with the long blond hair, at the same time she noticed him, and she gave him a gentle smile. She was tall and beautiful. Franz blushed and busied himself with holding his pillow and blanket.

Mama hugged Franz and his father before they walked back to the barracks and Mama to her room above the First Aid.

"Go back to bed for a while." Vati said. "School will start an hour later since everyone spent the night in the shelter. I'm going to work—it's time for my shift to start."

On the walk to school the next morning, Franz caught up with Josef and the two other boys from the Cantina.

"I saw you last night. Is that your first time there?" Josef asked.

"We went to a shelter in Augsburg, but it didn't last so long." Franz looked at the other boys, "I'm Franz Elmer."

"This is Karl Klein, in seventh year," Josef said. He turned his thumb toward the short, stout one, "and this is Hugo Braun, he's in fifth."

"The other owners of Slim, right?" Franz said.

They all laughed and nodded.

Aluminum tinsel lay everywhere, and Franz bent over to pick up a few.

"Stop!" Karl shouted. "Don't pick up anything dropped from planes. It's pretty, but it'll slice your skin. This stuff," he pointed to the ground, "is dropped from the planes to mess up our radar and listening devices."

Startled, Franz froze and stood up, then leaned over again to study the sparkling pieces more closely. "Thanks," he said.

"Last night you were with your mother, weren't you?" Franz asked Josef. "Was your father there, too?"

Josef shifted from one foot to another and no one spoke.

Franz wished he hadn't asked.

"My father was killed in Stalingrad," Josef mumbled. "We moved here so my mother could work. She works in the officers' kitchen with your mother."

"Oh," Franz didn't know what else to say. "I'm sorry."

"My father's in the Army," Karl said, changing the subject, "and Hugo's folks both work for the company."

"My parents work for the company, too," Franz said. "My mother cooks for the officers. My father runs a machine in the ammunition factory."

After they arrived at school, Franz and Josef went to their class and Karl and Hugo to their separate ones. Students and teachers alike took a while to settle down to study, but by the third period things seemed normal again.

The next two nights, sirens jolted Franz awake. By now he knew to get dressed, grab his blanket and stay with Vati, but fear accompanied him every time.

"Franz, tonight you move to the same building where Mama is," his father told him one evening. "I'm permanently on the night shift now, so let's take your things with us when we eat tonight."

They arrived at the Cantina early, but Josef, Hugo and Karl were there already.

"I'm moving over here," Franz held his suitcase higher.

"It's a rule that new boys get to make the beds!" Karl said. Josef and Hugo quickly nodded.

Franz smiled. This would be fun and he'd still get to see his parents every day.

"It's good here," Josef said as they took Franz up the stairs to their room. "It's close to food and to the shelter when air raid sirens yell."

Franz glanced along the hall and guessed these first rooms belonged to the women—through open doors he saw frilly decorations and pictures.

Karl led the way to the second from the last room. Light streamed in through a window on the end wall and two bunk beds stood on the left side and two on the right.

"There's my bed," Karl said, pointing to a bunk closest to the window. "You get the one on top."

"The younger boys hang around with each other," Josef said, then shrugged his bony shoulders. "One of them cries a lot at night, but he's getting better."

If anyone cried, Franz didn't wake to hear him, but lightening flashed through the edges of the blind, so he rolled to his other side, and went back to sleep.

The next few days, heavy storms and thunder rumbled almost constantly. The boys hurried to school, and at the end of the day, back to their room. Franz didn't mind the cold, wet days. At least clouds kept enemy planes away, and they didn't have to scurry to the shelter every night.

They settled into a routine of sorts. Mama worked days and Vati worked nights, so Franz had breakfast, and sometimes lunch, with Vati and dinner with Mama.

———

"The fork is too wide," Franz said, a week later. The four boys gathered in front of the First Aid Station. "Your aim's going to be hard to control."

"Can't I just chuck rocks at a rabbit?" Josef gave a gap-toothed smile, and pretended to throw with great force.

"If your target is a barn you can," Franz laughed, "but if you want to really aim at something you need a good slingshot. The secret is a narrow fork and long inner tube band." Franz held his own weapon up and showed them how far he stretched his left arm as he held the handle and his right hand pulled the pocket and rock near his eye. "What do you want me to shoot?"

"See the baby elm tree over there?" Karl pointed about twelve feet away.

Franz took off his coat, pulled back the sling, took aim, narrowed his eyes and followed the path. He let go. They all heard the solid thunk as the rock found its mark and cheers erupted.

"Can I try it?" Karl asked, but the distinctive hi-lo wail of an approaching ambulance stopped all thought of slingshots.

The driver backed up to the building so the boys scrambled to the top step to the side, out of the way. One medic opened the ambulance doors while another ran to enter the First Aid.

Three men screamed in pain as they stumbled out, holding their arms up, and away from their bodies. Parts of their shirts had burned away, and the boys saw skin hanging off arms and faces. The smell of smoke and explosives drifted in the air.

Franz gasped, as did the others. He wanted to run away and block out the sights and smell, but couldn't move.

Nurses swarmed outside to help guide the men inside. One man made raspy noises as he waved his arms uncontrollably. Franz heard enough guttural sounds to understand the words "Help me! I can't see! Please help me!"

Instead of a face, Franz saw what looked like multi-colored melted wax and no hair covered the man's head. Franz couldn't look away, but shrank closer to the building in horror.

The first medic spoke in a soothing tone as he put his hands on the man's unburned back to guide him up the stairs. As if everything hurt, the wounded man twisted away from the gentle touch, and moaned louder.

The medic's words remained simple, slow and steady, but loud enough to be heard. "Help is close, only a few more feet. We're going up some stairs. I'll tell you when to step up. In just a minute doctors and nurses will help you. Just move forward into the hospital."

Franz felt relief when the man finally calmed down enough to listen and respond to the words.

"The first step is here," the medic said, "and then another. I'm right behind you." One step at a time, they managed to make progress and finally disappeared from sight.

All the injured were inside and the door shut. Franz' legs felt weak and he collapsed, the other boys sat around him on the steps.

"What do you think will happen to them?" Franz asked hesitantly. "How can they live with burns that bad?"

"I stepped on hot coals one time," Karl said, "and it hurt so bad I couldn't walk for weeks. It was just on the bottom of one foot. I think I'd want to die if I were them, especially the last guy."

Franz agreed but didn't say it out loud, the others nodded.

A nurse came to get a box out of the ambulance. As she turned around, Franz could see tears rolling down her cheeks. She stopped when she noticed them. "You boys saw them come in, didn't you?"

Franz, and the other boys, nodded. "How, um," Franz stood up and stepped forward. "What will happen to them?"

She shook her head, "We'll do the best we can. They got caught in an explosion at work. Go home to your mothers or fathers. The doctors are working." She hurried back inside.

"What can a doctor do?" Karl mused aloud.

"Maybe put a gallon of salve on each of them?" Franz suggested without conviction.

Walking slowly, they went to their room, talked about homework they needed to do, but not now. Guessing Mama should be home soon, Franz wandered outside by himself and sat at the side of the building. He crossed his arms on his knees, tipped his head forward and closed his eyes.

"Franz?" his mother crouched down beside him. "I hear it's been a rough day. You want to tell me about it?"

Franz nodded, and then shrugged his shoulders. Where should he start? "We were making slingshots when an ambulance came." He took a deep breath. "The nurse said an explosion went off where the men worked."

Mama nodded and took his hand. "Those can be bad."

"It was so scary." Franz' voice dropped to just above a whisper. "We saw skin hanging from their arms and faces like chickens' skins sometimes slide off when they're fried." Tears filled his eyes and rolled down to drip off his chin. "It was horrible. They moaned and screamed. One of them couldn't see...," Franz tipped his chin down to his chest, and his voice wobbled as the tears fell, "...and he didn't have a face."

Hugging Mama fiercely, he sobbed as she crooned to him.

"I'm so sorry for those men and I wish you hadn't been there." One of her tears fell on his hand. "Bad things happen sometimes. But God created our bodies to do a lot of healing and maybe it's not as bad as it looked today."

Franz pulled back in frustration, "Mama, he couldn't see! His face burned away!"

"I know, *Liebling*, but listen." She pulled Franz closer and tucked him under her chin. "Things sometimes appear hopeless, but later get better. We all adjust and change. As bad as it looks now, they're still alive. Perhaps God sees good for them tomorrow or the day after."

Franz looked up, and Mama used her thumbs to wipe tears from his cheeks. "If you want to, Lili would be glad to let you sleep in her bunk for tonight. She can find another room."

His first instinct, to immediately say he would, hung in front of him. He hesitated. He might, if all his new friends stayed with their mothers. He sat up straight, sniffled, gave his mother a wobbly smile.

"No, I'll stay in the boys' room."

She nodded. They remained on the ground, leaned on the side of the building, and looked up at the clear sky. Mama pointed to an eagle overhead. It swooped and turned, its wings barely moved as it sailed in the breeze. He wished he were that eagle, flying above all problems and fear. They watched until the large bird flew out of sight. Relaxed now, they hugged again and went to the dining room.

At supper Karl' mother called to the other mothers "Do your sons stink as much as Karl does?"

Mama and the others smelled their boys and made a big production of waving their hands to clear the air. The boys knew their next stop would be the bathing building, on the other side of the First Aid Station.

They grabbed clean clothes and ran next door. Karl leaned closer to Franz. "There's Stephani!"

Standing in line with a clean, blue dress draped over her arm, stood the girl from the shelter. Her hair looked like silk as it covered her shoulder and back. She ignored the boys.

Franz gazed in admiration until he noticed the other boys elbow each other while pointing at him. He raised his shoulders, held both palms up and grinned.

"Get to the back of a long line of her admirers." Karl teased. "Josef is the only one who has talked to her and that was to apologize for jumping to catch a ball and knocking her down."

Franz laughed with the others, but didn't mention her earlier smile to him. The line moved and he stood before the bathing attendant, who gave each boy a towel and soap and told them which showers were available.

"Stephani gets a shower to herself because she's the only girl." Josef explained as he and Franz shared their assigned shower. Clean and dressed in their pajamas, they strolled to their room.

Franz hopped onto his bunk and Mama came in to tuck the blanket around his shoulders. She brushed his straight hair from his forehead. This evening he'd been busy and didn't have to think about the burned men. But now, pictures flashed on his mind and didn't go away when he closed his eyes.

Mama's long, slender face held no laugher, her brown eyes nothing but tenderness and sorrow. "If you change your mind, we'll make a place for you to sleep in my room."

"I'll be fine," he tried to sound confident. He wished he knew what to say to chase away the worried shadows in Mama's eyes.

"Yes," she said. "I know you will, but it might take a bit of time. Tomorrow is Saturday and it's half day of school for you, so Vati will sleep while you're off learning." Mama kissed his forehead. "We think you need to get away from here and think of something else. Vati's planning to meet you here for noon meal and you'll both go to town. Good night and say your prayers. I love you."

"Mama," Franz said softly, "I'm glad you're here."

Franz tossed and turned, unable to turn off his mind. The squeaking of three beds let him know the other boys had the same problem. In the still of the dark, memories refused to leave. He again heard screams, this time the monsters turned and looked at him. But those men were real, their injuries real, and not as temporary as a nightmare. Finally he slept.

———

"Yesterday I picked up your first ration stamps," his father said at noon as they walked toward the Market Square area.

"Are the stamps like money?"

"I wish they worked so good," Vati shook his head, "but no, they only let the shopkeepers sell us as much as our *marken* allows." He handed Franz the book with his name on front. "They're very important. Since we eat at the Cantina, we use them there. If we had our own home, we'd stand in line to get whatever we hoped to get."

"Without your stamp, we can't get milk or whatever you need and you'll do without. Of course, sometimes the food is no good by the time we get it. Mama or I will keep the booklet for you, but if one of us gives it to you, be very careful not to lose it."

"Okay. Why are they different colors?" Franz flipped the stiff pages of the booklet.

"For convenience, I guess. To buy sugar a white *marken* is torn out, for meat it's blue ones. It's written on there, but the colors make it faster. You'll notice you have more yellow than we do. Children get extra milk. Sometimes if the buyer for the Cantina kitchen is too late in line to buy food, they substitute. But vegetables and local fruit aren't rationed."

"If I were the boss, I'd ration vegetables and give sugar to everyone."

Vati's eyes crinkled at the corners as he smiled as he put the booklets in his pocket. "Want to go to a great, big bookstore?"

Franz found a book with colorful pictures of the stars and planets and another about clouds and what the different ones meant. Franz and his father happily spent the next few hours reading interesting facts about the world around them.

Sunday morning Franz woke at his usual time. He stretched every muscle, and leaned from his bunk to peek through the side of the black-out shade to see what it looked like outside. Cloudy, but not rainy.

He hopped down and purposely rested his foot on Karl' sleeping face and watched him flail around in protest. Franz just giggled.

"I know something you haven't seen before," Karl said. "Get dressed and I'll show you."

As soon as the outside door shut behind them and they buttoned their coats, Karl hesitated. "Maybe this isn't such a good idea. We're not supposed to know about them." He stood, biting a fingernail.

""Well, can you just tell me?" Franz asked. "I'm good at keeping secrets."

"No, you might not believe me." Karl frowned, and then plowed his fingers through his curly, blond hair. "Okay, I'll show you."

Franz almost told Karl to forget it, but his own curiosity removed caution.

Karl led the way to the far side of the Cantina, stopped and looked around, then motioned to Franz. They stayed close to the building and came around to the back. At first Franz didn't see anything but the trash bins. Shrugging, he sat down behind a bush next to Karl.

Karl put one finger over his lips.

They didn't wait long until a couple of men silently made their way to one of the trash carts. Franz moved to get a better view through the bush and gasped when he did. The men looked more like skeletons with skin stretched over them than like real people. Their noses and ears were far too big for their heads. Their coats were dark grey but dirty and worn thin and some metal buttons remained in two rows on the jacket's front. Franz recognized the Soviet Army fur cap from a picture he'd seen in Stanisic. The hat's skies and rear were up, since the temperature had risen, they didn't need maximum protection for their ears and neck.

Very quietly, the taller one reached a bony hand into the bin and picked up bits of bread and a chunk of chicken. He nodded his head and his mouth moved into something resembling a smile. As they searched for food, Franz heard them make guttural sounds of approval when larger pieces were found. They licked their fingers, and then slipped away as silently as they'd arrived, and walked past the hidden boys.

Franz could have convinced himself he imagined it, but for the odor lingering behind.

"Who are they?" he whispered.

"They're Russian prisoners of war." Karl shook his head. "I've seen these two before, but never any others. They work for the company and live in a camp that way." He pointed to the south. "They aren't allowed over here. As skinny as they are, they must not get enough food at their cafeteria. I think they come on the way to or from the work."

Karl put his hands on his hips and squinted at Franz. "Remember, you said you can keep secrets."

Franz hesitated, and gave a reluctant nod. How could he not tell Mama or Vati?

15

Winter/Spring 1943 – 10 years old
Leipzig, Germany

"DO JOSEF AND Hugo know about the prisoners?" Franz asked Karl.

"I didn't tell Josef because his father died in Russia. And if Hugo knew, he'd blab everything to his father and I know his father would do something really mean." Karl hesitated, then lowered his voice even quieter, "Some of us leave food there from time to time."

Still shocked by what he'd just seen, Franz nodded agreement.

All morning, Franz couldn't stop thinking of the Russian prisoners. On the way to the Cantina, he remembered the meals Mama or Oma used to make—made with the best of meats and hearty vegetables, and also loaves of rich, fragrant bread with fresh-churned butter. Back then he could go to the pantry and cut off a bit of bacon or beef whenever he wanted it.

Today being the first Sunday in March, *Eintopf* had been pre-pared for the noon meal. Vati sat at the table, so Franz grabbed extra bread when he picked up his bowlful. He started to eat, but stopped and really looked at his dinner. Stringy pork with lots of gristle, floated among peas, cabbage and carrots. It had cooked in the large pot for hours. It didn't taste good, but kept him healthy, even if he never had enough to eat.

"Franz, is something wrong?" Vati leaned over the table, his forehead wrinkled.

Franz felt tears behind his eyes. He couldn't stop the pictures in his mind of pitiful men digging through the trash bin for leftovers.

"I miss Mama's kraut and pork." He said the first thing he thought of, and Vati looked relieved.

"I do, too," Vati said, as he shook his head. "Just remember, living here is temporary. After the war we'll go back to Yugoslavia where Mama will cook for you, Kati and me." He leaned back in the chair, dimples bracketing his smile, "and we'll be a proper family again."

Franz liked thoughts of the future. They both picked up their forks and began eating. As Franz chewed his food, thoughts of the hungry men made it hard to swallow. They must dream of their old lives as well.

He knew he couldn't carry a plate or bowl of food outside, so he casually covered one piece of bread with oleomargarine then slapped another on top to make a sandwich. It wasn't much and didn't even have meat. After a discouraged sigh, he thought maybe any food would be better than none. When Vati turned his head, Franz tucked the sandwich into the side pocket of his coat. He wished he hadn't promised not to tell his parents.

After Vati went to work, Franz met up with Karl again and showed him what he had in his pocket. Karl had an apple and bread inside his coat. As they rounded the side of the Cantina, they heard a very angry voice. They stopped and listened, then continued to the end of the wall and peeked around the corner.

A barrel-chested man screamed at the Russians prisoners. He wasn't tall, but broad, with little hair on the top of his head. Franz saw him from the back but couldn't see his face.

The Russians stood still, without expression, and remained silent. Franz recognized them from before—dressed in Russian

Army jackets, and caps. Anger flared in the eyes of one of them, and his fists clenched. The other prisoner looked like a statue, no movement, and no expression. Franz thought if the prisoners ran, it might be worse next time.

"S-stay away from the women's quarters, you monsters! You don't belong here! Your s-side is over there!" The German's neck was red as he shouted and pointed to the south.

Franz recognized the stutter and voice of the man he'd over-heard in the barracks who'd been upset about Stalingrad.

The man's rage spilled over as he stepped forward, and for a moment his face turned toward the boys. Franz had seen him before but didn't have time to think about it. The man pursed his lips and spit into the face of the stoic POW. Then he hesitated, as if he realized he had no other weapon. "Get out of here!"

The Russians backed up several steps. They turned around and quickly faded into the trees.

"Let's go," Franz whispered.

They retreated to the front of the Cantina. Usually proud of being German, Franz felt sick, and ashamed because of the cru-elty he'd just witnessed. He looked at Karl's face, now drained of color. Could they have said or done something to help?

"You recognized Hugo's father, didn't you?" Karl whispered.

"No," Franz said. "I didn't. I heard his voice once before and remembered the stammer, but I didn't see his face then." He thought for a moment. "I kind of remember seeing him with Hugo in the shelter once. But why is he so angry with them? They're prisoners, and they're hungry. They sure don't want to be here."

"Now you understand why I didn't tell Hugo," Karl said. "My mother says war makes a lot of people meaner."

After waiting a bit, Franz and Karl nervously crept toward a tree stump behind the Cantina to leave their smuggled food. When they leaned over to empty their pockets, one of the POWs moved toward them. Frightened, both boys stepped back. They couldn't look away. Franz's heart began to beat faster from being so close to the grayish, foul-smelling man.

With one bony hand, the prisoner picked up the food and tucked it in his shirt. In a voice too high for a man, he said something that sounded like "*spuh-see-buh*", and must be "thank you".

Franz tried to nod, but fear kept his neck stiff.

Then starved man slipped away in the trees, and Franz exhaled in relief.

The sirens were so very loud. The four nights since Sunday there'd been no scurrying to the shelter and Franz thought maybe the danger had moved away. He grabbed his blanket and joined the line going down the hall, the stairs and outside, turning left to the Cantina. He glanced around. Following the Rule, he and Mama didn't wait for each other, but would meet in the shelter. The acid cloud hadn't yet spread, and he could see the end of one of the *Acht-acht* moving on the roof, looking for any possible attacks. What if they were bombed tonight? With a clutch of fear in his stomach, he pushed away the thought.

Franz squinted at the yellowish lights as he went down the steps into the shelter under the Cantina. He and his friends searched for their parents. Franz found Mama standing with Josef's mother, Margaret, by the wall, and then Vati came inside just before the door began to close. Mama waved for Franz to sit at an available seat by the table.

Hugo joined his parents nearby and stayed close to his mother. Franz hesitated to look directly at Hugo's father, afraid his feelings might show. Out of the corner of his eye, Franz saw Hugo's father ignore everyone, his arms crossed over his chest, his chin out and dark eyes hard and cold. Hugo and his mother whispered to one another.

"Stop! It hurts!" Off to Franz' left, twin boys about four years old screamed as they pressed pudgy hands over their ears. Their mother pulled them to seats and put one on either side of herself, hugged them together, and slumped.

"Every time we come here, someone's screaming," Franz said to Josef.

A short, bald, old man hobbled his way across the shelter with the help of his cane, and a woman with curly gray hair followed him. A young couple gave up their seats in front of Franz and, after thanking them, the elderly ones plopped down.

The old man turned around and offered peppermint candy to the wailing boys, but they were too upset to see it. Then he did a magic trick making a scarf disappear and show up behind one boy's ear. Nothing helped. A few minutes later, as the screaming continued, the man started thumping his cane, nodded to his wife and they began to sing.

The angels' soft voices sing lessons we haven't heard,
But hope within finds comfort in the words,
When darkness is over and the battle is done,
Hope for tomorrow's sunshine, after the rains are gone,
Hope whispers and we welcome her voice,
She shows us in sorrow we can rejoice.

Both little boys relaxed beside their mother as she joined in the song. Before long, many people sang along.

Franz thought the gentleman's deep voice and his wife's soft one sounded beautiful. He looked over to see if his parents heard the next verse. Mama and Vati had their heads together in discussion, but just before the song ended, Vati leaned his head against the wall and listened. He glanced over with a smile.

"How can you sing of hope—," a tiny woman with frizzled blond hair leaned forward, "when the whole world has gone mad?"

"Because," the man spoke gently, "we have the same hope in God during this terrible darkness as we do in the light."

"In God? Do you really believe such nonsense?" She rolled her eyes and turned aside as if she didn't expect an answer.

"Yes, I do. We can't trust the evil we see in the world around us, but we can trust the Lord. I have hope because I belong to God, in this short lifetime and for all eternity."

"You believe in a fairy tale," with each word the woman's finger pointed at him with a scolding motion.

"No, I believe in a sovereign God. What gives you strength and peace? Yourself? The world?" Something about the expression in the grandfatherly man's eyes reminded Franz of Opa. He'd had the same look of love and sadness the day they'd taken Adam to the station to leave for the German army.

Franz watched the younger woman open and close her mouth as if there were no answer inside.

He became sleepy and lost interest in the conversation. He leaned over the table to lay his head on folded arms and slept for several hours.

Suddenly the 'all clear' siren blasted. Franz snapped awake and adjusted his blanket over his shoulder.

The doors swung open. Franz squinted his eyes against the early morning light, and quickly joined his parents. Vati walked them both back to their rooms above the First Aid Station.

"We got two letters today," Mama said. "One from Oma that I'll read with you when we get upstairs," Mama said. "They're doing fine, but I just miss Kati so much." Mama's eyes teared up and she bit her lower lip. "The other thing is—," Mama pulled out a handkerchief and blew her nose.

"The other thing is, you're to join the *Deutsches Jungvolk* within two weeks," Vati completed her sentence. "Your uniform will be here soon."

"But come on, I want to read you the letter." Franz followed Mama to her room upstairs and waited until she had the letter in her hand.

> Our Dear Family,
> We're really looking forward to spring and the longer, warmer days. We're using Herr Haut more to help with the farm. His business is down now, so it's good for all of us. Tell Franz that his Opa (and Oma) really misses him.
> Kati had a cold last week, but she's back to her normal busy self. She found another litter of kittens and spends time every day playing with them. Opa let her bring one inside the house, can you imagine that? Every night she takes seriously the need to pray for all of you in Leipzig.
> We look forward to your return, but all are fine here.
> Do you have any news from Adam? More of our neighbors are leaving to join the war efforts. The Partisans are growing stronger and many think Tito will be the one to rescue us.
> Our love,
> Mother

Mama smiled through renewed tears as she folded the letter and put it into her pocket. "I'll be glad when we can go home." She reached across the space to pull Franz into her arms. "I am so very glad you're here, but I miss our precious little Kati every day." She wiped her cheeks, and put a smile to her lips. "I just have to remind myself why we're here. We've saved every dime we can, so when we leave we'll be able to start again with another butcher shop after the war."

"It seems so long since we were in Stanisic, doesn't it?" Franz said.

She nodded. "It does. Right now, we need to get some sleep, so you go ahead to your room. Your friends may want to tell you more about the *Hitler Jugend*. I'm not sure I like this, but it'll probably be fun for you."

Before he could ask what she meant, she turned him around and ushered him out the door.

The other boys weren't there, so Franz went to the wash room and joined them in washing hands and face and brushing teeth.

"My father said I'm to be in the *Deutsche Jungvolk* within two weeks," he said.

"That's not fair!" Hugo cried, "I've been here longer and I'm still a *Pimpf*! How do you get to jump up to *Deutsche Jungvolk*?"

"I don't know. My father just told me that's where I'm to go." Franz looked to the other boys for answers.

"When's your birthday? You'll be eleven, then, right?" Karl asked.

"Yes, on August 31."

Karl and Josef both nodded their heads. "That's why—Franz is between ten and thirteen," Josef said, "and you're only nine. It's not how long you've lived in Germany."

"What do we do?" Franz said.

"We go to meetings, march in parades and learn how to read maps, do survival things," Josef said.

"And we get to play war games!" Karl said. "We still do the hiking and camping like the *Pimpfs*."

A sudden knocking on the door stopped the discussion. "It's past time for lights out and quiet. Go to bed!" a female voice screamed.

Grinning, they all complied.

In bed, with a blanket pulled up to his neck, Franz turned on his side. Maybe this would be more like Stanisic. He missed having the freedom to explore the countryside.

16

Spring, summer 1943 – ten years old
Leipzig

"Y OU'VE LEARNED ABOUT traveling without a compass," their team leader shouted. "Now use what you've learned. Your enemy is straight north of here."

Franz adjusted his blue armband, a proud badge of being on the Blue Team. Over a mile away, Karl and the other White Team members would be ready. Both sides wore uniforms of khaki shirts, grey knee-high socks, and everything else black—their shorts, neckerchief and belts with a cross-strap.

"Remember your goal—to get their flag and as many armbands as you can. Don't let yours be taken, because you'll be dead." Their nineteen-year-old *Stammfuhrer* stroked an almost visible mustache as he marched back and forth in front of them. "Don't bunch together, but keep sight of your teammates because you'll need to help each other reach the goal. At the trumpet blast, go and win!"

Franz glanced up at the blue flag hanging high above their camp. He'd been relieved not to be assigned to stay and guard it. Sneaking through the lines to get the opponent's flag would be far more exciting. He and Josef hopped from foot to foot and punched each other like boxers. They were ready for battle.

An older boy, a member of the *Hitler Jugend,* raised his brass bugle, colorful tassel swinging, and blew loud and long. With shouts of victory, they were off.

Franz faced north, and as he did when using his slingshot, he looked toward his goal—where the White flag hung on its pole. When large trees or dense bushes appeared, he alternated going around them on his right, then left to keep himself on course. He'd never live it down if he got lost on his very first big battle.

Franz scrambled over fallen trees and small ravines and kept focused for ten minutes or so before he saw, in the distance, his first 'enemy' with a white armband.

He hesitated and glanced both ways. No one on his own team crept toward the White Team member. Squatting behind a bush, he waited. As his target went past, Franz jumped on his back and dragged him to the ground while tugging relentlessly on the coveted white band. The other boy pulled at his blue one, but Franz rolled over on his arm, denying access and managed to tear off the piece of victory white. "Sorry," he said without sincerity.

"It's okay. Now I can just go back to my camp without danger since I'm already dead."

Franz laughed and dashed away.

He tucked the trophy into his pocket after he waved it at several boys from his team. Josef caught up with him, excited by increased danger, since both teams were about halfway.

"Wouldn't it be great if we're the ones to get the white flag?" Josef whispered.

"Yes." Franz could see it happening. He'd hold it as high as he could and let the wind wave it in triumph and show them a plain, farm boy could win.

"Gotcha!" they heard in the distance, but couldn't tell if it were their team or the enemy. Without another word, they separated and continued north.

He saw Josef off in the distance, and then turned his head the other way when he passed a large bush. An older boy jumped out and pulled Franz's arm back, making him cry with pain. Swiftly, Franz put his boot behind himself and managed to hook his opponent's leg and bring him down. Franz pushed him on his side and straddled him.

"Can't breathe," the other boy mumbled, perspiration dotting his round face.

"You're still talking, so you're breathing." Franz slipped his long fingers under the white armband and pulled it off. He waved it in the air triumphantly and stood. "Now you're dead!" he said.

The newly 'dead' boy grabbed and held on to his foot like a steel trap, pulling Franz to the ground. It didn't help to jerk and kick. With effort, Franz relaxed his body as if he gave up.

White Team guy shifted his weight to use both hands to pull Franz' blue band. As he did so, Franz rolled away, broke his hold, and pushed himself up. As he turned his head, a fistful of last fall's leaves and dirt was thrown directly in his face. He shook it off and blinked his eyes. "You're dead!" he repeated as he stuffed the white band in his pocket and turned to leave.

"That's not fair! I got you first!"

"But I still have my blue band," Franz shouted over his shoulder, "and your white one, too, so it's finished!"

"You shouldn't be here, Yugoslav! I'll get you!" there was promise in the angry words.

Franz's eyebrows lowered, his eyes narrowed. In Yugoslavia he'd been referred to as "that German". No time to think about that. Franz kept moving.

The sun rose ahead, letting him know he'd turned too far east, so he adjusted his direction. Sounds of movement increased as both armies made more contact.

Bushes snagged at him, tearing tender skin on his face and inside his arms. His eyes kept searching as he plotted his course from one protected place to another. He cocked his head constantly, willing his ears to be attentive. He couldn't miss any warning. Wait. He saw something nearby—or did he? Moving gradually, he turned to look again.

Yes, a member of the White Team had someone in his sights. Franz looked at his next landmark toward the White Camp—a knurled tree with one branch stretched horizontally. Keeping that picture in his mind, he veered to the right, and caught sight of the enemy once more. He moved quietly and, at once, saw two things. A member of the White Team crept toward Josef, who watched the clouds above, unaware of his danger.

Franz' heart beat rapidly. Timing would be crucial. When he got close enough, he sprang on the White enemy like a cat.

"You're almost dead!" he said quietly, so others in the enemy team wouldn't hear.

He looked up and saw Josef, his round face quite pale, watching.

With Franz' concentration broken, the enemy pushed him off and escaped.

"Thanks," Josef said, his shoulders dragging. "I should have seen him."

"It's going to get worse as we get closer. Let's go!"

Franz retraced his steps to the tree he'd picked to keep on course. A few minutes later he heard the distant strains of the bugle trumpet's signal. Franz and Josef came together, and looked toward the sound. It came from the south, their Blue camp. They'd lost. Their flag was in the hands of the White Team.

They trudged back to their camp site. "Well, I got two guys," Franz said.

"I only got one," Josef said. "Our *Stammfuhrer* is not going to be happy."

Back in camp, as expected, their *Stammfuhrer* screamed at them for almost ten minutes, and then challenged them to learn from their mistakes, and win next time. Discouraged boys began to tear down tents and prepare to leave. Franz shoveled dirt over hot coals, and loaded his things on the Blue Team bus.

Triumphant, the White Team led the way back to Leipzig. Once there, tents, bedrolls, cooking utensils and their armbands and camp flag, were unloaded onto the parking lot and sorted into piles. Franz had his bedroll beside him and turned to pick up a tent as well.

Someone rammed into him, shoulder to shoulder. Franz recognized the sore loser.

"Your team deserved to lose, Yugoslav." His eyes squinted, but were open enough for hate to shoot out. "Because of you, it's not pure German."

Franz almost laughed, but shook his head and bent to adjust his hold on the tent. "Next time, you'll lose."

"Your Tito is in cahoots the Allies." The other boy took a step closer and raised his knee up in an effort to knock Franz off balance. "So you're our enemy."

"You're stupid." Franz sidestepped out of the boy's range, stopped and said each word clearly and slowly for emphasis. "I'm Yugoslavian, not a Partisan for Tito." Franz stood tall, his weight on both feet. "Besides, I'm German. My whole family is German."

Franz really wanted to slug this guy and knock the sneer off his face but that would be too easy. He narrowed his eyes, and then turned around to show his tormentor that he had the importance of a flea and walked away. When he glanced over his shoulder, his accuser had left.

The next week the sirens sent them to the shelter only three times. One evening Franz sat at the table in the study room across from his bedroom, fiddling with a pencil, staring at a book.

"You're not working," Mama said, as she rapped him on the back of his head with a ruler. She threaded her needle again and sewed the flap of his pocket securely on his uniform.

"I keep thinking of what we're doing in the *Deutsche Jungvolk*. Our *Stammfuhrer* makes us march, march, march—all the time. It's boring. We're all in trouble if one guy isn't in step exactly. I want to go on one of the rowing boat trips or another campout."

"Well, a parade is coming up next week and I'm sure he wants you to be perfect under his leadership." Mama laughed. "Right now, you're doing homework, and I want you to be perfect, too." She tapped his head again and he read the next arithmetic problem out loud, and worked out the answers until he finished the assignment.

"Tomorrow we go to a farm to save crops by picking potato bugs dropped from Allied planes."

"So, after school, you'll complain about bugs, bugs, bugs, right?"

"Probably" Franz tipped his head down to hide his smile, "It has to be more fun than counting off steps over and over."

The next day the sky was clear and the breeze gentle. The Nazi Youth bus left smooth city streets and bumped and rocked along dirt roads. When they got to the potato field, the farmer met them with some potato bugs in a box. The city boys were fascinated. Franz remembered the years he and Oma went through her potato garden and plucked beetles off the plants, and removed any leaves holding bright orange eggs on its underside.

Each boy took a jar as he went to his assigned area. At first, some found the small bugs with pale yellow stripes the length of their black bodies, fascinating. Josef held two together and watched their busy antenna battle, and their weed-like legs scratching for surface. Quickly bored, the next hour they competed for who would gather the most.

Franz and Josef sat together on the return bus. Josef had been quiet, but Franz didn't mind.

Josef looked out the window, and then turned to Franz. "Since our war game battle, I've been thinking about my father, and how he died in Stalingrad," he said quietly. "I wish he'd had someone to save him like you saved me."

Josef never talked about his father. Never. Franz shifted in his seat, uncertain what to say. "I hate war," he finally said. "I'm sorry about your father."

Josef nodded and returned to gazing out the window.

Discouraged at having so much homework, Franz carried three books as he joined his friends for the walk back to their dorm. His footsteps sounded loud on the wooden steps as they went upstairs. In the Study Room, books were dumped on the table.

"I didn't get my ration of milk this morning," Karl said, "I'm going to the Cantina to get some."

"I'll do my work later," Hugo said as he pushed his books to the end of the table and left.

"I'd rather get it done now," Franz said. He pulled out his geography book, sat down and studied the map of Europe. He and Josef worked in silence for a half-hour, and Karl returned.

As Franz stretched and leaned back in his chair, he noticed something near the wall. "What's this?" he asked, walking over to a short pipe sticking out of the floor. He peered down but saw nothing.

Karl and Josef left their desk and joined him in huddling down around the hole. They bumped together as each jostled to look.

"Is it an empty tube where an electric wire used to be?" Karl suggested.

"It's not for a light switch because that's on the other side of the door," Franz put his eye to the hole. "I can't see anything."

"Hear anything down there?" Josef said with a grin. He raked his hands through his reddish blond hair, and put his ear to the opening. "Nah, nothing's clear."

Bored with that, Franz returned to his books and the others followed.

"My milk is sour," Karl complained a few minutes later. He tapped the table with his pencil, and then walked over to the mystery hole.

"Pour it down the pipe and see what happens." Josef grinned and hopped from foot to foot as he and Franz joined Karl.

Franz nodded enthusiastically.

With a twinkle in his eye, Karl tipped the glass and the milk disappeared from sight. Nothing happened and Franz went back to study.

Two minutes later their door flew open with a bang and a small woman with a cloud of blond curls stood in the doorway and glared at them.

"You!" she shrieked and pointed first toward Franz and then the others. "Come to my office, right now!"

Afraid to speak, Franz raised his eyebrows at Karl, who lifted his shoulders and shook his head. Josef stared at the stranger.

The angry woman led the way downstairs, past the First Aid, to a large room where typists and clerks worked.

Like an avenging angel, she stopped and pointed at her desk. "Who did this?" She trembled with rage as she shouted.

Orderly stacks of typed papers were spread fan-like, organized in sections. The middle pile was soppy wet, and liquid had splashed over the surrounding papers. With a sick feeling in his stomach, Franz saw the ink had spread to make an unreadable mess.

He looked above her desk, and saw a very short pipe poking from the ceiling. In horror, he watched one lone drop of milk hover on the end of the pipe, and fall. It sounded like a firecracker in the silence surrounding them.

"Come with me!" She marched to the next office.

Franz glanced at Karl and Joseph, each looking as terrified as he felt. She shouted at them again and they reluctantly walked into the office.

A large man sat at the first desk. He stopped writing on a tablet, and looked at her. Then he stared at the boys. A picture on his desk showed a woman and two young girls, each smiling happily. The man was not happy.

"Children aren't allowed in here." He brushed his hand up in motion for them to leave, and returned to his work.

"I want Herr Budin to know what these little monsters did to his reports to the Fuhrer!"

At her raised voice, the other door jerked open and an officer with a black, bushy beard, and little hair on top, stepped out. He wore no jacket, but a wrinkled shirt.

"What's going on out here?" he snapped at the secretary. Deep creases formed between his lowered eyebrows. "Have you got those documents ready? You know the deadline!"

Franz felt her push his back. "They poured milk down a drain above my desk. Every single paper I worked on this whole day is ruined!"

Like lightening, the boss's anger turned from her to the boys. He glared at each of them, his nose flaring.

Josef took a step closer to one side of Franz, and Karl the other. Franz felt a bit braver, since they stood together, and he didn't feel alone.

"Which of you did this?" He roared. "Tell me now! Or by God, you'll wish you had!"

Not blinking his eyes, Franz stood silent. He heard nothing from Karl or Josef, either.

"Gunthar, get the Spanish Rod, and we'll get the truth out of them right now!"

Horror stories about the Rod had been passed along for years, but Franz had never actually seen one close up. He couldn't take his eyes away from the secretary as he reached up on the wall and removed it. About a half inch around and two and a half feet long, it looked tough and flexible. He expected to see blood dripping from it, but saw only a muddy yellow whip.

The bearded man grabbed Josef, and told him to bend over an armchair.

"Give him three swats," the officer instructed Gunthar. With the first whack, Josef whimpered. Franz knew he should protect Josef, the smallest of the three, but how?

"Harder!" the boss yelled. This time a high-pitched scream exploded, followed by a long moan.

"You're too easy! Hit him again!" the boss ordered. Franz had to do something, but he'd lost any power to move.

He turned his head away, unable to watch the third blow.

Josef seemed to give up. Slumped over the chair like a rag doll, he didn't move.

The officer grabbed him by the hair and jerked him up. White faced, Josef refused to look at the man, but kept his eyes downcast. His body shook with silent crying.

Franz flicked his eyes toward Karl, who stood rigid with his fists clenched at his side. Karl's face showed fear, but it was as though he had accepted what was to be.

"Tell me who did this?" the officer screamed. When no answer came, he shoved Josef aside and jerked Franz to him.

Franz leaned toward the chair and, with trembling hands, grasped the edges of the seat. He didn't look at Gunthar. The first lash caught him by surprise and he couldn't hold the sudden gasp. The chair came up as he reared back. He drew in his breath, fighting to gain control of the pain and his fear of the next two blows.

Gunthar pushed him back down

"Harder!" the boss screamed again.

Franz held his breath and bit his lower lip. It didn't help when the Rod hit again. Pain radiated through his body, flaming up his back and down his legs. His eyes watered and he could barely draw in a breath.

"Use force this time!" the officer yelled once more.

Lights dimmed and the room lost its color, as everything seemed to move around him. Franz pushed against the chair with his hands, and kept elbows straight. At the blow, he tasted blood, warm and salty, inside his cheek.

They shouted questions, but Franz refused to answer. If he opened his mouth, he knew he'd scream or cry. The man went into a greater rage, with dark, swollen blood vessels standing out on his red neck.

"Give me that!" The boss man rolled up his shirtsleeves and grabbed the Spanish Rod out of the secretary's hand and pushed Karl over the chair. Horrified, Franz looked at the man. His dark eyes had a strange green cast to them, like an animal in the dark. This was the face of the devil.

He swung hard once. "Answer me!" he screamed, spittle spraying from his mouth.

Karl bowed his head in silence, but his body shook and Franz felt the pain with him.

The rod came down again, even harder. Then a third time. The bearded man stopped, breathed heavily, and leaned back, lash in hand. And swung another time.

Karl's face showed no expression except a barely visible narrowing of his eyes. His body was held unbending, his legs stiff. He clamped his lips together and refused to say a word.

"Get out of here, you worthless vermin, and don't ever let me see any of you again!"

The typist didn't look them in the eye, but wiped away tears with her finger as they filed out the door and walked outside to the porch.

Franz looked around in wonder. Clouds drifted by in the blue sky, and people strolled along the sidewalk. Birds sang and flew above. Thunder and lightning would have looked more real.

Franz didn't feel pain yet, just a roaring in his head. He stopped, exhausted, and tried to think what to do.

"I'm sorry," Josef said, grimacing after he took a deep, shuttering breath. "It was my fault. I should have told him it was my idea."

"No," Franz said. "We all did it. Herr Budin could have scolded us or made us wash floors or clean latrines. He's the meanest man alive."

Karl groaned as he took a step forward. "I don't know about you, but I don't think I can walk." He moved a fraction of an inch, and then stopped. "And I'm gonna throw up."

"We need to get away from here," Josef whispered as he looked at the door.

Franz stepped close and put his shoulder under Karl's right arm. "Lean on me."

Karl had received the worst beating of them all. How could he bear it?

Without a warning heave, Karl vomited all over himself, and Franz's face and shoulder.

"Ooh!" Franz gagged and jumped away. With wrinkled nose, and lips turned down, Franz turned to cough. He wiped his cheek and shook his shirt. "Next time, use a bush, not me!"

"I'm sorry," Karl said. He mustered up a bit of a smile, and leaned forward. "You stink."

Franz looked at Josef, Karl and himself. Suddenly he saw what a pitiful group they were—in growing pain, and now he and Karl covered with disgusting, chunk-filled slime. Tearful laughter bubbled up first in Franz, then the other boys.

"Oh, that hurt to laugh," Franz said. "Think we ought to take a shower first?" He shook his head. "How are we going to get down these steps and walk over to the bath house?" He flicked more vomit off his shirt. "We need clean clothes." They looked up toward the stairs to their room above them. Then to the right to the bath house. There were too many, very high steps.

The First Aid door opened. The boys froze in fear that it would be Herr Budin.

"We hoped to find you here." Two nurses in their starched, white uniforms stepped outside.

At their obvious fright, the nurses held out their hands, with kindness in their eyes.

"We came to help." The taller of the two waved her hand in front of her nose, and her eyes crinkled in a half-smile. "I think a long, warm shower is the first place to start."

At the gentle words, Josef burst into tears, and Karl joined him. Not having to be strong now, Franz leaned forward and cried as well.

17

1943 summer – ten years old
Leipzig, Germany

"WE DIDN'T MEAN for it to mess up her desk," Franz explained. He took an offered handkerchief and wiped his eyes and blew his nose. Glancing at the door that led past the First Aid to offices they'd just left, his breath caught. What if Herr Budin came outside?

"We know you were just being boys," the short, brunette nurse said. She stood not much taller than Karl, and seemed like someone's sister. "First thing, let's move away from here."

The nurses fussed over them as they walked toward to a bench outside the bathing building. "You'll feel a little better once you're cleaned up."

"Our clothes are upstairs," Karl's shoulders slumped, "you know, above the offices."

"Yes," the blonde gently stroked his upper back and smiled. "We'll follow the milk trail."

"Our room is the second from last on the right side of the hall," Josef said. Josef and Karl tried to describe where they would find each of their clothes.

"Hugo is probably there now, he can help you," Franz said.

Within minutes, Hugo came down with the nurses.

"What's going on? Why did they get your clothes?" Hugo's questions were like cold water thrown on them.

Couldn't Hugo tell what happened, by simply looking at them? Franz saw tear tracks on Karl's and Josef's faces, and knew he looked the same. Oddly, their throbbing pains didn't show. The Spanish Rod had done its damage under their shorts.

"They'll explain it to you later," the short nurse said and the boys were escorted inside and signed in for their showers.

"My Opa undresses quicker than this," Franz said as he slowly lifted his foot to take off shoes and feeling the pull of bruised muscles.

"Ouch! My pants are stuck to my backside!" Karl rolled his shorts, then underpants, down to remove them. Several areas of his clothes were covered with blood.

While they undressed, they listened to the attendant and nurses in the check-in area.

"What happened to them?" Franz recognized the attendant's voice.

"The boys apparently poured a little milk down a tube and it landed on a stupid, hot-tempered little typist's desk," one of the nurses said. "She didn't have brains enough to handle it herself, but took them to Herr Budin. He went berserk and worked them over with the Spanish Rod."

"Oh, how awful! Those poor boys!"

"We've sent word to their mothers—Elisabeth Elmer and Margaret Wolf should have just ended their kitchen shift in the management section. Don't know about Erica Klein, but she works days, too."

Mama would be here soon. Franz closed his eyes and stepped closer to the water. Normally, two boys stepped in, washed quickly and left, but today all three entered together. Warm water rained down and Franz' muscles relaxed.

"I'd like to send Herr Budin to Siberia, where he'd be tortured until he dies a slow death," Karl said, his blond curls plastered to his forehead.

Soap went from one to another as they rotated around. Josef's bottom was bright red, Franz felt like a flame was behind him. Karl gasped when he turned his backside to the water. Where the skin had broken, the blood streamed down like a creek, but soon slowed to a trickle.

"He's a mad dog and should be put down." Josef's round face, usually cheerful and ready for activity, now looked like an angry warrior.

Franz soaped his cheeks and forehead, then looked up to rinse. What would be the perfect punishment? Something slow and steady.

"But first, I'd have Herr Budin chained down so he couldn't do anything. He'd have to watch us dump pigs' blood over him," Franz closed his eyes as he fantasized, "and then we'd pour ink on his precious letters to the Fuhrer, drip by drip. He'd probably burst a neck vessel."

They lapsed into silence standing under the warm shower. It took energy they didn't have to stand, so they turned off the water, dried, and dressed.

Franz heard his mother and Frau Wolf in the entry room. The boys bundled their dirty clothes, dropped the used towels into a hamper and followed the sound of voices.

"As furious as I am," Mama hissed the words, "I dread telling Stefan after he gets off work. His first impulse will be to grab the Spanish Rod and use it on Herr Budin. He deserves it, but I want my husband, and Franz needs his father."

"How badly hurt are they? I've got to see Josef for myself," Frau Wolf sniffled.

Josef hurried to his mother and rested his head on her shoulder. "We didn't mean to cause trouble. All we did was pour a little bit of milk down a tube!"

Mama's eyes searched Franz from his hair to his feet for obvious injuries. She took a deep breath and sagged as she exhaled. Franz tried to act strong, but tears sprang to his eyes at his mother's embrace. It felt good to be covered in sympathy.

Franz turned to see Karl alone and looking at the floor.

"Oh, Karl," Mama reached out and put her hands on the boy's cheeks. "Your mother's probably on her way home from work. Let's get all of you into your room." They walked across the lawn.

"We'll get one of the younger boys to sleep on your bunk tonight, Franz, so you won't have to climb," Mama said as they walked back. "Thank goodness Karl and Josef have lower beds."

"No," Franz said. "I want to sleep in my own bed."

Mama took his hand and squeezed it. "That's true, but it won't hurt to take it easy. Let me do the mother thing and fuss over you."

"A cherry tart will make me feel much better," Franz said, as he looked at her out of the corner of his eye.

"A bottom bunk I can find," Mama smiled, "but we'll see about the tart." She combed her fingers through his hair. "We'll bring supper up after we get you settled."

The next day, the boys were left strict orders to stay home from school.

"I feel fine as long as I don't run," Josef said as they walked to the Cantina for breakfast.

"I hate going up and down steps," Karl shuffled along, taking small steps.

"It hurts to lean over," Franz said. "I'll never be curious about a hole in the floor again."

Vati waited for him at the door to the Cantina. The other boys went inside and Franz and Vati met and held each other tightly. Franz buried his face in Vati's rough, tan work shirt and inhaled the familiar fragrance of pipe tobacco. He looked up into his father's eyes, so much the same as his own smoky-blue ones, and blinked away moisture. Franz's stomach rumbled, and with quiet laughter they both turned toward food.

"How are you, son?" Vati's deep voice sounded thick.

"Lots better."

Vati used their ration books for breakfast. Franz took his food, gently eased on to the bench and rocked from one hip to the other, trying to find a comfortable spot.

They ate with little conversation. Franz used his bread and oleomargarine for a sandwich and slipped it under his napkin. No matter what happened to him yesterday, the prisoners were always hungry.

As they walked outside, Vati looked around, saw they were alone and leaned his head down to Franz'. He held out his hand. "I'll leave the food in back for you." His voice was barely louder than a whisper. "Mama and I figured out you feed the Russians."

Speechless, Franz handed it to him and saw a little smile on Vati's lips, but his eyes were sad.

"Am I in trouble?" Franz bit his thumbnail and waited for Vati's answer.

"No." Vati's hand rested on Franz' shoulder and he looked around again and continued to whisper close to Franz. "But what you're doing isn't safe. Party members are everywhere and they watch and report. I knew a man who was executed for making a bad joke about Hitler. Very carefully, Mama and a couple of the other cooks also leave choice leftovers where they can be found."

Franz' eyebrows raised, "Mama? Wow, I didn't know that."

"Did you ever wonder how the prisoners are able to show up here?"

"Yes, but we were afraid to ask anyone."

"A couple of guards leave a hole in the fence and turn away when men sneak out. They can't escape, but they manage to scavenge for more food. Some guards take things very seriously for the *Nazideutschland* and would shoot fellow Germans for acts of compassion. We never discuss it where we can be overheard. Always remember, the walls have ears."

"How did you know what we were doing?"

"Your mother and I've seen you sneak extra food. Who else is leaving food there?"

"Just Karl and me." Franz looked down and kicked some pebbles around. He'd promised not to tell, but today it couldn't matter.

"Vati, why are they here. I mean, why are they here in Leipzig?"

"With so many men off in the military, there's a desperate need for laborers now. They're put to work doing non-technical jobs. Unfortunately, German troops need most of the available food and medical care. Workers, women and children come next, and that's rationed and things unavailable. I know it's not right, but prisoners are at the end of the line." Vati sighed, and lifted Franz' chin to look into his face.

"We trust you to be careful. It's dangerous, especially after yesterday. Tell me where to leave it and you go lay down."

Relieved to be free of the responsibility this one time, Franz quietly described the stump at the edge of the tree line. "Thank you, Vati."

The next two nights were spent in the shelter, where they listened for hours to the roar of planes overhead and explosions of bombs nearby. It helped when shelter sirens were turned off, but the rapid fire of the *Acht-acht* seemed to hammer on Franz' head.

He was tired, miserable and couldn't sit for long on the concrete floor and benches. A pillow helped, but not much. By now everyone knew what had happened to him and threw sympathetic glances his way.

The days were long, and Franz felt as if he moved from one week to the next in the midst of a dark cloud. More days than not, he went to school, then home where he did his school work. He woke as alarms went off, anti-aircraft smoke was activated and they spent the night in the shelter. In the morning, as they got the all clear signal, he walked back to his dorm room thru acid clouds that continued to make his eyes water.

"A friend of mine is going to his home in the Bohemian Forrest," Vati said at breakfast the next week. "We've made arrangements for you to go with Herr Zimmermann and stay for a couple of weeks or so."

"Why? What did I do?" Franz shook his head from side to side. "I don't want to go."

"This is not a punishment, Franz. It's only for two or three weeks. You'll take a break from what's happening here."

Franz bit the inside of his lip so he wouldn't look even a bit interested. A little thought popped up that it would be wonderful to wake to the sounds of birds and not sirens, but he must stay with Vati and Mama.

"The Zimmermanns are nice people, and you can help them do chores." Vati's voice was firm, and Franz knew his mind couldn't be changed. "You'll leave early Friday."

"But you can't— today's Wednesday—it's too soon!" He'd never shouted at Vati before, and made himself stop. "What if I don't like it there?"

"The last month has been bad, and we're worried about you." Vati gave a half-smile. "Have you even noticed summer is here and the days have been beautiful and sunny with gentle, cool breezes?"

Franz looked around and realized Vati's words were true.

"I didn't think so. Be ready Thursday night before bed."

Mama, too, ignored his pleas to stay in Leipzig. On Friday, she carried his suitcase and walked him to the train station with dawn barely lighting the way.

Scattered Gestapo stood alert, watching everything and everyone.

Franz normally left Hasag Company land only to go to school. He'd gotten used to the smaller Nazi flags there, and no longer noticed them. He stepped closer to Mama at the sight of so many, very large *swastikas,* Their sharp black edges on the blood-red background disturbed him, and he turned his eyes away.

At the sound of an incoming train, Franz found himself eager, as always, to see all the activity. The powerful hiss of steam drew him closer to admire and fear its awesome strength. While Mama looked around, he watched the hostler load coal and water on board. Franz had always been excited with every trip he took between Sombor and Stanisic. It had been different on his trip last year when Uncle Adam smuggled him into Germany. He'd been afraid after they left Budapest, until he was finally over the German border. He remembered the beauty he and Uncle Adam enjoyed all the way to Augsburg.

"Herr Zimmermann!" his mother shouted as she waved to a man standing under the big clock.

Franz wanted to grab his mother's hand, and go back home. He studied a thin man with a bony face, dark brown hair, bushy eyebrows, and deep set eyes. One side of his smile went higher than the other.

"Hello, Franz," Herr Zimmermann said. "It'll be nice to have a traveling companion this trip."

Franz frowned until he felt Mama poke him in the back. "Hello, Herr Zimmermann."

"Franz," Mama bent down to look into his face, "your ration book is in the suitcase. Your train ticket is in your pocket, right?"

At his reassurance, she folded him in her arms. "I've got to hurry to work now, but have a good time and remember we love you. Enjoy this adventure." With a final kiss to his cheek, she turned and left. When Franz looked over his shoulder to say goodbye again, all he saw was Mama's straight back as she walked in the direction of the Company.

"We'll take this line to Dresden," Herr Zimmermann said, "then switch to a *Feldeisenbahnen* to go over the mountains and forest."

"What is a *Feldeisenbahnen?*"

"It's a narrower and shorter train. The track is not as wide as these regular ones are." Herr Zimmermann's eyes twinkled. "My daughters always said it was the regular trains' baby. Maybe you'll agree with them, but I never could see it."

"Are they my age?"

"Oh, they're almost grown now. Come along, Franz," Herr Zimmermann said. "You'll never see land more beautiful. The Bohemian Forest is closer to God than any place on earth."

After they found seats on the Leipzig-Dresden, Franz pressed his forehead to the window. Early sunlight slanted in from the side, casting softness to everything.

Homesickness welled up in him as they passed farmland that made him think of Opa and Oma. The train slowed to go through small towns, then increased in speed. From flat farm land to rocky hills and forest, he watched it change.

"Dresden isn't far now," Herr Zimmermann pointed ahead to their left. "We'll go up a higher elevation which, I think, gets more breath-taking by the mile."

Franz watched a huge hawk soar ahead, and leaned forward to copy the hawk's gentle sway from left to right. It was just him and the bird, alone in peace and freedom. Franz could feel the cool breeze on his own face as they flew along. He must have seen prey, because he suddenly dipped and dove from sight.

When he glanced up at Herr Zimmermann, they both smiled, but said nothing.

In Dresden, Franz picked up his suitcase and they walked about a mile to catch the "baby train" Franz wondered what it would look like.

It was smaller, but very much a real train. It took a mile or two to get used to zipping right past the side of a forested mountain. If only he had a stick, he could hold it out the window and touch the trees. They arrived at a village and Herr Zimmerman led the way on a well-packed road.

"This is like an enchanted forest!" Franz threw himself back on a large rock covered with green moss. "When I was little, every day one of the nuns read us a chapter from a book called "Bambi, A Life in the Woods." It must have looked like this!"

Franz looked above at the towering pine trees. They blocked out all but a few spots of sunshine. The shadows held all sorts of possibilites of animals hiding. Perhaps a Bambi? To his right, a log had fallen across the small, winding creek. It, along with almost everything, was covered with moss of various shades of green.

A small bird with a brown head, gray back, reddish-brown markings under it's tail and over it's short black beak, sat on a limb close enough for Franz to touch it. "He's not afraid of me!" Franz barely moved his lips as he whispered.

"It's a Bohemian Waxwing." Herr Zimmermann said.

The bird twitched this way and that, cocked its head and Franz held his breath, sure it looked directly at him. Then it suddenly took wing and flew up away.

"Enough rest. It's not far until we reach my home and a good meal." Herr Zimmermann brushed dirt off his slacks. Reluctantly, Franz leaned over and cupped his hand to get one more drink from the creek. They walked along the gravel road and turned onto a worn path.

"Have you heard our National Anthem 'Kde domov muj'?" He waited till Franz shook his head. "My voice isn't the finest, but my love for Czechoslovakia is deep. Many times on my trip back home, as I walk down this road, I sing at the top of my lungs." With a wink and a deep breath, he began.

"Where is my homeland, where is my homeland,
Water's rustling o'er the meadows,
Pinewoods murmuring o'er the mountains,
Orchards are radiant with spring blossoms,

They strolled over a small bridge built over a rapidly flowing creek.

Earth's paradise on sight,
And that is that beautiful land,
Czech land, home of mine,
Czech land, home of mine.

The song wrapped around him and his dimples deepened when he grinned. "Thank you. I never heard that song before, and I like it."

Herr Zimmermann smiled and picked up his pace.

"Your father and I are both Germans and loyal to that heritage. At the same time, he's Yugoslav and I'm Czech and we're loyal to the homeland where we grew up. In a sense, it gives divided allegiances.

"Now the Sudetenland belongs to Germany so I can travel home freely, and I'm thankful for that. But my Czech friends didn't want to give up their land. As I said, our patriotism is split."

Franz' stomach rumbled, reminding him he hadn't eaten for hours.

"My family will be surprised. They expected me to come home a few days. But there wasn't time to write that they'd have a guest for several weeks, until I can come back and get you."

Franz stopped walking. Why didn't Vati or Mama tell him Herr Zimmermann would leave him here? His family might hate having a strange kid stay with them. What if Herr Zimmermann didn't come back for him?

18

Summer/Fall 1943, almost eleven years old.
Bohemian Forest, edge of Czechoslovakia

"CARLENE," FRANZ GROWLED as deep as possible, bared his stained lips and teeth, and held his blueberry-colored fingers up like claws. "I'm a forest monster!" He walked stiffly, and roared again. "I wish could stay blue when I go home—it would surprise my friends."

Herr Zimmermann's seventeen-year-old daughter looked over at Franz and giggled. "I missed a lot by not having a little brother!" Like her father, Carlene was thin, with dark brown hair and deep set eyes.

Franz plucked more berries from the knee-high bushes, careful to leave the green-pink ones and dropped juicy, sweet blue ones into the bucket. After helping Carlene for three days, words weren't needed as they slid the handles of both buckets onto an old wooden rod and each took an end and carried them back to the house.

From the moment he'd met Herr Zimmermann's wife and two daughters, Amalie and Carlene, Franz felt welcomed. Frau Zimmermann worked at a slow pace and rarely talked, but the first day she'd explained they gathered berries all summer long because their diet was mostly blueberries and potatoes. Franz helped them can and dry the berries in an outdoor oven and learned different ways to fix them in soups and stews. They were good snacks anytime. Frau Zimmermann showed him an old remedy of soaking berries in water to make syrups to treat coughs, diarrhea, arthritis, and most anything else. Their basement shelves were full of berries they canned for winter.

Each morning during the week, Amalie walked the long path from the house, until she crossed the bridge, and turned right at the gravel road. She helped a cousin keep up farm chores. The cousin's husband had returned from war missing a leg and arm, and full of anger. Each evening, Amalie returned tired and went to bed early, so Franz didn't spend much time with her. That left Carlene, who was a lot of fun and didn't mind answering his many questions.

Franz and Carlene set the buckets beside the house, grabbed two water jugs and walked to the creek under an archway made the year before. Bedraggled now, it would be rebuilt in the fall to protect them after the cold weather returned. "What are we going to eat for lunch? Blueberry soup?" Franz asked.

"Yes," she answered, "we have plenty left over. Tonight we'll have dried beef so you can add blueberry ketchup on top."

Franz laughed. "My mother and Oma won't believe you grow nothing but blueberry plants and tall trees." He stood in a splash of sunshine, twirled around, and looked up at the swaying branches. "I wish we lived in a forest!"

After filling the jugs, they splashed cold creek water on their hands, arms and faces and returned to the small house, built of gray rocks and wood.

The kitchen reminded him of Stanisic, where family came together whenever inside. The parlor, to the right of the kitchen had been dusted and cleaned, but not used since he'd arrived. Two bedrooms were to the left of the kitchen. Franz climbed a ladder to a little space in the attic to sleep. Unlike any place he'd lived, they had no electricity or plumbing.

When he saw the outhouse, memories of Stanisic tumbled in his mind. Digging the new, clean hole with Opa to move it to a new spot, the nighttime trips in the dark, and spiders who watched from corners. How quickly he'd adjusted to Germany's indoor bathrooms! It was interesting to use an outdoor toilet again—it reminded him of being with Oma, Opa and Katie.

"Franz," Frau Zimmermann said after they ate supper, "Carlene will take you with her to see Frau Huber tomorrow. We take berries to her every week or so and she makes us soap."

Carlene smiled and winked at Franz. "She may be the oldest person you've ever seen, and she's very interesting."

The next morning, after Franz and Carlene walked over a mile, they turned down a shadowed path. And there it squatted— a small cottage sitting in a pool of buttery sunshine.

Franz stopped, blinked and looked again.

Carlene watched him, a big grin on her thin face.

"Hansel and Gretel!" they said together and shared laughter bubbled up.

"It really does look like gingerbread and that the roof is tiled with cakes!" Franz lowered his voice.

"I hoped you'd heard the story! When you get closer, look at the windows. They're thick and wavy and make you want to lick the sugar."

"What does she look like?" Franz frowned in thought.

"She lives alone, has a large nose, and uses a walking stick, but she doesn't eat children!" When close enough, Carlene knocked on the door. "Frau Huber? It's Carlene."

The wooden door squeaked in protest as it opened. Sure enough, Franz saw an old woman not much taller than himself.

Carlene made the introductions and Franz carried the bucket inside. No iron cages. He smiled at his imagination.

While Frau Huber asked about the Zimmermann family, and Carlene about the numerous cats inside and around the house, Franz played with a gray, striped kitten. He felt a tap on his shoulder.

"I'll show you something you've never seen before," the old voice cackled, "wait a minute, dears." She went into the next room and returned with a sly smile, carrying a tray, covered with black velvet.

"Promise me you won't tell anyone what you see?" She cocked her head and narrowed her eyes a bit. "Some of these lapel pins are forbidden by Hitler."

Franz looked at Carlene, but she only nodded her head cheerfully.

"I won't tell anyone." Franz had to see them and stepped closer.

Frau Huber pulled back the material and held the tray in front of Franz. There were about a dozen of them, and he quickly knew which pin she shouldn't have. A round, gold one had a picture of the Russian hammer and sickle clearly displayed. They were dreadful enemies of Germany. He saw a couple of lapel pins with Christ on the cross, and others he didn't recognize. He looked back at the forbidden one. She covered them, and returned them to her hiding place.

Would Hitler really care if an old woman had lapel pins he didn't like? She might scratch with the pin, but couldn't hurt anyone.

"Thank you for the blueberries," Frau Huber said as she handed a small box to them.

Carlene took the soap, scarce in Germany now; she and Franz began the walk back. Dark clouds gathered in ever-widening bunches, cooler breezes pushed at their backs. They crossed the bridge as the first large drops of rain fell.

After a dinner of blueberry-potato pancakes, Franz tipped his head and listened to the cheerful sound of pecks on the roof. After a while, he got restless and wandered into the parlor, where he'd previously seen a small shelf with books.

"Go ahead and look at them," Frau Zimmermann said.

Franz sat on the floor and leafed through one and then another. Two were written in Czech and he set them aside. Franz knew German, Yugoslavian and Hungarian, but not Czech. He especially liked a book of birds, and studied them.

That night, Franz lay in bed with his hands beneath his neck and listened to the wind whistle through the pine trees as it flowed around the house. Hearing the soft greeting of an owl nearby, he smiled and stretched to see nothing but black sky out the window. It had stopped raining. No bombs, sirens, or nights in shelters, no acid clouds to burn his eyes and nose. Right here, in this forest, there was no war. He sighed, snuggled under the light blanket and closed his eyes.

"Franz," Frau Zimmermann said a couple of days later, "today is Amalie's day off, so we're all going to the farmer's market in the village about three miles away. We'll shop for food and you can see something besides blueberries."

It sounded like fun to Franz. With books to read, blueberries to pick, and a beautiful forest to study, he hadn't been bored. But it would be nice to see other people and a new place. With ration books in their pockets, they took bags to carry home their purchases and began their trip.

Not content to walk in a straight line, Franz took ten steps for each of the women's. He picked up rocks, chose a tree as a target point and usually hit where he aimed. A deer watched them as they went past, and Franz waved at it, causing it to dash away. Something lay on brown leaves, and on closer inspection, he saw a bird's blue egg that must have fallen from the tree above. He found a perfect branch on a small tree. Using his pocket knife, he sawed it off and shoved it into a pocket of his shorts. It would make a great sling shot.

They left the dense forest and entered an area with a few houses and one store. At the end of the lone street were a row of booths. Shoppers went from one to another, visiting as they tapped and listened to one item and squeezed others. The Zimmermanns bought a fresh rabbit, ready to cook. Carlene lifted two heads of lettuce, one in each hand and raised and lowered them to tell which was the heavier.

Frau Zimmermann removed *marken* from Franz' ration book and bought milk and oleomargarine.

Franz looked around, disappointed when he didn't see any boys his age. If he'd been in Stanisic or Leipzig, he'd be with friends and it would have been a lot more fun. When the women picked up bags for the return trip, he grabbed two heavy ones, ready to get back to the cottage. He'd seen an old inner tube in the cellar and would make a sling shot tonight.

Early in the morning, Franz sat very still in the shadows of the trees by the side of the house. His legs folded, the bird book open in his lap, he listened intently. There—the high trill of the Bohemian Waxwing. He saw the flash of gray and bright orange and smiled as he watched it swoop down to catch a flying insect.

Franz didn't mind sitting on the prickly pine needles while he watched birds and playful squirrels. Holding the new slingshot he made the night before, he waited for an opportunity to kill a squirrel for the family to eat.

Off in the distance, he heard a voice loudly singing the Czech national anthem. After two weeks and one day, Herr Zimmermann had returned! On his feet instantly, Franz tucked the book under his arm, the slingshot in a pocket and ran to meet him on the bridge over the creek.

"Herr Zimmermann!" he cried as he waved one arm in the air. He saw Carlene and her mother step out to the porch to wait, shading their eyes against the sun.

Herr Zimmermann wrapped Franz in his wiry arms in a bear hug and lifted him a few inches from the ground. "Have my girls been treating you all right? What have you been doing?"

"Yes," he answered the first question. "A lot of berry picking! Carlene took me to meet Frau Huber and we went to the farmers' market one day. I've read lots of books." Franz stopped and took a deep breath. He was so happy to see Herr Zimmermann, he couldn't stop smiling.

"I know people who are eager to see their son return to Leipzig."

Franz grinned again. He wanted to be with Mama and Vati and tell them all about his time here. If only they could come here, together, they would enjoy the quiet nights, chores to do and time alone to read or be outside. But his parents were in Leipzig, and he really missed them.

Two days later he and Herr Zimmermann were on the train heading west. It seemed to Franz that each chug of the wheels turning sang a refrain that chanted home. Vati greeted him at the station and took Franz to a recently vacated room where his parents had moved all three of them. It was two doors up from the old room with his friends. There was one bed for his parents and a smaller one for Franz. A chest of drawers contained most of their clothing and hooks on the wall gave a place to hang their nicer clothes.

"It was so funny! Try to picture Mirko Jelloneni with hog manure on his hands!" Mama said three days later. She leaned back in her chair and laughed. "When I got the letter from Frau Jelloneni asking me to see if I could check on him, I feared the worst. He'd never survive a work camp, not even a farm!"

Franz laughed along with his parents. It had been so long since he'd seen Frau Jelloneni, their landlady in Sombor. His "Yellow Nanny" took him to various stores where she had prodded him to speak in each shop's own language. He'd been shy, but it had been worth it, to make her proud and get treats from the clerks.

"Why did Mirko get sent to the camp?" Franz asked.

"Not because of the Yugoslavian Army, but he's an active member of the KPJ—Yugoslav Communist Party," Vati said. "Even the best work camps are not a good place to be, especially for a man who lives by his words and not by muscles."

"He did appreciate the box of food I took," Mama said. "But much of it was probably bartered away before I left the gate. You know Mirko! At least I can send a letter to Frau Jelloneni, to let her know her son may be thinner, but he's still working every angle, and surviving."

"Speaking of survival," Vati said, "let's go to the Cantina and eat."

"I'm dreaming of big, fat sausages with Oma's thick bread and real butter," Franz' mouth began to water just thinking about having real food, as they used to.

"Someday we'll eat like that again," Mama ruffled his hair, and then smoothed it back. "But today we're getting ersatz meat – overcooked rice patties mixed with onions fried in mutton fat. I do have a "welcome home" surprise dessert for you to have after we eat."

"What is it? Where do you have it?" Franz asked as his eyes darted around the room.

"Wait," was all Mama would say.

An hour later they were back in their room; Mama opened the bottom drawer of the chest and pulled out a plate filled with apple bread pudding.

"You've been back for two weeks, but we planned it for your home return celebration. Ingredients didn't come together in a day. I got extra sugar from the girls in the kitchen. Margaret managed to hide back some apples from the last shipment, and two eggs. So, Franz, your 'welcome home' is from the kitchen crew!"

Franz closed his eyes, and ate each bite slowly to enjoy it as long as possible. How long had it been since he'd had a real, true dessert?

They'd no sooner fallen asleep when the alarms went off again. Vati had left for his night shift, but he and Mama got up, wrapped their blankets around themselves and joined people migrating toward the shelter under the Cantina. Nothing had changed, and Franz wondered if his brief stay with the Zimmermanns in the Bohemian Forrest was only a dream.

The next morning was Saturday—Hitler Youth activity. He took his uniform from the hook and got dressed. He really enjoyed camp outs, survival wilderness training and first aid, but today he'd be in a parade. Not his favorite. He sighed and splashed water on his face and met Josef so they could walk together to join their *Kameradschaft,* at a bell tower in the cemetery.

"Attention! Formation forward!" their *Stammfuhrer* Winkler shouted. At their camping trip months before, he'd looked more boy than man. Now his face looked older—and tired. "Today you march in honor of the men who died for our country," he shouted with his hands waving over the graveyard. "They sacrificed their lives for Germany, determined to restore her former glory. Such brave men will not be forgotten!"

Franz and Josef fell in line and stood tall, faces forward. As often happened, he wondered about Uncle Adam. Where was he? Was he safe? They hadn't heard from him in a long time. He knew Karl and his mother worried the same things about Karl's father. He glanced over the lines of headstones. Three different spaces were freshly-dug and barren, with no maker to tell who they were. Did their families know they were buried here?

"Left face. March!" their *Stammfuhrer* ordered. Through the large cemetery they marched, being sure to match their steps with each other. Franz didn't feel patriotic, just sad.

"Want to race home?" he asked Josef when the parade ended. At a nod of the head, they raced through the cemetery and left its unmarked new graves behind.

Everyone spent the night in the shelter again. Franz rarely noticed people around him now and leaned over the table and rested his head on his arms. Hmmm—the *acht-acht* had stopped firing, so maybe they were through for the night. He looked up and immediately saw Stephani. She was the same girl, but now her long blond hair was no longer shiny and silky. She pressed her hands to her ears and rocked back and forth. Her eyes reminded him of the dead Priest's eye—open, but not seeing. Franz wanted to cry.

Instead, he turned away and leaned against Mama. He forced himself to think of something different, far away from here. He would think of Kati. Kati and the geese and her constant baby chatter. Eventually, his muscles relaxed as he remembered life in Stanisic. The all-clear signal blared and it was time to go.

A full moon lighted their way as they walked back to the First Aid Building and their bedroom. "We planned to wait and tell you later, but I think you need to hear it now," Mama spread one arm over his shoulders. "Vati has sent in paperwork to approve travel plans back to Yugoslavia."

Franz' sleepy, bowed head jerked up and he stopped and smiled at his mother. "Really?!"

"Yes, but it may take a long time for documents to come, giving us clearance to travel."

"Like next week?" he asked, watching for her nod.

"I'm hoping by August thirty-first, so you'll turn eleven in Stanisic."

19

End of 1943- eleven years old
Leipzig

"**W**HY DID THEY even bother to send us to the shelter?" Franz grumbled as he and Mama returned to their room. "The 'all clear' sounded as soon as the door closed."

"With the cooler nights now, at least our beds might still be warm," Mama said.

Partially dressed, Franz fell asleep again as soon as soon as he lay down. The whining roar of a bomber forced him awake. Puzzled, he listened for sounds of his mother moving around in the dark room, but heard nothing. She must not be awake. He burrowed under the blanket and tried to ignore the continuing, ever-louder bomber noise. The sirens hadn't gone off. It must be safe. Suddenly there was a horrible explosion, his bed bounced toward the blacked-out window. A series of explosions went off in chain reaction. Franz jerked up, heart beating fast. He tried to say something, but it came out as a whimper. His mother's hand grasped his arm.

"Franz, are you alright?" He barely heard her; the words came slowly down a long tunnel.

He nodded his head, leaned into her and waited. When he felt the room sigh and settle down, he figured the attack must have ended. He heard shouting, but with a delayed, far-away sound. A dim light came on in the hallway and people began to move outside. Franz and his mother felt around in the dark to find their shoes, but they'd been thrown to the wall by the blast and it took a few minutes to find them. Should they leave? Stay?

From the edges of the blackout shade they saw flames outside. They crept over and peeked out. Most of the beautiful trees and bushes grown and sold from the greenhouse next door were gone now. Stripped trees, stubble and downed limbs contrasted with the red sky. Small bomb fires lit the area and every minute or so another one would spontaneously appear.

"Why didn't the alarm go off?" His voice was strange, as if the words hovered in the air, not really coming from his mouth.

"I've heard the Americans' advance planes drop little aluminum things that make our radar miss incoming bombers," Mama said. "I think they call them 'windows'. I imagine that's what happened."

They watched as fire trucks ringed the area, battling one blaze after another.

"That was far too close," Mama said as she hugged him close to her. "I'll be so glad when we can leave. It's going to be soon, I'm sure of it."

Franz noticed tears rolling down Mama's face, and felt the wet chill on his own as well.

As he moved through the next days, he did normal things: doing school work though there was no school, leaving food for the Russian prisoners, and being with his parents and friends. But in his mind he couldn't stop chanting Mama's words, *we'll be leaving soon.*

The next week was August thirty-first and he turned eleven years old. The day was stormy, which offered rest because bombers couldn't fly when visibility was poor. People went to bed fully clothed and Franz always put his shoes under the blanket so he could find them quickly.

As soon as the sun dried the swamp-like mud created by the fire hoses, Franz and Josef met Karl in what was left of the nursery. Hugo showed up as well. They poked around, looking for something among the burned out tree trunks, maybe a treasure, or perhaps a weapon. They found a lot of the American metallic strips.

Holding a handful, Franz shook his head. "These look like tinsel for Christmas trees. But they messed up radar warnings, so we weren't warned." He dropped them and looked around again. "What can we do with all the soot? Paint something?"

"Who hauled off the limbs?" Josef stood with his the palms of his hands held up, and looked around.

"At night people load up carts or carry wood away," Franz said. "Vati thinks people outside Hasag Company are taking it home for heat this winter."

"My dad thinks with coal hard to get now, it's going to be a rough winter." Hugo looked toward the Company buildings where their parents worked. "He said the damn Russian prisoners are probably stealing firewood, and taking what rightfully belongs to Germans."

Franz and Karl looked at each other, but didn't respond immediately.

"My father is in the *Wehrmacht*." Karl spoke the words slowly, with great emphasis. "I hope, wherever he is, that he's not freezing or starving," Karl put his hands on his hips and glared at Hugo. "Even if he has to swipe downed trees to do it."

"The Company will be sure we have enough coal," Franz said. He hoped Karl wouldn't let this become an argument. "What difference does it make who takes the firewood?" Franz figured Hugo would repeat their words to his father. They better not draw attention to themselves. If Herr Braun watched them, he might see them take food to the prisoners.

As if reading his mind, Karl nodded to Franz. "Yeah, you're right. It's about time to eat lunch, anyway. I'm hungry. Race you to the door!"

The boys sprinted away.

Franz looked around the Cantina to see if Vati were here and saw him over in a corner. Why was Mama with him, she should be at work. Franz got his tray and joined them. As he got close, he could see Mama's eyes were puffy and red. Vati gave a small smile to reassure Franz as he scooted over on the bench for Franz to sit down.

"The other cooks insisted I take off early since it's the fifth of September," Mama sniffed. "Today Kati is five years old and I miss her so much I can't stand it!" she reached out and patted Franz' hand. "I never dreamed we'd be gone so long and I can't stop thinking of how much she's grown and wonder what she's doing." More tears flowed, and she wiped her face and sniffed her nose. "I thought our travel documents would be here by now and we'd be home!"

"Elisabeth," Vati's voice was soft, yet firm. "Things will work out. Each day is closer to when we leave."

Mama nodded, and sat up straighter. "You're right, Stefan." She blinked her eyes, forced a smile and took a bite of bread and looked at Franz more closely. "Where have you been? You're covered in black smudges from head to hand."

He started to explain, but was cut off by shelter sirens.

"It's the Amis—they're increasing daytime bombing now," Vati said. "Grab your food and let's go."

Since they only had to walk next door, they got to the shelter early and were moved all the way to the back, near the emergency escape tunnel. Franz never paid a lot of attention to it, but now he wondered what it would be like to leave that way, if the bombs blocked the exit doors. They barely reached seats as the first bombs went off at a great distance. More fell as the rest of the people scurried in and the door was closed. Closer and closer they came, till one shook the shelter itself. Franz noticed that the main sounds inside were children wailing as usual, but more adults cried as well. It seemed a very long day while the bombs exploded outside.

Franz put his hand in his pocket and felt his hastily wrapped sandwich from lunch. He hadn't wanted or even thought of eating, but now his stomach rumbled and he ate. With nothing to do, he sat with all the others as they listened to the explosions, the sirens continuing, and the rapid firing of the rooftop *acht acht* cannons.

Gradually, it got quieter. First the siren stopped, then bombs fell farther away, and the cannons stopped shooting. They had a time of relative quiet before the all-clear signal sounded and they began to slowly and tentatively file outside. Without wind, acid clouds hung along the ground. Franz lowered his eyelids to slits and tried to blink away the sting.

"It's so dark out!" Mama said. "We'd just started eating, so it's probably only about four o'clock. Can you believe that?"

Franz shook his head as he tried to accept this strange passage of time. "It's still Kati's birthday," he said aloud.

"Yes, I guess it is," his mother agreed. "But it seems a week ago since this morning."

Everything was gray, and Franz could see only a few feet ahead. He closed his eyes to slits against the burning air. It felt like he'd wandered into a cloud, as if he were in a weird dream. He looked toward the downtown area and couldn't find the tall buildings. Were they hidden in the smoke and swirling ash? Or were they gone?

Like sleepwalkers, Franz and his parents moved away from the shelter. The First Aid Station appeared to be undamaged, and peering through the dirty air, their rooms above looked the same as always. They kept walking. Something crunched with every step, so Franz knelt down to see what it was. Bits of glass, in various sizes littered the area. His eyes felt gritty and he closed them often to rest. All around, he heard people cough.

The bath building had been hit, and one side sat exposed. Franz pictured a giant, reaching down to grab the outer wall and flinging it to the ground.

"I'd better go to work and see if it's still there. The production part of the Company is the target," Vati said. He pulled Mama into his arm and looked down at Franz. "Are you both okay?"

Franz nodded, unable to find words for questions he might have asked.

"Yes," Mama said. "The worst is probably over—for now."

Franz' mouth opened to question her, and then he clamped it closed again. His parents couldn't honestly tell him they would always be safe. He figured no one else knew, either. He looked to the littered ground, his lower lip tucked between his teeth.

"If I hadn't been so upset about missing Kati, I would have been at work, serving food." Mama wrung her hands, "I'm sure my friends had time to get to a shelter, but I've got to find out for sure. We always clean up, and sometimes have to work past our shift to leave it ready for the next crew. Franz, let's go over there now," Mama continued. "No matter what happens, people need to eat."

Vati nodded and turned north toward the Company factories.

Franz and Mama made their way a half block west to the officers' dining room. They passed damaged buildings. A small fire flickered in the distance, then another flared up, and another. All the while, Franz kept his eyes squinted against the painful stinging of his eyes. Bits of paper and ash continued to drift around them, and he couldn't see but about five feet ahead, anyway.

"Franz!" A voice behind him called and he turned. Josef and his mother, Margaret, caught up with them.

"Have you seen any of the others?" Mama directed her question to Margaret.

"No, and I'm worried. I left as soon as the sirens went off, and didn't look back."

Content to let the mothers talk, Franz dropped back with Josef.

"We went up to our rooms," Josef said. "Some plaster fell off walls, but we still have beds."

"Beds are only good if we can sleep there at night," Franz kicked a large rock as hard as he could. "This war goes on and on and on."

"Sometimes I try to remember what it was like before," Josef said. "When my father was alive and we all lived in a nice apartment. He went to work every day and my mother took care of me and my baby brother and cooked for us." He sighed deeply. "But it's like I'm remembering a book I read once."

"I didn't know you have a little brother. Where is he?"

"I had measles, and he got them from me. And then he died." Josef flicked his eyes to his mother and continued in a whisper. "Two weeks later the *Wehrmacht* sent Vati to Stalingrad to die. I can't remember what either of them looked like. I close my eyes and try, but they're just shadows." Josef put his hands over his face and wiped tears off and away from his cheeks.

Franz didn't know what to say. Mama would have the right words, but his mind was blank. "That's too bad," he finally offered.

They could see the officers' dining room right ahead. It had been bombed on the corner and a lot of the roof dangled to the ground. Their mothers stepped up their speed, and went around to the back into the kitchen. Without electricity, it was dark except for a few lanterns.

Franz and Josef stood near the wall as the women met one another with hugs and tears and they all seemed to talk at once.

A few minutes later, Mama handed Franz a broom and told him to clear the floor.

"We'll go through the food supplies and figure out what we can do quickly." Mama reached toward a pan, but turned when another woman joined them. Knowing what to expect now, Franz moved away from all the women's emotional greetings.

He swept a pile of trash—flour that had fallen and spilled on the floor, glass from nearby windows, the ever-present ash floating around. By the time he found a dust pan, and returned, someone had moved his pile and people walked through it. So he swept again.

Usually he concentrated on chores to get them done, and leave time for something more fun. But today, he kept getting distracted. Snippets of conversations, sudden bursts of tears, people moving around and not getting anything done—all of this made him very tired. He longed for home. A real home. He longed for Stanisic.

The next two days it was as if the sun had left, leaving behind thick and dirty air.

No more bombs were dropped, but every time Franz heard a bomber flying over Leipzig, he tensed, ready to run to the shelter.

One morning he woke up to the sound of fierce winds racing around the building. Vati was not yet back from his night shift. In her white cook's uniform, Mama brushed her brown hair back and secured it with a barrette.

"Good morning, sleepyhead," she said with a smile when Franz sat up. "You might as well come with me again; at least you'll have something to do there."

"Do I have to wash dishes again? My fingers are still wrinkled from yesterday."

"No," her lips curved up before she turned away from Franz. "I think maybe you can graduate to pouring coffee for the officers and cleaning up in the dining hall."

"Anything is more interesting than cleaning hundreds of pans, plates and utensils," he said as he put his shoes on.

Franz stepped outside and smiled. "Look! The wind is carrying away the dirty air!" Now that he could see the results of the heavy bombing better, his smile faded. Few of the downtown buildings were tall now. Jagged corners and walls stood at random. Nothing was clean – not even the grass. Powdery ash and debris covered everything. But the clean air made it easier to breathe and open his eyes.

He found it interesting to work around the officers. They didn't see him as they ate and visited and he listened to them. He heard reports of the Russians taking possession of places like Orel, Bielgorod, and Kharkov. It didn't sound good for Germany. Then he heard one mention Yugoslavia and he stayed nearby, picking up dirty dishes. But all he heard was that Tito and his partisans were causing lots of trouble. The men gradually left and Franz kept cleaning and wondering if these things meant the war would soon end, or keep going.

Midmorning, Vati stuck his head into the kitchen and motioned for Franz and his mother to step outside. As soon as they did, Vati's mouth quirked upward into a big, dimpled smile. His eyes sparkled as they hadn't done in a long time.

Whipping a hand from behind his back, he waved a large yellow envelope before them.

Mama squealed and hugged it to her chest.

"Travel papers?" Franz asked.

Vati reached his arms to Franz. Mama opened the pack and looked inside. Her head fell forward and for a moment Franz thought it might be bad news.

"We're going home, Franz," Mama whispered, "we're going home!"

20

Winter 1943/44 — eleven years old
Stanišić, Yugoslavia (occupied by Hungary '41 – '44)

I T SOUNDED TO Franz as though the train chanted "home, home"
as they left Leipzig. If Franz had his way, they wouldn't have to
stop in Augsburg to wait for a connection to take them the rest of
the way. Mama was pleased to spend time with her sister, before
continuing. That evening, he listened to his parents and Aunt
Anna and Uncle Hans visit. He'd have to be patient tomorrow
and the next night.

"While we're here, I want to buy coats for Franz and Kati,"
Mama stretched out on Anna's sofa. "With all the bombing damage here, is there a store still standing, where we can shop?"

"Yes, there's one only a half mile from here. We can go in the
morning, if you want to," Aunt Anna said. So they made their
plans, and the next morning Franz trailed them as they walked.

Every once in a while he saw a building that hadn't been damaged by bombs or fire. Aunt Anna led the way into a large, brick
building. Several windows were boarded up, and part of the store
barricaded, but business continued. His eyes grew big when he
saw so many rows of clothes for children in the huge store. How
long would he have to be here? Hours?

Mama's eyes scanned the store and she ignored Franz as she
picked out several possibilities for him. "Turn around, Franz."

Mama instructed, as she picked out her favorite. "Turn," she instructed until he faced her again. "No, not as good as I'd thought it would be. Let's try this one." Again, he rotated while Mama stroked her chin between her thumb and fist. "Hmmm."

"What do you think, Anna? I like the three-quarter length. Big enough, so he won't soon outgrow it."

Aunt Anna felt the fabric. "It's quality wool, and the tweedy brown won't show every speck of dirt. The hems are deep enough to let down." Aunt Anna coughed into her handkerchief, as she did several times every hour. Last night Franz had asked Vati if she were sick. He explained her lungs had never been strong, but dirty air from all the bombing made it worse.

Franz sighed and wiggled his shoulders beneath the weight of the coat. Mama and Aunt Anna laughed. "Okay, you can take it off, now, Franz. We're finished with you, and I think I see the coat I want to get for Kati."

Happy to leave the store, Franz watched Mama pay for his coat and a soft yellow one for Kati.

"I wish you'd stay a while." Aunt Anna coughed again as they walked back to her apartment. "I may not see you for a long time."

"I know," Mama said. "We wouldn't be here now, except there isn't a train to Budapest until morning. All we can think about is getting back home and seeing our Kati."

Ever since Kati's birthday it was like Mama couldn't think of anything but his baby sister.

Franz led the way back to Aunt Anna's apartment. Augsburg looked a lot like Leipzig now— no longer beautiful. He noticed so many tall buildings had been destroyed; their materials tumbled about the ground. Whole blocks had burned away. People kept their heads down, shuffling along, herding their children to stay close.

"The school is a temporary shelter for those who have lost their homes." Aunt Anna said, as they passed the sprawling red brick building.

A Red Cross truck pulled up and a long line formed instantly. People held tightly to suitcases and bundles, or sat on them.

"Soup is given to displaced families," Aunt Anna continued. "It's very depressing. More show up every day."

We can't be bombed tonight— Franz thought, *just one more night and we'll be home.*

"How are things going with Hans?" Mama asked Aunt Anna in a soft voice.

"Oh," Anna took a deep breath, "about the same." And she shook her head.

Mama put her arm over her sister's shoulder and squeezed.

After a quiet night, in the morning they woke up eager for the day. Uncle Hans sat at the table and finished off his third bottle of beer while he complained about his boss at the brewery. Franz didn't understand why, but he'd noticed that Vati acted different with Hans than he did with Aunt Anna. He wasn't as relaxed and somehow his eyes didn't smile.

As Franz leaned over and tied his shoes, he watched them.

Vati didn't look at Uncle Hans, but focused on the cup of ersatz coffee he held. Vati nodded his head occasionally, but didn't comment. As Franz tied his second shoe, he realized that Vati didn't like Uncle Hans.

It was time to walk to the train station. Vati stood up and held a small blue bag, decorated with pink flowers, to Anna. "We've worked and sacrificed more than two years to save this money. If we try to take all of it now, the risk is too high that the *Wehrmacht* will search us and take it as overage when we cross the border. Can you keep it safe until we come back?"

Aunt Anna took the bag, glanced at Hans and frowned as she hesitated. "I need to put it in a place where you, and no one else, can find it if something happens to me." Her head snapped up, she nodded and walked into their bedroom. After opening the wardrobe doors, she pulled out a box of old family photos from her childhood. "No one will throw this away, or want it." She lifted out the pictures and buried the bag beneath them.

Satisfied, after tearful goodbyes, they walked to the station. Franz didn't enjoy the train ride as he usually did. He just wanted to get home. When they crossed the border, he remembered how scared he'd been when Uncle Adam smuggled him into Germany without the correct travel papers. Was it only a year ago he hid under guns and soldiers' bags, shaking with fright?

Finally they arrived in the fertile, flat farm land of Stanisic. There'd been no time to let Oma and Opa know they were coming. Franz put his beautiful new coat on and picked up one of the suitcases to carry to Church Street. Sunshine warmed them as they left the train station.

It was a relief to see homes and stores looked the same. Their village remained untouched by war.

When they came to the house, Franz looked over his shoulder at Mama and Vati, and grinned. The familiar squeak of the gate welcomed him. The yard was quiet. "Oma?" he called. "Opa?"

Mama crossed the porch quickly, opened the kitchen door and found Oma cutting up a chicken to cook.

"Oh! You're home at last!" she ran to them, wiping her hands on her apron and hugged each one. "Franz you're taller, but you're so thin!" And she hugged him again. "You all need some good farm food!"

"Kati's taking a nap right now." Oma took a deep breath. "She's had enough sleep, go wake her up."

She gave Franz another hug and giggled. "Opa will be thrilled to have you back."

Franz and Oma followed Mama and Vati to Kati's bedroom. Mama lowered herself to sit on the edge of the bed. "She's grown so much! And she's beautiful," Mama whispered. She traced the soft outline of Kati's cheek with her fingertips, waking her.

Instead of eagerly hugging Mama, Kati whimpered and scampered over the bed to reach Oma. She buried her face in Oma's apron, then peeked out and stared at Franz.

It felt odd to have her to keep distance between them. She'd grown and still looked the same, but somehow different now. Shyness hung between them.

"Hello, Kati," he finally said. "You remember me, don't you? I'm Franz."

She nodded briefly and gave him the barest of smiles.

Vati hunkered down to her level. "Mama and I missed you so much."

She hid her face behind Oma again. Franz wanted to tell her to stop being silly, but he felt a little strange at being together, too.

"We've come home, Kati," Mama said in a soft voice. No response. "Do you have any kittens?"

Diverted, Kati forgot her shyness. "I have a little black one. Want to see it?" At Mama's nod, she led them to the cellar, where a multi-colored cat watched over her three babies.

"Her name is *Flaumig*," Kati said as she picked up a round, yellow-eyed black kitten.

"I see why you named her that. She's got a lot of soft fur, doesn't she?" Mama stroked the fluffy kitten with one finger.

"Here, Franz, you can hold her." Kati held her gift to him.

But *Flaumig* only allowed him to hold her for an instant before she sprang to the ground and her mother.

"Come upstairs where it's more comfortable," Oma said. "We'll catch up on all the news."

Franz grinned when Kati lifted her hands for him to carry her up the stairs, as he used to.

Oma bustled around her kitchen pouring glasses of wine and slicing bread. Franz grabbed his suitcase and went to the porch and down to his room. It smelled stale, but oh, how safe he felt in the familiar room.

With a happy smile, he went to the porch and on to the outhouse. Inside, with dust floating in the dim light, he looked around as he pulled down his pants. The small structure's stink couldn't be ignored— Germany's indoor toilets with flushing water had spoiled him. But in every other way, he knew Stanisic was the best of all.

He returned to the kitchen and asked if he could run next door to Anton's. Mama, Vati and Oma were busy talking and smiled and waved him off.

"Franz, welcome home!" Frau Haut cried when she opened the door. "Anton isn't here right now. I think he's off with Adam Sujer, and maybe Stefan, and Tony."

After he walked out the Hauts' gate, Franz hesitated until he heard the sound of boys yelling. With a burst of excitement, he ran to his room to get his stick to play land hockey.

"Look! It's Franz, back from the big city!" Anton shouted.

The boys halted their game to greet Franz. "Dig a hole, Franz, and play." Tony leaned on his stick. Two years younger than Franz and Anton, his lanky body had grown. Now he was taller than Anton, but still shorter than Franz. "Let's see if you've forgotten the game!"

"Does a fish forget how to swim?" Franz picked up the shovel and added his hole to the circle, just as he'd always done. "Whose turn is it?"

It didn't matter if he were cheered on, or received taunts. This was home.

Within days, his daytime memories of Leipzig faded as he took up his old chores and enjoyed walking to and from school with friends.

A bitter, cold November, December, and January passed in routine. He did morning chores, met Anton, Tony and Adam and walked to school. The nuns made them do more work since they couldn't stay out too long. At home, chores needed to be done again. Mama supervised his reading and doing math on his old slate. One day was like the other. Only at night did he remember the beating by Herr Budin and the nightly sirens, acid clouds and staying in the shelter. Once in a while he saw pictures in his mind of the men burned in the explosion, but he quickly forced himself to think of something else.

—⟨⟩—

"Franz!" Oma stood on the porch and called to get his attention. "Please run to the general store. They promised to hold back flour for me."

"Can I take Kati with me?"

"No, you'd better just get back here. I need to get the bread started."

Though the day was overcast and cool, it wasn't windy. At least he was outside and not stuck in the house. One bag of hard-to-get flour had been held back for Oma. As he walked home, he heard a bicycle coming up behind him.

"You're the Hauts' grandson, the Elmer boy, aren't you?" At Franz's nod, he reached into his mail bag and handed him an envelope with Vati's name. It was typed, and not hand written. A German postmark was stamped in the corner.

Franz ran home, clutching the flour with one hand and the letter with the other, while his heart beat rapidly. Fighting fear, he reminded himself it could be unimportant.

Mama and Vati were on the porch swing, sipping cups of coffee, the steam rising in the air. Franz stopped, and without a word, handed the letter to Vati.

Vati looked at Mama and immediately slid his finger under the flap and pried it open.

Franz watched him read it once, and then again. Vati handed it to Mama.

"I must report to the German army next week." Vati stood and stepped over to the porch's square, yellow brick pillar. Hands in his pockets, he looked toward the orchard in the back.

Mama slumped over the letter in her lap. "We're supposed to be safe here." She mumbled something under her breath and straightened her back. "But of course," anger laced her voice, "to Hitler, we're not real people, simply tools!"

"Where will they send you?" Franz asked, his voice trembling. "Josef's father was killed in Stalingrad. If you go there, your fingers and toes will freeze and fall off." An idea flashed into his mind. "They can't find you here, can they?"

"The letter got here, and so would soldiers. Desertion is punishable by sure death."

Franz closed his eyes and took a deep breath. "When Jani and I little, we dreamed of growing up and wearing uniforms and have adventures. We didn't understand." Franz threw his arms around his father's chest and held on tight. He inhaled the familiar fragrance of his father's pipe.

"The war will be over soon, Franz. Even though I must join the *Wehrmacht*, it doesn't mean I'm going to die or be injured. In fact, I'll probably be back before you know it."

"That's what Uncle Adam said," Franz whispered. "And where is he?"

Vati looked over Franz's head to Mama.

"Let's not borrow trouble." Vati put his hands on Franz's cheeks, tipped his face upward and looked him straight in the eye. "For now, let's enjoy being together."

For the next week, little was said about Vati's leaving. Each morning Franz and his father worked together taking care of the cow, horse, and hogs. Vati helped him chip through the ice in the water tanks so the animals could drink. As they worked, they shared good memories of when they lived in Sombor near Jani. How they'd cleaned out the attic where the Tumbling Pigeons stayed, and their performances in the sky. Talking of Vati's butcher shop reminded Franz of how different life was then.

The days hurried past.

"Franz?" Vati pushed open Franz' bedroom door. Mama followed, carrying a heated brick, wrapped in a towel. That was another thing he'd gotten used to in Leipzig, where a small heater generated warmth.

Vati sat on his bed and Mama as well. Franz didn't want to hear what they would say. He busied himself arranging the brick at his feet under an abundant, thick goose-down quilt.

"I'm catching a train before morning to report to the base in Germany."

"Tonight?" he murmured. He couldn't think of anything to say. Okay? Beg him to stay? Goodbye? With Vati's hand on his, he said nothing.

"Just help your mother, Opa and Oma, and play with Kati. I'll be back before long."

Franz flung his arms around Vati's neck and hugged him tightly, silent tears falling. After a moment, he let Vati lay him down, and kiss his forehead. Mama pulled the quilt up to his neck and kissed him good night. They turned out the light and left.

He lay in the dark for a long time, tossing and turning before finally falling asleep. Vati was gone in the morning. Because of a lump in his throat, Franz had a hard time swallowing bacon and bread before leaving for school.

———

"Why aren't you talking, Franz? You get in trouble today?" Anton gave him a friendly punch in the shoulder as they walked home from school.

"No," Franz said. "Horst told me the *Wehrmacht* has sent his uncle home after he got shell-shocked and his memory messed up. His land lay fallow while he was gone and the rabbits took over. The day after tomorrow, they need people to drive the critters out so he can plow over the warrens. Each helper will get a rabbit as payment. All I have to do is bring a stick or something to make noise and show up."

"It's on Saturday, and if I hurry to get my chores done, I can go," Franz continued. "I had no way to earn money while we lived in Leipzig. I won't get paid for this, but I can get food for dinner."

"I thought you'd be on my team to play Land Hockey Saturday!" Anton's lips turned down and his eyes narrowed.

"Why don't you come with me? It'll be fun."

Anton mumbled 'maybe' and they parted as they came to his gate.

Saturday dawned dreary, wet and cold for the first of April. Franz fed the horse and milked the cow in dense fog. Through breakfast, he wiggled with excitement. He ran to his room, grabbed his new coat and hurried to meet Anton. They joined Horst and the others for the hunt just as the sun burned away the cloudiness.

A man cradling his gun stood on a fallen tree. "There are two basic rules," he said. "First, stay in a line. We've got to scare them and make them run. Second, don't step into a hole and sprain an ankle. Several years of leaves and dead grasses hide rabbit holes underfoot."

Franz picked a place for himself and Anton. The whole row moved forward, and everyone banged their sticks together and on any bushes or small trees in the path.

"We're good at this," Franz laughed a few minutes later as they stepped forward. "We can talk, make a lot of noise and swing at bushes with our sticks."

The hunter stayed well ahead of them, and watched. The first shot flushed out a nearby rabbit. A second shot hit it. One of the drivers picked up the small carcass and tossed it on his cart.

"That's the first one," Anton shouted.

Shots increased as rabbits ran from their cover. When the sun began to set, two blasts fired rapidly to signal the end of the hunt. Franz and Anton waited to get their rabbits.

"Our mothers will be happy to see what we've got!" Franz hugged the rabbit to him and hurried home.

"Mama! Oma!" he called out when he found them in the back garden, digging up potatoes with Kati helping. "Look what I have!"

Neither of the women looked pleased. "Franz!" Mama stood up and shook her hand in a chopping motion for emphasis. "Look at what you've done to your new coat!"

"Oh, no . . ." he said as he held the rabbit out to his side. Thick smears of blood covered the front of his new coat. Franz felt sick. "I'm sorry. I just thought about how good he would taste."

Still aggravated, Mama took the rabbit and handed it to Oma. "Give me your coat and I'll try to wash out as much as possible. And next time think, Franz. Think!" She knocked on his head to emphasize her words.

She stalked off with the coat, still mumbling.

"Can I hold him?" Kati asked Oma as she reached for the soft fur.

"No, Kati, he's too dirty," Oma said. "Let's clean up this meat to enjoy tonight." Franz cut off the little brown tail and found string to tie off the end and gave it to Kati. He and Oma smiled as they watched her stroke her 'pet', nestled in her tiny hand.

Mama washed and scrubbed for a long time and did manage to get a lot of the blood out, but a shadow-stain remained.

"Something sure smells good." Opa said as he entered the kitchen.

Mama, much calmer now, pointed to Franz. "Our hunter brought home the supper."

While they ate the delicious meat, Franz told about the hunt, and confessed he'd ruined his new coat.

"What's done is done," Mama said with a tight smile. "Your coat will never be the same, so just eat the meat slowly and enjoy every bite!"

"Franz," Opa ate a portion and hummed appreciation. "It's delicious."

The weeks became warmer, the days longer as spring peeked up its head.

"Come here!" Mama enthusiastically motioned with her hand one morning as Franz headed to school.

Curious, he looked at Oma's flower section and saw bits of green. He thought for a minute, but didn't know what it could be.

"Sunflowers!" Mama said. "It's officially springtime, and it won't be long till these babies are big enough to open up and start tracking the sun. We'll almost be able to see their growth every day!"

Franz didn't quite get her excitement, but grinned back.

"Do you think your Mother is being silly? Maybe, but after the time we had in Leipzig the past year, when we didn't know what would happen from one day to the next, seeing them comforts me. They're beautiful and hardy and stubborn. They go through terrible winters, but always return. They promise spring and summer." She chuckled and dusted off her hands. "Go on to school and learn a lot today."

21

1944 – eleven years old
Stanišić – occupied by Hungary '41 – '44

"DID OMA TELL you our Saint Maria celebration is next month? People from other villages will join us, so Stanisic is sprucing up. We'll need a lot of help from you." Opa stroked his mustache as he leaned back in his chair on the sidewalk in front of the house. "It'll be good for us to forget war and work for a little while."

"Oh!" Mama exclaimed with a big smile, "I didn't remember that we have a Saint's Day coming up! Let's see . . . July sixth is just four weeks away."

Franz grinned. He loved festivals where people laughed, sang and visited. Even if they couldn't get sugar and flour, the women always filled the tables with good food.

"What do you want me to do?" he asked.

"Help clean up around here – the yard and sidewalks first, and if you do a good job," Opa's eyes twinkled, "you can help paint the house."

"Franz, he means with real paint, not mud." Mama teased.

"There must be a story behind that," Opa said. He and Oma looked from Franz to Vati and Mama.

"When we lived in Sombor," Mama began, "Franz and Jani accidently got their ball over a neighbor's yellow enclosure. This man really didn't like people, especially children. He wouldn't let them have it back. The boys retaliated by smearing mud all over his wall."

"I still think he really deserved it." Franz saw a familiar twinkle in Opa's eyes.

"You boys had to scrub hard to get it clean, didn't you?" Mama smiled at the memory.

Each school day, Franz worked after school and his regular chores were done. He gathered broken limbs from the orchard, cleaned dead foliage from the winter, and ran numerous errands. Opa did minor repairs needed around the windows and roof and bought cans of paint.

"I've got our brushes, Franz," he said early the next week. "If we wash them clean every day after painting, they'll stay soft and usable. Come on, we'll work together."

"Hmmm, this is kind of fun," Franz said after they'd worked for several hours. He pointed to the newly painted part, "It really looks better, doesn't it?"

He continued working after Opa left to meet workers who would scatter the animals' manure on the cornfield. Franz enjoyed hearing birds sing, chickens cluck, and the soft voices of the Hauts, Anton's parents, next door. Absent were sirens, bombs or explosions.

The Hauts had painted for the past two days. Franz heard Frau Haut say it was time to eat, and noticed they leaned the ladder against the power pole before they went inside.

He stepped back and admired the wall he just finished. Feeling satisfied, he picked up his bucket and walked around the corner to the end of the house.

"Stop! Get down!" a man's scream shattered the quiet.

Franz dropped his paintbrush and followed the sound to next door.

Anton stood on the ladder like a statue. His face had turned white, his blue eyes wide. Above his head, he held the electric line with both hands. Franz didn't think he even breathed, but he was alive.

Several rungs below Anton, Herr Becker grabbed him by the back of his *lederhosen* with one hand and jerked to break Anton's hold. Then he pulled Anton to himself and set his feet solidly on the ladder rung.

"We're slowly going to the ground," the man said to Anton in slow, clear words.

Franz didn't move. He just watched them gradually come down. Frau and Herr Haut arrived in time to take Anton in their arms.

At last, Anton howled in pain, breaking his silence.

Everyone talked at once. Finally, Herr Haut shouted, "silence!" and turned to the man. "Herr Becker, what happened?"

"I was in my front yard watching the clouds and saw him climb the ladder. I shouted to him to stay away from the electric wires, but I was too late."

"My hands got stuck," Anton's voice quivered. He looked at his shaking palms, now bright red. A few tears rolled down his cheeks.

Herr Haut shook hands with the rescuer and thanked him fervently. "I'm relieved the lines up there are low voltage. Again, we thank you so much."

Frau Haut took her son inside to apply salve.

The next day Franz ran over to see Anton.

"Lots of skin peeled off." As if they were awards for bravery, Anton proudly held up bandaged hands. "My mother said I have to protect them from getting dirty."

"Well," Franz said with mock seriousness. "I guess you won't be able to do much work for the celebration, will you?"

"No," Anton tried to look disappointed, but his upturned lips gave him away. Then he shrugged and frowned. "The bad thing is I can't even eat without help. Mother fills my plate with healthy food so I can heal fast. You know I like to eat mostly desserts at feasts!"

The village continued painting the houses and cleaning both inside and outside. The women had hoarded flour and sugar as well as other scarce foods for their annual celebration.

On a beautiful, clear day, Franz used the hoe to make a channel for planting in the garden. He heard a very faint droning hum and couldn't figure out what it was. He cocked his head as he listened. It gradually became louder, until Oma and Mama came outside and they all walked outside the walled fence to the sidewalk. Many neighbors drifted there as well. Everyone stood motionless and tried to figure out what it could be. Tanks coming? As the sound got closer, they looked up and saw airplanes flying very high up, heading north.

Franz had never seen anything like it, nor had any of the adults. There were hundreds and hundreds of small silver specks against the blue sky. Worm shaped puffs formed behind them, and reminded Franz of the leeches trails. They were interesting, but also scary. What were the strange cloud-like things?

"Those are Allied bombers and fighter escorts," Herr Becker shook his head and sighed.

"According to the news on my radio," Herr Haut said, "the Americans and British defeated Rommel in Africa and established an airfield there." He scratched his chin and continued to look above. "Now they can fly over Italy, Yugoslavia, Hungary and Austria."

"If they turn west over Budapest, they can attack Germany from the East," Herr Becker said. "German defenses are concentrated in the west."

Herr Haut met Herr Becker's eyes and nodded. "They've increased bombing farther into Germany."

Mama stepped close behind Franz and put her hands on his shoulders. He twisted his head around to face her. "Vati?" he whispered.

She raised her eyebrows and shook her head. "We need to really pray for his protection."

What about Aunt Anna, and his friends in Leipzig? No one said anything, and after the planes were out of sight, everyone went back to work and kept busy.

Franz had just washed the last bucket of potatoes for Oma when he heard the far-away growling sound again. He ran to the street and watched the planes come back, heading south. Anton joined him.

"There aren't as many, are there?" Anton asked.

"No." Franz's eyes scanned the sky. "And they aren't as close together, either."

"A lot of them were probably shot down or too badly damaged to fly." Herr Becker spoke as he and Herr Haut joined them. "I'm afraid we'll see a lot more of this."

"I heard the Luftwaffe hid some of Messerschmitt's ME109 fighter planes." Herr Haut said "They're scattered throughout the countryside, so if American and British bombers fly back without fighter escorts, the ME109 can pick them off, one by one."

Franz squinted his eyes at the planes above, and thought. That meant more people dying – men who were fathers, sons, uncles. Dead was dead, no matter whose side they were on.

Franz felt quiet tears run down his face.

"Boys, we were about your age in the Great War. We thought it would never end, but it did. This one will, as well." The last of the planes drifted out of sight. "We have something to look forward to tomorrow—Saint Maria's day of celebration."

Franz shoved his hands in his pockets, and nodded.

The next morning Franz jumped from bed, dressed in work clothes and hurried to the kitchen. After they'd eaten, he tossed fresh hay to the horse and cow and replenished their water. After he milked the cow, he ran to get the slop bucket from the porch. Filled with potato peelings, corn cobs, egg shells and various unidentifiable things swimming in dark liquid, he carried the bucket to pour into the hogs' trough.

Chores finished, he washed up, dressed in his best lederhosen, slicked down his hair and put on his coat. His family and the Hauts walked together to church.

"Look!" Anton shoved up his coat sleeves and held his clean, pink palms up for inspection, "the bandages are off and I can do everything for myself now!"

"And that's good?" Franz cocked his head and his dimples deepened as he grinned.

"I'm tired of being treated like a baby." Anton rolled his eyes. "My mother helped me with everything, except when I went to the outhouse."

Franz laughed, but felt instant sympathy for Anton.

Many visitors from other, smaller villages came to Immaculate Heart of Mary for the annual Holiday. Taking advantage of extra commotion, the boys melted into the large crowd.

"Let's sit there," Franz whispered into Anton's ear and tipped his head to a rapidly filling pew. It would be more fun not to sit with their parents. They leaned forward, making themselves small. In the midst of admiring how quick they'd been, Franz felt a tap on his shoulder and turned to see Mama right behind him. She tipped her head forward and raised her eyebrows, but Franz didn't miss the message in her eyes. Frau Haut sat behind Anton. They couldn't have fun.

Anton slumped in his seat and looked out the corner of his eye to Franz. "We almost made it," then they grinned at each other.

Bored, Franz listened slightly as the priest droned on . . .

"Saint Maria showed an astounding ability to forgive the man who violated and murdered her. Is her life and death just a story from a long time ago? No, our Lord has issued a challenge to us in our time. Somehow, we must forgive and not be filled with hate."

Franz thought of the old man in the shelter who had said his faith was the same in good times and bad times. He could trust God in both. Was he saying the same thing?

Finally, he heard the close of the service.

"Dominus vobiscum, Et cum spiritu tuo, Oremus"

As Franz repeated the words, he translated them to himself. *May the Lord be with you, And with your spirit, Let us pray.*

On the way out of church, Franz heard adults greet one another, and welcome visitors by inviting them for the mid-afternoon meal. Parishioners streamed outside and scattered toward their homes. Tables had already been placed on sidewalks every block or so. Franz and his friends weren't idle for a moment. As soon as they carried a tempting dish from one house, another woman stepped outside and called for help to carry hers.

Everyone brought his own plate and tableware. The line filed past the tables as people helped themselves to delicious food. While eating, men gathered in their groups and women in theirs.

Franz and his friends sat on blankets spread over the ground, cross-legged, their plates in their laps. Busy eating, they listened to the men talk about the weather, war, their crops and animals, the war again and the scarcity of wheat and tobacco.

Tony Baumgartner brought marbles and a vigorous game kept them busy as the sun moved lower in the sky. Franz eyed the dessert table from a distance, and decided to see if anything were left. While he nibbled on the last, small piece of *streusel*, he wandered to stand by his grandfather.

"Things are tough right now," Herr Peitz was saying. "But I'm still convinced Germany will win and take her place as a world leader. The Russians are the meanest of the Allied powers. And the closest. Germany must overcome them; it's just taking longer than we thought it would."

"How you can place so much confidence in Germany?" Herr Kalanj said. "It's like a giant Ping-Pong contest."

"What are you talking about? This isn't a game!" Herr Peitz leaned forward threw his hands in the air.

"No, but I understand what you're saying. Yugoslavia, for instance," another man turned to answer. "Tito's Partisans were almost destroyed by the Axis in May, but he managed to hold on and revived his followers. They rounded up the Italian forces, and eighteen days later took control of Split. They won, then lost, then won again."

"That's my point." Kalanj wagged his finger from one side to the other, mimicking the ball. "Germany seized it back the end of September."

"I'm talking Germany overcoming Russia," Herr Peitz waved his hands in front of his face as if to shoo away minor issues.

"Same thing," a round, red-faced man said. "Most wars are won battle by battle. Look at Kursk. The Russians took it in February, and Germany brought in a gigantic tank battle in July and now has control."

"Kharkov fell to German hands," a thin, blond with a Hungarian accent said, "and by February, the Russians regained their city. Germany captured it back it in March, and Russia battled again and won Kharkov in August."

"You men are sounding dangerously traitorous! Germany needs our loyalty now!" Herr Peitz growled.

Franz noticed they shifted uncomfortably in their chairs. Something about the words sounded familiar to Franz. Suddenly it came back to him—about five years ago when he was just a little kid. It had been Opa's saint day when they'd slaughtered the hogs. Could this really be the same man who had hotly voiced his loyalty to Hitler? Opa looked over his shoulder at Franz and winked. He remembered, too.

"Gentlemen," Opa, tall and lean, stood up. "Today is Saint's Day, and should be a time for neighbors to feel safe enough for open discussion."

Several heads nodded.

The church bells rang six times and everyone gathered dirty dishes and chairs and took them home.

"Carry the candles for all of us," Oma handed Franz a box. "Your mother and I will bring the flowers." It was time for a procession to the cemetery.

Franz knew this last activity would signal the end of Saint's Day as they left flowers and candles on the graves of loved ones. Kati looked sleepy, and truthfully, so was he.

"Franz," Opa said one day after school, "now that the sun's out, let's do a thorough job of cleaning out the barns."

Franz changed into his old work clothes, grabbed his favorite slingshot and stuck it into his back pocket. He stopped at the cellar and cut off a hunk of ham before joining Opa.

Waving his arms in front of him against a swarm of horse flies, Franz grabbed his pitchfork, and scooped up a mixture of cow manure and hay. He carried it to the mound outside and threw it on top. "Today at school our teacher talked about how God supplies food for all creatures." He wiggled his legs and swatted near his ear. "That may be, but I sure hate these blood-sucking flies! And so do the cow and horse."

Opa chuckled. "Not one of God's best creations."

Just then, a swallow swooped past, his forked tail open as he sailed. Before he flew out of sight, Franz grabbed his sling shot and aimed.

"Stop!" Opa said with force. "Never shoot a swallow. They eat these pesky flies and other bugs that have no good use that I can see." He stepped away from the cow, motioned for Franz to join him. "Watch him fly. Isn't that beautiful?" They leaned on the barn wall and admired the motion of the bird as he went down to catch a bug. "Notice their songs. They sound alarms, call for other birds, and just sing for enjoyment."

Franz thought about Vati and wished they could go back in time and be watching the pigeons together.

"If you see a wild cat around here stalking a swallow, you use your weapon on him."

Franz shook his head and hands in mock fright. "Not if Kati is around! She'd come after me!"

Opa's weathered face turned to observe one of the cats slinking along the top of the lower barn door. His eyes were fixed on a swallow preening in a puddle. "Can your slingshot get him or shall I reach around the door for my shotgun?"

22

Fall 1944—twelve years old
Stanišić, occupied by Hungary

"UGH!" Franz plunked the milk pail onto the kitchen cabinet. "Who wants fresh, warm milk?" he asked. "There'd be more, but Katie's kittens cried and told me to give them Kati's share."

"They don't talk!" Kati frowned and her lower lip came out.

"He's only teasing you, Kati," Mama said. "Eat."

"Good morning, son." Mama said, cheerfully. She handed a plate to him, and Oma filled it with two eggs, bacon and poured a glass of milk. She didn't say anything, but patted his head.

Kati sat in her chair, swung her feet under the table, kicking Franz in the shin. He grinned and reached over to tug a lock of curly, blond hair.

With a gap-toothed smile, she stopped and began nibbling, like a mouse, on her bread.

Mama sat down with her coffee. "I'm tired of the war running our lives," she said. "We've always planned for you to go to gymnasium after fifth grade, so let's do it!"

Puzzled, Franz frowned as he looked at the map in his head. "There's one in Stanisic?" He glanced between Mama and Oma and put another piece of bacon in his mouth.

"The nearest one is in Sombor."

"No!" The word burst out of him. Mama planned to send him away? Oma's back was turned to him. "Why can't I just stay in school here? It's good enough."

"'Good enough?'" Mama repeated his words and leaned over the table, her eyes narrowed. "I want you to have a better future. From here, you can go to a trade school or nothing. With the superior education of gymnasium, you can go to university." Mama picked up his last report card and waved it in the air. "Franz, don't settle for what's easy now. Last semester you scored an A in eleven subjects, and a C in the other three. Use the mind God blessed you with!"

He crossed his arms and glared.

"Relax," Mama sighed and leaned back in her chair. "You turned into a mule before I explained. It's once a week. You'll go by train to Sombor, stay for a day of instruction, get your assignments and come home. You'll study here and take homework back with you the next week. To apply, we'll stay with Manci and Peter. How does that sound?"

"I'll take the train, and go there and home again in one day?" At her nod, he relaxed. "I'd like that."

She held up three fingers and ticked them off. "We'll have to fill out an application, get a photograph to attach and take the test. Then we'll see."

"Test?" He muttered and sat up straight. "What if I don't pass?"

"You will, but we'll never know unless you try."

"Okay," he said, feeling dubious, then perked up. "I'll get to see Jani!"

Two days later, they waited at the station for the train to Sombor. Hair prickled at the back of his neck at the sight of so many German and Hungarian soldiers. They all looked serious, knotting in small groups and keeping their voices down. Why here, in Stanisic?

The whistle of an incoming train distracted him. Franz sat by the window but didn't enjoy the scenery. He was excited about being with his cousin again, but thoughts of the coming exam bothered him. He glanced at Mama, who had her head back, eyes closed. They'd both be disappointed if he failed. Again, he looked out the window and absently bit a fingernail. He *had* to pass the test.

"Do you think Jani has changed?" Franz asked as they pulled into Sombor and waited to get off.

"I'm sure we've all changed." Mama brushed a lock of brown hair behind her ear.

They walked up the street to the Merkels' home. Everything looked the same, except the houses seemed smaller and paler. Franz led the way to turn on the sidewalk to Jani's. A little girl a bit older than Kati sat in a chair, dressing her doll.

"Dori?" Mama asked as she kneeled beside the small chair. "We haven't seen you in a very long time, but we knew you when you were younger. I'm Aunt Elisabeth and this is Franz."

Dori looked from one to the other, as her wispy, brown hair fluttered in a breeze.

"You used to play with our Kati. She's about your age."

Dori's face lit up in recognition. "She had a book with baby animals in it."

Mama's eyes lingered on Jani's sister, as she stood up.

Franz heard accordion music. He grinned. Many times he'd stood at this same door, and listened for the end of Jani's practices. Then they could run off and have fun.

He stopped thinking and just listened. Back then, Jani had struggled to make one hand do a lot of buttons, the other a keyboard, and at the same time stretch out the bellows properly. He'd gotten discouraged often, yelling "I can't do it!" before calming down and trying again.

This sounded like a performer on a stage. Franz looked up at Mama, her eyes wide, brows raised. "I guess that's Jani."

Mama knocked on the door. The music stopped, they heard footsteps and the door opened.

"Elisabeth! Franz!" Aunt Manci froze, then reached to hug them, laughing and crying at the same time.

Jani had grown taller, his face leaner, his thick brown hair covering the tops of his ears. "Hello," Jani said after he studied Franz a moment or two. His lips quirked. "What are you doing in Sombor?"

"Taking a trip to check out gymnasium and see you." Franz shifted from foot to foot. He'd told his friends at home he came to see his cousin, and barely mentioned the real reason. He didn't know why, but felt shy about it somehow.

Aunt Manci ushered them into the kitchen, where a pot of soup simmered. It smelled wonderful.

"You know Jani started gymnasium last year, don't you? He still plays the accordion," Aunt Manci said. "We're very proud—he's been accepted into the music conservatory! He'll start next month." Jani stood tall and nodded his head slightly.

"I'd forgotten that Jani is a grade ahead, even though he's only a few months older." Mama said. "And here we are again, making plans for our boys to receive superior educations."

A shadow covered Aunt Manci's face. "If all goes as it should. There are so many rumors filling the air, mostly about the Russians coming."

Jani stepped closer to Franz. "Want to go to our old park and look around?" He swiftly changed the subject, edging to the door.

Franz turned to check with his mother, only to see Aunt Manci leading her into the front room. "Tell me everything, Elisabeth. Our letters aren't enough!" She looked over her shoulder and laughed at the boys. "Go, but be back in time to eat!"

Franz grinned at Jani. "It's not as far as it was before, and the park has shrunk!" He said as they came to the entrance.

Standing below a horizontal branch on a massive oak tree, Franz pointed to a spot above their heads. "The best place for our cans-filled-with-mud trick!" Franz laughed. "It was funny, wasn't it?"

Jani agreed and they walked to the bandstand in the middle.

Franz kicked a rock over to Jani's side of the path, and Jani kicked it back.

"What's gymnasium like?" Franz asked when he kicked it once more.

"Some subjects are tough, but I like it. We learn a lot more." Jani bent over to re-tie a shoe. "It'll be more fun with you here."

"*If* I pass the test." Franz said. "It's hard, isn't it?"

"Yes, but if I passed, you will, too. Besides, I'll need your help with arithmetic," Jani said. "At the end of the year we built a kite and studied each part. It taught us how science and mathematics could make it better."

"We did that when we were five years old! Well, except for the studying part." Franz shook his head. "Sounds interesting." They headed back, ready for Aunt Manci's soup.

The next morning, Franz and his mother walked to the registration building. He turned to look up the main street, past stores with apartments above. Beyond the treetops he saw the Serbian Orthodox Church at the end. The white steeple, decorated with pink trim and topped with the gray spire with the cross pointing to Heaven. It looked beautiful and clean, not like a place to cause nightmares.

Gone was the steeple's gaping hole. Franz stopped and stared. It had been a long time since he thought about the Chetnik-Priest, his face covered in thickened blood. Though reluctant to touch him, Franz had reached past the lone, unseeing eye and felt cold skin. He and Jani had raced down the steps to find help. All this time later, Franz' hand shook a bit as he relived that day.

Turning such thoughts off, Franz caught up with his mother.

After his picture was taken, they filled out several pages of forms. An hour later, he entered a room with seven other boys about his age and sat at a timeworn desk, pencil in hand. He took a deep breath, flexed his fingers and picked up the test pages. How would he finish so many questions and problems? *Just one at a time,* he reminded himself. *If I can't do it, I'll go to the next one and come back later.* He heard the scratching of the other boys' pencils and focused on his paper. When he faced questions about Hungary's history or economics, he wished he hadn't found them boring in school. He laid his pencil down and shook the death grip from his fingers. *Don't stop. Move on.*

Exhausted when he finished, he gave it to the examiner.

Mama waited on a bench in the hallway. "How was it?" she asked.

"Tough." He shrugged. "I knew or guessed at most of them. I hated to leave some blank, but I couldn't even think of any possible answers. Then it was time to stop."

"Don't worry about it." Mama said. "We'll find out tomorrow." Relaxed now, they strolled back to the Merkels.

The next morning they returned for the results. Seated on a hard bench, Franz jiggled his leg as they sat in a long, brown hall and waited for his name to be called. The lady smiled when she stepped out with his file, and brought him a little book. He opened it and saw the stamped verdict. Mama leaned over.

"Accepted!" They hugged each other in celebration and in high spirits went to Jani's and shared the news. By afternoon, they were on the train headed back to Stanisic, busy making plans.

Instantly, his heart beating triple time, Franz woke from a deep sleep. He'd been dreaming of cannons in the distance and he thought he was still in Leipzig. No, this was Stanisic, and early light peeked through his window. Might as well get dressed.

"Did we have a thunder storm last night?" Franz asked at breakfast. "It sounded something like *acht-acht* cannons far away."

"It wasn't thunder," Opa's eyebrows pulled together, his voice gruff. "Go listen to the Crier today, and tell us what he says."

Opa sounded worried, but that couldn't be so. His grandfather never fretted over things, he simply thought of solutions and fixed them.

One glance at Mama and Oma and his uneasiness grew. Neither looked at him, or each other.

At ten o'clock, when Franz arrived at the nearest announcement intersection, he recognized the Crier's uniform.

The man beat a marching song on his drum as he walked forward, stopped and completed the tune while people assembled. "Hirek! Ma Mo Hirek!" the Hungarian Town Crier reached to the loop on the drum strap, pulled out the paper, and unrolled it. "Today is September 20, 1944. Russians continue their move to the west, taking territories. The Hungarian Army is destroying railroad tracks in an effort to put up roadblocks to hinder their progress." He continued his announcements, but Franz didn't listen.

Hold back their progress? A shot of panic moved down Franz' spine. Why didn't the Crier say stop the Russians? Franz turned and ran home. What was going to happen?

Apparently the news had already come. A group of Mama's friends gathered around her on the sidewalk. Some of their voices were shrill, others filled with sniffles, but they didn't shout. Staying close to the wall, he walked by and went through the gate. Opa wasn't home. He'd said something about going to the vineyard in Legin, but with eleven fields he could be at any of them.

The sound of Kati's happy chatter led him around the barn to find them. Oma and Kati were busy plucking feathers off a dead chicken. Who could he talk to? If only Vati were here.

He wandered away, not wanting to be with the women. He sat on the ground, opened the gate a little, peeked through it and leaned on the wall. He'd wait for Mama.

"The men from Batschsentiwan, from seventeen to fifty, are being forced into German uniforms." Franz didn't know her name, but recognized the woman with wild and curly gray hair. "All they had is rifles as they marched out of town to the train station. No one knows where they are. What good can these last-minute soldiers do? No training, pitiful weapons?"

"It's too late!" a stout, grandmotherly woman cried. "The Russian Army is coming and we can't do anything. They're beasts who don't feel the cold and can go without food and drink for weeks at a time."

"They'll rape us all!" another woman hissed.

Franz lowered his head to his knees and squeezed his eyes closed. Could it be worse here than bombing in Leipzig? He thought of the Russian prisoners, starved and miserable. They'd been men, thankful for any food and kindness. Confused, he felt both hope and fear.

"Gerta said they tie women across the opening of cannons before they shoot, then laugh when their bodies are blown to pieces." Frau Haut twisted a handkerchief in her hands.

"My husband got some tarps and is building a top over our wagon to load what we can. We're leaving for Hungary." Frau Penz looked around at her group of friends and neighbors. "We have three growing girls and we're afraid to stay here. The Wehrmacht will protect us on our way."

Mama didn't say anything, and Franz moved his head so he could see her. She listened, chewed her lower lip and clasped her hands tightly.

"My brother lives in Austria, so we're leaving soon to stay with them." Tears rolled down Frau Braun's thin cheeks. Mama gave her a fierce hug. "What will your family do, Elisabeth?" Frau Braun asked.

Franz held his breath as he waited for Mama's answer.

"We've talked, but no decision has been made. I want to run—I want to stay."

Just then, Franz felt Mama's eyes on him. He wiggled back, away from the opening.

She excused herself from the group and joined him.

"Oh, Franz . . ." she said quietly, as she sat beside him in the grass.

"If they come, maybe it won't be so bad." Franz said. "Remember how Hugo's father, and lots of men who worked for the Company, hated all the prisoners, spit on them and did everything to be mean. But we weren't all like that. Some of us tried to help the Russians."

"I don't suppose all of them will be cruel to us, either." She squeezed his hand. "We don't really know what's going to happen. Fear makes people imagine the worst."

Again, they sat in silence. "What did you do today?" Mama asked.

"The Town Crier said Hungarians are bombing the tracks to slow the Russian advance." Franz said. "Mama, where do you think Vati is?"

"I don't know, *liebling.* Or Uncle Adam, or Tony Baumgartner's father, either." She took a deep breath and let it out slowly. "We have plenty to do besides sit and worry the day away!" With that, she stood up, brushed grass off her skirt, and clapped her hands.

"Do you need me to help you find something to do?" Mama waited for his answer, but Franz gave her a wobbly smile and turned and ran over to Anton's.

Opa supervised the harvest from early morning to early evening. All the care for the horse, cow and hogs fell to Franz, both before and after school. Oma and Mama worked the kitchen garden and canned everything possible for the winter ahead. Now he went to get the news every day. At first, the villages mentioned were far away, but every week the Russians occupied another place. And they were coming this way.

Franz tried to ignore the distant sounds of *acht-acht* cannons, but always searched the sky. With each explosion, he trembled for just a moment. Sound carried for miles in their flat, agricultural land and he knew the danger could be far away. But he couldn't quite believe it enough to relax.

While doing after-school chores, Franz heard the gate open, and then slam shut. He stepped from the barn, pitchfork in hand and watched Anton, Adam, Stefan and Toni march in with their sticks swinging and Tony carrying a ball under his elbow.

"Over here!" Franz hollered and waved. "Let me guess . . . Land Hockey! Am I close?"

"Smart, isn't he?" Tony grinned at the others, who were nodding.

"I can finish this later," Franz said as he reached over to hang the fork on the wall. Quickly, he pumped water to wash his hands, and got his stick.

They played three rounds and the sun lowered in the sky, when Franz heard a sound he'd heard before, but didn't recognize. He looked up the street and saw a big motorcycle, with a sidecar, in the distance. He'd never seen one around here, but had in Leipzig. Curious, the game forgotten, he started running toward it, the others following close behind.

The driver stopped by Franz's house. As they got close, Franz could see he wore a gray field cap of the German Army.

The man swung one leg over the seat and stood beside his bike, never looking away from the boys. His uniform hung on thin shoulders. His face had no softness, only bones and angles. Something about him seemed familiar.

Abruptly, Franz stopped and stared. He didn't know what to do.

"Who is he?" Anton asked from the side of his mouth.

"Go get my mother and grandmother." At Anton's still posture, Franz's elbow swung into his friend's ribs. "Now!"

Anton ran, Adam and Tony stepped back a few steps.

Franz wanted to ask the stranger if he were Uncle Adam, but couldn't. He simply stared, then closed his mouth and cleared his throat.

"Hello," the visitor growled.

He'd been a little kid when Uncle Adam left. Now Franz searched his face, noticing deep-set, brown eyes, like Opa's. He was the same height, taller than other men in the village. This man had pale skin, limp hair, and serious face. Uncle Adam was strong, with sun-warmed skin and thick black hair. He'd always been ready for fun. Franz stared at the man who stood by the motorcycle.

No, he just looked a tiny bit like Uncle Adam. Both relief and disappointment flooded him at this conclusion.

"Can. . . can I help you?" Franz asked.

The gate swung open and Oma and Mama hurried out.

Mama's eyes went directly to Franz, then slid to the stranger. She gasped, her fingers splayed on her cheeks. Oma, tears already pouring down her face, reached out an arm as she neared the man. "Adam!"

23

August 1944- twelve years old
Stanišić, the time of the Russians

"Y OU'VE LOST SO much weight!" Tears rolled down her cheeks
as Oma hugged her son. "Have you been sick? Are you
home to stay?"

Franz ran ahead to open the gate. Oma and Mama each took
one of Uncle Adam's arms and escorted him to the porch and
into the most comfortable chair.

"I'm not exactly sick," he said. "We weren't too far from here,
and I could use the bike, but tomorrow I have to go back. We're
retreating from Russia." Uncle Adam leaned his head back and
closed his eyes.

Franz stopped. His heart began to race. So that's why the
Russians were coming to Yugoslavia! Mama stopped moving,
except her eyebrows came together. She fell, rather than sat on
her chair beside Adam.

Withdrawing meant running away, didn't it?

Franz sat on the porch, leaned against a yellow-brick pillar,
and clasped both hands around his knees, and curled into a ball.

No one said anything. The words "retreating from Russia"
echoed in Franz' mind. Mama and Oma remained silent, their
eyes unfocused.

"I'm not asleep, just enjoying the peace." Uncle Adam sat up. "I've dreamed about being with all of you. I know you have a lot of questions and I'll tell you about me later. Right now, I want to hear your news. Elisabeth, I'm relieved to see you. I didn't know if you'd been able to leave Leipzig."

"We came back a few months ago. Right away Stefan was conscripted into the Army." Mama blinked away sudden tears.

"I'm sorry. I don't suppose you know where he is, do you?"

"No." Mama straightened her back. "I worry, but it helps to keep busy each day."

"Your uniform is black," Franz interrupted. "I see you have the SS bolts also."

Uncle Adam nodded. "Yes, I'm in the SS, with a fighting division. That means I'm on the front lines. I didn't want to be a guard, so this is better. I'd rather be here." His eyes darkened as he looked down at his lap.

Franz noticed Kati peeking around the kitchen door, and waved his fingers for her to come. It was all she needed to skip to Mama's side. With a glance at Franz, she turned a shy, but sunny smile on Uncle Adam. Mama put her arm around Kati and kissed her soft hair. Oma laughed quietly. Franz swung his leg along the side of the porch as he watched Uncle Adam's face light up with surprise.

"This can't be Kati?" At Mama's nod, Uncle Adam shook his head and chuckled. It sounded rough, kind of mixed with pain. "It has been a long time. I guess I expected a baby, not this little charmer. It's good to see you, Kati."

"Hi," Kati squeezed beside Mama and looked pleased, then ducked behind her arm.

Uncle Adam turned his gaze to Franz. "I can tell, by the deepness of your dimples, you're glad to be back. Other than family and friends, what did you like best the first few days?"

"Food, most of all!" Everyone laughed. "Not family or friends?" Franz repeated thoughtfully. "The first few days. . . I enjoyed the chickens grumbling and the rooster doing roll call in the morning. You know how the Punkte complains when we're late milking her? I took my time a few days so she'd call for me."

Uncle Adam grinned and nodded. "Anything else?"

"I didn't miss the outhouse, or the smell of it, but I liked the sound of its door banging shut." Franz stopped, feeling silly.

A soft expression came into Uncle Adam's brown eyes as he thought about it. "I miss those things, too. It's the little events, like sounds and smells, that surprise us, isn't it?"

And Franz relaxed.

Oma went to the kitchen and brought out a boxful of green beans. As she and Mama snapped them, short beans were dropped into a clean bucket. Uncle Adam joined in, and Kati inched forward to help.

"Is it fun to drive?" Franz gazed toward the gate.

Uncle Adam smiled, and in that moment Franz saw the Uncle Adam he remembered. "The motorcycle?"

"Yes."

"Come on, I'll let you see the BMW for yourself." Adam stood and swept his hand to let Franz lead the way.

"Tony!" Franz shouted when he saw his friend on the sidewalk. "Meet my Uncle Adam." Franz turned to Uncle Adam. "This is Tony Baumgartner. His father went into the *Wehrmacht* just before Vati did."

Introductions over, both boys circled the vehicle. "Look at these knobby tires! Bet they don't slide."

"No, they don't," Uncle Adam grinned. "Soldiers can go almost anywhere on these. Mud, ice and snow are nothing. It's able to weave around anything in its path."

"What's this for?" Tony pointed to a protruding part.

"It's a side car." Uncle Adam removed his duffle bag and flung it inside the gate. "It can carry a person, but mostly hauls weapons. Sometimes it's used for courier or scouting work."

"We sure could have used this in the Hitler Youth!" Franz laughed in delight. He could see himself zipping through the woods, dodging trees and rocks. He moved around to the front.

"You've blacked out the headlight." Franz brushed his hand over the rounded glass. "When we lived in Leipzig, every light had to be hidden at night so planes couldn't figure out where they were, or see where we were, either."

"Hop on, I'll take you around the block," Uncle Adam said as he swung his leg over the front seat, and pushed the kick-start.

Franz hopped on the seat behind him, and Tony into the sidecar.

"This is noisy!" Franz shouted into the incredible roar. "Woo!" He shouted in victory as he held his arms out like an eagle's wings.

"My hair's blowing away!" Tony hollered in the wind.

All too soon, they were back at the house. The boys jumped off and opened the big gate for Uncle Adam to drive through.

"Think Anton and Stefan will believe what we just got to do?" Tony shouted in excitement.

Franz hesitated. He glanced at Tony, then Uncle Adam. He might miss something if he left, but he wanted to brag to his friends.

"Go on. I'll help you with the livestock this afternoon." Uncle Adam glanced at the barns and pasture, and then turned to the porch. "I'll visit with the women, so go be with your friends."

"Kati's asleep now and nothing will wake her," Mama said that evening. She sat at the kitchen table beside Uncle Adam and took his hand. "Now, please tell us where you've been."

Uncle Adam glanced at Franz, and hesitated.

"You can speak freely in front of him," Mama said, and Opa and Oma nodded.

"I'll tell you now, but I won't talk about it again." Uncle Adam said each word distinctly. "First, I was sent to Greece, to Thessaloniki, then Volos. I wish I could find words to tell you how beautiful the Aegean Sea is. It's bright and not like any blue I've ever seen. Long stretches of sandy beach make anyone want to take off their shoes and stay. I was there almost a year. Summers are hot and dry, winters short, and temperatures mild. In peacetime, it would be a wonderful place to visit."

Franz leaned forward, listening intently.

His uncle tented his hands. "The Greeks hated us." He shrugged. "We occupied their country, ate their food and couldn't be ignored. No surprise we were surrounded by hostility." He suddenly snapped his fingers. "I almost forgot to tell you I got the candies you sent. There was plenty to share with my buddies. It takes parcels so long to arrive, that sometimes guys receive ruined food." His nose wrinkled and he waved one hand in front of his face. "We appreciated anything. But the candies were delicious and we tried to take our time with them. Thank you."

Uncle Adam hesitated.

The clock ticked loudly, in tune with Franz' heartbeat. Uncle Adam couldn't stop now!

"Then came Russia." Uncle Adam got up and poured himself another glass of wine. His hands shook slightly. "It was bad everywhere along the Eastern Front, but especially Stalingrad in the winter. It's the backside of hell. But instead of perpetual fires, it's constant cold beyond anything you can imagine. We suffered in minus twenty-two degrees for months, and we weren't dressed properly. Food came sporadically and was never quite enough."

Franz felt a shiver run up his back.

"I couldn't hate them, their leaders yes, but not them. They were hungry as well."

Oma's face paled. Opa bowed his head.

"Go on," Mama whispered, and then bit her lower lip.

"Everything froze. Vehicle motors, tires, anything that needed to move. We hated to relieve ourselves because we feared injury from frostbite. Our hands and feet were always a problem. Far too many of our brothers simply froze to death."

Mama's finger wiped the corner of her eye. Opa's fisted hands crossed on the table.

Franz heard the words, and believed them only because they were from Uncle Adam. Franz couldn't think about it now. Later, he would.

"Snow got so deep at one time we burrowed little rooms, to sleep out of the wind. We scooped it up and melted it in our mouths for water," Uncle Adam continued.

"You okay, Franz?" Mama's sad, brown eyes looked into his smoky blue ones.

He couldn't speak, but gave a jerky nod. Taking a deep breath, he relaxed his face and body. If he appeared too upset, Uncle Adam would guard his words, or Mama would send him to bed.

"The Russians kept coming, and coming," Adam continued. "Our troops grew smaller, theirs seemed inexhaustible. We should have been allowed to retreat then. Our horses barely managed to move from one step to the next. They suffered the same as we did."

"Along with the shortage of food, we had insufficient ammo. Russian equipment runs on diesel, rather than petrol and it rarely catches fire when hit. Many of their crews escaped to fight another day. We battled against women and children sent in as part of the Russian front. They were all gaunt, too, but dressed warmly." Palms together, Adam's lips pressed against his fingertips. "What devilish goals did Hitler and Stalin gain by having two starving armies fighting each other? The whole damn thing was insane!" He pounded the flat of his hand on the table as he spoke.

Overwhelmed by the pain in Uncle Adam's eyes, Franz looked down. His heart beat rapidly, and something heavy twisted in his chest.

"You're right. It is crazy, and evil, too." Opa's voice had never sounded so low. With trembling hands, he tamped down tobacco in his pipe. "I didn't think anything could be worse than my time in the Great War, but I could never have imagined what's happening now. But remember," he said as he focused on each of them, "there *will* be life after war, and it's coming to an end." Opa turned his deep-set eyes to Adam and wagged his index finger. "We'll always have our land, Adam, and you'll come back. Through working the soil, planting seeds, watching them grow, and bringing in the harvest, all your memories of war will begin to heal."

Franz squeezed his hands beneath the table and gazed at the others. Mama and Oma cried silently. Oma blotted her face on her apron, and Mama used her handkerchief.

When Franz and his parents returned to Stanisic, leaving the terrifying bombing and the fear in Leipzig, he gradually stopped thinking about it so much. And he'd had protection and food there. Not quite enough and not tasty, but food.

"Opa's right," Franz spoke aloud before he thought.

Suddenly, Uncle Adam gave a twisted smile. "I know. The trick is remembering it more often."

"You said food was scarce," Oma ventured hesitantly. "What did you eat?" Her forehead wrinkled as she leaned over the table.

"Rations when they arrived. Actually, we ate anything – dogs, rats, horses frozen to death, any plant life available. If not for the danger of frostbite, we would have boiled our leather gloves to eat." Adam sipped his wine. "This war may be won or lost according to how well-fed the army is."

Franz studied a framed photo hanging on the wall of Uncle Adam standing slightly behind Opa and Oma as they sat on the porch. Dressed in black, formal clothes, their expressions serious, the picture brought a lump to Franz' throat. The old Uncle Adam had been strong and healthy. How much he'd changed!

"Thoughts of home and the smokehouse, pantry and cellar filled with food, kept me going. Some men gave up, but I'd think of all of you and had reasons to push on."

His long legs stretched before him, Uncle Adam laced his fingers behind his head. "Next time, I'll be back to stay." He nodded to Opa, as if the words were a promise.

At once, Oma and Mama moved to his side and hugged him at the same time. "You need a good night of sleep." Oma's voice quivered.

Adam agreed, and within minutes, everyone had gone to their own beds. Franz tossed and turned, unable to stop thinking of all he'd heard. Nightmares of his father far away and suffering kept coming. In one, Vati walked over a field of ice. He struggled alone, calling for help. Franz tried to take a down-filled blanket to him, and had pockets filled with food, but he kept being pushed back. Vati couldn't see or hear him. Franz woke, screaming for Vati to come.

—※—

Awake early the next morning, Franz' first thought was Uncle Adam. What time would he leave? Franz dressed and raced to the kitchen. With his hand on the door, he heard Adam's voice, and it didn't sound gentle.

"Just keep Kati close to you at all times, and don't let her out of —."

As Franz opened the door, Adam stopped and Franz felt all eyes on him.

"Just the young man I'm waiting for," Uncle Adam said, in a quick change of tone. "Before I go, I'd like to help muck out the barn one more time. Then I can leave in a fragrant cloud of cow and horse manure." He smiled and winked.

Franz laughed. "Maybe we can oblige you with some horse flies, too."

"What's the plan? Do we eat or work first?"

"I usually get the work done, then change clothes and wash up." He glanced at Mama. "Can I stay home from school?"

"No, your Uncle Adam is leaving as soon as you get finished." Adam slung his arm over Franz' shoulders. "I'm ready!"

Franz looked up at Uncle Adam as they walked off the porch. "Can't you stay here? You could hide."

"I wish I could." Uncle Adam stopped and pulled Franz into a fierce hug. "Deserters are shot on the spot and you never know who'll turn informant to collect a reward. I might be willing to chance it, but I'd put all of you in the same danger. My survival odds are greater out there. We'll be together again later, when it's safe."

Punkte gave a loud moo from the barn and broke the moment.

"She's getting upset," Franz grinned. Uncle Adam got the bucket, and like old times, began to milk the cow. Franz replaced hay and water and together, they both did a basic job of cleaning the stalls before they joined the rest of the family.

The sidecar held the duffle bag, and Oma carefully positioned jars of canned red cherries, soft orange peaches, and green beans and those were only the ones on top. Franz thought it looked a bit like Christmas, but couldn't smile. Mama bustled out with packages of cured bacon and ham.

"What's your best guess on where you'll be sent, son?" Opa asked the question, but Mama and Oma stopped activity and waited for Uncle Adam's answer.

"I know we're slated to go west. Anything has got to be better than Russia," he said with a shrug.

"There's a possibility of Denmark. For protection, Germany has kept forces throughout the war. But maybe we'll be near Belgium. Troops are being built up to protect Germany from English forces. Also, we hear rumors of a German offensive, maybe to split the Allied line in half. Some people think it might break the Americans' spirit to fight. Without them, the other Allies couldn't continue."

"Either place would be closer to supply lines of food. I don't know why Hitler continues. The Allies have had control of the air ever since they grounded the Luftwaffe months ago." He brushed his hand through his hair. "But I have to go. I love you all."

With last hugs, he swung his leg over the cycle seat, stood up and gave the kick-start all of his weight. "I almost forgot to warn you the Russians will take the horse for food. There's nothing you can do about it. But hide the cow somewhere if it's possible."

With final goodbyes said, he left in a sudden roar. Franz, hands in pockets, watched him leave until he stood alone, looking at nothing but a cloud of dust from the dirt street.

24

Fall 1944 – twelve years old
Stanišić, still living at their home

"WHO ARE THE new guys living with our neighbors?" Franz nudged Anton, and nodded to a girl about their age, and two boys a bit older.

"They're from Germany. My father said their parents sent them to farming villages like ours. It's safer here, I guess."

"Safe?" Franz raised an eyebrow. "With Russians sweeping through Yugoslavia?"

Anton shrugged. "They aren't friendly."

"I'd hate to go somewhere away from family." Franz said thoughtfully. "When my parents left for Leipzig, I was with my grandparents. Then I left here, but it was because I went to my parents."

"I'd hate that," Anton said. Silently, both boys walked home.

"Good day, Franz. Your cow settled in as part of the herd very quickly last night. I think she likes the company," Herr Balli spoke in German, but not as a native. "You did not have trouble finding my place, did you?"

Franz looked around in the soft dawn light. To his right, he saw a small house at the end of a rutted trail. Straight ahead, an old wagon sat in front of a barn, faded to various shades of grey.

"No," Franz said, speaking Hungarian. "Opa explained where to turn, and it's only a mile. It was strange not to hear Punkte doing her usual moaning this morning."

"I will show you must do every day." Herr Balli stood about five feet eight inches. He had a round, ruddy face, etched with smile lines, and bright blue eyes. Fair hair poked out his ears. A pipe clamped between his lips looked as if it belonged there.

"I am sure your cow is complaining now!" The older man turned back to the barn, the fragrance of his pipe tobacco floating behind him. "As soon the wagon is ready, I will show you the corral."

Franz followed him into the barn and helped bring two oxen outside and hitched them up. The same size, both animals were short-legged and stout, but one was black and the other red, with identical horns gradually curved upward.

Seated in the wagon, they rolled forward. "It is about three miles away." Herr Balli flicked the reins to keep the oxen moving. "Since these boys are just big babies, you will have no trouble getting them hooked up by yourself."

As they traveled, Franz saw fewer homes, and more pastures. Trees were losing their dry, and sometimes colorful, leaves. He relaxed in the rhythm of the wagon's rocking. "Would you rather I call you Balli úr or Herr Balli?" he asked in Hungarian.

"I am around so many Germans, the herr will be fine. It is good that you speak Hungarian, Franz. Not just because I am more comfortable, but it may help you in the days ahead. How did you learn?"

"Mama and I visited with Yugoslavian and Hungarian customers in our butcher shop in Sombor, as well as Germans. I'd listen to Mama and the customers were friendly to me and it was easy to learn."

The sounds of many persistent long, lowing *murrr* sounds in the near distance grew louder. Franz's dimples deepened in smile. "I know who is crying the loudest."

Herr Balli turned to face Franz, and nodded. "They are thirsty."

"Yeah," Franz said. "Is the pond far from here?"

"The nearest one is miles away." Opa's friend grinned, and shifted his pipe to the other side of his mouth. "We have a well."

Franz saw a small shack, with a corral beside it. He laughed as he noticed all the cattle stood facing the wagon, every head moved with a great deal of grumpiness. "Dogs would welcome us cheerfully instead of all the complaining!" Franz had to shout over the noise. He jumped down and ran to open the gate for the oxen to enter. Once inside, they unhitched them.

"The well is over there," he said, pointing his finger.

Franz was glad to be able to get a drink. He drew up the bucket of water and dipped a ladle for refreshing water. He got the blue enamel milk pail, with white spots, from the wagon, and pulled Punkte away from the others. The herd grew louder, but he ignored their big eyes and slobbering mouths, and squatted for about fifteen minutes to milk her. He put the pail in the wagon, popped the lid on, and turned around.

The farmer's eyes twinkled and he leaned on the well, and then swept his hand out to indicate the other animals. "They're waiting."

Now surrounded by steers and a few heifers as well as their own cow, Franz remembered hearing something about the nearest pond being miles away. He looked around the corral and, in a flash, understood what he needed to do. He had assured Opa he'd take care of the whole herd as a way to thank Herr Balli for saving Punkte. And he would. Even if it was a bigger job than he'd guessed.

There were so many, very thirsty cattle crowding around him.

He straightened his back, and got to work. Over and over, he pumped water from the well. "There are twenty-two of these big beasts," he grumbled under his breath. His arms had never been so tired.

At last, the animals milled around and gathered in a group. At a nod from the older man, Franz unlatched the gate and watched them rapidly leave the corral and fan out to eat rich grasses on nearby open pasture.

"They will be content roaming until noon."

"What happens then?" Franz had to ask.

"They are thirsty." The little man chuckled as he watched Franz. "They will need water again, and rest for an hour or more." He nodded to the little shack just outside the corral. "There is a bed inside for you to nap. When they get restless, turn them out to pasture again. Guess what we do about four o'clock?"

Franz groaned. "Water them again?"

Franz finished his early morning chores at Herr Balli's, and hurried home to clean up for a chilly walk to school. He placed the milk pail on the kitchen table and turned to the door when someone called his name.

"Franz! The Russians are here," Anton shouted from the yard. "Come on, let's watch!" Unable to stand still, Anton hopped from one foot to the other, his brown hair standing out like a thistle.

Franz didn't hear sounds of battle. And he sure didn't want to get in the middle of one.

"My father just came from the drug store and told me!" Anton stepped back, ready to run.

Terrible pictures tumbled in Franz's mind of all he'd heard. He was afraid, but very curious about them, too. "School will close anyway!" With that decision, he was ready to go.

Stefan and Tony, leaving their yards, joined them and together they all raced to the primary street on the north side of the village. Franz' heart began to thump, in time with the marching of feet. He didn't say anything, and neither did his friends. The troops drew closer, coming by foot or riding huge, thick-haired horses. They wore tan uniforms, with green patches on their collar points. Well-worn and scruffy black boots reached almost to their knees.

These very skinny men didn't look German or Hungarian. Most had rather flat faces, and large cheekbones, with dark, wiry hair. None of them had beards.

Franz stepped back from narrow-eyed glares. He remembered the women's hysteria weeks ago when they feared this day. Would these soldiers tie living women to the opening of tank cannons before shooting?

A few reminded him of Uncle Adam as they glanced at the townspeople with sadness. His uncle had sympathized with the Greeks' resentments when he was stationed there. Franz, remembering the prisoners in Leipzig, shoved his hands in his pockets and gave a brief nod to one who met his eyes. Many had heavily scarred faces and arms. Four rows of men, including the ones who appeared friendly, turned off at an intersection. A large military truck trailed behind the group.

Franz nudged Stefan, next to him, and whispered to others, "Let's see what they're going to do."

The march continued, past two more intersections and they stopped and broke formation. Horses fed on nearby grassy lots as soon as they were released. Two men carried a table and chairs from the house behind them.

Franz, afraid to draw attention, pretended he didn't see those who growled sharp words and shoved their comrades out of their way. He understood those who stepped aside, and kept their mouths closed. Why should they battle each other?

When a camp fire was started, and food brought out, Franz felt uncomfortable watching them divide up meager portions. Now he understood why Uncle Adam said the Russians would likely eat their unimpressive horse.

"My father wants me to deliver some shoes," Anton said.

Ready for a reason to leave, Franz and his friends ran back to the neighborhood.

Like ants in springtime, Russians spread up from the south into the village during the next few weeks. Each afternoon, from a distance, the boys followed their progress.

⸺

October 20, 1944

Franz cut a chunk of bread off the loaf and grabbed a piece of smoked sausage from the pantry, wrapped it up, and put both into the satchel over his shoulder. He grabbed the milk pail from the kitchen, and waved to Mama as he headed to Herr Balli's.

The slurred rumble of Russian voices came before he saw them. Yesterday, Church Street had been the same familiar place it had always been, and Franz knew every German family.

How could he have slept through this? He blinked his eyes, unable to believe the Russians had quietly moved across the street in front of his house, just two blocks up.

Without his friends, he hesitated, and then continued to walk past them. Part of him wanted to look straight ahead and not make eye contact, but, as always, he was curious. He received the usual mixture of hate-filled stares, but also pleasant nods from a few. Taking a deep breath, he tried to look relaxed.

Don't look over your shoulder, he chanted as he passed.

Normally, he enjoyed this early morning walk. He listened to the birds, studied clouds and watched for cattails, which signaled he was near the end of his walk. But today, he worried.

The whole village was now occupied. What happens next? So far, there'd been little shooting and the Germans managed to keep living normally. Or as much as they could while looking over their shoulders and wondering what they should do. Thankfully, Adam had warned Opa to hide the cow and Herr Balli had agreed to take her.

Franz turned off the main road and walked to the barn. "Time to go," he told the oxen, just for the comfort of hearing his own voice. "After you're hitched up, we'll go to the corral." Right now, the quiet made him jumpy. He sighed with relief at hearing the door to the house slam shut.

"Good day." Herr Balli called from the well-worn path to his house. "Is there a problem? You look pale." He cocked his head as he studied Franz's face.

"They're on our block now," Franz said, knowing he needed no explanation. "I saw them as I came here."

The old Hungarian patted the back of the black ox. "Let my wife know when you come and go, if I do not see you. That way, we will know you cannot come. I will manage to take care of them, somehow."

If I can't come. The thought echoed in his mind as he drove to the corral. Fear pumped through his heart. He finally realized they were at the mercy of the Russians, who controlled Stanisic now. Work camps had been set up in other villages, and people taken away. What would happen here?

His world may have changed, but the cattle were just as pushy and cranky as always. Punkte needed to be milked. He relaxed as he did routine work beneath the sunny sky.

After Franz did the milking, he cared for the cattle, hitched up the oxen and rode the wagon back to their barn. Switching from one hand to the other, he carried the heavy pail home.

As he turned onto his street, Franz saw organized activity. An officer studied a map on the table spread before him. He glanced up at one house, returned to the map, and looked at another home, and again he made notes. Was the map about the people who lived in Stanisic?

He shouldn't have come this way. He hoped they didn't notice he carried three gallons of milk.

—⁂—

"Every night since my father left for the army, my mother cries. Sometimes I put a pillow over my ears so I won't hear." Tony's voice was almost a whisper. "Does your mother do that?" His face was turned toward the Russian soldiers, but his eyes gazed at the gray sky.

"I don't know," Franz hesitated as he thought about it. "My room's at the end of the house. Mama and Kati's bedrooms are on the other side of the pantry. I wouldn't hear if she did." Franz shuffled his feet as he and Tony stood under the branches of an old oak tree.

A slightly-built soldier said something in Russian, and interrupted them. Neither of the boys understood. Franz spoke a few words in Hungarian. No understanding. Then Yugoslavian. Nothing.

Reduced to gestures, the soldier, not much older than Franz and his friends, put his hands up in gesture of 'what now'? He shrugged, and flipped his hand forward to invite them to look around. Anton and Stefan walked up behind them and joined in.

Reluctant at first, Franz gradually became comfortable climbing on the truck and tank, and looking at weapons.

"Don't pick it up," Franz hissed at Anton, who had his hand on a weapon. "They're watching."

"I wasn't thinking," Anton mumbled. "I think it's a Mosin-Nagant rifle."

"These fellows need baths." Stefan whispered. "They sure do scratch a lot."

"Yeah," Franz wrinkled his nose.

The next two days, Franz woke early, took a clean bucket and walked to take care of the cattle and milk the cow. He carried it around behind houses on his way home.

With the noon watering, his friends met him at the edge of the German section and they all walked home past the encampment. A man with a round face, and high-pitched voice, motioned them over.

"Shrept," is the way it sounded as he patted his chest and obviously told them his name.

Confused, Franz repeated it back. "Shrept."

The Russian shook his head and said it again. Anton took a shot, "Shep?"

"*Nyet,*" he said. "Shrept," he said very slowly, pointing to himself, as if it would help. Franz and Anton looked at Tony and Stefan. They both shook their heads, each made a try.

"*Nyet,*" he said again as he shook his head.

"We can understand his word for no," Franz said. "So let's call him Nyet Man."

Nodding as though he understood, the man leaned back and smiled. Having given up on making them understand his name, he returned to his work. Though many of his comrades snapped harsh, guttural words, the Nyet Man seemed to ignore them.

"Franz, what are you doing all day, off with your friends?" Mama passed him a potato as the family sat around the kitchen table the one evening.

"Well," he said as he tried to figure out how to explain. "We're hanging around the Russians and watching what they do."

Mama, Oma and Opa all stopped moving and looked at one another.

"Franz, that doesn't sound like a good idea to me," Mama shook her head. "They're here as enemies and not as welcome guests."

"We stay away from the bad ones. But others laugh and let us climb on their trucks and look around.

Franz quickly downed a glass of milk. "We've noticed a lot of them have ugly faces and arms, like they've a million tiny scars."

Both Mama's and Oma's eyebrows shot up and together, they said "Smallpox!"

"What's smallpox?"

"A disease that causes terrible blisters," Oma said. "Scabs form over the blisters and fall off, leaving scars. But it's not contagious by then."

"Oh," Franz nodded, but wanted to tell them something else. "More troops came into the village today and they're beginning to move this direction."

Again, he watched all three of the adults communicate with their eyes. "Just be alert, Franz, and listen to the little alarm inside you," Mama said.

The next day, Franz realized his head itched a lot. His friends scratched, too.

That afternoon, he stopped in the kitchen to get a something to eat after being at Herr Balli's.

"Franz, what's wrong with your scalp?" Oma saw him rubbing and tipped his head toward a lamp and turned it on. "You've got lice from those nasty Russians!" she screamed and stepped back. Her lips opened a bit over clenched teeth and she pointed to the door. "Get out of my kitchen! Now!"

"It's a good thing I baked bread earlier so it's still hot," she pushed him to the outside oven. "Get every stitch of clothes off and don't worry about my seeing you! Your mother and Kati are over at the Hauts."

As Franz stripped, she removed embers from the outside oven. Shivering, he ran to hide behind a nearby bush. Using a stick, Oma picked up each item and tossed it into the oven and slammed the door shut.

"Get over to the pump and wash yourself from top to bottom. And I don't want to hear any protests about how cold the water is. Just do it!"

Stalking off, she went to the shed and brought back kerosene and a raggedy blanket the kittens slept on. She handed it to Franz to wrap around his waist. "Any possible fleas are better than lice," she said as she poured the thin, clear liquid into an old cup. "Lean over." Oma dribbled small amounts on his scalp and scrubbed his head.

"That burns!" Franz screamed, the indignity of being mostly naked, forgotten. "Stop, it's enough! You've got them by now."

She rapped her knuckles on his head and poured more and began to rub again. "I know it burns, just try not to breathe deeply. We've got to get rid of them or you'll share them with the whole family." Oma coughed and turned her head away. "Go ahead, wash your head at the well, and get dressed. Don't you ever go near those disgusting soldiers again!"

"You might as well burn that blanket now! I'll get a comb so we can get rid of every tiny egg."

Mama no sooner got home than Oma told her about the lice, and Opa learned of his disgrace at dinner. Franz kept his head down and forked food into his mouth rapidly. Kati kept asking about the little bugs. Where did they come from? What did they look like? Worst of all, she needed reassurance they wouldn't get on her. A lot of reassurance. Franz wished he could give her a mean look to make her shut up, or better yet, put a gag in her mouth. But he'd be in trouble all over again. He sighed with relief when the subject finally changed.

"After you finish here," Opa said the next morning, while Franz fed the horse, "put the cleanest straw we've got onto the loft over the old cow pen." He spoke quietly, and started to turn away, then stopped. "Don't mention this to anyone," he said over his shoulder.

"What's going on?" Franz, hands on his hips, followed Opa to the door.

"At night, drunken Russian *teufels* roam around and rape our women," Opa roared. He closed his eyes, and when he spoke again, he kept his voice lowered. "Kati's in danger, too. She'll sleep up here with your mother and Oma."

A cold shiver swept up Franz's back. Because of the animals around him, he'd known for years what happened between males and females. And he'd heard about the violence of rape. Fueled by mingled fear and anger, he scooped up the freshest straw. While Franz tossed, he thought of his family sleeping up here, listening for movement below. He made it thick enough so they could burrow in it. They'd be warm and not be seen. What else could he do to protect them?

Each morning, before he went to Balli's, he fed and watered the horse and cleaned out his stall. Mama, Kati and Oma climbed down the ladder, fully dressed, and made their way to the kitchen. Franz ate, and walked the mile to Herr Balli's to get the wagon and drive to the corral. When finished, he brought milk home.

Everyone in the village remained tense. People began to disappear. Some said they were being taken to Russia to work the mines there. Others were sure they'd been shot and dumped in a trench south of town.

"You forgot one letter, Kati. Read them and see what you didn't write," Franz said as they sat at the table.

With a deep sigh, she tried again. "A, b, c, d, ..."

The big gate squeaked, followed by the harsh sound of a shod horse on the brick walkway. Opa's wagon didn't follow. Franz got up and looked out the window. Sitting tall in his saddle, a Russian soldier had entered the yard. He looked all around, as if he belonged here.

"M, n, o, p ..." Katie's soft voice recited. She hadn't noticed the noise.

Franz peeked through the curtain as the horse slowly walked to the barn and the man viewed inside, and rode back.

"Q, s, t, v— I got it, Franz! I didn't write the 'u' down." Katie grinned at her mistake.

"Well," Franz picked up her slate and took her into the living room, where their grandparents slept. "You do it over, every letter. Surprise Mama with your perfect list. Be very quiet, understand?"

Franz led her to sit on the floor on the other side of the bed, out of view. "I'll be right back. Remember; don't make a sound until Mama calls your name. And stay right here until then!"

Franz stuck his head out the kitchen door. The riderless horse stood at the end of the porch. The man had stepped into Franz's room.

He heard the soft murmur of Mama's and Oma's voices talking in the pantry, between his room and the kitchen. Franz hurried.

With a sinking heart, he saw it was too late. The soldier had a Mosin-Nagant rifle slung over his shoulder and, in stiff strides, headed toward them.

25

Winter 1944/45 – twelve years old
Stanišić – Russian occupied

F RANZ STEPPED FORWARD, then hesitated and turned back. Was it
safe to leave Kati alone? She was perfectly quiet, and Mama
and Oma might need him. Peeking back once more at the kitchen
door, he stepped away. His heart beat rapidly, as he reached the
pantry the same time as the soldier, who glanced at Franz without interest.

"Where can we keep these cherries safe?" Oma's voice was
soft as she took inventory of their supply. "We have plenty to get
us through to the spring yield."

When the soldier stepped into the pantry, Franz moved to
the doorway.

The Russian's rifle was slung over his shoulder.

Oma held a canning jar to the light from outside and dusted
its top with her apron. Then she saw the uniformed stranger, and
froze.

The man looked around, muttered, and pointed toward the
cherries.

Oma shook her head and hugged the jar. She returned his
hostile stare.

"Give me that!" The man spoke Hungarian adequately, but
not fluently.

Oma huffed to her full height while her eyebrows lowered. "No, it's not yours," she replied smoothly in Hungarian.

Mama took Oma by the shoulder. "Just give it to him," she urged her mother in German.

"No, it belongs to us!"

The soldier lowered his firearm and pointed it directly toward Oma.

She looked like a stubborn mule, so Franz stepped into her line of vision. As Oma's eyes focused on him, Franz saw the fire of anger dim. She might be stubborn for herself, but she'd never place family in harm's way.

"Please, mother, give the cherries to him. Now."

Oma handed the canned fruit to Mama, but her eyes were narrowed at the Russian.

Satisfied, the Russian leisurely studied the shelves of food. He jammed the jar of cherries into his pocket, turned, walked back out and got on his horse. At the bang of the gate, they all let out a deep sigh.

"Mama, are you coming?" Kati, cradling her slate board, called from the doorway.

Franz ran to her, grabbed her by the arms and shook her. "I told you to wait for Mama, and not come out!" His shout was whispered as his heart beat even faster at the sight of his precious little sister. If Kati had come out earlier, what would the soldier have done to her?

Kati burst into tears and Mama and Oma rushed to her. "Next time, listen to Franz! He protected you from a bad man." Mama wrapped her in an embrace.

Within minutes, Kati calmed down. "I'm sorry," she said, and slipped her hand into Franz's. Franz hugged her as he looked up at Mama, who gave him a tremulous smile.

While Mama and Oma prepared the evening meal, Franz hurried back to his job at Herr Balli's, but his mind continued to replay what happened. The soldier had clenched his jaw in anger when Oma said 'no'. He'd pointed his rifle at her deliberately. It hadn't been a false threat. Feeling weighed down, Franz couldn't shake the feeling that everything was worse.

By the time he got home, the aroma of *schnitzel* and green beans greeted him. He glanced over the table. They always had plenty to eat, due to his grandparents working their land. Every season, food was preserved for the months ahead. In Leipzig he'd had not quite enough, nor had it been this good. Gazing over the table, he felt the same thankfulness he'd had when they returned here.

"Hmmm. *Schnitzel!*" He inhaled deeply. "My favorite!"

"If the damn Russians can take our food, we'd better beat them to it." Oma slammed plates on the table.

Franz's eyes met Mama's. No one spoke as Opa came in and washed his hands at the sink.

"You've heard about the refugees?" Opa asked Franz before anyone had a chance to tell him what had happened.

Franz shook his head. "You mean the kids from German cities?"

"Yes." Opa sat down at the table. "Last night some of them played a game that involved pretending to get hanged. The chair slipped away too early and a fourteen-year-old boy's neck broke before they could do anything. The other kids ran away in fright."

"How tragic!" Oma exclaimed, eyes wide, as she put glasses of milk by the children's plates.

"It was an accident?" Mama asked in a whisper as she glanced at Kati, who appeared to be absorbed in coloring a picture.

"Some think the young man just gave up and wanted to end it all." Opa's words were heavy, but he cut off a piece of meat, and chewed slowly. He looked at each of them with his piercing, deep-set eyes. "We never give up," he said with a harsh voice.

"No matter what happens, or how bad it is, we <u>never</u> give up." He reached out to Franz' shoulder. "Understand?"

"Yes," Franz said with all the seriousness of a promise.

Bitter weather came with the New Year. It snowed during the night, and a light dusting continued to fall. As always, Franz looked around in the quiet, early morning before he lifted his voice to say good morning to Mama, Oma and Kati.

He heard the ladder being pushed to the opening above. Then it appeared and began come down. He guided it to the ground and the women climbed from their nightly hiding place. Kati ran to the outhouse, and Oma was eager to get to the kitchen. Franz put the ladder away, out of any Russian's sight during the daytime.

Mama helped him care for the horse. As he brought water from the pump, she forked hay into the feeding-box. Shared work went faster, but he really loved the time they spent together, just the two of them, without Kati or Oma.

Franz gave the horse a vigorous rubdown. "Opa gets to use you for another day." He picked up the pitchfork and carried what had been soiled outside to the manure pile. Mama brought new straw to replace the bad.

"Look at that gray sky. Colder weather is coming," Mama said quietly, as they washed in cold water from the pump.

"This is the Hogers' house." A harsh voice came over the wall as Franz and Mama neared the kitchen door.

Mama threw an arm out to stop Franz and lifted one finger to her lips.

"Nikolaus and his wife, Theresia. Their daughter lives here, too. Married name is Elmer. She has two children, the younger is under ten." The speaker was German, and Franz had heard the voice before, but didn't recognize it. "Hoger's son and son-in-law are in the German army."

An indistinguishable answer rumbled from a Russian speaking poor German. Franz and Mama made eye contact. He recognized fear in her, and knew she saw the same in him. Plus her eyes were narrowed and her jaw tensed.

Their voices a low mumble, the two men continued their walk and moved beyond hearing range.

Quietly, Franz and his mother walked on the grass toward the kitchen. Mama opened the door and Franz followed her in, and then drew the door shut with little noise.

"You remember Herr Muller, who lives the next street over?" Mama asked Oma and Opa.

"Yes," Oma placed her spoon, still holding a bit of oatmeal, on the cabinet. "His wife died last year and their children are grown." She cocked her head and raised her eyebrows. Opa stepped closer.

"He's become a snitch!" Mama hissed the angry words. "We heard him giving information to a Russian. Muller told him about Stefan and Adam!"

Oma's face paled and she steadied herself against the cabinet. Opa sat down and bowed his head, hands tightly fisted on the table.

Wanting nothing more than to stay home with his family, Franz knew he had to go care for the cattle. Their cow would be suffering with the need to be milked. Forcing himself to do his job, he went to the pantry to cut off his chunk of ham and slices of bread. He walked to Herr Balli's, took care of the cattle, and carried the milk home. As he drew close, he heard a man with a megaphone making an announcement, and ran to join others at the sidewalk. He sat the blue enamel milk pail between his feet, for safety.

A Russian stood in an open-top jeep as it was driven up the street. "Workers will be taken to labor sites farther away.

We'll inform those chosen in person, but names will be posted several places in the city. Disregarding summons will not be tolerated."

———

Two days later, Franz squeezed through a group of people gathered around a Deportation List posted on the school door.

EACH PERSON ON THIS LIST MUST:
Report to the town square Wednesday, January 24, 1945, at eight o'clock in the morning.
Bring one suitcase, packed for ten days.
Absentees will be found and shot, or a family member executed in their place.

He read the notice twice. It seemed unreal. Feeling nervous, he started at the top of the attachment, ran one finger down the list, and began reading names. He went past those he didn't know, and stopped after the first ten. Were they all women? Reading the first names quickly, he stopped. "No men are on the list," he whispered to himself.

After going straight down the list looking for Elmer or Hoger, he sighed with relief. Mama's name was not there, or Oma's. But Oma was too old to be sent to work, anyway. He went back to the top of the list, looking again for people he knew.

Bauer, Edith. She worked at school, keeping track of the students, and was always nice to everyone. Franz felt a burst of grief for her and her family, and then continued reading.

Huber, Ursula. Franz remembered her as a woman who loved her flowers and seemed to hate people. Few liked her, but seeing her name, Franz regretted that he hadn't ever tried to be friendly.

Lang, Ilse. Her husband helped Opa at sunflower harvest time. She came when they celebrated the seeding. Her husband was gone. Where? Probably the army.

Baumgartner, Katarina. Franz held his breath and read it again. Oh, no! Tony's mother! Heart pounding, he finished the list.

Feeling queasy, he ran home. He pushed open the small gate and found his mother by the laundry basket, shaking out clothing.

Holding a clean, half-frozen shirt in one hand, Mama reached for a clothespin with the other. She nodded around the clothes gently moving in the cold breeze. "I'm glad the sun is out right now, the clothes will smell fresh." She stopped speaking when she saw Franz's face.

"Tony's mom is on the Deportation list," Franz said, and blinked his eyes rapidly.

Mama dropped the shirt over the line and carelessly put the pin on. She reached out and held Franz, who was now as tall as she was. "Oma and Katie are inside. Let's tell Oma and you and I'll go see the Baumgartners."

Oma closed her eyes and, with her right hand, touched her forehead, chest, left shoulder and ended with right shoulder. Opening her eyes, she took the basket and called to Kati to join her at the clothesline.

Mama hooked her arm through Franz's. "I wonder if there's anything that can be done." She chewed her bottom lip.

"I saw Frau Lang's name, also."

Mama squeezed his arm, but said nothing.

Quickly, they were at Tony's home, which was full of weeping women. He glanced around and saw many little figurines of babies and children on small tables and corner shelves. Franz had never thought about it before, but Tony's family now was four women. He lived with his mother, his sister, Berbl, Aunt Lissi, and her mother, Eva. Tony's father had been drafted into the German Army months earlier.

"The rumor is that we're being taken to Siberia, to work in mines." Frau Baumgartner sobbed on Mama's shoulder. "What can I do?"

"Mines?" Franz repeated. "Siberia?" Horrible images came to him. Bitter cold with deep snow and fierce winds. Isolation. Wolves. Death. He looked at Tony, who nodded with grim agreement.

Not long ago, Tony had said his mother cried every night after his father went to the army. How would she survive being taken away?

"Probably coal," Tony said through gritted teeth. "Look at her!" He threw up his hands as he gestured at his mother. "She's not physically tough. What work in a mine can she do?" Shaking his bowed head, he spoke more quietly. "She said she's glad it's her and not my aunt, because Aunt Lissi is strong, like my father. She's convinced that Aunt Lissi's better able to protect Berbl and me. Also, her store provides for us because it distributes rationed goods."

Watching his mother comfort Frau Baumgartner, Franz had the weird feeling he wasn't seeing his mother at all. Mama was in charge, pouring her own strength to her friend through their clasped hands. They could have been the only ones in the room; they listened and talked just to one another. Whatever Mama whispered, made Frau Baumgartner sit up straight, nod her head, and wipe her face dry.

On the way home, Mama was silent. Her eyebrows pulled together in deep concentration.

"Is there any way she can get out of it?" Franz asked.

"I don't know, but I'll find out. Her notice had a Yugoslavian official's signature on it, not Russian, so maybe. I know some of them, and speak their language, so I'm going to try."

Franz noticed a fellow leaning against a brick post of the general store, staring at Mama. Before Franz could say a word, Mama saw the man.

With an intake of breath, she stumbled. "Another German snitch! See the red armband, with black hammer and sickle, on is arm? He dares to swagger and be in plain sight!" Her voice was firm, though her lips hardly moved. She took Franz's arm and stepped off the sidewalk. "Let's cross to the other side of the street."

Franz glanced over his shoulder for a closer look. The traitor stared at him, tilting his chin a notch higher. He certainly didn't look ashamed of himself. He should have.

On the way back to Balli's for the afternoon watering, Franz started to call out to Stefan, who sat on the ground by the wall surrounding his home and yard. Then Franz saw his friend was crying. Without a word he sat next to Stefan and waited for him to talk.

Stefan used his shirt sleeve to wipe his face. "Last night some Russians came next door and raped Erna!" Again, he wiped his face. "She's only seventeen. We could hear her screaming." He buried his face in his hands, ignoring the boys' rule against crying. "I still hear her screams."

Franz had wondered if it were really necessary for Mama, Oma and Kati to sleep hidden in the horse loft. Now he knew.

26

Winter/spring 1945 – twelve years old
Stanišić – Russia occupied

"HELLO, YOUNG FRANZ!" Herr Balli found Franz in the barn, hitching up the oxen. "We will have a heavy snow soon." The old man moved his pipe to the other side of his mouth and puffed it several times. He tipped his gaze up to the gray skyline with low clouds. "That is a sure sign."

"Snowstorms used to be fun," Franz said. "We'd stay home and make snowballs and forts. But nothing's good with the Russians watching us."

Herr Balli gave an understanding nod. "If the weather is too bad," he said, "stay at the corral. I want to go with you today and know you will be fine on your own. It would not do for you to get lost on your way home."

Franz glanced off in the direction of the corral and pasture. Nothing but flat land. If everything were white, he'd have little to guide him. A gust of bitter wind blew around him. It would be lonely up there, by himself. Huddled in his old coat, outgrown, and still marked with the shadow of rabbit blood, he shivered. How long ago he'd proudly carried the dead rabbit home, which landed him in so much trouble when Mama saw the drying stain. Odd, but it was only a year ago.

After the oxen were ready, they moseyed the three miles to the cattle.

The older man gestured off to the west. "Partisans are setting up camp in Gakova for the Russians. I have heard they are filling it with women and children." He clicked the reins on the oxen to step up their speed. "We will not like the changes Communism brings." Looking at Herr Balli's profile, Franz noticed he clamped down hard on his pipe.

"Tito's Partisans are Communists, and so is Russia." Franz tried to remember what he'd heard. "But what does that have to do with us?" he ventured.

"To them, anyone owning land is a capitalist enemy. The state, Russia, owns everything for the collective good. All land will be taken away and their government manage our farms and businesses."

"Opa's properties can't be taken, can they?" Franz' eyes opened wide

"Yes, they will. Our only hope is the Allies winning the war." Herr Balli sighed and shrugged. "Right now, the Bolsheviks need Hungarians, so I am protected. Later, they will swallow my land, as well."

Franz and the older man fell into silence. Franz wondered what Opa would do if he lost his acres. The land and farming were Opa and he was his land. But to hope the Allies win? How could Herr Balli say that?

At the corral, Franz hopped down to lead Punkte over to milk her. Seated on the old tree stump, he slipped off his mittens and began the relaxing rhythm of pulling on her teats. How could communists take away what belonged to Opa? That wouldn't be fair! He'd worked so many years to purchase good land for various crops. It couldn't happen, could it? Around and around thoughts swirled in his mind, of their land, and Tony's mother. Would Mama, or anyone, be able to help her? Punkte moved away and Franz realized he'd begun to milk her harder and faster. He patted her, and mumbled he was sorry. The rest of the time he relaxed and milked her as usual.

Punkte's milk dwindled and Franz wiped her off, and put the lid on the milk pail. He helped Herr Balli finish pumping water for the animals, and turned the cattle out to pasture. All the while his thoughts kept returning to Opa and their home. Oma said the things we worry about never happen, so maybe everything would stay the same.

They strolled to the shed. Franz had rested inside other days, as he waited for the cattle to return to the corral. What would it be like to actually spend the night here? The room was okay, though not like home.

"My suggestion is that you stash food here, in case." Balli took his pipe from the corner of his mouth and pointed toward an old stove. "You can use that for heat, if you have something for fuel."

Franz looked at the simple heater, but no wood or charcoal was there.

"Cow dung?" Franz asked.

Balli's eyes twinkled and he nodded. Franz ran out to get a pile of very dry ones, and pulled a handful of last summer's grass along the fence line and went back to the shed.

Balli reached to a nearby shelf made of rough wood and picked up a broken file, about one-fourth inch thick by one inch wide and two inches long, and a brown cattail. "I left this here last time I stayed, but you'll have to bring more to keep on hand." Balli felt around the shelf for a white flint stone. "Found this along the railroad track." He took some fuzz from the cattail, and put it on the stove's hot plate. "Lean over, and strike the flint with the edge of the file."

At first, it didn't work, but Franz tried again. And again. Finally sparks flew down and the fuzz started to smoke. He leaned forward and blew gently, till it flamed. He beamed, pleased at success.

"Take four cow patties, and stand them up like a cone around the fire." Herr Balli sat on the chair and watched. "Very slowly, drop a bit of your grass in the middle."

Franz reached over and got a little more grass and added it. The flame became stronger. He unbuttoned his coat as the fuel began to generate heat. "It's warmer already." He grinned and rubbed his hands together over the small fire. "If I make it bigger, I bet I could cook with it." He rocked back on his heels, admiring his work. "It seems like it would stink more, doesn't it?"

Herr Balli chuckled and agreed. "Tell your Opa you are welcome to sleep here or stay with my wife and me any time it is not safe to go home."

Franz opened the kitchen door later that morning to the sight of Mama on her hands and knees scrubbing the wood floor in the kitchen. Splash! The rag went into her bucket. She squeezed it out, slapped it down and scrubbed viciously. When upset, she always took it out on the floor.

He felt queasy. What happened with Tony's mother? Knowing he might hear bad news, Franz shut the door with a loud click.

"You're home at last!" she got up and stretched her back. Her lips turned up on one side in a half smile. "Oma and Katie are in the bedroom taking a nap, so I got busy cleaning the floor." She brushed a lock of hair from her forehead, and sighed. "I went to City Hall this morning. My Yugoslavian came in very handy. I talked to one official after the other."

She pulled out a chair and, and motioned for Franz to join her at the table. "I talked to them about Katarina. At first they wouldn't even listen, but I did manage to get one man to look in his records for her orders to be on the train to Russia." She slumped and shook her head. "It did no good, but the last man said if I had come earlier, he might have been able to help."

"So Frau Baumgartner's not safe?" Franz thought of Tony, and his heart twisted.

"No, I was too late. She's gone. I'm sorry." Tears formed in her eyes, and she brushed them away. "But now I know who to talk to, and to do it quickly, not wait overnight." She bit her lower lip. "By the time I got home, another woman came to see me. She had just received orders that she has to leave tomorrow. I went right back and pleaded with him to help keep her here. She has small children, so he said that'll help. We'll find out early in the morning." Her hands on the table folded into fists. "I'm afraid this is only the beginning."

Oma yawned as she came out of the bedroom, and poured a glass of water. "I thought to stay and help Kati go to sleep, but it seems I drifted off as well," she explained as she patted Franz's back and pulled out another chair. "How are things at Herr Balli's?"

"He wants me to stay there if the weather gets bad. I think I'll store food up there just in case."

"Good. Anything you take will be hidden from the Russians!" Oma's eyes narrowed as she spoke. "We can line your coat with food. I hope you don't get stuck there, but if you do, you'll be fine. And we can hide our supplies right under their noses!" Oma sneered in anticipation of besting the Russians even in a small way.

That day and the next, Franz stopped on the way to the corral, gathered cattails for the fire, and collected dried patties and stored them in the cabin. With smoked meat and canned vegetables and fruit, he knew there was plenty for a long stay, if needed.

The third morning, walking to the kitchen, he saw large flakes of snow drifting down. Bundling up, a few minutes later, he hugged his family and headed north.

By the time he stopped at Herr Balli's, hooked the oxen to the wagon, and got to the corral, it was clear he wouldn't be going home that day. Eyes blinded by snow, he milked Punkte, and stopped frequently to blow warm breath on his hands. Putting gloves back on, he watered the cattle, and scooped snow away from the gate so it could be pushed open enough for them to file out. Two large steers headed east, followed by the rest of the animals.

"I hope you know where you're going," Franz mumbled to the cattle as he closed his eyes against the cold wind.

Back at the cabin, it was time to renew heat.

At first, he paced as worries came in bunches. If Tony's mom had to go to Russia, what would happen to her? To Tony? Would they send others to Siberia, the worst place in the world? Who would be safe? His family? Neighbors? He stared out the fogged window, and then thoughts circled on his father. It had been so very long since he left. Where was he? Hesitantly, he wondered if Vati were even still alive.

Franz wiped moisture from the window and peered out. Nothing moved on the road and snow continued to fall. He lay on the bed and watched a spider enlarging her home. He poked a hole in it and watched her repair the damage. His eyes drifted closed frequently, but worries dogged his mind. Finally, the animals returned and it was time to bundle up again, let them in and close the gate. Stomping his boots against the cold, Franz pumped bucket after bucket and watered the whole herd. The cattle's big, hairy bodies radiated heat and formed a wind-break around him. Tired again, it was a struggle to get through thick snow to the cabin, while the animals huddled and rested in the corral.

Back in the shed, he built another fire with the flint and file over cow patties. Within minutes, warmth returned.

Tired, he curled up under a blanket to rest. What were those squeaks and scratchy sounds? He poked his head out and gazed around.

Three big rats ran from place to place, their noses twitching. Then Franz saw several holes in the floor. "Scat!" he screamed, causing two of them to scurry away.

"Get out!" he shouted at one who sat up and looked at him before turning and escaping. Franz went through his pockets and found his slingshot. Picking up the flint stone, he sat on his bed, back braced on the wall, his knees up. Franz rested his head and waited. Scrabble, squeak. Without noticeable movement, Franz squinted his eyes and searched for the source. One rat sat up, scanning the room. Franz pulled back the rock, aimed and let it go. Bam! He got him. Silence reigned. Picking up the rat by his tail, he took it outside, and finished it off with a large rock.

His heart sank when he picked up the flint stone. It had broken in two pieces. Fortunately, while one was very small, the other was large enough to use. He'd better find something else to use as a missile. If it broke again, it'd be really hard to start sparks.

Finally, he heard the herd as they came back, snorting and grunting. He welcomed the activity. Up and down he pumped water, listening to the rhythmic sound of metal moving against metal.

That night, he slept with the file, and banged it on the edge of the bed when the rats sounded too close. He hugged the smoked meat close to him. He'd have to find a way to store it here safely.

Unable to sleep deeply, he worried about neighbors from Stanisic being sent to Russia, and what they might suffer. Not only the cruelty of their captors, but their famous sub-zero temperatures? How would they survive?

Where was Vati? Uncle Adam? When would the war be over? Ever?

Snow no longer fell when the sun came up the next morning. Franz eagerly ran through his chores. Putting the milk pails in the wagon, he hooked up the oxen and was on his way. He dropped off one pail with the Ballis and hurried home with the other.

He felt he'd been gone a long time, but it was only two days.

As he reached home, two smiling Russians led their horse to the street. Franz started to object, and then closed his mouth. It was useless. One of the soldiers carried a lumpy flour sack over his shoulder. Both of their pockets bulged with canned food.

Stomach churning, and anger simmering, Franz dashed inside. What if they had hurt his family? His heart beat rapidly.

"Mama!" he cried as he opened the kitchen door. Kati hurled herself into his arms, and Oma turned from stirring a pot on the stove. He bent to tickle Kati then glanced at Oma. "I saw our horse leaving."

She nodded, stirred the food again, and sat down at the table with a sigh. She patted a place for Franz. He had a feeling whatever she had to say wouldn't be good. He waited.

"After you left, they came for your mother." She blinked back tears. "A much heavier blizzard hit Sombor. The soldiers took many able-bodied people, and said they had to walk there to clean off the airfield. The Russians can't land when the snow is so deep, I guess. She was told that she'll return home after the job is finished."

"In Sombor? They walked?" Franz's voice rose and he jumped from his chair. "That's fifty miles away!"

The kitchen door opened and Opa entered.

"Mama had to walk all the way to Sombor in the snow!" Franz' angry voice held accusation. Did Oma and Opa even try to stop it from happening?

Opa tossed his cap on a hook. Without the familiar sparkle in his eyes, he turned on the sink water and began to wash his hands. Opa looked old now. Was that new, or had Franz just not noticed it? He wanted to cry.

Like a light switch, he felt his anger turn from his grandparents to the guilty ones. The evil Russian army. "Why didn't they just use people from Sombor? They didn't need Mama!"

"They're showing their military power by moving people wherever they want. We're farmers and shopkeepers, Franz." Opa's dark eyebrows pulled together, his voice dropped to a whisper. "So many are being sent to Siberia, and that would have been far worse. Men not eligible for military and women over thirty were rounded up for this project. They're expected to remove snow with their own shovels." He slapped his hand on the table. "I've tried to think of what I should have done to keep her here, but I don't know what would have helped."

"She wore layers of clothes to keep warm." Oma used her apron to wipe away a tear. "We packed food, and she carried as much as she could. She took the best wooden shovel."

Kati climbed onto Oma's lap and hugged her. Franz watched precious, innocent Katie. His grandmother and little sister faced each other, communicating with their eyes. Oma lowered her face and pressed it to Kati's small cheek.

Franz exhaled through his lips. He tamped down anger and fear churning inside. For them, he needed to be strong.

He wasn't the only one who was afraid and wondering if Mama would come back.

Franz thought of the distance to Sombor. "It would take two or three days just to get there, wouldn't it?"

"Yes," Opa answered. "My guess is that it'll be more than a week before we see her." Franz noticed he didn't say "if'.

Franz worked at Balli's as usual the next day. He had too much time alone, time to think. That night, at home in his own bed, he tossed and turned, and worried about Mama, but also Vati. Would they be together again? Who would be sent to Siberia next? Or other camps?

Like one of the tumbling pigeons his father raised before the war, Franz felt tossed into the air, uncertain when or if life would settle into place.

27

Winter 1945, twelve years old
Stanišić – Russian occupied

A THIN, DIRTY WOMAN stood at the gate, holding a shovel. Franz narrowed his eyes for a closer look, stepped forward, and stopped. "Mama?" he cried, still unsure, and ran closer.

She leaned on the gatepost, shadows of pain in her eyes. "I'm home. I'm really home," she whispered.

Franz grabbed the shovel and pushed it to the wall. Embracing his mother, he felt lightheaded with relief. Very aware of feeling her bones, he loosened his grasp. He leaned back to search her face. Framed by dull, tangled hair, her eyes seemed large in her face. Franz's heart squeezed as he compared this pitiful sight with the mother he'd seen two weeks ago.

Tenderly, he slipped his arm around her back. "Lean on me," his voice came out a croak past the lump in his throat. She limped as they walked. "Oma!" he cried. Much of the snow had disappeared, but he watched for icy patches that could cause a fall.

The kitchen door opened and his grandmother and sister came running out. "Elisabeth!" Quickly, Oma hurried to Mama's other side. They helped her past the kitchen, into the living room and eased her into a soft chair. Mama leaned back with a grimace.

Then she saw Kati in the doorway, and beckoned to her. Like a hesitant butterfly, the six-year-old climbed onto Mama's lap and, with a peaceful sigh, snuggled into a hug. Tears rolled down Mama's cheeks onto her daughter's blond curls.

Oma reached for Franz' hand and they both squeezed.

Kati had been quieter than usual the past twelve days, refusing to let Oma out of her sight. Every day Franz explained why he must go to Balli's, but it had been hard. Missing their mother, Kati wanted the rest of the family where she could see them.

Too weak to do anything beyond sit, Mama leaned her head back and closed her eyes. Oma gently removed Mama's dirty, worn shoes, and peeled off the socks.

Mama moaned, and pressed her lips together.

Franz heard Oma's indrawn breath the same time as his own, when they saw the wool stockings were covered with fresh red and dark brown blood.

"Throw these in the burn pile." Oma whispered, as she tossed them behind her, out of sight.

"I'll get warm water." Franz muttered as he scooped them up, and turned back to the kitchen. Angry beyond anything before, Franz wanted to pummel a Russian, any Russian.

Teeming with rage, he filled a large pan with water and turned on the heat. He marched outside and threw the filthy items into the barrel used for burning refuse. There'd been no reason for her to go through two weeks of hell! They could have used workers close to Sombor. He kicked a bale of hay, scattering a family of cats. Damned Russians! He needed to scream, curse, and throw things. He banged his fist on the outhouse on the way inside. A deep breath chilled his anger. He had to stop throwing a tantrum. It wouldn't help, and would add to his mother's pain.

His emotions better controlled, he returned to the kitchen and picked up the warm water, soap and a towel and carried them to the living room.

Mama flinched, and bit her lower lip as Oma dunked her feet in the water to soak. Oma lathered her hands and washed first one foot, then the other. Franz carried a hassock over to elevate his mother's tired and blistered feet. Next, he got a blanket and draped it over both his mother and Kati.

While Mama and Kati rested together, Oma went to the kitchen and reheated left-over soup. Since his mother was too weak, Franz fed her one spoonful, then one more and another, until she shook her head.

"We were never warm," Mama said, her voice thready, and slow with the effort to talk. "Just less cold." She gazed at them all with love in her eyes. "I'm so glad to be home!"

"Snow blew constantly on the way there, and we had to lift our feet to keep moving." She looked down at Kati and pulled her closer. "It took two long days to get there, but got to sleep a few hours in a barn. We'd all brought as much food as possible, but it wasn't enough. We shared with those having less. At the end of the first day there, our food was gone."

She hesitated, and closed her eyes.

"Right now, you need to get in bed and sleep," Oma said. "You can tell us after your father gets home."

"No, just bring me a pillow and blanket, please." She tightened her arms around a dozing Kati. "I don't want to move."

While she slept, Franz hurried to Balli's, took care of the cattle, and dashed home again.

———

The evening meal finished, Franz and Opa sat on the porch while Oma helped Mama bathe, wash her hair and dress in clean clothes.

Franz huddled in his coat as he watched Opa go through his nightly ritual with his pipe. He dumped out the dottle, blew to clear the stem, and mixed ground almonds in the bowl to stretch out his rationed tobacco. The routine of Opa's motions as he lit, and puffed his pipe, comforted Franz.

"Mama's going to be alright, isn't she?" He finally voiced his worry, his warm breath flowing in the cold air.

Opa didn't respond, but stared off toward the barn. Just as Franz reached out to touch his arm, Opa cleared his throat. "A few days of rest and farm food and I'm sure she'll be fine." He smoked in silence. "From the time she was a little thing, your mother's always been strong."

The wind whipped up at the same time Kati motioned them inside to the living room.

Mama coughed into her handkerchief. "It's so good to be home, with all of you." Mama's voice was stronger than it had been this morning. "God answered our constant prayers."

Franz lowered himself to the floor and Katie curled beside him. Their grandparents sat in chairs.

Mama bowed her head, as if pulling her words together. "We started work before daylight and finished sixteen or seventeen hours later. Few breaks and very little food. At night we slept on the ground in an open hanger. Those on the outside had the worst of the cold, so we mapped out a rotation system where different people formed an outside ring, and the next night those workers would be in the center, where it was warmer." As she remembered, she pulled her blanket around herself.

"Snow is so heavy. We had to move it far away from the runway. The soldiers kept screaming at us, and used their rifles to hit the slower ones." She picked up her glass from the small table beside her, but her hands shook too much. Oma tipped it, and very slowly dribbled water into Mama's mouth.

She turned her head toward Opa. "Do you remember Karl Schmidt? With a shortened leg?" At his nod, she continued. "We didn't know what started it." Tears rolled down her cheeks. "One of the soldiers started screaming in Russian and he pulled his gun up and shot Karl. Before anyone could go to him, we heard rifles being lifted. We were surrounded by them. We couldn't bury Karl or bring him back. They dragged his body off like he was trash." She wiped her eyes.

"We had just enough food to keep us working. We ate snow to satisfy our thirst." Mama coughed again, and got her breath.

"Finally, they told us to go home. An airplane landed on the cleared runway, and higher-up officers hurried up the stairs. The big shots were eager to get away." Her eyes had a far-away look as she gazed at the wall. "Like machines with no emotion, our feet took one step and then another, all toward home. We didn't talk, but stopped to dig up the rootstock of cattails, and found an old field of asparagus."

She fell silent. Franz leaned forward to see her better. She had fallen asleep again.

Sitting on the edge of the porch, Franz scrapped mud off his boots. Spring rains had been heavy, and the dirt roads refused to dry.

Mama used her foot to push the swing, and faced the gentle sunshine coming through the clouds. She looked so much better than she had several months ago.

Franz' eyebrows shot up when he heard a car stop outside the wall. A door shut, then another. Mama looked alarmed, so he got up and walked to the sidewalk. Three Russian officers entered the gate.

"We must talk to Nikolaus Hoger. Is he here?" One of them asked in badly spoken German.

"Yes," Franz said. His mind whirled. What could this mean? They hadn't been taking away men Opa's age. The speaker looked down his nose at Franz, and snapped his fingers, clearly impatient.

"I'll get him." Opa was behind the barn, doing an inventory of supplies for planting. They got to the house just in time to see the men in uniform enter the kitchen door.

Opa pushed himself between the officers and his family of women. "I'm Nikolaus Hoger. What do you want?" His voice gruff, eyebrows lowered over his deep-set eyes.

"We come to inspect your home," the spokesman said. Without waiting for a reply, they fanned out through the house.

Franz seethed. Never had any man shown such contempt for Opa. Always, people asked for his thoughts and experiences, and listened with respect. These men treated him like a homeless dog with mange. Franz glanced at Opa, who stood tall, arms crossed over his chest while he glared down at the invaders.

Kati hiccupped, her eyes large with fear. Franz slipped behind everyone and pulled her into his arms. He sat on the floor and hugged her trembling body, until she was calmer.

The three men conferred in Russian. The spokesman approached Opa. "It appears that this will be an acceptable place for General Petrov and three other generals to stay."

From his seat by the wall, Franz could see that Opa, Oma and Mama were all perfectly still, as if they were too surprised to breathe. It hadn't been a request, but an order.

"You will provide meals and beds for them." The soldier tipped his head in a curt nod, and they marched out.

Oma fell into a chair, Mama against a doorway. Opa looked to Franz.

"Meals?" Oma and Mama repeated together.

"Are we supposed to pretend they're our guests? I'd rather poison them." Oma muttered.

"Father Bernard would tell us that we should feed our enemies," Mama rolled her eyes upward. "Anyway, I don't see how we have any choice."

"Chicken feet and a lot of dried plums would be good." Franz suggested.

Oma snickered.

"We'll do our best to show them that German Yugoslavians are gracious and decent people." Mama corrected, but her eyes smiled as she patted his cheek.

"We'll sleep together in your room." Opa paced to the living room, and back, already making plans. "I wonder why they're coming *here*, and not another house? What do they want?"

Franz felt chilled.

Kati grabbed her dolly, and hooked it over her arm.

As Franz turned to go to his bedroom, Kati followed him, making them into a parade of two. He opened the door and looked around the small room. His was the only bed. How could all five of them sleep here?

"When I was in Leipzig, in the Hitler Youth, we camped out in the woods sometimes," Franz said. Perhaps if he helped Kati see something good in it, he could as well. "We'll pretend that's what we're doing tonight."

Kati's lower lip stuck out. "Why can't I sleep in my own bed?"

"Because Russians will be in the house tonight." His heart tightened at her alarmed expression. "We'll be together back here."

"Oma and Opa will use my bed," he thought out loud. Franz pushed his box of treasures and clothes into a back corner to make room. "Guess where the rest of us sleep?"

"On the floor?" Kati's eyebrows perfectly mimicked Mama's expression of disapproval, where her eyes turned hard as they narrowed.

He ruffled her hair and nodded. "You'll probably be between me and Mama."

"Maybe I'd like that," she said, looked at her doll. "She'll be with us."

After Franz took Kati to his mother, he went to care for the animals. Finishing as quickly as possible, he raced back home.

While the women worked on the food, Opa and Katie helped Franz bring down-filled comforters to his room. Without a source of heat, it was always cold at night. Spreading layers on the floor for Franz, his mother and sister, they left the thick, down-filled comforters on top.

By late afternoon, they were ready. Both women and Kati ate in silence. Katie gathered her chosen toys and a kitten. She understood she must stay in Franz' room.

Quietly.

"The less they see of our precious girl, the better." Mama told Franz. "Just yesterday two little girls about her age were snatched on the other side of the village. The parents were told they were on the way to Russia, to learn the 'glories of Communism.'"

At six o-clock they heard a vehicle pull up and the gate open. Franz tensed, and peeked out the kitchen window. It was the four generals. They didn't march, but strode, with chins up. Their green-grey uniforms were neat, and boots shined with polish. Not at all like the rotten, lice carrying, regular soldiers he'd been seen seeing for months.

Opa opened the door and introduced himself. Mama and Oma stood silently by the stove. Franz studied them. They tipped their heads to Opa and also to the women.

"My wife and daughter have the meal prepared," Opa said. His posture was stiff, his voice not quite cordial, not quite rude.

"We're sorry to inconvenience you." The older general, with sparse grey hair and a white beard, said in accented German. "I am General Petrov, and these are Generals Ivanov, Sodorov and Drygin." His palm up, he indicated each one. "We appreciate your hospitality, however it is given."

An awkward silence stretched out. "Have a seat if you will," Opa finally said.

A discussion of the fine spring weather followed. Like actors in a play, everyone said their parts. Franz remembered reading *The Emperor's New Clothes* at school, and understood how the little boy felt.

Franz sat beside Opa at the table, with the men. Mama and Oma served stew, cornmeal muffins, and fine wine from their own vineyards.

"Herr Hoger," said General Sodorov, who looked younger than the others, and had a full, black beard, "we have been informed that you are a farmer. What do you grow?"

"A variety, so if it's a bad year for one, it'll be a good one for others. We raise sunflowers, wheat, potatoes, and have some vineyards. Before the war, we had hogs, and cattle." Opa spoke carefully; seeming to weigh his words to be sure he wouldn't invite more trouble.

The men listened to Opa, and Franz relaxed when he saw they appeared courteous.

After the meal, Franz helped pick up dirty plates. Cherries and peaches were served for dessert. Complimenting the meal, the men sounded sincere. No matter how nice they might act, they were enemies. Franz stayed alert.

"Herr Hoger, we were told that you used to have a brick factory. Is that correct?" General Petrov asked.

"Yes," Opa replied slowly. His guard up, he sat stiffly.

"What's the process to get brick production going?" The man leaned forward, his head cocked to the left as he listened.

"I always dug clay in the fall, let it sit out during the winter and formed and cured them from April to about October. We'd fire the bricks in November. It takes about a year for each set of bricks to be completed." Opa gazed at each of the four men, then leaned back and waited.

"A year? How can the process be accelerated?"

"Well, if you're after quick, it's possible. If you want a fine product that will last for years, it takes time."

The older man closed his eyes and stroked his beard as he thought. Watching their expressions, Franz wondered at their interest.

Petrov leaned back and crossed his leg over his knee. His socks were so white! Not just the usual pale gray or yellow, but bright white. Franz couldn't see the others' feet and wondered if they all wore such fancy leggings.

A picture of his mother's stinky, bloody stockings flashed through his mind. He blinked it away. He couldn't think about that now.

Oma and Mama completed the washing and drying of dishes. Franz saw them whispering, and knew they'd want to go to his room with Kati, but was now a good time?

The General noticed, and turned to his partners. "Gentlemen, I think it's time to retire for the evening. We have an early morning and long day ahead."

Chairs scraped the floor as everyone rose. The quietest man turned to smile at the women. "Thank you for this excellent home-cooked meal."

One man went to each of the bedrooms and the other two went to the living room, where bedding was laying on the sofas. Franz and his family made their escape.

Emotionally and physically exhausted, they talked little. Feeling comforted by being together in the crowded room, Franz fell into a troubled sleep within minutes.

The next morning, all but Kati woke early. Franz dressed rapidly and headed to the outhouse. Pangs of hunger drove him inside before going to Balli's. Hearing the rumble of male voices in the kitchen, he opened the door cautiously.

Oma cooked breakfast, and glanced over her shoulder. At his raised eyebrows, she winked and dished food onto plates.

General Petrov asked Opa more questions about brick making, which Franz thought was strange. The general was fighting a war, not building a house. The other men remained quiet, but appeared attentive as Opa and the senior general talked.

Franz cut off a hunk of ham, and tore off the end a loaf of bread.

"We pull out today," one of the Generals said.

Did he mean them only? Or more? Was a change coming?

He almost turned to stay and listen, but a thirsty herd waited for him and he had to milk Punkte regularly or she'd dry up.

After his chores were finished, Franz heard the sounds of stomping feet, snorts and moans when he was but a street away from home. Curious, he dropped off the milk to his mother, "Something's going on over there," Franz pointed to the next block.

"Before you leave, look what we found when we cleaned the table this morning!" She opened her hands to show a pile of coins. "Each of the generals left five Rubles under his plate! Maybe some of them aren't so very bad."

Dropping the coins into a cookie jar, she turned and studied his face. "I understand you're very curious, so go check things out. But be very alert and carful, Franz!"

He nodded seriously and ran to find his friends. Tony called his name.

"The Russians are leaving!" Wiggling through the crowd to watch the departing troops, the boys saw the artillery division march past. Next came cavalry, both horses and tanks. They must have rounded up all remaining cattle in the village, to feed their troops farther away. Marching behind the animals, soldiers of lesser ranks goaded them.

"Too bad they've eaten all the hogs here," a nearby man groused. "I'd like to see them side step through their shit!"

Franz and Tony smirked, until they heard a little boy's voice. "Is the war over?"

"What about my mother?" Sobered, Tony whispered. "Can she come home? Will she be forgotten?"

Franz remembered how he felt when Mama was taken away. Even if he knew what to say, he couldn't speak past the constriction in his throat. Looking at the ground, he blinked away moisture. He was so thankful his mother was home.

Tony and his sister, Berbl, needed their mother, too.

28

Spring, summer 1945 – twelve years old
Stanišić – Occupied by Russians, and Tito's Partisans

"FOLLOW ME." BREAKFAST eaten, Mama crooked her finger and led Franz and Kati to the back of the garden.

Wispy, white clouds drifted across the sky, casting shadows in the grass. At that moment, Franz felt as if the war couldn't touch this day. The sunflowers, just over Kati's head, nodded in their half-open stage.

"It won't be long until these sleepy heads are awake." Mama touched a few of them tenderly.

Franz put his hands on his knees and leaned down to his sister's height. "She says that every year, doesn't she?" He grinned at Kati. "Especially just before Opa harvests his fields."

"This year is especially true," Mama said. "They're still simple and cheerful and dependable in this messed up world. Nothing matters but turning their faces to the sun and bowing to us when the sun goes down."

"Can I have this one, Mama?" Katie whispered as she pointed to one flower.

The mood of the moment changed for Franz. It made him sad that talkative Kati had become this quiet little girl. She knew she had to stay close to family and couldn't play out on the sidewalk.

She couldn't squeal with joy as she ran, like she used to. She'd become an 'old' child.

"Yes," Mama pulled scissors from her apron pocket. "It will be so much prettier next week, but you can get another one then." She cut it off and tapped Kati's small nose with a petal.

Franz heard the rumble of an engine coming up the street and looked toward the gate. There were few tractors in Stanisic, and they belonged to the richer, Hungarian farmers on the north end. It got closer and closer.

Mama sent Kati inside and followed Franz.

The huge green tractor had giant tires on the back and smaller ones in front. It slowed down on the dirt road, a cloud of dust following. Mama gasped and put her hand to her chest as the vehicle stopped in front of their house.

"Jani?" she called out. "Jani!" She ran to greet the man climbing down from the steel seat.

Puzzled, Franz stood still. The only Jani he knew was his fourteen-year-old cousin in Sombor.

The man turned to embrace Mama and she clasped his shoulders tightly. Tears flowed down both faces. Franz narrowed his eyes. Suddenly, he recognized a skinny and sun-darkened Jani, much changed since the trip to Sombor to test for *Gymnasium*.

"What are you doing here? How long can you stay?" Mama slipped her hand under Jani's elbow, and pulled him close. "It's so good to see you!" She stopped and laughed. "I'm not giving you a chance to answer, am I?"

"I'm in Legin now, on what used to known as the Futto farm. The Russians 'liberated Sombor' and shipped us here," Jani said as he and Franz studied one another.

Franz stepped forward at the same time as Jani, and wrapped his arms around him and squeezed. They held on, rocking back and forth, saying nothing. Franz realized he'd really missed Jani. Smiling, they turned back to Mama, who cried again.

"Tito's Partisans have me working on a farm. Can you believe that?" His thumb pointed over his shoulder as they walked to the house. "I operate Russia's American tractor. An opportunity popped up to sneak over to see you."

"City boy, you're on a farm?" Franz first reaction was to laugh, but Jani was no longer his fun loving, accordion-champ cousin. His arms were muscles and bones, with no fat to soften his skin. He seemed so much older now and Franz felt the sadness behind the smile.

"Not actually farming." Jani sighed, his words quiet. "Marshal Tito has us plowing up fields to show his total power over us. Everything belongs to the State."

It took a moment for Franz to absorb what Jani said. There'd been rumors about Communists replacing churches and individual ownerships. Weeks ago Herr Balli had warned Franz it was coming. But Jani spoke of Legin, the location of Opa's biggest vineyard. Not that many miles away. Franz' felt as if an icicle had fallen down his back.

"Tell us about your family?" Mama held his arm tighter, as she led him to the porch. Franz remembered that Aunt Manci had been Mama's closest friend in Sombor, not just Vati's sister. They'd canned fruit and vegetables, sewed, planned for the future and giggled as they shared everything.

Conversation paused when Oma motioned them to come inside. "I saw you out there and thought you might like something to eat." She remembered Jani from the few times he came with Franz to Stanisic, and hugged him before they all sat down. On the kitchen table were two hastily made sandwiches and a pitcher of milk.

Jani stared at the meal. "Thank you. I needed to see you, but it's true I hoped you still had something in your pantry and smokehouse." With an unsteady hand, he grabbed a sandwich and ate every crumb quickly. Jani picked up the other sandwich, and drained his milk. He drummed his fingers on the table, just like he used to do. In that second, Franz caught another glimpse of his boyhood buddy.

Oma refilled Jani's glass.

Franz felt a clutch in his chest as he watched his cousin take a mouthful, swallowing only after holding it in his mouth. How thankful Franz was for the cow! She was safe only because of Herr Balli's kindness in hiding her in his herd.

"Jani?" Mama clutched his hand and brought him back to the question. "Your family?"

"I don't know." He glanced out the window and Franz saw a lump move up and down on the front of Jani's bony neck. "We were all thrown into a labor camp in Sombor. Then they sent some of us young men up here. My mother, and Dori, and my Aunt Lissi and Great Aunt Eva, are still in the camp there. The German army drafted my father months ago. Our Elmer grandparents," he glanced at Franz, "were sent to a camp for old people, where they'll likely die."

"Oh, no!" Mama moaned. "Not our Manci and Dori!" Franz's mother hunched over, her hands laced tightly together.

Jani reached over and stroked her back. "I hear news from time to time. So far, they're okay. Somehow, I'll get word to you, Aunt Elisabeth, when I hear."

Franz studied Jani's hand. It was rough, his fingernails bitten down, with dirt ground into his knuckles – not like his previous soft, musical hands. Franz tore his gaze away.

"How are all of you?" Jani asked, glancing at Franz.

"We're not as bad off as many. Every family is in pieces now," Franz said. "But we've lost all our livestock, and our supplies are shrinking."

With visible effort, Franz's mother sat straight and gave Jani a wobbly smile. "I find myself praying more than ever. Manci and

Dori and all your family will be in my special prayers. The list grows longer every day."

A deep silence settled on the small group.

"We heard Hitler committed suicide." Franz broke the quiet.

"Yes," Jani's right eye twitched at the corner as he nodded. "On last day of April, just before Germany surrendered."

"If only he'd killed himself long ago!" Franz growled.

"He started this war," Mama said. "But now one devil has replaced another, right?"

"Yes," Jani said. "Stalin's powerful and evil, and Tito is learning fast from a master."

Oma sprang to her feet and turned on the faucet to wet the dishrag and, with jerky motions, wiped the table. She stepped over to the picture of Adam on the wall, reached up and touched his face. It was taken shortly before the army took him and put him in the SS. Sighing, she returned to her chair.

"Tito's troops are here." Jani said. His eyes were sad and forehead wrinkled. "I'd say you should run away, but where? In Sombor, the Russians took over. It's Marshal Tito's job to come in to set up work and prison camps." Jani hesitated. "He's getting better at his job," he said each word slowly and distinctly. "Town after town. Just be prepared. Hide valuables and food. Likely, you'll be used for work."

Franz noticed that Jani looked to him and Mama, but kept his eye contact from Oma. Was he thinking of their Elmer grandparents in a camp for older people, to die?

"If things get really bad, we'll somehow leave." Mama leaned forward, her voice steady and determined. "We're not that far from the Hungarian border. We'll pass your camp and I promise we'll come get you. Together, we'll escape if that means survival."

"What's a camp?" Kati asked. She had been quietly drawing on her slate board near the bedroom doorway. She faced those around her and waited for an answer.

Four pairs of eyes quickly glanced at one another. Franz' heart beat faster. No one jumped in to answer Kati's question. Franz had only a hazy idea of what being in a camp meant. He thought of the Russian POWs in Leipzig. But they were enemy soldiers, not families. The silence made him more frightened.

"From what I understand," Mama spoke slowly, "people are gathered together, away from home. Grownups work making factory parts, or do other labor." She bit her lower lip, and looked up to Jani for his reaction. "Children stay with their parents."

Oma busied herself wrapping up food for Jani to take with him, but Franz noticed her hands shook.

"I've got to get back." Jani forked his fingers through his short, brown hair. "I won't be able to explain being away for too long. An opportunity came today, but probably not again." Jani tucked the food into his jacket and thanked Oma.

"You know just about every neighborhood has snitches, don't you?" he asked softly. "They tell the Russians anything they want to know about German families. Who has money, Nazi connections, anything that will get them food and protection."

"Yes," Mama whispered. "We know who some are, and we're careful."

Jani turned to give farewell hugs, and squatted down to look at Kati, standing close to Mama. "It's good to see you, Kati." He reached out and gently took her hand. "Someday my little sister, Dori, will come play with you."

She studied him seriously, then her lips turned up just a bit, and she nodded.

With a wave of his hand, he strode to the gate, Franz beside him. The boys stood on the sidewalk, surrounded by sunshine and a breeze that shifted Jani's hair.

Franz hated to see his cousin leave. Jani's chin quivered as he said goodbye. Many images tumbled in Franz's mind. Angry at a neighbor, he and Jani painting the man's massive wall with mud, and for punishment, scrubbing it for hours. Searching for leeches to sell. Listening to Jani play beautiful accordion music. The three days of shooting in Sombor, where people stayed home, hiding. Afterward, they had found the dead Serbian Orthodox Priest. How terrified they'd been as they ran for help.

When he looked at Jani's eyes, Franz felt the bond, far closer than mere blood.

"Someday this will be over," Franz said as he and Jani embraced one another.

"It's hard to imagine going back to a normal life." Quickly, Jani hopped on the tractor and drove away without looking back.

It was the magical time of morning between dark and light. Few people moved about the village this early. Normally, Franz loved this part of the day, when soft sunlight peeked between houses and around trees. He usually listened to various birds, the winds that went from silent to whistling, and the barking of area dogs. A few Russians patrolled, but more often he saw Tito's Partisans marching with their machine guns. Franz learned to watch for them. He'd cross the street and walk a steady and relaxed pace, in shadows if possible. His face showed neither friendliness nor anger or fear.

Today was different and the dark clouds matched his mood. He and Opa headed for the vineyard in Legin, near Balli's.

"I'm glad Herr Balli has someone to take care of the cattle in exchange for milk," Opa said as he put his thumb and forefinger together under his nose and slowly separated them to smooth his brown mustache.

Opa had a shovel over his shoulder. Franz carried the hoe and a bagged lunch of meat and cheese.

"Stop scowling, Franz," Opa said. "It might seem like we're really crippled without the horse, but I have you to take his place."

The twinkle in Opa's eyes made Franz more frustrated.

"After we walk six miles every morning, till by hand all day long and walk home, we won't see anyone or do anything else. Besides, the vineyard's going to be taken away from us soon."

"Maybe." Opa instantly sobered. "There's a big chance we'll lose the land to the Communists. But what if things change and our enemies go away? Grain from last year's wheat is in the attic for storage. The hogs and chickens are gone. Fortunately, the sunflowers are hearty enough to survive. If we waste this time our yield of grapes will be too small at harvest. We can't just sit down and quit."

Not convinced, Franz kicked a rock. The women would be unprotected with both of them gone. They wouldn't have their daily milk. At six years old, Kati needed him to play hide and seek, or the I Spy game with her when he had time. Mama and Oma were busy all the time. Franz found comfort in Opa's promise to be at home each night and all day Sundays.

The sun moved higher in the sky and the temperature warmed. As they passed fewer houses and more fields surrounded them, Franz's bad attitude melted away with the clouds. As soon as they approached the vineyard, Franz stopped and his shoulders sagged as he looked down the long rows. He looked up and down and from row to row. It was too big to till by hand!

"We'll start at the north end," Opa said as he led the way.

"I counted eleven rows," Franz croaked when they reached Opa's starting place.

"Yes."

"They're almost a mile long!"

"Yes." Opa's deep set eyes looked down at Franz. He raised one eyebrow. "Better get started."

Franz clamped his mouth shut. It was like arguing with a rock.

He picked up his hoe and swung at a clump of weeds. Encouraged because the ground was very sandy and easy to cut, he chopped again. By noon it was hot and they sat under the shade of a Maple tree along the west edge of the grape vines and ate their lunch.

During the following weeks, each day was similar. One day while they rested under the shade of the tree, Opa told about his experiences in the Great War, and what it had been like stationed in bitter cold Russia. He'd met Shurri Balli in those days and they'd stayed close friends.

Another day Franz asked about Opa's stories of his two trips to America, working to save money to buy his acres. What wonderful adventures he had! Franz chuckled at the familiar tales.

"Tell me about Leipzig, Franz." Opa said on one of the hottest days. "You've said very little."

At first, he told about his friends and seeing the factory workers badly burned from an explosion. As time went on, Franz shared about the bombings and the POWs from Russia.

"I hated going to the shelter," he confessed. "But I didn't want us to die, either. One night bombs fell next to our barracks. It was so scary, and fires kept breaking out. After that I wanted to go to safety." Opa nodded with understanding.

Every day seemed the same during the following weeks as temperatures increased. Opa ignored the occasional rains. Exhausted by the time they got home, they ate, visited and went to bed.

Franz was thankful for Sundays. The family stayed at home and did nothing more strenuous than attend Mass.

Flopping onto his bed Sunday night, August nineteenth, Franz felt a flicker of pride. They were doing the tilling without the horse or other workers. His arm muscles were larger, legs stronger. The grape vines were growing fruit and looking healthy.

He didn't mind the work now that it was routine. But every morning and evening they passed increasing numbers of Partisan soldiers. Usually they ignored each other, but sometimes one would stop them. Replying to them in Hungarian had satisfied the soldiers so far. What would happen if it didn't?

Franz rolled over in bed one way, then the other.

He told himself to stop thinking and go to sleep. Tomorrow would be a Monday just like all the others.

29

August 20, 1945 twelve years old
Tito's Partisans force them from home

"CRASH! BANG! THUMP!" Franz woke instantly, surrounded by fear and confusion.

"Get dressed, come outside!" A strongly accented voice shouted.

"Bam! Bam!" He heard their kitchen door hit and the same terrible order.

Franz' hands fumbled as he grabbed clothes in the dark room and dressed. Scrambling out to the porch, he saw soldiers in the shadowy light of sunup. Oma came out of the kitchen, dressed and her black scarf in place. She hadn't grabbed her apron, which she always put on early. Her eyes darted around in confusion. Opa followed with deep grooves between his eyebrows, carrying Kati, who tucked her face in her grandfather's neck. Mama held Kati's socks and shoes as they stepped outside. She took and held a deep breath until she saw Franz.

Three Partisans pointed guns at them. Franz ran to his family.

"Opa?" he whispered, wanting to hear words of encouragement.

Opa put his long, strong arm over Franz' shoulders and pulled him close. He shook his head.

"Your house and assets have been confiscated by the Communist State!" The booming Partisan stood with his feet braced in fighting stance. "Go to the street. Now!"

Confiscated! Taken away! Franz' mind screamed that it was too sudden. There were things they should take. The garden needed weeding again. He looked back at Tito's soldiers and their big guns. Early morning sun glinted off the blackened barrels, long as river snakes, but more deadly. Each soldier's finger curled around the trigger, in unspoken menace.

Stuck in the middle of a nightmare, he glanced around and saw all their neighbors to the north in silent huddled groups. Anton's parents held him and his two sisters. Every family did the same.

"Today Stanisic is being cleansed of Germans," a gray haired man in a faded uniform announced through a megaphone. "Move to the middle of the road and face south."

Jani had warned them this would come here eventually. Now it was their turn.

Franz shuffled with the growing crowd going south on Church Street. Oma held his hand and turned her head to look back. He could do nothing to comfort her as tears dripped down her cheeks. He took a last lingering look at home. The living room window facing the street, the familiar gates he'd banged as he came and went. More people crowded behind him until the house was out of view.

There was little conversation. Children seemed to take turns crying in different places on the street. One wanted down to use the outhouse. A little girl begged for her doll while her mother put her finger to pursed lips. In the timid light of morning, soldiers rammed their rifle butts on doors and demanded people come out immediately. The dreadful echo repeated numerous times on all five long streets. At the fourth cross street, they turned to the right and were led to Market Place and soccer field in the southern, Yugoslav area of Stanisic. He'd been to a carnival here with his friends. It was now fenced with a single strand of barbed wire. People continued to be funneled through the wide gateless opening.

Franz had never seen so many people. More kept coming. "Are they all from Stanisic?" he asked Opa.

"Yes." Opa looked over the crowd. "Ninety-five percent of the village is German. There will probably be about six thousand of us when they finish."

They stood and waited and waited. The sun rose in the sky and the heat climbed. How could the white puffs float peacefully through blue sky now? It should be mountains of black clouds. People looked around and, one by one, lowered themselves to dry grass. An hour later, they leaned on each other and even rested their eyes.

A horrible scream from the other side of the field pierced the air. No one dared react. Franz looked around and scooted closer to his mother. Another cry of pain.

Franz's heart thumped against his ribs. He looked at Opa, then Oma and Mama for answers questions he couldn't ask.

"I'm pretty sure a baby has decided to be born." Mama leaned over to confer with Oma. Franz couldn't hear the words, only a soft murmur and saw their narrowed eyes as they searched in the direction of the sound.

Franz blew out his mouth and relaxed in the quiet, only to be jolted by another high pitched moan. He understood she was in pain, but couldn't she be quiet about it? He bit his thumbnail. Soldiers kept looking over that way and nervous soldiers could be dangerous.

"She probably doesn't need our help," Mama said. "But if everyone thinks that, no one will check on her." After another muffled scream Mama stood and shaded her eyes as she located the woman. Oma nodded and they meandered in that direction through groups of seated people.

One of the patrolling soldiers outside the barbed wire stopped and watched them. He raised his gun. Franz held his breath and nudged Opa. The gun was lowered at that moment.

"I think he's just being alert and sees what they're doing. If your mother can help someone, she can't be stopped." Opa's deep voice expressed frustration as he crossed his arms over his bent knees. "That young Partisan might be relieved when her baby comes, but then he'll have to listen to a newborn crying." Opa's lips pressed in a straight line as he watched their women kneel in the distance.

Kati crawled onto Franz's lap. He held her head against his chest and covered her other ear to block the sound. There was a rhythm to the continual screams and he began to anticipate them.

"Is it always like this?" Franz asked Opa.

"Sometimes, sometimes not. I'm sure if she were safe at home it would be easier." Opa shook his head. "On all of us."

Franz pressed Katie's ears and steeled himself for the next one. It didn't come. Instead of feeling relieved, he felt edgy. He could handle the repetitive screams better than waiting for another shriek that didn't come. After a while the silence became comfortable.

"I want Mama," Kati said as she wiggled. "I need the outhouse."

"She'll be back in a bit," Opa said as he and Franz shrugged and looked around the market place. There was no privacy.

"Come on. I'll take you to that post and you can squat over the weeds." Franz took her by the hand to a spot where no one sat or walked. As he heard her pee, he looked around. Two steps away was the barbed wire. Keeping Kati visible in the corner of his eye, Franz looked both ways. With no guards nearby, he emptied himself on the dry grass beyond the fence.

Kati slipped her hand into his when he turned back. "When will Mama come back with food?" Her little voice turned shrill. "I need a drink!"

"Soon," Franz answered as they reached Opa and sat down. "She'll tell us about a new baby over there." Kati loved babies. Maybe she'd think about that instead of her own misery. He turned his back to the sun to shade his little sister. Perhaps if she weren't so hot she might forget her thirst. He wished he could.

"We just witnessed the birth of a very tiny girl." Mama announced as she and Oma joined them. Her eyebrows pulled together and she sat down and opened her arms to Kati. "She's beautiful, but came far too early."

"Nikolaus." Franz watched his grandmother put her fingers on Opa's shoulder. "Herr Stertz died over there." Her voice wobbled. "Erna is afraid that soldiers will take his body away if they know he's gone." Oma sat down and hid her face on her husband's shoulder. "Sounds as if he had a heart attack."

Opa covered Oma's hand and cleared his throat. "So a new life came and an old one left."

While his grandparents mourned together for their friends, Franz' heart broke. They'd aged years since last night.

By noon, Franz' stomach growled and he couldn't stop thinking of the water well and food in the pantry at home.

It was growing so hot. Not a piece of shade to give rest and no breezes. His mouth was dry and his head ached. He looked around again, but saw nothing that hinted of water.

He dropped his head, closed his eyes and tried not to think of what had happened or of the future. It was impossible to turn off his mind.

"I'm going to find my friends," Franz couldn't sit on the hard ground and wait for another minute. He saw Stefan and they joined forces with Tony and Anton and began walking around.

"We've got to know what's happening outside this field," Franz said.

"They aren't doing anything but keeping us here," Anton said as they watched the patrolling soldiers.

"That skimpy fence isn't to keep us in here for long. Just temporarily," Franz said. "They have something else planned."

"Look up Second Street," Tony said as they got close to the edge of the enclosed soccer field. "What are they carrying out of those houses?"

Franz narrowed his eyes as he watched one man carry away a large painting. He couldn't see what the others took, but they also had their arms loaded.

"It's things that are worth something," Franz said. "They're ransacking as far as I can see down the street. Let's see if they're doing it everywhere." They walked farther on.

"Same on Third Street," Anton said. They stood and watched the activity before moving along the perimeter. Most streets were quiet. They came back around to Second and Third Streets to watch Partisans still emptying houses of valuables.

Despite the heat, Franz felt cold prickles along his spine.

"We'd better stay with our families." Franz chin trembled as he looked at his best friends. "See you later," he said.

He thought of his father and Uncle Adam. Where were they? What about those sent to Russia? His remaining family must stay together!

Five armed men entered and weaved their way through the crowd, separating some people from the others. The second time they ushered a woman and little children out, he knew. Herr Balli said Gakova was being filled with mothers who had babies and very young children. They weren't able to work.

Mama gasped and bit her lower lip. Franz followed her eyes. It was a woman stumbling along, holding a very tiny baby against her breast.

"Maybe she's being taken to a place to heal from childbirth," Mama said without strength.

Oma sat still, tears quietly tracking down her wrinkled cheeks.

What would happen next? Franz didn't say a word.

A gun was fired. He must have been expecting it because he wasn't surprised. Partisans led a large number of people away and turned them to the north and west. They went past Second Street. Where were they taking them?

"Looks like about a thousand people leaving," Opa guessed.

Soldiers stood shoulder to shoulder to stop the flow and motioned for those remaining to be seated again. Almost a visible thing, dread covered everyone old enough to be watching.

"I'm thirsty," Kati repeated as her eyes filled with tears. She looked closely at her mother's pale face.

"I know, Liebling, we all are." Mama closed her eyes and hugged her. "Try not to think about it. Do you feel the little ant on your leg?"

Franz stopped listening as their voices droned on about the ant's journey to her knee. Mama kept herself and Kati diverted. Armed guards took more people away. Pictures of the POWs in Leipzig darted in and out of his mind. They'd been starved, dirty and ill dressed for the weather. He wished he could stop remembering. This wasn't the same thing. Was it?

Soldiers returned and people in their section were motioned out. His family walked closely together. Panic simmered inside, but Franz kept his eyes on Opa's head, above the crowd.

They were herded to the block of houses on Third Street. This couldn't be too bad, could it? About seventy people were separated to enter the first house. His family went into the next one in a group about the same size. Franz felt a flip of hope at the sight of a bricked well. Water! Once inside the crowded house, he looked around. No soldiers came with them. That was a relief! It was a real home with furniture, which felt strange. Kind of the same as being with a dead body, but the life was gone. They were being held against their will, but in someone's home.

Pictures of another family hung on the wall. What happened to them?

Oma and Mama joined other women searching the pantry and cabinets in the kitchen. Doors opened and closed and finds announced. Corn. Preserves. Some dried beef.

Two men carried a couple of large canning pots from the crowded house and filled them with well water. Opa stepped out to the yard and gathered with a few other older men. Franz followed and saw a lot of head nodding and worried faces. They scattered and Franz followed Opa.

"Please," he motioned to a group to come close. He addressed them quietly as he watched for guards. "We have food here, but we don't know how long it will need to last. If we all cooperate and eat only what is needed to survive, we'll manage for a while."

Looking around at the crowd, Franz saw Tony Baumgartner standing with his sister, Berbl. Franz didn't know her well. She was his age and Tony two years younger, but she always stayed at home. He lifted his hand to draw Tony's attention and his friend gave a grim nod and worked his way behind the group to join Franz.

Franz and Tony slipped outside to check the pump. They joined people who were lined up waiting their turn for water. None from their neighborhood was in this group. People stayed in the house or very close to it. After getting a drink and taking some to Kati, he looked around. A large metal cup hung on the fence near a household garden. Using its edge to dig at the soil, he uncovered stored potatoes. Tony found a stout tree branch and helped. After a quick wash, the potatoes were taken to the kitchen where women prepared anything brought to them for soup.

Beets, potatoes, carrots and parsley were piled on a side table. Pickled vegetables, sacks of flour and dried prunes were available for other meals.

Shots rang out, followed by cries. Everyone froze.

Franz squatted down and looked around. He and Tony exchanged frightened, puzzled glances. They moved slowly and silently to peek outside the front window and looked out at the street. Three men in uniform pointed toward the soccer field, then split up and walked in different directions. They waited a few minutes before they explored the house and porch

"Do not leave the boundaries of your assigned premises under punishment of death!" Russians shouted through a megaphone as they drove up the street. "You will be shot if you take one step over the property lines!"

"The barn and stalls are inside the yard. Think it's safe to see what's in there?" Tony asked.

"Probably. If we don't move fast and draw attention." Franz' eyes and ears didn't relax their vigilance in watching and listening for danger. Tony did the same. The barn had three stalls and it was obvious that they'd been empty for some time. The tack for horses still hung on the wall. Wheels had been removed from the wagon. The roof seemed to be solid.

Franz and Tony returned to the overcrowded house. Franz closed his eyes and inhaled the aroma of mingled vegetables in the soup. His stomach growled painfully.

"Groups have to share bowls or cups and spoons because there aren't enough." Mama explained as she met him. "Opa has ours over there."

Kati ate first and cried because it was too hot. After one spoonful, Mama encouraged Franz to take another. It passed to Mama, Oma and Opa last of all. Cooled now, Kati quickly ate several mouthfuls.

After the third go-around, Franz noticed that the adults were each taking one small spoonful and telling Kati and him to eat more.

He looked around at each man, woman and child. When had everyone become so thin? A layer of fat would help. After the livestock were taken, and even before, people had cut back on all supplies of food to keep some for later, when less was available.

Weakness and fear weighed heavily on him. What would happen? What could he do?

"While you were outside did you see any place we can sleep tonight?" Mama leaned closer to whisper in his ear. "The house is very crowded."

"It'll be cool with the sun going down," he said as he thought out loud. "We could use an old horse stall. There's straw and it might be clean enough."

Two hours later they picked out the dirtiest straw and found places to settle in to get some needed sleep.

Very tired but still hungry, Franz stared at the gray oak planking on the stall. Is this where they would stay? It didn't seem like a work place. Perhaps they'd be moved again. What then? Just wait and starve?

He rolled on his other side, barely seeing the others in the moonlight shining through the end of the shelter. Was it possible that only last night he'd gone to bed grumbling a bit about working the vineyard all day today? Yesterday seemed part of another lifetime. The Russians came on October 20 last year, ten months ago.

Franz shivered. He heard soldiers patrolling as their boots pounded the dirt street, rifles squeaked with movement and the friendly smell of cigar and cigarette smoke drifted in. He listened to their soft talk without understanding their words.

Unless their captors brought them food, something would have to be done. Soon.

30

"LAST NIGHT, I shot a bunch of Partisans. Then I plunged knives in their black hearts." Franz whispered and groaned as pain twisted in his belly. "Their sneers fell right off their faces. Then we weren't hungry or have diarrhea." He leaned against the porch pillar and lowered his eyebrows and clenched his fists. "I woke up wanting to make it come true."

"Russians are worse," Tony said, hitting his hand on the pillar. "They made my mother go to Siberia. And she's not the only one. If we kill Partisans, we need to wipe out every Russian."

"We'll add Russians." Franz nodded at the growing list. He jabbed a tall stick into the dirt over and over. "The ones who sent your mother away. And the rapists. We'll make them suffer for what they did to the women and girls."

"No." Tony narrowed his icy blue eyes. "All of them."

"Some officers stayed at our house one night," Franz said. "They treated us politely. Stalin tells them what to do and they have to do it. Our fathers are the same and they'd be with us if they could."

Tony's lips pressed together.

"Think about this," Franz continued, pointing his stick. "Partisans are almost all Serbian and we're German, but we're

— 357 —

all citizens of Yugoslavia! They were neighbors!" He stopped. His voice was too loud. He looked toward the street. "They weren't forced into the Communist Party of Yugoslavia!"

"Now they have our homes and my aunt's store," Tony said. "We have nothing."

Tony closed his eyes and bent forward, gripping his stomach. He frowned at the long line at the outhouse. "I've got to go. Quick!"

"Forget that," Franz mumbled. "I found a bucket behind the barn. Come on!"

As they pushed off the edge of the porch, Franz's glance, as always, searched for and found Opa, Oma, Mama and Kati. When something happened, they needed to rush together.

Tony always did the same with his family.

"Aunt Lissi insists I eat most of the little food she gets," Tony said. "Berbl treats me like a baby because she's thirteen. I'm the only man in our family now."

"Ignore it." Franz said as he quickened his steps. Another pain shot through his belly.

They hurried as fast as they could while tightening their buttocks. Relieved, they finally made it to the back of the barn. Franz showed his friend the rusted, misshapen bucket.

"You go first," he said. Tony already had his shorts lowered. Then it was Franz' turn.

Feeling better, temporarily, they walked back from the barn along the end of the yard. They went to the only narrow place they could view the street through a gap where the stone walls joined. Sometimes they saw Russian uniforms, but more often watched Tito's soldiers wearing the familiar cap with red stars.

Today it was three Partisans standing together. One was an officer. Franz moved to one side, out of sight, when the soldiers faced the house. He peered out again. The officer waved his arm to the south as he talked. Franz turned his ear to the opening to hear better. He jerked up and leaned forward when he heard several words. His heartbeat increased.

Tony cocked his head and raised his blond eyebrows in question. They stepped away a few feet.

"I couldn't hear much," Franz said. "*Zarobljenid* and *posao* mean prisoners and project. I think they're planning a work camp."

Franz peeked out again. "They're coming here!" Heart pounding, he looked for his family and moved nearer them. The soldiers, one tall and lean, the other heavier, entered the yard and stood with feet braced. They studied the silent group of people.

"You!" the stocky Partisan shouted.

Franz froze when the man pointed several women, then his mother. He couldn't breathe, but moved under the apple tree, closer to Mama. One of the few older men was also picked.

"Follow that soldier at the gate!" The Partisan bellowed and stepped aside.

Mama reached for Franz' elbow and grabbed Katie by the hand. "We stick together," she said softly. "Heads up."

The guard didn't flick his eyes as they all filed past. Franz exhaled quietly and his back muscles relaxed. Kati clutched as if she'd grown onto Mama's leg.

The group of nine adults and three children shuffled to the street and followed a new route. Franz squeezed his mother's hand by pressing his arm to his side. He studied everything around him without swiveling his head, searching for a source of food.

"Our Father who art in heaven," Franz prayed without speaking. "Give us this day our daily bread; and forgive us our debts, as we forgive our debtors." He stopped. Debts were doing wrong things. He would not and could not forgive the Partisans. He couldn't be expected to do that! "Give us our daily bread," he repeated. "Amen."

He glanced up at Mama. He wondered if she, too, were praying.

The guard led them several blocks away up to the door of a large house, opened it and stepped inside. He gestured for them to enter as he spoke in Yugoslavian. Franz listened to that and the interpreter's echo in German. "We found grain stored in your attics. Now take these tools," he pointed to a pile of wooden shovels in the corner. "Some of you will move wheat from the dining room and bedroom into the living room. Others will carry from there to trucks outside."

"You are disposable," another Partisan shouted. "You must remove every grain of wheat out of the house by the end of the day."

Franz's eyes narrowed. Intense anger and fear shot through all him. They'd do it. Kill them as easily as gophers in a wheat field. He gazed at the others in their work group. Their eyes stood out on white faces. The threat had been taken seriously.

Without a word, they moved inside. Furniture was stacked along the walls of the living room. In the dining room and adjoining bedroom, six jagged holes had been chopped in the ceiling above eight foot high pyramid shaped piles of grain.

Franz picked up two shovels and handed one to his mother. Kati and another little girl and boy played in the kitchen, out of the way but nearby.

Less than a week ago he'd been with Opa as they hand tilled the vineyard. His muscles were still strong. Without good food he had little energy. He kept hearing the words 'by the end of the day, the end of the day'. He never rested, but shoveled at a steady pace.

After emptying the house, and filling the trucks, they each received a plate with a half cup of shredded corn boiled in water. Franz could tell it had no salt, oil, or fat, but ate it eagerly.

As they walked back, Franz moved one foot, then the other and stayed with the exhausted group. He was too tired to think or pay attention to anything.

Once inside the crowded group home, Franz sagged onto the floor in a corner of the kitchen. He crossed his arms over his raised knees and rested his head. Mama joined him in silence. After a few minutes, Opa, Oma and Kati made their way to them. Franz lifted his tired head and remembered what he'd brought.

"See my pockets," Franz said, pulling fistfuls of grain from their hiding place.

Mama smiled. Then she emptied her pockets and Kati's as well. Her shoulders slumped. "With this many people, what good is this going to do?"

"If everyone brings something," Opa said, "we'll survive another day, another week."

"I've never eaten raw grain, but I'll bet it won't cure diarrhea." Mama's fingertips pressed her eyes.

"We can't quit." Opa moved closer to his daughter and folded her into his long arms. Mama's shoulders shook as she wept.

Franz searched Opa's deep brown eyes. Without words, Franz promised he wouldn't give up. Opa gave a brief nod.

The next day soldiers led the same group to a big, beautiful house on the Main Street of the village, where the richest people lived.

Greeted by the sight of grain piled high along the outside walls, Franz noticed the wheat was deepest near the windows. No holes had been chopped in the ceilings. Why did the Partisans pour grain here instead of taking it directly to their supply stations? Just to give their prisoners more work?

Every person squirreled away as much grain as possible, without drawing attention.

Small children sorted through grass for clover and dandelions. Roots, leaves and the rare flowers still on them would be boiled to provide a meager soup and ersatz coffee. Franz had eaten dandelion greens before but this was too late in the season to taste good. They'd already done their flowering, and would be bitter. Anything helped the ache in their bellies. At least they gave off a sweet smell.

After glancing around for the whereabouts of guards, Franz slipped into adjoining rooms to search cabinets and crawl spaces. He was rewarded by finding a wrapped slab of smoked ham under a loose board in the dining room.

One end was thicker and wide. Quickly, he peeled the paper away and tore off a hefty chunk. Oh, it was so good, it made his hands shake. One more piece went into his pocket, and then it was wrapped again. He was able to slip it underneath his dirty and rumpled shirt, to rest on his back.

Glancing around to be sure there were no guards watching, he went close to his mother.

"How do I look?" he asked.

"Besides being filthy from wearing the same clothes for many days?" Then her lips barely turned up. "Your back seems padded." She turned her face away. "What is it?"

"Ham." He didn't hide his feeling of satisfaction, and gave her the piece in his hand. He sighed with frustration. "Not much to share with sixty people." So far, there'd been no fighting or stealing where they were housed. Everyone obeyed the communal living rules.

Another small bowl of shredded corn was their reward at the end of the day.

They trudged home, wondering what came next.

Early in the morning, two days later, Franz moved the curtain away from the window just enough to peek out at the trickle of rain. He let the curtain hang and stepped back. He'd stopped thinking of food every minute. It became normal to never feel satisfied. People worked hard to control crabbiness, but sharp words and muttered curses sprinkled through the day. There was little to do.

Everyone in the crowded house suddenly became quiet at the sound of boots on the brick walkway to the porch. Franz searched quickly for Opa. Mama and Kati and Oma did the same. Within seconds they stood together.

Tony, his sister Berbl, Aunt Lissi and her mother, Eva, huddled together.

The soldier knocked on the door and entered at the same time.

"Who knows how to milk cows?" It sounded more like an accusation than a question. "And speaks Yugoslavian?"

Should they raise their hands? Not answer? Milk made the decision. Franz and his mother each held up an arm.

"You'll do. Follow me."

Franz glanced over his shoulder at Kati and their grandparents and found Tony and his family. He hated to leave.

He joined hands with his mother as they walked through the cool drizzle coming from gray sky. Where were they going? For how long?

They arrived at a large and formal house. It must not be to shovel more wheat since it was just the two of them. His jaw clenched and he squeezed Mama's hand until she wiggled her fingers.

The soldier went to the front door and knocked.

A small woman with stooped posture opened the door. She chewed her lower lip as she faced the soldier. Franz looked at his mother and she appeared puzzled as well.

"You will help this family." The Partisan said. He shifted his gun to his left shoulder and turned to leave. "When you're finished, return for roll call."

"I'm Yaga Dolenec," The lady said.

"I'm Elisabeth Elmer, and this is my son, Franz." Mama spoke in the woman's language.

"Oh, you speak Yugoslavian," her smile turned genuine. "I guess you're to help us milk the cow. The pigs are way out back." She raised her shoulders and lifted her palms face up. "We were shop keepers in Croatia until the Partisans moved us here. We know nothing about farming."

She behaved as if they'd come to welcome her to the neighborhood.

Mama motioned to the barn in the large yard. A cow faced the house and moaned. "We're used to it. We had a cow, hogs and a horse, chickens, and a garden."

Franz noticed movement behind the woman. A little girl about three years old peeked around her mother's skirt at them, her thumb in her mouth. She quickly ducked back. A slightly older boy poked his head around his mother's other side and studied them. He had the same dark hair and brown eyes and deeply tanned skin.

The cow complained again, needing to be milked immediately. Franz turned his head back to the woman. He felt conspicuous as she studied him and Mama. As scrawny as they'd become and dressed in the same clothes for ten days, she might be wondering if she'd catch something from them.

Frau Dolenec's eyebrows pulled together and she frowned. "Help yourself to milk," she said softly. "I'll get you the pail." She brought it to them, but also included a long-handled dipper for drinking. Franz heart skipped a beat. It was all he could do to mumble a quick thank you past the lump in his throat.

Walking into the barn, he inhaled a long, slow breath. "It's good to smell a cow again, and hay and even manure." He grabbed a small stool off a work bench and walked around to the cow's right side. He sat and positioned the bucket between his knees and scooted close. "Here we are, Frau Cow. Going to fix both our problems."

The cow was restless until Franz began the rhythm of pulling her teats. Most went into the bucket, but Franz squirted generous amounts into his open mouth as well. Mama sat on the ground and scooted close so Franz could aim shots to her. They both smiled in stolen pleasure.

"Another day or two and this old cow would dry up," Franz said.

Mama scooped milk with the ladle and handed it to Franz.

He drank eagerly, and gave the dipper to his mother. She did the same.

Closing his eyes, he savored another mouthful. The taste and warmth rolled around in his mouth before he swallowed. "Mmmm." He licked his lips for every partial drop available and handed the ladle back to his mother. His heart twisted and he felt a stab of guilt. "Kati needs this more. How can we take some back?"

"I was just thinking the same thing," Mama said. "The Dolenecs seem like nice people. Perhaps . . . perhaps they won't care." She got up and forked out dirty straw and found a supply of hay for feed. "Maybe we'll be able to work here for a while."

Franz glanced outside the barn door at uneven ground nearby. "I wonder if some roots have been left behind." Franz went outside and pointed toward the fence. "The grass has grown up this summer, maybe there was a garden."

Mama nodded and picked up the pail. "I'll take the milk inside and you search around."

Franz went back to the barn and found a trowel on the bench and brought it back with him. He was right! There were potatoes, and carrots and beets. He enjoyed feeling alone again. Bending on his hands and knees, he dug. Oh, this felt so normal. Cool air blew, fall settling in, and he was working the soil. Little by little, his pile grew. He grabbed a carrot and took a bite.

"That's dirty," a small voice declared.

Franz turned his head and saw the little boy. Would he bring trouble?

"You got to wash it first," the child informed Franz. His soft smile showed two holes where he used to have middle top teeth.

"I'm Franz. What's your name?"

"Bogdan," the boy said. "We had to move here, but we didn't want to." His lower lip stuck out.

Franz rolled over to a sitting position. "A lot of that is happening." Franz squirmed. "Want to dig with me?" he asked.

Eagerly, the child bent to help find treasures under the grass.

A half-hour later Franz heard someone on the walkway. Heart hammering, he quickly tossed the grass he'd removed and covered his stash of food. He must take some of it!

"Tata! Tata!" Bogdan shouted and ran to a man with the same olive skin and dark hair.

The man caught the boy as he jumped to him. Herr Dolenec's eyes softened at his happy child. His eyes narrowed, clearly wondering about having a stranger talking to his son. Apparently he was satisfied, he nodded slightly. Franz heard the soft patter of the man's voice as they went to the house.

Franz's heart caught as he remembered times like that with his own father. Tears leaked out and fell to the ground. If only they could go back to when he was little. His family had each other and plenty of food and safety. He remembered laughter and working together. Missing Vati was a familiar ache inside.

The rest of the afternoon went quietly. Franz and his mother took shears to cut last summer's untended grass. After stuffing vegetables into their pockets, they carried a half-filled basket to the Dolenec family. They returned to the cow and milked her one more time. Mama produced a jar she'd found abandoned behind the house and they filled it with the wonderful, life sustaining beverage. How to carry it home? If a Partisan saw them, he'd take it away and possibly shoot them because they'd broken some rule.

Mama managed to hide it in her hair kerchief. Shaking it out, she tied a knot and formed a sling to lay the container on its side. She held Franz's arm, hiding it between them. They hoped.

At the house, they walked into a scene from a nightmare.

A loud, guttural scream cut across the room. One of the men banged a chunk of wood against his own head over and over. Eyes bulged, with vessels in his neck enlarged as he beat himself, oblivious of trickles of blood running down his face.

"Herman, Herman," the woman beside him stood crying as she tried to catch his hand. "It's me, we're safe today."

"Shut him up!" another man snarled. "He'll bring guards inside!"

Opa stepped toward the couple. Franz exhaled and felt some of the tension drain. Opa would know what to do.

31

August 1945 – turned thirteen years old
Temporary house, then First Camp

"EVERYONE CALM DOWN. He's shell-shocked," Opa said. "Does he have a favorite song?" he asked the wife as he patted her shoulder.

"Yes." The word came out as a squeak. "He sings *Lili Marlene* to me. My name is Lili."

Opa looked around the now silent room, except for the man hitting his head and growling. "Who knows this song?"

A bit of shuffling and several nodded or said they did.

"Otto," Opa pointed to an old friend whose hand was up. "Please lead and everyone join in."

Vor der Kaserne vor dem grossen Tor
Stand eine Laterne, und stebe noch davor,
So wolln wir uns da wiedersehn
My Lili of the lamplight,
My own Lili Marlene.

By the end of the first jaunty verse, the troubled man leaned back, his eyes focused on people in the room. By the middle of the second verse, he sang some words. As the third began, he smiled and joined in as if there'd been no problem. The song ended with him hugging his wife.

"Opa," Franz whispered later that night they lay in their straw bed in the barn. "How did you know to sing?"

"When I was in The Great War, we had soldiers go crazy. Their anger, fear and guilt would just explode. We learned to sing before things got dangerous." Opa fell silent and Franz closed his eyes. "It didn't always work, but worth trying."

———

They came for Opa a week later.

Mama had just finger combed Franz' dirty hair before their daily walk to the Dolenec's.

A Partisan stepped into the house and looked around. "Nikolaus Hoger, come with us."

Opa turned to Oma and kissed her forehead. He cradled her face with his big hands. In an oddly tender way, he adjusted her black scarf as he gazed at her. Standing tall, he followed the soldier out of the house and past the yard.

The gate clicked behind him. Everyone remained frozen for a few seconds, and then turned to speak to one another.

Mama hugged Kati and wiped a tear from the corner of Oma's eye. "Franz and I come back and forth from the Croatians' house. Perhaps Father will as well."

"I hope so," Oma said as she hugged them goodbye. "I'll be alright. You've got to go."

Franz and his mother walked along the sidewalk in sunshine. He felt like throwing rocks at the birds twittering in the trees. How dare the weather be so cheerful and the dumb birds sing! It should be dark and gray. A gust of cool air whipped around them, reminding him again that they had no coats, or even another set of clothes. Winter was coming and he'd been thinking about what he and Opa could do.

Why did they take Opa away by himself? Where? Franz felt a stone weight inside, much like when the German Army claimed

Vati. And when Uncle Adam left for the last time. Where and how were they? His thoughts circled back to Opa and then to his father.

He and his mother continued in solitary silence.

"How will Vati find us?" Franz asked.

"What?" Mama shook her head as she came back to the present.

He repeated his question.

"I don't know," she replied. "During the night I can't stop worrying constantly about him and assuming the worst. In the daytime, the battle is easier. Your father would want us to get food and milk from the Dolenecs today. Thinking ahead will drive us mad." Her brown eyes teared, but her voice became firmer as she talked. "Does that make sense?"

Franz nodded.

He tensed as they walked past a row of shops, trying to appear relaxed as he watched for soldiers.

Two Partisans stepped out the pharmacy door. One of them looked directly at Franz, but was busy chatting and waited for him and his mother to pass. If the soldiers had stopped them, Franz knew he and Mama would tell about their assignment with the Dolenec family.

Maybe if he didn't shake and sweat, Tito's troops would accept a believable story before they shot. Some of them might, but not all.

Frau Dolenec and her children had donned jackets and waited for them, as usual. Franz thought they looked like sparrows since everything about them was shades of brown, including their clothes.

"Bogdan is excited about trying to milk again," Frau Dolenec said. She held Dajana on her hip and smiled at her daughter. "This one is still afraid."

"For now, you just watch from a distance." Mama reached out to pat Dajana's leg. "Bogdan, you remember that we talked about being careful to not surprise the cow? She could step on you and flatten your foot!"

The boy giggled, nodded his head and held the milk pail in front of him. They all trooped to the barn and Franz helped him tie the cow's halter to the hook. Franz once again showed how hand movement got the milk, and then put Bogdan on the little stool. Though he watched and tried, his hands were simply too small and too weak.

When Mama tried to help, the little boy crossed his arms and scowled.

"I do it meself!" He pressed close to the cow and tried again. Failing once more, he jumped up and ran to the corner of the stall, bursting into angry tears. He picked up a handful of straw and threw it at the cow. "I can't do it!"

"You will someday," Franz sat beside him and held up his own work-roughened and long fingered hand and Bogdan's smaller, softer one. "When your hand is as big as mine, it'll be easy. I promise."

Reluctantly, Bogdan gave a watery smile and hugged Franz.

"My turn." Frau Dolenec sat on the stool and showed them how much she'd progressed. She reached up and squeezed with her thumb and forefinger holding the teat so milk didn't go back into the udder, but into the pail. She didn't pull or jerk but successfully pressed milk out.

Bogdan clapped and cheered, which made them all smile. His mother finished draining the cow's udder and picked up the bucket.

"A couple of officers came to see us yesterday while my husband was home," Frau Dolenec said as they walked back to the house. "They wanted to know how the lessons with the cow and hogs have been and said you won't come after today."

Franz and his mother stopped and looked at each other, questions in their eyes. Opa. This had something to do with Opa leaving this morning. Franz wanted to run back to Oma and Kati, to be sure they were there.

"You didn't know?" Frau Dolenec bit her lip and motioned them to follow her.

They shook their heads. Franz stared at the milk pail. Their supply would be stopped, and none to take back to Kati. What would they do then?

"Come have some wine," she said, her eyes shaded by her lowered eyebrows as her lips curved in a smile. "If you stop comparing it to blood, Franz, you'd grow to like ours."

Franz tried to smile but his thoughts darted from one worry to another. Where was Opa? They needed clothes for the coming winter. And food— always the necessity for more food.

He had to turn away from his mother's and Frau Dolenec's discerning eyes. Franz went to the well to bring up water. Wind kicked up as clusters of gray clouds moved their way. Dipping a quart sized metal cup in the bucket, he carried it to the yard table. For the moment, he could pretend nothing had changed in the past few minutes. Frau Dolenec had laid out three tall glasses and a couple of short ones for her children and a pitcher of Croatian wine. As she'd been doing all week, she had two small sandwiches, sliced in halves, for Franz and his mother.

Franz never asked what the meat was. Being edible was enough.

Frau Dolenec poured her and her children's glasses full of the dark red, thick liquid and Franz and his mother's about half full. Mama diluted theirs with water. They each quickly devoured one half sandwich and pocketed the other to take with them.

"I wish we had been left in our homes and you Germans in yours. The Communist government punishes all of us to prove that everything belongs to the State. But what can we do?"

You can give us extra food. Franz instantly felt guilty at his angry thought. He looked at his feet so she couldn't see his face.

The Dolenecs didn't have much either. They had the only livestock in the neighborhood and the Partisans checked on them regularly. They were allowed to keep only part of the milk and kept hidden the dwindling supply of wine they'd brought with them.

"When we lived in Croatia," she murmured, "my husband was a respected attorney. Here, he fits people for shoes and makes a pittance. That is spent on the few rationed goods we can get."

"Someday this will be over." Mama reached across the table and squeezed the other woman's hand.

"You're right. I'm terrible to complain to you when you also lost your home, and have even less food than we have." Frau Dolenec slipped her hand between buttons on the front of her dress and pulled out a handkerchief. She wiped her eyes, sat up straighter and cleared her throat. "What else do I need to know?"

Mama glanced at him. "Franz?"

"Clean the stalls and corral every day," he said. "If the cow stands in manure and urine she'll get foot rot and that can be horrible. Let her out to the back pasture as soon as you finish milking her. Clean the stall while she runs." Franz stopped, out of suggestions.

"Another thing," Mama said. "We've been here only in the mornings, and milked her once a day. You get less milk, but it's richer. Now that you know how, you should milk in morning and evening since it's so badly needed."

They all walked to the back and Mama showed where the hog pen should be repaired and stressed the need to keep water available for them and the cow. It began to sprinkle and the women and children returned to the house.

At last Franz had a few minutes alone. He scooted to the top of the wooden rails. A curious hog pushed at his feet until Franz kicked him in the nose. For the first time that day, he allowed tears to fall. He tried to ignore the pain in his belly and chest.

Opa, please come back! What would they do without his grand-father? He was the glue that kept them together, strong. Franz decided he needed to do more, and whispered familiar words. *Holy Mary, Mother of God, pray over us for our protection. Bring Opa back to us, safe. Amen.* He felt more hopeful. Hopping off the fence, he followed the women's voices.

"In the spring," his mother's voice sounded tired. "Watch for potatoes, peas, cabbage and onions to push their way up."

"Thank you so much for your help. I wish I weren't such a slow student," Frau Dolenec said. "Good luck to you."

"We appreciate the milk and food you've given us," Mama said. "Goodbye."

Franz waved to Bogdan.

"That poor woman," Mama muttered as they walked away. "She's about as equipped to farm as Kati is. Less, actually. They just might trample food under their feet and starve because they don't see it."

"I don't know how you can pity her," Franz said. "She's got a home, her family is together, and they eat enough to survive. She's not hated by Russians and Partisans like we are."

Mama tucked her arm through Franz's. "True, but I feel sorry for her. She's lost a lot, is scared and not prepared for this life.

"At the same time, my heart truly breaks for Katarina," Mama continued. "Off in Russia away from Tony and Berbl, under con-ditions we can't begin to imagine. Their problems aren't the same, but they each have to struggle with their own. None of us knows the future."

They turned toward their temporary home in the rich peo-ples' area of town, the precious last jar of milk between them. Light rain turned heavier and within seconds their summer clothes were soaked.

Few soldiers were outside. Franz kept alert to movement around them but was relieved not to feel eyes watching them. The fear he'd kept pushed down rose again. Would Opa be there? Why was this the last day to help on the farm?

As they usually did when they returned to the house with food, they quietly went to their 'bedroom' horse stall. Franz' knees shook with relief when he saw his grandfather waiting. Opa stretched an arm around him and Mama.

Franz' self-control collapsed and he joined his mother in weeping.

"We're okay. I have news." Opa's deep voice rumbled comforting words. After worrying all day and now seeing Opa, Franz laughed with relief. He sank on the straw with the others.

"Katie," Mama whispered and handed her the jar of milk. The saved half sandwiches were handed to Oma and Opa and quickly eaten. "What happened?" Mama asked Opa.

"They told me to name less than thirty people to go to a house they have ready for us. I'm to start the brick factory working." Opa's eyes had a little of their old sparkle, if only for a moment. "Deciding which people was difficult. If we're not useful to the Communists, we die."

"Who's going?" Franz asked. He leaned forward and scarcely dared to breathe.

"Lissi Baumgartner, so Tony and Berbl come with their aunt." Opa smiled as Franz sighed in relief. "You and Kati are the only other young people. The few men still in Stanisic are older. I have four men who worked for me at harvest. The rest are women." Opa's head lowered. "I wish I could take more."

Franz rolled over on the hardwood floor, every part of his body cold and sore. It was his first morning in their work camp beside the brick factory. Dark by the time soldiers finally came last night to lead them a mile and a half south on Main Street to the end cross street, then east three miles, before they arrived. Weak from hunger never satisfied and nervous from hours waiting for the sound of Partisan boots, no one had had much curiosity about their new home. They'd each found a spot to collapse in the house and the only conversations were short and quiet.

Soft light filtered in the dirty windows. Franz lay still as thoughts of foods he used to eat first thing in the morning danced through his mind. A generous slice of smoked ham and thick piece of Oma's bread. Any time he had been hungry he went to the pantry. Was that a dream? Which was real, then or now? He shivered again at the sound of wind as it whistled around the corner of the house and rattled the windows.

Part of him was eager to get up and explore and search for food. The miserable part wanted to stay as he was, with his arms tucked close to his chest for warmth. Movement from the corner of his eye caused him to lift his head. Opa motioned to him, and other people. With a deep sigh, Franz sat up to put his shoes on and saw Tony nearby. He and his Aunt Lissi stretched, stood up, and joined him.

It was a house like many others. A parlor, kitchen and as Franz headed outside, doors were open to two small bedrooms. The previous owners had been taken quickly the same as all of them. The family left everything. The kitchen table and chairs, utensils, beds in the bedrooms and comfortable furniture in the parlor were all there, waiting. Everyone expressed thankfulness, but a bit of regret for the owners.

"Let's go see the brickyard." Opa said. "It'll be easier for a few ladies to figure out sleeping arrangements and poke around cabinets and hiding places without all of us getting in their way."

As the workers drifted out, Franz and Tony fell in line beside Opa. The stopped and looked over the area next door to their west. Some old brick ovens stood surrounded by volunteer trees, and tall weeds. The area was a refuge for small animals, snakes and rodents.

"I don't see any guards," Franz said, craning his neck.

"They're here. I heard them moving around the parameter last night." Opa stretched his shoulders and neck, his eyes alert as if he were hunting a rabbit.

32

H ANDS ON HIS hips, Opa scanned the neglected brick factory. Franz shoved his fists into his shorts pockets for warmth. Mama nudged him and glanced at his grandfather. They both smiled, knowing how naturally Opa always took responsibility. Franz looked around the area and studied the massive brick kiln. It was as almost as big as Market Square. He walked over to one end and peered into the darkened interior. A small red wagon, covered in grime, sat forlorn and forgotten in a pile of ash.

"Go through the oven and remove any finished bricks." Opa pointed to several women huddled together. "Search for forming molds," he added to another group.

"Franz! Tony!" Opa called out. "We're going to need a lot of clay. Find a wheelbarrow and tools."

Franz saw a shed to his right. Good place to find what they needed. He pulled weeds that had grown over the summer before he could open the door.

Two Partisans walked up and stared intensely at their prisoners. Franz watched as the younger man's nose wrinkled in distaste while he gazed at them.

"You!" The gray-haired one spoke sharply and motioned to Opa.

Standing tall, with his usual authority, Opa joined them. After a quiet discussion, he eyed Franz and Tony and appeared to ask a question.

Franz's heart raced, and his legs felt weak. What was happening? Would he and Tony be taken away? He forced himself to continue working and breathe normally. Finding the wheelbarrow inside, he grabbed it by the handles and jerked it outside.

"Boys," Opa shouted. "Come here."

"This can't be good," Tony whispered.

Franz felt weak as he and Tony reluctantly shuffled over.

"You boys go to the bakery every day, beginning today," the older soldier said. "Find a cart or something to bring back worker rations for this camp."

Rations! Did he hear correctly? He glanced from the man to his grandfather. Opa seemed pleased. Franz studied the soldier and nodded.

After the Partisans left, Franz hurried to the oven and eagerly pulled the little red wagon outside.

"You boys have the single most important job here. Getting us food." Opa put one large hand on each boy's bony shoulder. "You'll be together so you can notice twice as much. Be careful."

"Should we leave now, Herr Hoger?" Tony asked.

Just as Opa said yes, Franz's mother and Tony's Aunt Lissi came to find out what the Partisans wanted. The mere mention of food subdued their worries.

Tony picked up the wagon handlebar and they headed about three blocks north on Flower Street to the pastry shop.

"Now we'll have a chance to see what's happening around here," Franz sighed. He filled his lungs with cool air.

"It's kind of strange, isn't it?" Tony asked. "We've been gone little more than a month, but it seems forever."

In case they were watched, Franz tried to appear unconcerned and not too curious. He kept his eyes on the street and
glanced up from time to time, but never to the sidewalks.

"It sure is deserted," Tony murmured. "No neighbors coming
and going."

"We used to close our eyes and hear hogs, cattle, chickens
and dogs," Franz said. "They'd talk to each other and snort and
move around. I miss that."

When they reached the shop, Franz wondered if the same
cheerful people were there. Tony opened the door to enter.

The unknown middle-aged couple didn't greet them, merely
viewed them with inquiry. Uncertainty flooded Franz. What if
the man told them to leave and gave them no food?

"We're here to get rations for the brick factory," Franz spoke
clearly and pretended he wasn't nervous.

The man turned a page in his ledger with his short stubby fingers. They looked like sausages, but the thought didn't bring a
smile to Franz's lips as it would have before. The man checked off
a line in the book.

"You're to get two loaves of fine Russian bread," he said in
awkward German. "And vegetable sauerkraut soup." His eyes
twinkled as if telling them a joke.

"There are thirty of us there," Franz ventured, hoping to
receive more. He glanced at the woman, whose eyes were full of
pity. Neither adult gave a response.

While the man wrapped their bread, she ladled watery soup
into an aluminum cooking pot. Franz guessed it held a little over
three gallons.

"Thank you," the boys said together as they carried the food
to their wagon, and shook their heads at the meager amount.

On the way back, Franz felt less conspicuous and looked
around. There was a sign on the door of the first house they
passed.

He came to a dead stop and leaned over to read the seal.

"GOVERNMENT PROPERTY!
YOU WILL BE SHOT ON SIGHT!"

In disbelief, he read it again. He turned to Tony, whose mouth hung open as well.

They resumed walking as though in a fog. Many houses stood like bodies without life. They were the ones with chained gates, untrimmed grass between the wall and sidewalk, and the horrible seal on the door. Other homes appeared to be the same as always.

Franz smelled pipe smoke. He stopped and, like a dog, sniffed for its direction. Despite the cold, beads of sweat popped out on his forehead. If they did run into a Partisan who asked questions, they had an acceptable reason to be here. Would they accept that?

Tony frowned when Yugoslavian voices came from the next yard with the tobacco aroma.

"There's no notice on the door," Franz whispered. "These people are new here. I wonder why they've come up from the south."

They trudged in silence. Franz remembered the Croatians and how they'd been forced from their home and shop and 'relocated' to Stanisic.

We're being moved around like pieces of a chess game, he thought. *Just to prove everything belongs to the glorious Communist State!"*

"Our homes are so close," Tony said. "We could just walk to Church Street, turn back north and we'd be almost there." Tears formed in his eyes, but didn't fall.

Franz bit his lower lip and looked toward the west. If only they could go sit down and eat with their families there. Stop! There was no time to daydream. Today he had to get back to their present 'home' with the little food they had.

On the way they noticed many houses with the seal and a few without.

Greeted enthusiastically when they entered the camp, the two loaves were cut and passed around to everyone. Oma took one bite of her small portion of the Russian bread and crumbled the rest.

"Nothing but rye, sugar beet waste and straw! Why, if we'd fed it to the animals, they would have refused!" She glared, but ate it anyway.

Franz joined others in the house to receive his cup of soup. A few small bits of potatoes and corn floated around the sauer-kraut. Mostly, it was water. No salt, no pepper, no seasoning. He sipped it until the last drop.

Far too soon the food disappeared, leaving no belly satisfied.

Franz listened to the others talk about how much or how little had been accomplished in the brick factory that day.

Perhaps tomorrow there would be more food to load into the wagon. Maybe they'll find out they made a mistake in the amount. With that hope, he spent a restless night.

Though this house had belonged to the previous owner of the brick factory, it wasn't home to Franz or the others now. He could hear the women in the two bedrooms shuffling and turn-ing, trying to get comfortable. The older woman and those who needed it the most got the beds. The men did the same bedded down in the living room. The men slept in chairs and sofas. With his knobby knees and skinny arms rubbing the wood floor, Franz tried in vain to sleep. Morning was welcomed with stretches and moving around. He walked outside.

Someone had washed the soup container and returned it to the wagon for them.

Today they would do their job of walking into town to get food, instead of hauling clay here, and being with the same people day after day. Franz ducked his head to hide his pleased expression. He probably shouldn't be so eager to go.

Mama hugged him. "Oh, Franz, I can see you're smelling adventure." Mama shook her head, her shoulders slumped. "But this isn't like when you and Jani explored in Somber."

"I know," Franz mumbled. "We'll be careful."

"Let them be boys, Elisabeth," Opa gently scolded. "If they find something of interest in this damned war, that's good." He looked down his long, straight nose at Franz and Tony. "Stay alert and notice every danger or opportunity."

"It's different now," Mama said, her brown eyes clouded. "You have no rights, no power. Remember that you're both needed. Be careful."

It was with relief that they were on their way. More relaxed than he had been the day before, Franz freely studied the area. A group of five Partisans walked toward them on the other side of the street. Franz forced his feet to keep walking the same way he'd been doing. The soldiers glanced over, but reacted as if the boys were a couple of dogs and kept talking among themselves and passed by.

Franz heard Tony exhale the same time as he did, and they smiled at each other.

A few houses closer to the pastry shop, stood a man by an open gate. He watched them. With broad shoulders and maybe as tall as Opa, he swung a large club at his side.

"Hello," the man sounded like a purring cat. "I saw you walk past yesterday. Are you from the brick factory?"

"Yes, we're on our way to get rations." Franz offered a hesitant smile. The stranger spoke in regular German, so he was probably harmless. Except for the weapon in his hand. Franz tore his eyes from the big stick, and focused on the gray, bushy eyebrows resembling a caterpillar. The boys gave a pleasant nod.

"My name is Herr Haas. Is your family with you at the camp?"

"Some are," Franz answered, intentionally vague. He didn't trust the man. "Others are gone." Franz found it difficult keep his eyes off the frequently shaken bat.

"I'm alone now." The deep, gravelly voice said each word with emphasis. "I came back when I was discharged from the army." He looked down and cleared his throat. "Neighbors said my family has been sent to Russia. Now my friends are gone, too. It's terribly quiet around here." He hesitated and his eyes teared as he studied first Tony, then Franz. ""You remind me of my sons. I guess they're in Russia. I don't know. But I'll find them someday."

Franz didn't know what to say. He and Tony both shuffled their feet.

"Come and visit a little bit."

Franz was about to say they couldn't, but Tony's head tilted to the side as he looked around the man to his yard.

"Sure," Tony said.

They walked cautiously in the open gate, pulling the loaded wagon behind them.

Bam! The club banged the gate as they moved. Both boys jumped and stared at each other. This was not a good idea.

"Sit, sit," Herr Haas motioned to the steps of his porch. He smiled, his thick eyebrows twitching. "Let me show you what I found yesterday." He turned to a box and tilted up its lid. He pulled out a brown rabbit. "I need to cook him, but he listens to me talk. I guess I'll do it tomorrow or the next day. Want to hold him?"

"Sure," Franz said. He wondered how much meat they could get from the critter as he pet the soft fur and felt the full belly.

As if reading his mind, Herr Haas took the wiggly animal and returned him to his box.

Franz stood up and explained that they needed to be on their way.

"I really enjoyed meeting you. Please come back to see me." Herr Haas turned around, clutched his weapon and returned to his house with heavy feet.

The boys let themselves out without a word, pulling the wagon.

"He's not quite right, is he? Why do you think the Partisans left him?" Tony asked after they'd walked away. "He sure is lonesome."

"The Partisans probably decided he wouldn't last too long anyway, with no one to look after him." Franz said. "I think he's harmless."

"His club makes me a bit nervous," Tony said.

"Me too," Franz agreed.

They rushed toward the pastry shop and were given the identical food as before. The same amount.

They didn't need to talk to be aware that this food wouldn't keep them alive for long. Franz' shoulders curled forward and he saw Tony drag his feet as they took the rations back with them.

"Have you noticed that Partisans ignore us when they see us?" Tony asked.

"Yes. "Franz bit his lower lip. "It's like we don't exist, isn't it?"

In the days that followed, Franz and Tony stopped to see Herr Haas frequently and came to like the odd man. Franz was even more thankful that he had Mama, Kati, Oma and Opa with him. And Tony had his sister and aunt. But Haas had no one and he eagerly greeted them every time.

One day when Herr Haas guided them inside the yard, he looked thoughtful. No one spoke for a moment.

"Do you know why I carry this club?" Herr Haas asked.

Franz stood at alert and glanced at Tony. Barely breathing, he shook his head in answer.

"Because it keeps death away." He spoke with great seriousness. "When he comes to get me, I just hit him with my stick and he leaves." He stared intently at Tony, then Franz. "I'm telling you this, but it's a secret that not many people know. That's why they die."

Fear ran up his spine and Franz froze. The birds were louder, the wind sharper, but Franz was totally speechless. This was so strange. It was as if Haas had just said he was from another world.

Haas changed the subject and talked about the weather. Franz couldn't concentrate and soon they were on their way home.

Back at camp Franz was quiet as the bread was cut and dispersed. He ate his bit of soup and studied the others in the group. He held back tears of rage and fear. Mama and Oma along with the others had begun to elevate their swollen feet and legs in the evening. They continued to lose weight. They had to work to stay alive, or they'd be sent to one of the other camps to die. How much longer could they manage on so little?

Should they all take big clubs with them to beat off death?

33

October 1945 – 13 years old
First camp in south Stanišić

FRANZ LEANED CLOSER to Tony as they put the aluminum pot in the wagon. "Let's go a different route tomorrow and see if the Partisans ignore us. We've got to find more food and clothes. Clean clothes."

"Well, I hated to say anything." Tony wrinkled his nose and waved his hand in front of his face. "But you stink."

Franz snaked his foot around Tony's leg to pull him down. Tony jumped aside, staying upright. They both laughed and it felt good. Franz flung his arm over Tony's shoulders.

"Tomorrow might be interesting," he said.

"I'll settle for boring," Tony answered.

Sleep didn't come easily, but Franz wasn't the only one who moved uncomfortably on the wood floor. He kept thinking of various plans for the next day. If they took Auter Row Street and turned off on the cross road past the pastry shop, they could go south and get their food. Franz rolled to his other side, pulling the kitchen dishtowel around his shoulders for warmth.

In the morning, he washed his face and hands with cold water from the well, and wondered what the day would bring. He felt shaky inside, but excited, too.

Tony brought the wagon and they pulled it the new route. Three soldiers were gathered at the corner. One glanced their way, but continued talking to his companions.

A tight knot loosened in his chest and Franz looked at Tony, who raised his eyebrow and smirked.

"We're not important enough to notice."

At the pastry shop, the man gestured for them to get their own food as he continued stocking his shelves. Ugh. Franz clamped his mouth shut to keep complaints inside. Corn gruel again and no bread. They filled their pot.

Franz would have said good-bye or thank you, but the woman was not there and the man's back turned. They returned on Main Street and talked only where they couldn't be heard. Which language would be better anyway? Tony only spoke German. But would Yugoslavian or Hungarian help or hurt?

"Wait! I've been looking for you," a man yelled.

Franz and Tony froze at the voice of authority behind them and glanced at each other. Tony's his eyes showed fear but he didn't outwardly react.

Franz' leg muscles tightened and his heart beat rapidly. He held his breath and turned to look over his shoulder at a man in an officer's uniform.

"Come, we can talk while we drink coffee." Another man ahead of them replied. Franz heard retreating footsteps and the conversation gradually muted.

It took a while for his breathing to settle to normal, and by that time they'd returned to the camp.

Everyone ate their meager 'meal' of shredded corn. It was the same as yesterday and the day before – tough and tasteless. Salt would help, but it would still be bad. Complaints of stomach cramps grew daily.

Franz sat cross-legged in the yard with Tony. "Think we can climb that wall?" he asked. Tony tipped his head and hitched his shoulders. "If we had a ladder, sure. Why?"

Walking close to the brick enclosure, Franz leaned against it. He locked his hands together. "Step up and see if I can get you high enough," Franz said. The support at his back steadied his grip.

Tony placed his foot in the human stirrup and climbed to Franz' shoulders. He bent his knees and hopped up. In one swift movement, he perched on the top.

Franz laughed in triumph.

Tony braced himself, a leg on each side. Leaning over while his knees and feet squeezed the wall, he reached down as far as he could.

Franz sprang up, stretched to grab the hand and pulled up quickly. Both boys dropped to the outside.

Returning to the camp side was smoother and quicker. They grinned at each other as they sat on the wall.

"What are you doing?" Kati's seven-year-old voice sounded as bossy as any mother.

From his perch, Franz looked down at his little sister. When had she gotten so skinny? Being the youngest in the camp, everyone tried to slip her extra to eat. Her pretty blonde hair had changed into something resembling hay. Franz blinked his eyes and looked again.

"I'm going to tell!" Kati ran for their mother.

Franz and Tony waited.

It wasn't but a minute before both families gathered, peering up at them. Opa's eyes twinkled. Franz' and Tony's families looked confused.

"Is this a game you're playing?" Hands on hips, Lissi frowned.

Both boys jumped to the ground.

"Got places to search?" Opa gave them a knowing nod.

"What are you planning to do?" Berbl's blue eyes widened as she reached for Tony with shaking hands.

"We're all starving." Tony, the same height as his older sister, hugged her. "We have to do something."

"Where should we start, Opa?" Franz stepped closer to his grandfather, needing his wisdom.

"Check houses that feel safe, Franz. Go slowly. Before the Russians came, a lot of people put a false wall around the chimney in their attics to hide valuables, smoked meats or whatever seemed important. Also, you can see the street from the vent up there."

The next morning they got up, dressed and left before the Partisans came to check the progress of the brick factory. Clouds covered the sunrise in the cold, damp air.

Franz and Tony walked past the first block, looking for a place to leave the wagon while they checked some houses.

"Look," Franz said. Holding his hand close, he pointed at an overgrown lot.

Tony nodded and pulled the four-wheeled cart into tangled weeds and grass leading to a small tree. It couldn't be seen. They'd pick it up in a couple of hours to get their usual rations.

Feeling naked without the wagon to explain their presence, Franz watched the dirt road for anything noisy. He read the signs on the doors announcing they were government property and trespassers would be shot. He'd seen people shot in Sombor, and also in Leipzig. One moment there was life. Instantly, he could be on the ground dead and bleeding. If there were time to run, which way should he go? He bit his lower lip and looked away. They had to do this! At the cross street, he turned and went halfway up the block. Franz stopped. Backyard gardens were on the other side.

His hands shook. It wasn't too late to stop and just get the rations. He glanced at his friend.

Tony's elbows pressed into his sides and he breathed with his mouth open. When he saw Tony was nervous, too, Franz' courage strengthened.

Franz put his back to the wall as both boys scanned the area. He listened, almost expecting someone to shout at them to stop. It was quiet.

Cupping his hands, Franz nodded at Tony. Up he went, swiveling around sideways on the wall with his hand stretched down. As they'd practiced, it took about two blinks of an eye for them to get up, over and drop down on the inside.

Franz' legs trembled as he sat beside Tony. They listened for footsteps or voices. Relieved, Tony pressed his hand to his heart. Franz made a sign of the cross, and they shared a slow smile. They did it!

There was plenty of cover with remnants of corn stalks, beans, sunflowers and berry bushes. Almost an hour passed without activity. They took their time crawling to the end of the first house. Franz heard wind, and leaves rustling, but nothing else. They stopped frequently. Almost every home in Stanisic had a back room where tools and horse tack were kept. With any luck, they'd find something to help break inside.

Pry bar in hand, Franz forced open a window facing the garden. The neighborhood silence magnified each noise. He looked around. A bird sang in a nearby tree, and its familiarity filled him with comfort. He gave a slow exhale of the breath he'd held.

Inside, they went straight to the pantry, and walked up the stairway to the attic. Franz watched through a one by two foot wide ventilation hole facing the street, alert for Partisan patrols. Tony took the bar and tapped the walls around the chimney.

Carefully looking up and down the street, Franz listened. Thunk, thunk, thunk. Solid sounds. Tony moved around to the side, finally rewarded by a hollow echo.

Franz hands itched to be the ones tearing the fake wall down, but they mustn't be seen here.

"Ah!" Tony's head was in the hole, his voice muffled.

Franz tried to keep his eyes on the street, but glanced frequently over his shoulder.

Tony held up a roll of German money and a large smoked ham from a well-fed hog. Holding his fists up in victory, Franz returned to the view outside.

Downstairs, they took a sheet off a bed and found men's shirts and pants hung in a wardrobe and they put them with the meat. Franz stood and looked down. Where was the owner of this house, these things? Russia? Dead? Coming back?

"I'm sorry," Franz whispered to shadows as he glanced around the room. "We have to take this. I hope you understand, wherever you are." He blinked his eyes and his back straightened as he thought of the needs of the workers at the brick factory. They took their haul out to the garden and hid it amidst dense stalks.

"Let's get the rations now. I don't think they'll miss us anyway." Franz said. "Our things will be safe here until we come back."

It took but a few minutes to get out and retrieve the four-wheeled cart. At the pastry shop, the man gestured for them to get their own food as he'd done before. He visited with a friend and ignored them. The same horrible stuff again, and it smelled like hog slop. They filled their pot and left.

They walked slowly to the wagon's hiding place and pulled it into the jungle of weeds and small trees. Soldiers were patrolling, so they ducked out of sight and waited until it was safer to return to the same block.

Two more houses were searched after they followed routine observations. Warmer clothes for women and another blanket, and kitchen utensils were found. In one horse trough, Franz burrowed to discover an old gunny sack and a bag of potatoes nestled under soured hay. Several onions were dug from a small garden.

"This is as much as we can carry over the wall," Franz whispered into Tony's ear. "Let's wrap some in the sheet." They rolled the material with clothes, ham and money and tied the ends together.

"This bag smells like cow manure, but it'll work." Tony stretched the opening of the bag from the barn and dumped the blanket in first, and Franz finished filling it.

They crawled to the back of the garden and waited until dark.

Tony motioned he was ready to go up the wall. Then Franz raised the bundle when Tony reached for it. There was a soft plop when it dropped to the grass on the outside.

Tony lay forward to fit the wall.

Franz listened intently. Quiet. He lifted the gunny sack high as possible, and felt Tony lift it.

As soon as Tony's hand reached down, Franz grabbed hold and quickly they dropped to the sidewalk.

Each carrying a bundle, they stayed on the grass, went to get the wagon and returned to camp very tired, but thankful to be safe.

"Hello," Franz said as they opened the door and tried to look sad. "We have the same old shredded husks." Then he turned around with a flourish and showed the bundle on his back. Tony did the same. "And real food!"

Franz beamed as he watched everyone's excitement when they saw the ham, potatoes and onions. Within minutes the pot was loaded with water and set to heat. Potatoes were washed and cut into bite-sized chunks and ham sliced. Clothing was given to those with the most need and about the right sizes.

The water didn't boil fast enough, declared some. Others wanted to eat it raw. But Oma and the other women who'd claimed ownership of the kitchen insisted on patience. The fragrance of cooking onions kept everyone restless.

Mama sat between the boys as they leaned against a tree and put an arm over each one. "We're all so thankful." She hesitated. "Did you have any trouble?"

"No," Franz answered. "We were cautious." He grinned and put his head on Mama's shoulder. "And lucky."

"People are calling you our Robin Hoods." Mama shook her head and closed her eyes. "What every mother dreams of for her son." Then she laughed and ruffled their heads. "Does your trick have a name?"

Franz and Tony looked at one another. "You're a ladder," offered Tony.

"And we're robbing confiscated homes." Franz cocked his head as he thought. "We can call this our Robber's Ladder."

Both boys liked their new name.

"Dinner is ready!" Oma called for people to gather.

"Let's pray," said their most devout man. "Father, Thank you for bringing real food by way of these boys. Guide each of us to do Your will. Amen."

Franz joined the swiftly moving line. The only sound he heard was people busy eating and an occasional expression of appreciation. Within minutes every drop had been eaten.

Tomorrow, Franz vowed, we'll go to more houses. This was good, but not enough.

Having more satisfied stomachs helped people get settled in for a better night's sleep.

Franz woke Tony, and they left early again the next morning, dragging the wagon.

"We haven't seen Herr Haas lately," Tony said. "I'll bet he misses us."

"Let's go that direction," Franz quickly agreed. "We'll explore the block across the street from him after we stash our supplies."

As they neared his house, there was no sign of Haas waiting by the gate. They shoved the wagon onto an overgrown area next door.

"We're earlier than usual," Franz said. He opened the gate gently and poked his head inside. "Herr Haas?" he whispered.

No answer. Tony pushed the opening wider and they walked along the path in the dim light of the rising sun. Every few seconds one of them would call out the man's name.

"What's that?" Franz pointed to a dark shape on the ground.

Closer, they saw it was their friend. Lying on his back, stretched out, his head turned to one side, and eyes fixed open. He still clutched his club.

"Is . . . is he dead?" Tony whimpered from a distance of about six feet.

"Yes." Franz backed up a few steps, then turned and ran to the gate. He had to get away. Had to escape the horror of seeing their friend's hideous, lifeless face. Tony was as close as a shadow until they were out of the yard.

"What was that stink?" Tony's chin trembled. He held up one palm to stop the answer.

"He messed himself, I think. His club didn't keep death away." Franz shivered, and straightened his shoulders. "We can't think about him or help him now. It's more important to find food."

They went north a half block, then walked along the cross street until they were even with the backyard gardens. They stopped, listened, and carefully looked around.

"Robber's Ladder?" Franz braced his back against the wall, his hands cupped. Quick as a monkey, Tony climbed up Franz and reached the top.

Following the successful routine, they crawled on their bellies close enough to watch the first house. The unkept back yard looked deserted. Eventually, they reached the shed and felt around until Tony found a large hammer.

The sun had risen to cast long shadows where they could move about.

Franz tried the windows and the plain back door. All locked. For a few minutes, they waited to hear any small noises from within. Franz took the hammer and with one swift downward thrust, the knob fell off. It was far too loud, and then the knob fell with echoes. After minutes of no response, they went inside and up the stairs to the attic.

This time, Tony watched the street from the vent and Franz tapped, searching for hidden spaces. It sounded solid all around. Discouraged, Franz sat on a box to think. Why were things pushed together in a pile in the corner? Hmmm. He lifted a box, old curtain rods, a much used quilt frame, coffee grinder and a stack of books. Beneath was flooring that didn't match.

Franz grabbed the hammer and used the claw to remove a loose plank. He reached in and pulled out a thick portion of smoked bacon, wrapped in paper. He grinned and opened the end to show Tony. They each tore off a piece before Franz rewrapped it. There was a box of family pictures, and a bundle of old letters. As he put them back in the hole, Franz wondered if the owners would be able to come back for them. He hoped so.

He restacked the pile and picked up the coffee grinder to set aside. Could they make flour with it? Just in case, they stuffed their pockets with remnants of wheat stored here.

Hiding everything in the garden, they retraced their steps to get the wagon and went for their rationed goods. They saw no one, but helped themselves as usual.

The rest of the day they went through two more houses. A bag of dried, white beans would do for several meals. In every house they managed to scoop up wheat. At the last one, a nice wicker basket was found so they could carry back their treasures.

"Aunt Lissi won't believe that I wanted to take soap back." Tony leaned close to Franz' ear to visit as they lay in the garden waiting for the cover of darkness. "We'll be clean, but that won't keep us warm. We still need to find more coats."

"This Black Hawthorn has a lot of berries." Franz pointed to a thorny bush nearby. "Let's pick them."

"Because it stinks and tastes awful, Aunt Lissi says it's healthy." Tony wrinkled his nose.

"I know. I hate it, too. But it'll make the women happy." Franz sighed. Unenthusiastically, he picked from the bottom of the bush and Tony joined him. Each berry went into a pile, and dumped into the container.

The basket was awkward to get over the wall, and difficult to carry back to the wagon. Relief flooded Franz when they successfully reached the camp. Again, they were greeted with eagerness.

Franz ate his bit of smoked bacon and chewed as if it were an amazing delicacy while waiting for the beans to cook.

"Boys," one of the older women hobbled over to them on her swollen legs. "You're saving our lives, such as they are." She seemed to run out of words as a lone tear rolled down her cheek. She returned to her seat.

Franz felt like crying and apologizing for there not being more. These people worked hard all day at the brick factory trying to meet quotas.

"Do what you can," Opa's deep voice interrupted Franz' thoughts. "Don't beat yourself about what you wish you could have done." His deep brown eyes seemed to see inside Franz. "What else happened today?"

Franz blinked away tired tears. "Remember we told you about Herr Haas?"

"Yes, the man you've been visiting. He worked several harvests for me."

"We found him in his yard. Dead." He hesitated and turned to Tony, who had just walked up.

"He still held his club," Tony looked off in the distance, and then stared at his feet. "Death caught him anyway."

"We didn't know what to do." A heavy weight of guilt pressed on Franz for running away. "What will happen to him? Will someone bury him?"

"There wasn't one single thing you could do, either of you boys," Opa said firmly. "By Tito's rules, Haas shouldn't have been left in his home." Opa patted Franz' shoulder. "Only Germans married to Hungarians and listed as Hungarians can stay. All of Haas' family was German. One of the guards likes to talk. One day he bragged that when one of us dies, we would be stuffed in a gunny sack and thrown in a big hole with other bodies. That's probably his fate. But remember there is a better life after this one on earth."

Franz bowed his head, stomach churning. No funeral, no people gathered to say nice things about the old man. His family would never know what happened.

34

November 1945, 13 years old
First camp, two weeks later

"G O BACK INTO our house one more time, but only when it's safe. Don't get reckless." Mama leaned in close to Franz as she poured a cup of stinky Black Hawthorn tea for him, and set the kettle back on the kitchen stove. She waited, so Franz made himself sip the horrible tasting drink. "Get the family pictures out of their drawer, and our birth certificates tucked underneath. We'll need them later." Mama wrapped him in a fierce embrace.

"Later?" Franz rubbed the back of his neck. Had he missed something?

"We're getting less wood for the kiln, and our quota has dropped." Mama turned to face him, and grimaced in pain at the movement in her swollen legs. "We've heard nothing, but we all feel something in the air. This time, I want to be prepared."

Tony opened the front door and gestured. It was time to go.

Franz picked up their large key ring and shook it. In every house, they added to the loop, and now could reenter many houses and the cabinets inside. He tossed it to Tony.

Franz hugged his mother and left with his friend. "Guess where we're going." Franz said.

Tony nodded slowly as they walked toward the street. "My aunt and your mother have been talking. I know where to look in the store's hiding place."

"I wonder why the guards never noticed we stopped getting our rations." Franz felt in his pocket, as he did every morning, to be sure he had his slingshot. "Oma says she's been praying to Saint Michael for our protection. I guess it works."

Everything felt different today. Tension vibrated in the air and sound magnified as Franz and Tony moved with stealth toward their destination. Bare tree limbs pointed toward dark clouds, as if they could poke them and bring rain. Leaves still littered the ground, flattened and still.

While part of him stayed on high alert, Franz thought about the women in the camp. He and Tony had found a sofa with a strong, rough fabric, used a straight razor and cut most of the back out, thinking it might be useful for bedding. Their next trip out they wrapped rags around canning jars of fruit to protect them and keep them quiet.

One night everyone in camp complained about their cold feet. In no time at all, the women began planning how to make house slippers. Sitting around a circle, they'd torn the material into half-inch wide strips, took three pieces and braided them into ropes. The sewing machine was used to sew upper layers to enclose the top of the foot and the toes. For soles, feet were traced on the upholstery fabric and sewed onto the braided rags. Nothing was wasted.

Don't let your mind wander, Franz scolded himself. After going on daily searching trips the last two weeks, Franz felt a fluttery, empty feeling in his stomach when he neared home. He glanced both ways as they headed to the wall where they would use their Robber's Ladder. Staying low, they crawled through fallen leaves and used the key to enter.

Franz wandered around the rooms, but it didn't feel right. Tears were close to the surface and a dull ache filled his chest. The house smelled different, like it had died. It was too quiet.

He stopped. The sofa was gone. Probably Hungarians took it. The empty spot flooded him with memories. It had been a favorite place to read. Kati did her letters here and hid behind it when the Russians rode though their yard and took Oma's prized cherries. Katie's kittens loved to crawl on the back and look out the window. Now impressions in the rug, where the furniture had been, were all that remained.

He'd searched the house thoroughly last time. Here, where there had always been abundance, he found nothing edible in the pantry or kitchen. On his hands and knees, he examined every room, not just the kitchen. He started to say something, then remembered Tony was in the barn searching one more time.

Franz went to Mama's oak chest and opened the box of photos in the bottom drawer. On top was one of Mama and Katie in matching dresses. It must have been taken shortly before the Chetniks battle with the Hungarians changed everything. Mama pushed young Kati in a stroller and looked focused on where she was going in downtown Sombor. Franz' finger traced the blond curl on Kati's head. She'd been so little. They still had Vati and Franz played with Jani most days. Life had been simple.

With an angry snap, Franz pushed the lid back on and shoved the flat box under his arm. The birth certificates were in a large envelope and he tucked that inside his shirt, flat against his chest.

"Goodbye." He looked around the rooms, memorizing them. A heavy sadness pressed against him, making breathing difficult.

He hid the items in the garden and they moved on to the house next door, where Anton Haut had lived. Franz glanced over the fence where the Weiss family resided and a slight smile came to his lips. He remembered the day he and Anton climbed the ladder to get the bird eggs and Anton had broken some roof tiles. Frau Weiss was some mad!

Where was his old friend now?

He blinked away the memories and concentrated on why they were here.

More wheat was found in attics, and four jars of peaches.

They retraced their steps and went to the house next to Lissi's. Their first discovery was a large sand-colored tarp that had been little used. It could be folded around everything to carry back. In a corner bedroom, Franz pressed his face to the floor and saw a dark shape. He shoved the bed away from the wall and peeked inside a brown bag. Pickled carrots and a surprise of three large smoked sausages! Stashing them with the other items, they continued to Tony's aunt's house.

Franz watched Tony's face change after he used Lissi's key and entered. Tony tipped his head down, closed his eyes and bit his lip.

Understanding, Franz left him alone and went to the attic to peek out the vent hole. A Partisan came up the sidewalk, the red star prominent on his cap, his afternoon shadow long. Eyes narrowed, the man looked from one side of the street to the other.

Lips pursed, Franz gave sparrow chirrups to alert Tony downstairs. All was quiet. Franz stepped back out of view, then looked with one eye and saw the soldier had passed, continuing to scrutinize the area. Franz went downstairs.

Tony held a picture of his parents, tear tracks on his cheeks. His mother was in Russia now, and he didn't know where his father was. Somewhere in the German Army, the same as Franz' father. Wordless, Franz followed as Tony led the way to Lissi's store.

Tony pulled the keys from his pocket and inserted the right one to open the shop. They slipped inside, careful to shut the door with a quiet click.

The shelves were empty but littered with dust and bits of trash. Franz remembered the way it had been. The counter used to hold delicious small candies and the corner was where he found supplies for Oma and Mama. He leaned over a barrel. Empty. There were German books on the shelf, so not of any interest to the Serbs or Hungarians. He held them and circled the room.

Tony twisted a small turn screw on the back of a lower shelf. Wiggling it loose, he reached inside for a bundle of cigarettes, currency that could be traded to anyone. Tony's light brown eyes widened as he saw how many there were.

They went through two houses that faced Main Street, and found more canned goods. They gathered everything together and placed them on the tarp and pulled the corners together.

Franz closed his eyes and rested when they returned to the garden area near the wall. Darkness came rapidly.

Suddenly, orders to stop were shouted by both Serbians and Yugoslavs. Franz tensed at gun shots in the distance. Beside him, Tony jerked and they scooted closer together. Screams pierced the air. He could hear running, but it echoed from various directions. An uneasy silence followed.

Was it safe to leave? He had to be with his family. He lay perfectly still from head to toe, only looking around for movement. Who was shot? Why? Were they found raiding houses?

Gradually, the fear eased and his breathing calmed as nothing more happened.

Nervous, with shaking hands, Franz hefted the filled tarp to Tony on the top of the wall and they struggled back to the camp, trying to stay in the shadows.

As soon as they walked in the door, their families swarmed around. "We heard shots, and were so scared!" Mama and Oma cried.

"We joined together and prayed," said another.

"Thank the Lord, you're here!" Lissi put her hands on Tony's thin face.

Then they unrolled the tarp and saw the treasures.

Oma and the other chief cook held the fragrant sausages in the air to cheers and carried pickled carrots and canned goods off to prepare their meal. Lissi swooped in to grab the cigarettes. The wheat was gathered and taken to the table where their coffee grinder waited to turn it into flour.

Mama claimed the tarp to make pants for Franz and Kati. A man who read avidly picked up the books and moved them to the shelf.

Franz handed her the envelope he pulled from inside his shirt and the box of pictures. She weaved her way through people and sat in a corner. One by one, she looked at the pictures, crying over many of them. Franz sat down beside her.

"You look so much like your father." She sniffled and gave a weary smile as she held up a picture of her and Vati on their wedding day. "If only he could be here with us!"

"I'm glad we have the pictures," he said. "Sometimes I can't remember what he looked like. Pictures will help Kati, too."

They looked through a few more photos, some made them smile.

"Franz," Kati tugged on his hand. "Did you bring me a kitten?"

"No," Franz closed his eyes a moment. Truthfully, he'd forgotten her request. "I'm sorry. I didn't see any."

Her lower lip stuck out, and then she threw her arms around him.

"Next time?" Her blue eyes were moist. "It would make Oma feel better, too."

"Yes, it would. I'll try." He pushed the hair from her face and patted her head, then looked at Mama. "Oma isn't improved today?"

"No," she said very softly. "She's dizzy and listless. Her legs ache all the time. Something that might help would be pigeon soup." Mama's face relaxed and she gave a little laugh. "After all these years of scolding you for practicing shooting at birds, I want you to take your sling shot out back to the old corn shed. Pigeons are in the rafters."

"Maybe it's a good thing I didn't get to take down every bird I saw, because there would be none left now." He chose not to remind her about how adamant she'd been that birds should be free to fly, as God created them. "Bet I could get at least one this evening after we eat."

"Good," she said simply, with a deep sigh.

"We're not getting enough for 30 people." Franz whispered to Tony that night as they lay in a nest of old blankets. "If we go south, maybe the Yugoslavs will give us food." Franz hated to even suggest such a thing. It felt like failure. Begging could expose them to greater danger, but all the camp might benefit.

"Just march up and knock on doors?" Tony said each word slowly and separately, expressing skepticism.

"We could walk around like we belong. If they're friendly, we could ask. My Yugoslavian is good enough."

Tony bit his lower lip and nodded. "Wish ration goods didn't give us stomach cramps and constant runs. We could go back there."

"Don't tell anyone what we're going to do," Franz said.

35

November, first of December- 1945, 13 years old
Camp One

"GOOD DAY." FRANZ tried to ignore feeling nervous and spoke in Yugoslav to a woman hanging clothes out to dry. A little boy, playing with a toy truck nearby, got up and stood at his mother's side. He stared at Franz and Tony, his brown eyes curious, his face framed with black curls. "It's nice to have such a sunny day," Franz said. Then he felt stupid because clouds were gathering. He wiped his hands on his pants.

She smiled and Franz felt encouraged.

"Do you live near here?" she asked pleasantly.

"No," Franz said, tense with the ready story. "Our father is gone and our mother is sick." He stopped, and then forced himself to continue. "We could really use some food." He didn't want to cry like a little kid. This was much harder than he'd expected. He had to get food for their camp.

"I... I'm sorry," the woman gathered her basket and little boy and backed away to her house. "We barely have enough to survive ourselves." She bit her lip, and turned and hurried to her home.

"Well, that didn't work." He felt sick with guilt. What would Mama and Opa say if they knew he was begging? Franz glanced at Tony, who looked down as they walked.

Tony barely nodded. "Other people might help."

The yards were quiet until they saw an old man replacing rotten pickets on his fence. "Can we help you with that in exchange for some food?" Franz asked directly. *Please, please, say yes!*

"No, and get out of here!" The man snarled and shook his hammer in the air. "I'm tired of you people bothering me. We're all having a rough time." He glowered and picked up his next board and ignored them.

"Sorry," Franz mumbled. He felt his face heat with embarrassment.

By mid-afternoon, Franz felt like a deflated balloon. "Tomorrow it's back to the German section," he said. "All we got here is tired feet and humiliation."

"At least empty houses don't hate us," Tony said. "Somehow we'll find what we need."

They went home, shoulders slumped and empty-handed.

Franz took his sling shot to the old corn crib, picking up a handful of rocks on his way. *Take your time,* he cautioned himself. *Don't spook them.* He leaned against the wall until he was part of the landscape. He waited patiently until he chose one pigeon sitting by himself. Very slowly, he raised his weapon, pulled back and got a good aim. *Wisk!* The pigeon was hit right on his head and simply fell over backward without a sound. More was needed.

Again, he must be patient. If the birds were frightened, the flock would leave. Sitting quietly, he watched them pull one leg up and settle in for a snooze. Fighting a desire to hurry, he positioned another rock in the pocket. Selecting the next pigeon, he pulled back, and let go. It dropped to the ground.

Clenching his teeth, he slowly picked them by their feet, and took them outside. With nimble fingers, he plucked them clean, and put their feathers in an old flower pot for use later. He'd learned to waste nothing. Once inside, he handed them off to the cooks.

He'd helped Oma become healthier on a supply of pigeons for soup the last two weeks. This should help everyone tonight.

It was a light meal with no spoken complaints. It didn't matter, because Franz felt weighed by failure. He swallowed past thickness in the back of his throat, thinking how stupid his idea had been. If they'd gone into homes without food, they could have gotten blankets if nothing else, or items they could use.

After they'd eaten, Franz sat by the shelf of books, looking for something of interest.

"I'm glad you thought to get these," Mama said, joining joined him. "A lot of people read in the evenings."

Franz looked up, saw a lady march toward him, bowed his head and whispered, "Who is she?"

Mama smiled, and greeted the woman. "Hello, Frau Zisler."

She nodded. "I've thought of some things I need you boys to get from my house, Franz." She gave him directions to her home, and told him what she wanted, and where he would find them. "Our suitcase is under the stairway. It might be used to bring things from other houses, too."

He listened carefully and repeated the directions back to her. With a relieved sigh, she left.

"Franz, don't ever feel you haven't done enough." Mama said. She reached out and raised his chin and looked into his eyes. "When they give you specific requests and you and Tony bring them back, it's priceless. Some things are memories they don't want to leave behind. Others are for a future." She reached and held his hand while they sat in comfortable silence. The heaviness in his heart lifted.

The next two weeks, he and Tony continued their daily raids, primarily filling requests. On one of their trips they got Mama's silverware and jewelry. Then they retrieved more of Lissi's things as well as possessions Tony's mother had left in safe-keeping. They looked for hand baggage when possible. Everyone knew they would never go back to their homes. That dream had gradually died, even for Opa.

Always, Franz stayed alert and reacted to each gun shot, each new sound. Cold wind whistled around them as they walked, but the longer nights made it easier to get to their destination, search more houses and get back to the brick yard shortly after dark.

While most people worked at the factory a couple of women stayed at the house to protect Kati and keep the coffee grinder busy turning wheat into flour. At night, Franz could hear the sewing machine humming along using fabrics they'd found to make shirts and pants.

Now they gathered anything of value to pay for eventual escape. Hiding places were all over the camp house. The Partisans never came inside.

"Why are Opa and Oma looking so worried?" Franz asked Mama one evening.

"I'm not sure. Our quota for bricks has been cut again."

———

Staring out the window at clouds blowing away from Stanisic, Franz put the book about stars and planets back on its shelf. The night had been filled with lightning, thunder and angry rain pelting the windows and roof. Temperatures dropped close to freezing. Everyone moved slowly, getting ready to make another batch of bricks.

Franz motioned to Tony. "We'd better go now." They trekked out behind the shed in back, which had become the men's open air latrine. The women got the outhouse.

"I wonder how much storm damage there was last night." Tony mused. He cocked his head at something and began walking toward the front of the house.

Creaking and clopping sounds of a horse and wagon on the street grew louder. Franz buttoned his pants closed and ran to join the others. "It's stopping," he said. Dread moved from his heart and mind to all of him. Everyone stood still as if turned to wood and watched also. Franz felt a shiver go up his spine. Why a wagon? And who?

"Not soldiers," Mama said beside him. A horseman sat high on the wagon and a woman next to him. The woman climbed down with a big basket on her arm. She almost dropped it, but quickly turned to grab it with her other hand as well

"Stop! You're not allowed to come here!" A large, scowling Partisan guarding the camp waved his hands, shouted and hurried toward the visitors. "Move along! These are German enemies. You don't have any business here!"

"Get out of my way!" The woman pushed past him with her head held tall, and all the command of a queen. "I heard my people are here and I am bringing them some food." She brushed past him as if he were a child. He reached for the container, but something about the woman changed his mind because he let his arms drop and allowed her to pass.

Franz cocked his head. Did he know that voice?

"Oh!" Mama exclaimed. "It's...it's Julienne Jelloneni!" She rushed out the door, totally ignoring the guards and their disapproval. Franz followed close behind and took the heavy basket while the women hugged each other and cried. It was the lady he'd called Yellow Nanny when he was too little for school.

Oma and her friend Erna each grabbed an end of the handle and took the precious gift and hurried inside.

"I have to turn around and return to Sombor." Their friend stopped and looked at Franz, hands on hips. "That boy is a right skinny man now, but I'd recognize him anywhere." Her voice dropped down so she couldn't be heard by the guards. "What about your younger one?"

"We keep her out of sight as much as possible," Mama whispered. "Sometimes they go through looking for little girls." She stepped back and shook her head. "Thank you for whatever wonderful things are in the basket." She spoke in a normal voice before the guard should decide to come closer.

"When Mirko found out I was determined to come, he said to thank you for the food you took to him when he was on the farm work camp. I wish I could do more for you." With a wave at Franz, she got back on the wagon, biting her lips, her brow furrowed.

"Who was that?" Opa asked.

"Our landlady from Sombor." Mama glanced up at the soldier still on the street. He stared at her intently, but she turned back to Opa. "She was always very kind, and a good friend to us all. It took a lot of courage for her to come here and bring food. I hope she isn't punished." She inhaled a raggedy breath.

Inside the house, Franz opened their gifts and pulled out enough smoked meat to last a week if they were careful. Three cabbages wedged into corners, and down at the bottom, a treasure. Real coffee! Then he found candies. Franz and Mama smiled, remembering how their friend used to take Franz to stores for sweets and Mirko brought some back from his trips.

Franz held up two jars of peaches, letting the light filter through the rich color.

"Thank you, Yellow Nanny," he said out loud to the door, willing the words to follow her.

The next day Franz and Tony found money, jewelry, another blanket, some clothes, green beans that had been canned, a nice haul of wheat and two books as well. One of poetry that some of the ladies would like and a child's book for Kati. Women asked for family pictures and told Franz where to find them. They'd gone into three of the people's houses and quickly found their treasures.

"It's a good thing that woman brought food," Tony said when they filled a gunny sack. "It's getting harder to find." They lay on their sides, waiting for dark.

"If they close the brick factory," Franz whispered, "What will happen to us? Will we stay with our families? Can we still keep searching around here?" Franz' mouth was dry, and his throat felt closed up.

They didn't talk, each mulling over their own thoughts until the sun set. Franz got up, braced against the wall so they could do their Robbers Ladder and take the sack to the others.

The first thing Franz noticed was that everyone was inside the camp house. Usually there were groups bundled up and sitting outside to visit.

Tony opened the door and they stepped into to a scene of chaos.

Instead of the usual lack of activity, people scurried around carrying clothes, or papers, or photos and stacking them in piles. Cooked food was on the stove, but that didn't seem to be the only priority now.

"Franz!" Kati ran to him, tripping over a woman's shoe as she knelt on her hands and knees, reaching under the sofa.

"Kati Elmer!" Her face mottled with anger, the woman grabbed her injured foot. "Can't you stay out of the way? We don't have time for brats underfoot!"

"I'm sorry," Kati burst into tears, running to Franz.

He picked her up and hugged her. "You're okay. It was an accident." When she nodded against his chest, he lowered her to her feet and took her hand. "What's all the commotion?"

"They're taking us away in the morning," Opa said from across the room. He came closer and put his hand on Franz' shoulder. "We'll all wear as many clothes as we can and hide our important papers and valuables in pockets and pinned inside wherever possible. We're each allowed a bundle or suitcase for food and other things."

Distracted by Oma calling for him, Opa moved on to the living room. He hollered over his shoulder that the boys should get themselves some soup.

The small amount of food in the pot was quickly divided. They leaned against the wall while eating, with Kati tucking herself close. There was order in what had at first seemed like total confusion. But tension ran high as people got in each other's way, and disagreements popped up.

He studied things placed on the table. The coffee grinder, a box holding wheat not yet ground, and a sack of flour were at one end. Canned green beans, and a half loaf of bread at the other.

"Tony!" Berbl called from the women's bedroom doorway. "Aunt Lissi wants us to separate what each of us will carry." She put her hands on her hips and clenched her teeth and shook her head. "We need your help. Now!"

A dimpled smile flitted across Franz' face. She sure could act like a bossy mother!

"I'd better help before someone falls apart." Tony held his bowl up and tipped each drop into his mouth before joining his sister.

Stacking his clothes together didn't take long, and the sling shot rested in his pocket.

Kati shadowed him as he moved around and followed him to find Mama.

"These are Kati's things for tomorrow." Mama didn't look at Franz, but tapped her finger against her lip as if ticking off a list. "We'll probably have a long walk in the morning."

"We need to take the frying pan and stock pot to cook with!" A shrill voice from the kitchen shook, as if the woman were near tears.

Franz walked into the room to see Frau Werner's red face.

"You know they'll take it away from us, so why carry the extra weight?" Frau Lackner protested. "Our feet give us enough problems as it is."

Shaking his head, Franz walked outside. Hearing people argue made his stomach hurt.

All night people shifted frequently in their beds, or fumbled around to get something from another room or drawer. It didn't bother Franz. He couldn't sleep anyway. Worries and questions swirled in his mind. At last the sun peeked up.

Everyone got one slice of bread and began the process of dressing. By the time Franz layered summer clothes, then winter, and jacket and coat, each pocket filled with something, he was ready.

Franz and Tony looked at each other and laughed.

"We look like we've been fattened for slaughter!" Franz said. The sight of extra Partisans surrounding the camp chased away the brief moment of humor. One guard motioned for people to form lines.

"Kati, stay between Franz and me," Mama leaned over and touched her forehead to Kati's.

Huddled between their coats, Kati held on to their sleeves. Mama and Franz picked up their bags.

"Where are Oma and Opa?" Kati looked from side to side, panic in her question.

"Right behind you." Opa's deep voice brought comfort to Franz as well.

As they shuffled up Flower Street, waddling in the burden of clothing, Franz saw Herr Haas's house. Would he come this way again? The bag grew heavy but he couldn't switch hands. Kati held tight.

"I remember that place," she said a mile later. "Is that where you used to get me candy?"

"Right now the pastry shop doesn't have candy, but we'll come back when they do." Even as he said the words, Franz wondered if that would be true.

"I'm tired." Kati sighed dramatically. "How far have we gone?" she tugged at Franz' hand for an answer.

"About three miles," he said. "Count every time you step on a rock or even a pebble, it'll help the time to pass." He wished he could carry some of the cumbersome clothes for her.

He looked down Kati's little blond head. Seven years old and how long had it been since she'd played with another child?

36

December 1945 – 13 years old
Camp Two, north of Stanišić

KATIE WIGGLED HER cold fingers in his grasp. Franz looked down at her, an apology in his eyes. He'd forgotten her and hadn't realized he was gripping so tightly. An advantage of putting on as many clothing layers as possible was that they weren't freezing, except for hands and noses. He pursed his lips and watched the plume of fog shoot from his mouth. The sky had filled with gray clouds. Was snow coming?

Guards continued to march forward and then back again, watching them. They held their guns pointed downward and fingers ready on the trigger. With each step they took, Franz could hear their magazines rattle in their canvas pouches. Did they really think any of them could make a run for it? Or did they hope someone would?

No one spoke, but he felt tension all around him. What was ahead? Where would they go? His mind raced and jumped from one thing to another. They were together now, would they stay that way?

He glanced at Mama, but she faced straight ahead, with no expression he could see. Everyone made short, jerky movements as they followed the Partisan who led them.

"The old brick factory is ahead." Opa spoke in a low rumble. They had passed Church Street and Main Street.

Franz' heart beat faster. Right by Herr Balli's.

Guards ushered them past the factory, then turned to the house behind. It was larger than the last camp, covered with peeling, greyed paint.

Feeling self-conscious with the Partisans watching, Franz looked around, trying not to stare to the west and see if he could catch sight of Balli's place past the hedge. His heart thudded with excitement. *We'll be next door.* Franz felt such relief mentally and physically. This would be another work camp, and not one for extermination. *And closer to their cow and her milk.* He shied away from the fear that they would be heavily watched and unable to get it.

A guard stood on the porch, holding an AK47. Like a bolt of lightning, hatred raged as Franz stared at the star with a hammer and sickle on the front of the Russian's hat. It represented Communist power over them, the red stars on both Partisans and Russians.

Kati was wedged in between Franz and Mama on the sides, and Oma in front, Opa in back. She couldn't be seen.

"You'll stay here," the soldier shouted in very poor German. "Get the brick yard organized and in production. You'll notice guards at each corner with machine guns. Local laborers will bring you food each morning and evening as long as you're useful." He stepped aside from the door. His hard, dark eyes bore down on each of them as they shuffled past. He moved to the street.

There were more bedrooms in this house, and Franz and Tony, as the only boys, were given a corner in the parlor. They peeled off several layers of clothes and stashed their belongings behind a red, stuffed chair in the room.

They followed Opa and his small group to the abandoned factory to see what needed to be done.

Opa stood beside the idle kiln and pointed out things to do by the end of the day.

"Franz, Tony, come here," Opa said. "Find something to cut down these weeds so we'll have space in this main area."

After a little looking, Tony found a sharp sickle, and Franz grabbed a rake.

"I guess we won't be able to go on our excursions." Franz felt a curious sense of loss.

"I'm probably going to miss it. Is that crazy?" Tony tipped his head to the side and furrowed his brow.

"We never knew what we'd find. No two trips were the same." Franz hesitated, and thought of his mother and grandmother. "Our families will feel relieved that we're safer."

Franz and Tony traded tools and worked through the day, opening a flat area for stacking bricks, and hills of clay and the molds and the leveling boards.

Exhausted, like everyone else, Franz closed his eyes at the stinging shock of cold well water poured over his head. He washed his hands and drank from a ladle that did nothing to stop the ache in his belly.

Leaning on the kitchen corner wall, he closed his eyes. Thump! Thump! He sat up. All eyes were focused on the loud knock at the front door. Opa opened it. Franz craned his neck to see.

"Your food is here," a Stanisic neighbor almost shouted. "Clean the containers and put them on the porch to be picked up with your morning delivery." An average height man, he looked up at Opa in recognition, blinked and left.

"Let's get it inside." Lissi quickly opened the screen door and held it while Opa's friend, Sebastian, helped Tony carry the soup inside.

"It smells eatable," Tony announced.

Oma hobbled over and sniffed. "Well, it's mostly mangold leaves. It tastes a bit like beets, so I guess if that was good enough for our hogs, it's good enough for us."

The line formed and soup parceled out.

Opa's shoulders sagged and his head drooped. For the first time, Franz noticed how old his grandfather had become. He collapsed into the nearest chair and sipped his portion slowly. "That man used to work for me from time to time. Now he's doing errands for our enemies."

Without a word, Franz helped his grandfather remove his boots, and sat on the floor beside him. He forced himself to eat slowly. Perhaps his stomach could be tricked into responding as though there was more volume.

"I always had the clay dug in the fall," Opa said. "We let it set out during the winter and made bricks April through October. We'd fire the bricks in November at 2000 degrees. It takes about a year for each set of bricks to be completed." He stopped. Franz thought Opa had fallen asleep, and stood up.

"They expect production out now," Opa continued, "during the coldest months." He looked around the room. "We're pale, constantly exhausted and our legs hurt. I don't see any trees for fuel. If we air dry them, they'll be bricks, but they'll crumble within a few years. Even now, I hate to turn out such inferior products." He sighed and rubbed his face vigorously, then gave a lop-sided smile to Franz. "Tomorrow will be better."

"You've two more workers with me and Tony", Franz said.

"I'd love to have you, but if they think one of our people isn't needed, it's off to a death camp."

It was the 'but' that had Franz sit down again, a feeling of dread in his belly.

"You need to find a way to get back to Balli's." Opa stopped a moment, as if gathering his strength. "You're looking too much like a man. Tony's two years younger and still a kid. If they decide to take you to another camp or into an army, they will. You can bring us milk and spend time with my old friend."

Franz opened his mouth, and then closed it. He wanted to plead to stay all the time. What if they were moved and he wasn't with them? He could help here. A couple of things stopped him. Opa was right. Anyone judged nonproductive would be sent away and milk was desperately needed.

People began to drift to their beds for this first night here.

Unable to relax, Franz slipped on his shoes, got up, opened the squeaky door and stepped outside. Hunkered down, he went to the edge of the property and hid behind a large bush. He saw a guard at the corner to the right, and another to the left. Lighted cigarettes made them visible in the half-moon. A few minutes later, both men walked toward him, weapons on their shoulders. His heart thundered in his ears. Run? Stay? Too late to move.

The soldiers stopped and chatted. Their voices had the rhythm of greetings but too quiet to be understood. They continued on their way, trading corners with each other. The warning played in his mind, 'guards on every corner with machine guns.' So all four corners were the same?

Franz scooted under the branches and must have fallen asleep because he jerked awake at the sound of Partisans talking. The moon peeked from cloud cover, making them visible. One lighted a cigarette for the other, and kept going. For a short period, as they each headed to the other corner, their backs were turned to Franz. An excellent time to dash across without being seen!

In the morning, he would find a place to get through the three-foot thick hedge. Without a sound, he went back to the house and slept.

———

"Herr Balli, the Hungarian farmer I worked for when we were still at home, is just on the other side of those boxwoods." Franz whispered to Tony. Their breakfast finished far too quickly, he took a tiny bite off his lone piece of bread. "Opa wants me to work for him again, and bring milk from our cow. If she hasn't dried up, anyway."

Tony tilted his chin down and frowned. "I'll miss having you around."

"I'll be back and forth, I think. Come on; help me figure out a way through."

"I know where a butcher knife is hidden. I'll get it," Tony sprinted to the house and returned.

Leaving the visible sides as intact as possible, they hacked away branches in the middle and low enough to crawl through. Hidden, Franz cut back leaves on the other side so he could peek both ways for patrolling guards.

"Where's Franz?" Opa's question to Tony brought a smile to Franz and he turned around and stuck his head out on the yard side of the border. "Ah! There he is," Opa said in mock surprise. "It looks good, boys."

"When should I go?" He couldn't stop the quiver in his voice. If only the cow would be safe here!

"Work with us today and leave before milking time." He stared vacantly at the bushes, his words slow. "Layer clothes for weather changes." Opa turned to the factory.

Franz and Tony followed him. They spent most of the day digging past the top soil, down to the clay and filling the wheelbarrow for women to carry to their work station.

Midafternoon, Opa came over to watch them a moment. "Franz, go now. The guards are getting bored and hungry and inattentive."

Franz nodded, and awkwardly wiped his clay-caked hands on his pants.

"See you later," Tony said. He hesitated as though he would say more, but rammed his shovel into the ground and resumed working.

Katie and Oma were in the house. Kati played with paper dolls a woman made for her. The cardboard mother and children cutouts all had speaking parts supplied by Kati.

Oma nodded at him and the light dimmed from her eyes.

So she knew he was leaving and there was nothing to say. Franz added clothing. He'd probably need some both places. He bit his lower lip and thought of the uncertain days ahead.

He looked around and saw no guards. Everyone from camp was at the factory except for Oma and Kati.

Standing by his escape hole, he listened and looked around. Quiet except for birds and a gentle, cold breeze. He dropped down and scooted in, out of sight. On Balli's side, Franz lifted two limbs and checked from both directions. He heard footsteps and the rattle of ammunition. Lowering the branches slowly, he waited.

Two guards crossed paths with a simple word exchange. Looking again, their backs were facing Franz. Keeping his breathing even took effort. He checked. Now. He scrambled out and hurried to the pasture behind Herr Balli's house. He stayed out of sight by entering the barn. Once inside, his hands shook and he tucked them under his arms and paced until he felt calmer.

The oxen were not here, so Herr Balli must be gone. The stall hadn't been cleaned. Franz grabbed the pitchfork and began working. Gradually, he felt warm and calmer and peeled off two layers of clothes. Tired and with nothing to do when he finished, he sat on a bale of hay and closed his eyes to rest.

His shoulder was shaken. Blinking, he saw a thinner Shurri Balli. His ruddy face still had smile lines though recent months had given everyone little to smile about. Franz inhaled the familiar aroma from the ever-present pipe in his mouth.

"So you're back, are you?" Herr Balli stood to his full five foot, eight inches, shoving his hands into his pockets. "I'm glad to have you, but I'm guessing things aren't going well." He sat on a nearby upside-down bucket.

Franz quickly explained about the first brick camp, and the present one.

"You'll see a smaller herd today." Herr Balli sighed deeply. "Things have gotten worse even for us Hungarians. We have to be creative to keep some of our beef. If a stray joins our herd, we don't register them. I've sent a few healthy animals to the knacker's yard." The old man winked at Franz. "He fails to weigh the carcasses with the heads, so that amount can be kept back for our use or to sell illegally."

"That sounds like what Opa would do." Franz chuckled, picturing headless cows being weighed.

"Time to go off to the corral."

The oxen were already hitched, so they tossed blocks of hay in the back of the wagon and left. Franz was content to ride companionably without talking. He didn't think of his family or problems, but leaned on the backrest. This was like it had been months ago, going the familiar path. Before the nightmares became real.

As they pulled up to the corral the cows were huddled and ready to enter the gate for water.

It took a long time to crank up enough for the thirsty animals. When he came before, he'd been eating good food at home, and now he could tell how much weaker he was and his stamina less.

Patient no longer, Punkte voiced her displeasure at being ignored. Franz sat on the stump and relaxed into the routine of milking. He smiled at the smell and lifted a teat to catch a mouthful. Mmm, good. He didn't swallow right away, letting his tongue enjoy the taste and feel.

When her udder was emptied, Franz joined Herr Balli by the fence. They both looked off in the distance, to the west.

"Remember the camp in Gakova?" Balli said. "More German women and young children are brought each week. And more perish." He raised his bushy eyebrows.

Franz squinted and studied the camp across the prairie. "It looks crowded."

"Yes. A few sneak over to get milk so their babies might survive. Just want to let you know what to expect."

Infants dying? Franz ached at the thought of it. What could the mothers do? He and Tony had spent every day searching for food, keeping their group alive. Not well-fed or really healthy, but surviving.

He didn't want to see or even know about these mothers and their precious little ones. It would be easier if he could wear oxen's blinders.

37

December, 1945 – 13 years old
Camp Two and Balli's farm

From the corner of his eye, Franz saw movement outside the corral.

"Please." The woman's eyes were large in her gaunt face. She held up a small baby, who showed no interest in his surroundings, its arms like twigs. "Please, I need milk for my child." She timidly handed Franz a clean vessel.

He walked over to the stump, and she followed him outside the fence. Franz pulled his milk pail over the lower rail, sat and placed it between his knees. It was difficult not to stare at his visitor. He pulled the cow's teats and then filled the lady's container without looking. Franz wanted to say something, but his mind and tongue were paralyzed.

"Thank you." Tears filled her eyes as she grasped the handle with one boney hand, holding the bundle against her chest with the other. She glanced over her shoulder. "I'll be back."

Discouraged by the great needs, he resumed milking. The baby looked like a brand new bird – all skin and no fat. The mother made Franz' family look much better. How had she managed to carry her child so far?

He looked off in the distance and watched her leave. How would they do? He closed his eyes, but they didn't fade away.

Looking up, he saw the woman as a speck in the distance. He reached up to his cold cheeks and felt tears freely rolling. Wiping them away, he picked up the milk pail and carried it outside the corral and placed it in the back of the wagon.

A second woman drew close. She looked familiar. Was she a friend of Mama's? He tried to see past dry, frizzy hair, and unusually red gums.

Suddenly, he remembered. "Your baby was born in the market square, wasn't she? I think my mother and grandmother helped you." He felt foolish. This couldn't be the same woman. That baby would be bigger, but the lady carried a wadded blanket, held as if a baby were inside. Franz blinked and bit his lower lip.

"Oh, you're German!" A wee smile lightened her expression for a moment. "My name is Ilse." She looked down at her little bundle. "I was so very scared and thankful for their kindness." The mother opened the blanket to let him see the quiet infant, who looked like a sleeping doll. "Will you please put milk in this jar for her?"

"Be glad to." Franz lifted the milk pail. The baby had to survive until things got better.

He filled the container to the brim and tightened the lid before giving it back. As his hand met hers, he felt a spasm in his chest. What would happen to them?

All day Franz thought of the babies and their mothers. Thank heavens Herr Balli kept their cow safe. No other Germans in the village had been allowed to keep one. Finished with the late afternoon milking, he hitched the oxen and returned them to their barn. The Balli family invited him to eat with them and showed him the bedroom he'd share with the little boy.

Franz visited with Frau Balli and her daughter, Ada, and grandchildren Margit and Csaba. Margit tended to boss her younger brother, who couldn't seem to sit still for a minute.

Eager to return to the brick factory with the milk, he slipped through the hedge and looked around. He felt as if he'd been gone a very long time and not simply one day. How good it was to see his mother, grandparents and Kati waiting for him in the house. They were very thin, but not near death. Warmed by Kati's enthusiastic hug and the light of welcome in her eyes, he sat down and leaned on the parlor chair. She drank his portion of the ration since he'd eaten with Herr Balli. Her head dropped down and she drifted into a deep sleep.

"What happened today?" Mama sat beside him on the parlor floor.

"There would have been more milk," he paused, feeling a weight in his chest. "It was the women at Gakova. They came with their babies. Some of them escape and walk all the way to get food." Franz looked at his small audience. "It was awful. They're in bad shape. It's hard to tell if their little ones are even alive." He looked at Mama and Oma. "Remember the one born after we were rounded up?"

Mama's eyes looked haunted, and Oma pressed her knuckles to her mouth.

"They came today." A knot formed in his throat and he couldn't say another word.

Heavy silence followed his story as others had stopped what they were doing and listened. Maybe he shouldn't have told them, life was hard enough already.

"Franz, if it weren't for you and Tony getting food the last few months, we'd be in that shape." Mama looked from him to Tony, who had joined them. "You give the milk where the greatest need is now."

"Let's pray." Frau Guckerle grabbed the hands of the women beside her. "Heavenly Father, how can we pray for these people suffering so much? Please let the cow be like Elisha and the widow's oil. Provide enough for them and us as well. We thank you. Amen." She did the sign of the cross.

The days fell into a pattern. Always, they came with their babies. More every day. At first, Franz wondered why they went back to Gakova. He finally decided at least there was shelter from weather, some warmth, and they had each other. It was safer than alone.

Two weeks later, as the sun brought light up in the east, Franz stared off toward the west. The women's camp had grown rapidly and was many times its original size.

He saw two people in the distance moving toward him. Since they realized he was German, they'd relaxed and trusted him. And more came. He squinted and noticed something being tossed to one side of the camp. This was new. He looked more intently, but he still couldn't tell what it was. It happened again.

Fifteen minutes later a couple of his regulars, Gertrud and Ilse, nodded a greeting as they got close enough to sit on a crude bench by the shed. Other women came one by one, but these two always came together.

"Any news?" He poured milk from his pail into their containers.

"I was hiding by the fence yesterday, out of sight, when I overheard Tito's Partisans complaining." Ilse glanced around, a habit of caution ingrained. "One of the guards grumbled about how few of them were expected to control 30,000 prisoners. They just kept throwing up makeshift buildings and bringing more Germans." Ilse looked down at her baby, stroking her small face. "The shortage of those watching us is helpful. And one kind man turns his back and makes it easier to push through the hole in the fence."

"What's happening on the south? I saw a pile of something." Franz looked again, still unable to recognize what he saw.

The women looked at one another and hesitated.

"We're crowded," Gertrud said. "The little food they give us is divided and not multiplied." She shook her head, now shorn of its blond hair. "So many simply starve. Others die from typhoid fever." She glanced at Ilse, the taller and younger of the women, then at Franz again.

"Every morning they carry the dead to the front of the house." Ilse cleared her throat. "They lay three of them side by side and then do the next three on top, turned 90 degrees. Stacked like wood, four layers high."

Nausea rose in Franz. Those bundles were bodies! He stepped over to the edge of the corral and retched. "I'm sorry," he said, and stumbled to the well and pumped water to wash out his mouth. "What happens to them? Are they just left there?" He remembered the few funerals he'd been to, where respect was paid to ones who died.

"Every day Partisans come and put them on a wagon and go to the outskirts of the village. They're tossed into a deep hole. If one of them moves, they get shot." Ilse's voice grew hard as she spoke. "I've heard them laugh about it."

"Celebrate with your family tomorrow." Herr Balli helped unhitch the oxen late the next day. "I'll take care of the cows."

Franz trudged home, carrying the milk pail. The cold weather and evaporating snow on the ground was the only way it felt like the village Saint Day. No celebration meal, no Mass with a priest. Frau Guckerle wasn't discouraged, though everyone else was subdued.

A day with his family. What would they do? Work at the brick factory, rest and perhaps read the books they'd managed to bring with them? Share memories of past years?

He longed to go back in time, and have the holiday with joy, and plenty around them.

After Franz snuck through his place in the hedge, he was greeted by an anxious camp. The soldiers had poked their heads in, and left. Rations weren't provided.

Franz' evening milk was all they had.

By morning they waited for the familiar bang on the porch for their food. It didn't come.

The morning dragged on with little activity. Midday, as he headed to the well to get water, Franz noticed the honking of a gaggle of domestic geese coming from a Hungarian neighbor's place. Many were drawn outside of the camp house by the sound. Franz drew close to the back of the yard, listening to energetic flapping of wings and the sounds of the birds cheering each other on.

"Come over," he whispered. "Don't give up, try again!" Their chatter grew frantic.

"Please, please." Franz wasn't sure this was a proper prayer, but it was heartfelt. A wide grin covered his face as a dozen geese sailed over the wall and glided to the brick factory area.

Bending over quietly, he picked up a tree branch from the ground, swung quickly and hit a goose on the head. Out of the corner of his eye, he saw other people grabbing them and twisting their necks with a snap. Franz knew he'd never plucked the feathers off a goose so fast, and those around him appeared to be in a joyful race.

He held his naked bird over his head like a trophy and laughed as others did the same.

Already, Opa and his friend, Sebastian, had started a fire behind the kiln.

For this brief time, it didn't matter where they were and why.

"Praise God! This is a miracle!" Oma beamed and sat on a bench. She pulled Kati to her lap and folded her cold little body in a warm hug.

"Did He send them to us?" Kati asked.

"Yes! We didn't have food and it's our Saint's Day." Oma laughed like a young girl. "Suddenly we have this wonderful bounty without our doing a thing to get them." She looked at the heavens and smiled.

"We need to catch the fat for later," Lissi said. She and Mama carried a couple of large pans and scattered the burning leaves away, making a cleared space under the fattest geese and soon drops of grease sizzled as they fell.

Watching everyone laughing and singing bits of hymns, Franz' heart felt light. He sauntered over to Tony.

"If our puny ration had come, I'll bet the soldiers would have scared off the geese."

"No," Tony answered. "They would have just taken them all."

"Did you ever smell anything as good as this?" Sebastian challenged as he turned a bird on its skewer.

Sitting around the campfire felt like it used to. Cold ears and noses didn't matter. Franz' dimples deepened as he watched Kati. She stepped as close as she could for the warmth, but was afraid of the fire itself. She looked up at him, and grinned.

By the time the meal was cooked, the sun lowered and temperatures dropped. From time to time someone went inside for another layer of clothing, but mostly no one wanted to miss any part of this special day.

Admiring a well-cooked goose leg, Franz ate every tiny bit of its meat, sucked each section of the bone, and then got another piece. Always aware of everyone's hunger, he stopped.

"No offence to the women," Opa addressed the group. "I do think this might be the most delicious meal I've ever eaten."

"I agree," Franz' mother said. "God has provided the best! We'll never forget this holiday!"

Everyone gave murmurs of agreement. Franz met Tony's light brown eyes and they nodded to each other. None other would be like this one.

The sun was setting. They'd have to put out the fire before dark and hide all traces of feathers, bones and feet. Opa and Sebastian stood and carried their remnants to the pit dug for the purpose. Franz joined them and before long everyone had erased evidence of their day.

By twos and threes they drifted into the house. The prisoners of Gakova on his heart, Franz went back to sleep at Herr Balli's. How many women would come tomorrow?

38

January 1946 – 13 years old
Camp two and Balli's

H ERR BALLI SWITCHED his pipe from the right side of his mouth to the left and waved Franz inside the kitchen. A very cold spell, with intermittent sleet, crept in with January. "Come on in, boy," Balli said and patted Franz' shoulder as he entered. He nodded at the women. "They made a pretty good soup and are eager to put some meat on your bones."

Franz still felt shy with Frau Balli and their grown daughter, Ada. Always pleasant, but they didn't say much. Ada's girl and boy smiled easily. Csaba seemed about Kati's age, and his bossy sister, Margit, a bit older.

After he ate, and took the milk to the camp and saw his family, Franz returned and followed Csaba to the bed the family provided for him. He fell asleep almost instantly listening to the little boy chattering. It felt good to sleep in a Hungarian family home where Partisans wouldn't be marching around, watching. Ever since they'd been rounded up, he knew it might happen again.

The next morning Franz left before dawn to return to the corral. The rolling wagon lacked rhythm as it went over rocks and into puddled dips in the road. His red neck scarf wrapped around his mouth and nose, he looked at the stars. Are the mothers at Gakova gazing at the heavens right now? Through the freeze, fewer had come for milk. He fidgeted while gently tapping the reins to hurry the oxen.

His thoughts stayed on the women. Maybe they had enough provisions and didn't need the milk right now. He wished he believed that. The pile of stacked bodies continued south of their camp. As he pulled in close to the shed, he looked around. No one here yet.

The oxen eagerly walked into the pen after he unhitched them. Next the work of pumping water from the well for thirsty animals. He milked the cow before turning them out to open pasture. Cow patties were gathered and tossed in the shed's wood stove and he struck the flint on the file to start a fire. He set the milk pail nearby to keep it warm. At last, he stretched out on the bed for a short nap, his hands under his head. The sun would rise soon.

Feeling lonely, Franz sighed and thought of his father. Where was Vati? And Uncle Adam? By himself now, he could let down his guard. "Are you alive?" The spoken question seemed to hang in the air as he rolled over on his side. "We miss you, Vati. Katie doesn't remember much. Please come back." Tears rolled down his cheeks as he tried to picture his father, and to remember his voice. "Can you find us here?" No answers.

Franz opened his eyes to timid daylight. He heard scuttling and squeaking. The rats!

He looked at the wooden floor. Gigantic ones ran everywhere. None climbed on the bed, and he felt encouraged. Herr Balli gave him a solution last winter, and it was time to try it.

Moving slowly, he stood on the bed and reached to the shelf nearby for a wire. He eyeballed their lengths and picked one a little wider than the rats. Franz slowly squatted down and grabbed one by his neck. Somehow his hands steadied enough to pinch up the hide and shove the wire through its skin firmly. He dropped him to the floor and watched the rodent aim for an escape hole.

Sitting back, he waited.

As the critter ran down the hole, the wire ends scraped the sides of the tunnel, pulling painfully at the rat's neck. Unnerving screams caused chills to run up Franz's spine and he put his hands over his ears. Gruesome shrieking went on and on, and seemed like it would never stop.

In a mad dash, all the others escaped through their holes. A weird quiet finally settled around Franz. He fell back on the mattress, listening. He could picture their wiggling noses drawing closer just below. Franz' heart beat rapidly. Herr Balli had guaranteed he would never see a rat in the shed again. Phew! His hand stunk!

Rolling to his side with the blanket the Balli family provided, he tucked it around himself. Franz lay quite still in the soft light shining through the window, listening for the sounds of rodents. Nothing. Only a cold wind whistled around the corner of the shed.

Stretching under the warm blanket, Franz knew he had to get up. With the thaw he expected more visitors. He hated to leave the comfort here. Stopping those thoughts, he threw off his covering and built up the fire.

He'd no sooner gone outside when a woman stepped around the corner of the shed and hesitated. She clutched a ragged blanket around her shoulders.

Franz lifted his hand and waved. "*Guten Tag,*" he said. He watched her face relax and even give him a timid smile at his familiar greeting.

Like the others, she carried a wrapped bundle, but this one wiggled. When she drew close, he heard soft crying.

"How are you doing over there?" he nodded toward the camp. She was so skinny, her eyes lacked energy.

"Not good." She shook her head. "To them, we're worth as much as a beetle. Yesterday one of the women I share a bed with died and four of us carried her outside. Her baby died the day before." The flat way she spoke made it seem a normal daily happening.

Just then, the child in her arms peeked out, and studied Franz seriously.

"What's his name?" he asked and reached out to pat one little kicking foot.

"Kurt." She lifted him higher and bent her head to plant a kiss on his forehead. "Will you fill this for him, please?" She handed Franz a large jar from under the blanket. "Thank you so much."

The lady reminded him of his mother. Both capable and gentle, even now.

While he filled her container and tightened the cap, she rewrapped the baby and made a nest below his feet, where she tucked the warm jar. Franz watched her slow steps returning to the Gakova camp, and shook his head. If only there were warmer clothes to give her, and a generous, real meal. Tears filled his eyes. Even if it gave them only one more day, the milk helped.

He watched the cattle meandering around, eating what pitiful grass they could find. Balli needed to bring hay.

More dried cow dung was gathered and he went to the shed to warm his cold hands. A knock on the door and he stepped outside to greet another mother. This one held her chin high, lips pressed together.

"I left my girl back there," she tipped her head toward the camp. "But I need you to fill these." She held two large pitchers.

"I'm sorry," Franz stammered. "I want to help as many as I can with what I have. I can't give you so much."

"That woman who just left is one of the richest women in her village!" She leaned forward, reminding Franz of a hissing cat. Her nose flared and eyes narrowed. "You shouldn't have given her any. Not one drop!"

Franz stepped back as if she'd struck him. His mouth opened, and then closed. His muscles tensed, and heat spread up his back to his head. Clenching his hands, he didn't let himself say anything until he'd calmed down a little.

"Her baby needs the milk just as much as yours does." Speaking slowly and politely, he looked at her hard, beady eyes. She might as well not have ears. "Whatever wealth she had is gone and can't help her now. Everyone is trying to survive."

"She wears silver jewelry under her clothes, so she is still richer than the rest of us."

Franz thought of the things he and Tony had taken from their old homes, silverware, cigarettes and other things they might use eventually to pay their way out of here.

"Babies' don't eat silver." He grabbed one of the pitchers from her and strode over to the milk pail. He filled it part way, hesitated, and with thoughts of a hungry and innocent one, he poured more.

"This is for your child." Turning away from her, Franz didn't watch her leave. How could one woman begrudge another food for her baby? Picking up some rocks, he threw them as hard as possible toward a distant tree. Damn war! It didn't matter about the previous life of a prisoner. Another rock went sailing. Hunger was hunger. He shook his head and stomped inside for shelter. Gray clouds blew in from the north.

By early afternoon, all the milk had been given away. After the evening milking, he hitched the oxen and put the precious full pail by his feet. Slowly he followed the familiar trail to his eager family and friends.

"I sure would like to have some of my grapes again." Sebastian complained for the third night in a row. "You can bet in all the turmoil my little garden acre missed the harvest."

Franz walked over and looked out the window. "I'll go with you," he said. "The moon is nice and bright."

"Really?" Sebastian sat up straight and leaned forward. "It's not too far, just on the east side of the last cross street." Sebastian picked up his shoes and put them on.

"We'll need baskets and knives or scissors." Franz grinned at Sebastian's obvious surprise and pleasure.

The older man led the way at first, but they both quickly realized Franz had the experience needed to move through this area without detection.

"It's right up here," the older man whispered. "I let the corn grow thick last summer, so it ought to make a good place to hide."

Parting the dry stalks with as little noise as possible, Franz put his hand in a few places until he felt a space. Stepping inside quickly, he held the opening for Sebastian.

"There's a small road on the other end of the garden," the farmer said.

"I'll go to there, and you lie down here," Franz murmured. "There might be guards around."

Franz went out the other side of the corn, past remnants of the produce planted in the spring. He hunkered down and moved slowly, along a row of grape vines to his right side. By the light of the moon, fruit was visible. He stayed close to the tall plants and edged his way to the narrow road. Looking both ways, he saw a Partisan walking toward him, with a little Dachshund trotting at his heels.

The dog stopped a moment and sniffed Franz' way, giving one bark and a low growl. Franz dared not move. His heartbeat felt far too loud.

"Now, don't you think of going after another skunk," the soldier said firmly to his pet. "I might have to let someone eat you after all."

The dog looked at his owner and wagged his tail as if he understood and they continued on.

Franz ran back to Sebastian. "Wait here and I'll keep an eye on the Partisan. When I'm sure he's gone I'll be back to get you," Franz said. "You guessed correctly, there is still some fruit."

Returning to the road, Franz watched the guard slowly go to the next cross street and turn the other way. He sighed in relief, looked around and retraced his steps.

"Sebastian?" No answer to his whisper. Franz went through the corn, repeating his call. Still no answer. Where was the Opa's good friend? Had he followed Franz to the grapes? Run away? Why didn't he answer?

Thump! Franz stepped forward and bumped something. The bucket and scissors. Might as well go back to the vines again. Feeling nervous about the missing man, Franz cut grape clusters and filled the basket. Unsettled, and feeling a heavy dread, he returned to the camp house. What if Sebastian had been picked up and taken away?

He hurried as fast as he could.

Entering the gate, he stopped. There the older man sat on the porch, his shoulders drooping. Franz started to say something sharp, but in the light of the moon, Sebastian looked up with a sad and guilty look on his face.

"I'm sorry, Franz," he mumbled. Drawing a deep breath, he sat up straighter. "I got scared and just took off. I hope you forgive me."

Franz understood fear. All worry and anger melted away. He held out the bucket, full of soft and bruised grapes. They were edible.

"Thank you for getting these." Sebastian shook his head. "You keep them. I'm so sorry for chickening out."

"No, they're yours. I've got to get back to the Ballis' for the night." Franz slipped through his hole in the hedge and looked around. No activity, so it was safe to leave.

Only three women had come this morning and there'd been a two week break in the cold weather. There should be more. Franz stood at the shed window and stared off in the distance toward Gakova. He bit his lower lip at the familiar stack of bodies there, only now he saw additional piles.

He narrowed his eyes. Someone was moving his way. Gertrud, with her son in her arms.

Franz put his coat and muffler on and hurried out to meet her. He didn't use the usual greeting of *Guten Tag.*

"Where is Ilse?" Please let there be a good reason she's not here, Franz prayed.

"Her daughter died two days ago and she died last night." Gertrud's eyes looked bleak, but dry. "This morning we took her out to the new pile." She closed her eyes and swayed a bit. Franz took her arm and helped her to the bench. He poured milk for her, and watched her sip.

"Soon, the Partisans will haul them off to be dumped in a hole," she continued, then stopped. "So many die each day," she whispered,

She handed Franz her large jar, and neither spoke while he filled it. Franz tried to grasp the idea of Ilse and her little girl being dead. The baby Mama and Oma had helped deliver. If only they'd been able to hang on until things got better. With thoughts of his mother and grandmother, he decided he'd not tell them. The loss would hurt them and not do any good.

Frustrated, Franz watched Gertrud shuffle away. Would she be back? When would this nightmare be over? Would it ever stop? His heart ached with failure. He hadn't given them enough. But he'd thought if each had some, it would help. Perhaps he should have taken five women and let them really have milk as well as their babies. But what would he have said to those he turned away? That had been the choice, he reminded himself. Give everyone some until no more available each day. Or he could have turned most of them away and given more help to a few. He'd chosen to help as many as possible.

He gathered more cow patties as he went to the cabin. The sun shone, and the sky was clear, but the temperature hung a little above freezing. Regret lodged painfully in his chest.

With fewer women coming, the days dragged on longer. For the first time in his life, Franz spent a lot of time alone. Silence became more comfortable.

Herr Balli had left some matchbooks so he didn't have to use flint and steel to start every fire.

How much pain could he take? He struck a match and watched the flame. Without a friend to dare him, he dared himself. Bringing the flame closer and closer to his thumb, he was curious. How tough could he be?

39

February/March 1946 – 13 years old, Kati 7
Camp Two, north of Stanišić

EVEN THROUGH HIS coat, the welcome sun heated Franz' back. He pulled the milk pail through his secret passage in the hedge. Watering all the cattle and oxen, milking, turning them out to pasture had all taken twice the time and too much energy. After that, time dragged until afternoon milking.

Opa was outside with several of the workers, laying out bricks to cure in the dry, somewhat warm weather. Franz waved first at Opa and then nodded to Tony, who must be working hard because he'd taken his coat off. Several others were sitting to the side, sunning, as they took a break from the work. Where was the rest of the family? He meandered to the house to find them. Katie would be with the little black dog that slunk toward camp one day. She'd immediately named her Cookie. She clutched the sad little mutt so tightly and begged so earnestly, that no one could deny her the dog, despite being another mouth to feed.

When Franz opened the kitchen door, his stomach dropped and he couldn't move. Mama and Oma, their faces drawn and tense like cornered animals, shifted toward him from where they sat on a davenport. As soon as their eyes met Franz, they sagged back, exposing Katie cowering in the middle. Mucus ran from her nose, and she wiped at it with her sleeve. She hiccupped, staring at him silently with red rimmed eyes.

"What happened?" Franz asked as he lowered the pail and kept his eyes on his family. No answer. He rushed straight to Kati and bent down. He framed her face with his hands, and leaned over to kiss her forehead.

Kati hiccupped again and gave him a wobbly smile.

"They came looking for her today," Mama said. Breathing raggedly, she hugged Kati to her breast.

"I should have hurried faster when I saw them," Oma looked down at Kati's blond hair. "But I was trying to appear calm so they'd go away." Her eyes bleak, she looked at Franz again. "Kati didn't come when I called. I panicked. She wasn't in the attic." Oma's voice wavered. "I was so afraid . . ."

"I hid from them," Kati whispered, "so they wouldn't take me to Russia."

"What happened?" he asked again. Franz felt his heart twist as he sat back on the floor. His greatest fear. She could be snatched, as other little girls had been. Looking from his sister, to mother, grandmother and back to Kati.

"My dog sat when I told her 'sit'. Then I heard the outside door open." Kati's tears stopped and her voice gained strength. "On tiptoes, I carried Cookie to hide under the bed."

"The men went through the house, but I couldn't understand what they said. The stomping came closer and closer and I scooted farther back, holding onto Cookie." Hearing her name, the dog hopped up onto Kati's lap and licked her neck.

"Tall boots stopped right by the bed. Cookie wiggled away from me and ran out. She growled and twisted one of the uniform pant legs," Kati said. "The soldier kicked her under the bed and I held Cookie's mouth closed, so afraid the he would bend over and see me." Another set of tears rolled down her cheeks. "We didn't move because they might be waiting."

"Why didn't you answer Oma?" Franz asked, and sandwiched her hand between his.

"I was too scared." Kati sniffled again. "They might knock Oma down and find me."

That night they all went to sleep feeling nervous. Franz heard prayers being said from different rooms.

───※───

The next week while staying with the cattle, Franz kept thinking about the close call with Kati. The morning dragged on. Only two women came and got milk for themselves and their babies. After Ilse and her tiny girl died, he didn't talk a lot to the new ones. The piles of dead bodies at Gakova camp grew and then disappeared. Then they grew again. He grieved, but it would be worse if they became friends. No, it was better not to know them.

After the late milking, he hitched the oxen to the wagon and returned to Herr Balli's. Franz poured enough for the old man's young grandchildren. Sniffing appreciatively, he peeked at the soup the women prepared with stringy meat and cabbage, and cooked for hours until tender. Along with the others, he got a bowlful and a piece of bread.

Around the table, the children did most of the talking about the day. After he ate, Herr Balli stood by the stove with file and flint stone to light his pipe.

"I'm curious. Why don't you use matches?" Franz asked. "They're easier."

The two women smiled at each other.

"Yes, father, tell about the day the matches attacked." Ada's brown eyes twinkled as she laughed.

Margit and Csaba, looked at each other and then listened with Franz.

"I tried these new matches a long time ago." He tipped his round, ruddy face and for a moment made Franz think of der Heilige Nikolaus. "When they first came out, I liked being able to strike one anywhere and kept them in my jacket pocket. One evening I needed fresh straw from a tightly stacked, tall mound. I used a five foot long wooden-handled harpoon – just a little shorter than I am – to push inside and pull the straw out." He took a draw off his pipe, allowing a fragrant curl of smoke to escape his lips couple of times.

"Always in a hurry, I pulled and pushed the harpoon in and out as fast as possible." Herr Balli stopped, studied them, and seemed satisfied with an attentive audience. "Guess I worked up some friction."

Franz grinned, guessing what came next.

"Next thing I knew, my jacket was ablaze. I got it off," he reenacted his motions, "and grabbed the paperboard folder and threw it away. Well, the whole pile of straw and two nearby ones caught on fire. Faster than a blink, I had a much bigger problem. I was frantic and yelling for help and beating it out."

He held up his pipe in salute. "So my reliable old flint stone and file stay with me."

Franz laughed at the idea of Herr Balli flinging off the fire, only to make it worse. How funny this story would be to his family. Pushing away from the table, Franz gazed at the children.

Csaba and Margit had normal hair and rosy skin. He thought of Kati, who looked pale, her hair dry and thin. He remembered how she used to be so healthy and energetic, but slowly things changed. If only Kati could eat as well as these children!

Franz shook his head, hating the flash of resentment. The Balli family always welcomed him to sleep here and fed him each evening. They hid Opa's milk cow in their Hungarian herd.

"Thank you for the meal," he said, with sincerity. The burn in his stomach eased. Picking up the milk pail, he hurried back to camp.

He had to see Kati's face, to know she was safe another day. Cookie gave him the most enthusiastic greeting. Everyone else appeared miserable and barely moved. Kati was sleeping on a blanket on the floor. Several grumbled because they were unable to meet the brick quotas. Mama's back hurt. Diarrhea sapped what little strength they had left. Opa was silent and Oma watched a bug crawl by.

"I need to get away." Tony slipped up beside him. "Since we have this break in the weather, let's have an adventure before it gets too dark." They put their coats on and did their old Robbers Ladder routine to get over the wall and strolled toward Legin

Oddly, Franz felt free. This was fun, walking down a Hungarian road with his friend. Time dropped away. The fading sunshine even cooperated. He grinned at Tony, who nodded in happy agreement. Neither said a word. Large trees, bare of leaves, lined the road. Franz noticed Magpie nests up high.

"I'm going up to see if anything's in them." Climbing like a monkey, he saw no abandoned eggs or birds. Disappointed, he made his way down.

Just as his foot touched the ground a soldier came along the road, pushing a bicycle. The man looked directly at him. No time to hide. Why were they so foolish as to come here? A heavy, sour weight landed in his belly. They'd have to bluff their way through.

"I'll do the talking." Franz whispered to Tony. "We'll not be German."

Tony nodded, and did his best to show a relaxed expression.

As the man approached, Franz first acknowledged him in Hungarian, then Yugoslavian.

The Partisan grinned, crooked teeth stained by tobacco, and greeted them in Yugoslavian. Armed with a tommy gun over his shoulder, a revolver on his side and several hand grenades on his belt, he drew closer.

Franz blinked, forcing himself to look at the man and not his weapons.

It was clear why he walked his bike. For every step, he stumbled twice. At the moment, he was a happy drunk, which Franz didn't trust.

"Do you want to shoot my tommy gun?" he asked, and held it out.

"No, thank you," Franz said. "I'm afraid of them." Tony also acted respectful and shy.

"Shame! A boy like you afraid of guns?" The soldier shook his head in disgust. "Better get over it. You're old enough to help in the war effort." Studying each boy, he turned away, still shaking his head and muttering.

Franz and Tony watched him stagger several yards. They sighed in relief before the man decided to get on his bike. As soon as he mounted, he fell off the other side.

Both boys froze. Ordinarily they would have thought it funny, but they couldn't laugh.

Like lightening, the Partisan got up, pulled out his revolver, pointed at them and started firing. The first bullet hit the tree limb Franz had just swung down from! The boys ran.

One zinged far too close to his left ear, and Franz knew the next one might not miss. One round pinged off a large boulder, others splintering nearby branches. Instinct, not thoughts, gave him speed.

Blood pounded in Franz' ears. He saw Tony out of the corner of his eye. A block later, Franz had to stop. He leaned over, a sharp pain in his side, and braced his hand on a fence. His eyes darted around. If anyone had been outside, at the sound of shooting, they must have run to the safety of their homes. Not a sign of the soldier behind them. The ache in his side eased, so they continued. Despite the quiet, Franz breathed easier when they finally arrived at the edge of the brick camp.

"If you'd still been in the tree . . ." Tony said, voice halting, and his face looked like bleached muslin.

"Or if he'd used his Tommy gun, he wouldn't have missed us!" Franz hands shook and his knees felt wobbly.

"We don't tell about this, right?" Lips trembling, Tony's eyebrows pulled together.

"Won't help anyone." Franz hesitated, and then turned to the younger boy. "I should be helping in the brick factory. I'm lucky, the Balli family shares what little food they have with me. It's getting worse everywhere." He chewed his thumbnail.

"The women of Gakova need you. Besides, we wouldn't have fresh milk every evening if you stayed here. We'd be much worse off." Tony heaved a sigh. "The brick factory will close soon. Without wood to fire them, we can't keep up." He looked up at the sky. "What's going to happen to us then?"

40

March 1946 – 13-1/2 years old, Kati 7
Leaving Camp Two and go to Camp Three, both north of Stanisic

"SOMEONE'S COMING!" LISSI hissed.

Kati silently picked up her blanket and her lone doll. Franz followed as Mama hurried to the back room with Kati in tow.

"Put her on top." Mama pointed to the wardrobe.

Franz stood on a nearby chair, lifted Kati and swung her up. She and Mama blew kisses to one another and Kati pushed open the lid on a small attic entry, tossed her doll in and hopped up to pull herself inside. The cover slid closed.

Mama and Franz returned to the living room just before the front door opened. How could he not know about this, a well-practiced routine? Because he was gone so much. Too much. He should have been here to help protect his family.

Like kings, the Partisans surveyed every room. Oh, how Franz hated them! From their uniforms with the hateful red star, a symbol they owned the world, to the way they shoved people aside looking behind them, swearing and domineering. They were evil clear through, at least to all Germans.

"Where is the girl?" The guard looked around the room for an answer, one eyebrow raised.

"She died." Lissi said, tears filling her eyes.

Franz stopped breathing, sat on the floor, and kept his eyes down so he wouldn't give anything away. He couldn't bear it if anything happened to Kati. She was as necessary as sunshine.

After a thorough searching, the leader growled at the other soldiers and they left.

It was another long ten minutes before Kati was brought back down. Grief welled up in Franz for the life Kati lived now — always quiet and in danger. When he was her age he was roaming around Sombor with cousin Jani, without care. She sat in Opa's lap, with Cookie in hers.

"How often do they come?" Franz asked, hating that he was at Balli's with the cattle so much. He should be here, helping watch over Kati!

"Someone always stays with her now," Mama whispered.

Franz stood up, walking with pain from the boils on his legs.

"Sit down," Mama said. She took the iron and heated towels to press on the sores. "Once they come to a head, they'll break and drain, then heal."

He felt better, but didn't know if that helped or it was having Mama fuss over him again. Probably it was because Kati was safe. For now. Reluctantly, he picked up the milk pail, and after hugging Kati and his mother, headed to the door.

"Franz," Opa said. "Take that to Balli and stay tonight. In the morning, let him tend the cows and come back. You need to be with the rest of us. We've dismantled the factory."

Franz searched Opa's serious face, and nodded.

Another ending, saying good-bye to Herr Balli and his family. He trudged to the hedge, and peeked through the opening to see if any guards were patrolling. Off in the distance he saw the back of a lone soldier, so slipped through and walked to Balli's house. What about the milk? If they were moved, they wouldn't be able to have the sure pail each evening. What about the few women who showed up at the corral for their babies? Would Balli stay for them or would he return to his other responsibilities?

Approaching the house, he saw the older man sitting on the porch step, waiting for him. Franz's throat closed and he couldn't say anything.

"So, it's time, is it?" Balli's bushy eyebrows rose, no smile on his face.

"Yes," Franz said. He put the pail down and sat beside this man who had looked out for him and taught him about getting rid of rats, starting fires with flint and file, and kept him, as well as their cow, safe. Franz always knew he was welcome here. "I'm to stay tonight, then go back early in the morning."

Silence covered them. Franz looked down at a knothole in the wooden step between his feet.

"Let's go inside," Balli said. He stretched his arm over Franz' shoulder. "The women have our supper ready. Csaba and Margit are really going to miss you."

The next morning Franz woke early. As he left the bedroom he shared with the children, he looked back at them. Maybe some-day he could tell them how much their grandfather had done for him, and his family, even though they were hated Germans.

Herr Balli was by the stable hitching up the oxen, but when he saw Franz he waved him over.

Looking at Shurri Balli's ruddy face, Franz wanted to find words to tell Opa's good friend how protected he'd felt here and how much he learned.

Herr Balli walked slowly to meet him, and never had looked so serious. Only slightly taller than Franz, he reached out and gave a long, tight squeeze. The gentleman stepped back, moved his pipe to the other side of his mouth and shook his head.

"We'll be praying for you, and your whole family." The old man's eyes filled with distress.

"Thank you for everything," Franz murmured. He returned to the camp and his family, with pure white snow falling against his face. He felt so tired, sad, and very old. Hard to believe a year ago he and his friends played and hollered in blizzards. Those times were gone.

"Did you bring me a snowflake?" Kati met him at the door; her eyes open wide in hope.

Franz forced a smile, but his heart felt heavy. Kati wanted what any normal child would, but she was too used to her lack of freedom to go outside.

"I will when there's enough to put in a ball," he said. "Then I'll throw it at you!"

She giggled and ran to tell Mama, who was busy ticking things off on her fingers.

"We've hidden things too well." Mama forked her fingers through her hair. "Escaping will be expensive," she whispered. She barely looked at Franz. "Son, put those clothes on and stay close to your backpack."

Knowing the drill, he quickly put one item on top of another, and picked up his rucksack. It was very heavy. Tony and Berbl also had hefty bags on their backs as well. They copied the men and stayed out of the women's way. Tension filled the room, though few words were spoken.

"They're here." From the kitchen window, Sebastian's voice sounded shrill. Suddenly the door banged open.

"Grab your things and get in lines!" The Partisan shouted, unneeded in the quiet house.

Franz stayed close to his family, as they filed outside. His breathing grew heavy and labored. Opa and Oma huddled together, Kati tucked between them under Oma's large coat. Franz turned his eyes away.

Mama had a suitcase, as did Oma and Opa. Lissi carried a small one and the other people had assorted cases and bags.

With clothes piled on clothes, everyone looked like they'd gained weight.

Oh, God, please keep my family together, Franz prayed as they stopped to watch guards giving orders. He glanced over his shoulder at Tony. He, too, stayed close to his relatives.

"Those over here, follow this guard." The soldier in charge pointed his gun straight out and gestured to his right, separating the people into two groups.

Squeezing Oma's hand, Franz thanked God for His answer. Tony and his aunt and sister squeezed in right behind. His knees felt wobbly as they trailed a soldier taking them—where?

Snow began to fall rapidly, thick and soft. Franz blinked often to see those around him and squinted his eyes.

"Go faster; we don't have all day for this!" A guttural voice bellowed as a guard swaggered by in his uniform, complete with a Russian hammer & sickle. Turning his head, Franz felt a jolt of lightening hit him when he recognized the man. The snitch from their neighborhood. Franz looked away, and wondered if he'd been recognized.

The informer stepped right up to Franz' mother.

"Well, so we meet again." His words sounded well-oiled. "And you're wearing a khaki colored shirt, like a good Nazi. I wonder what would happen if I tell everyone your brother is in the SS." He cackled and leaned toward her suggestively.

Franz felt the hair on his neck rise and his body turned cold.

Mama didn't answer and Oma and Opa kept their faces averted. No one missed a step.

Franz looked out of the corners of his eyes, trying to keep track of the traitor.

The group shuffled to the closest cross street, turned east, and went past Main Street. Franz turned his head as he got close to Church Street, eager to see everything. On the corner to his right was Lissi's store, by the vacant lot where they used to play land hockey. What fun they'd had! Anton Haut was an enthusiastic ringleader.

He could barely see the house where Tony lived, behind the shop. It appeared blurry in the snow, as if the very shadows of Tony's family had left.

Only three doors down was Opa and Oma's house. Franz needed to look at it one more time, but couldn't see it from here, even if the air had been clear. He glanced at Opa and he was doing the same thing, but being the tallest in the group, he refused to gawk in front of their enemies.

Like sleet falling on his head, horrible thoughts pecked at Franz' mind. Where were they going? They passed Flower Street, on the way to the railroad tracks. Would they be taken away, possibly to Russia? Did the trains even use the damaged tracks now? To a prisoner of war camp? Terrified at these possibilities, Franz gazed at each loved person around him. They were together. That calmed him a bit, so he pushed down paralyzing fear and concentrated. *We're together, we're together.* Walking behind Oma and Opa, he saw Kati's little shoes moving as she stayed hidden between them under Oma's oversized, long coat.

Suddenly, they turned left and entered the house where the Stiglic family had lived. It was smaller than the other camps. Franz looked around. It was a regular yard with a small, dead garden and a well for water.

Mama and Oma joined the other women in searching the house. Franz and Tony followed with their sisters.

"There are fewer of us, so maybe they'll bring us more provisions." Frau Guckerle said aloud, but closed her eyes as if in prayer.

"More likely we'll be forgotten," another chimed in.

"No sign of this being a work camp," Opa said. He stood by the door, hands in his pockets, staring out at the open fields behind them. "I'll look around." Opa slumped as he stepped outside.

"I was afraid we'd be in a camp like Gakova," Mama said at Franz' shoulder.

"We have to be worth feeding," Franz mumbled to himself.

"There's a rumor about a Yugoslavian guide from our village who might take us to Hungary for a price." His mother tapped her fingers on her chin. "If they bring us something to eat, get a good look at the carrier or call me." The rest of the day, she hung around the window, watching the porch.

By afternoon, Franz gave up the vigil. He searched the house for anything helpful, and found nothing. Looking out each window, he formed a general map in his head of the area and joined the others in the kitchen. Something clattered on the porch.

Mama jerked to attention and closed her eyes before opening the door. Their food had arrived. She stepped out alone.

Oma and Opa also stared at the closed door. Franz sat with them and waited. What was she doing? Opa sat still, so Franz did the same. Inside he felt jittery and wanted to know what his mother was up to.

The door opened and frigid air rushed across the floor. Two women stepped out to get the food. Mama bit her lip and looked around before coming to her family.

"It was the same man and he'll take the message." She sat down on the floor beside Franz and sighed as though every bit of her scant energy had drained. "Now, we wait." Her eyes held new hope.

"Please come with us!" Mama's hand rested on Opa's arm, her back bowed down. "If you stay, it will be the same thing. Less food, until there's none. Once we get over the Hungarian border, our chances will be better."

"If you get caught in those nine miles, what will happen?" Opa threw his hands up, and paced the room. "The war is over, communism will go away. I'm going to be here to get our home and farm land back." He scrubbed a hand over his face. "It could go either way. We're staying."

Franz looked at Oma. She inched closer to Opa and nodded.

"What about Adam?" Mama whispered. "We're in greater danger now from the guard."

"I know." Opa's proud shoulders sagged. "We'll be here for Adam when all this is over."

Oma stood by Opa, tears rolling down her sunken cheeks as she watched her daughter, and Franz and Kati. She met Franz's eyes and studied his face as he memorized hers.

"You do what is best for your family, Elisabeth, and go with our blessings."

"We'll slow you down anyway," Opa said. "You'll have to hurry and not stop and rest every ten minutes."

"We don't want to go without you," Mama pleaded. "Won't you please change your mind?"

Their set faces were sufficient answer.

"Tomorrow morning we leave early. We'll go by the camp where Jani is and get him. Then we wait at the abandoned rail car until the guide comes."

Franz looked around. No one said what he thought. *If* the guide comes.

With nothing more to say, Franz checked his packed bag. His mother, Lissi, Eva and Tony and Berbl did the same. They each had money and valuables Franz and Tony had brought back from their weeks of searching for food. Silverware and jewels were wrapped in clothing to prevent noise as they walked. Instructions were to bring only what they could carry all the way.

People drifted off to bed, hoping for sleep. Franz looked at the calendar on the wall. Tomorrow would be March 15, 1946. The date felt branded into his brain.

If all went well, this was their last night here. Franz' eyes couldn't stay closed. He punched the blanket he used for a pillow. Stanisic was home, with Opa and Oma.

What if they get picked up before ever reaching the meeting place? He almost moaned out loud, but stopped himself. If the guide didn't show up, they'd have to come back here, wouldn't they?

"Franz?" whispered Tony.

"Guess you can't sleep either." Franz said, as he listened to the sound of restless people wiggling in their beds. "I keep trying to picture what will happen."

"I'm glad Aunt Lissi wanted to go. Better than sitting and starving."

Tony didn't say more and Franz wondered if he'd fallen asleep.

"Franz," Tony's soft voice stopped again. "Are you scared?"

"Yes." Franz admitted freely. "Either way, I am."

"Me, too." This time Tony didn't continue.

In the morning, Franz moved with quiet precision. He layered his clothes again, along with the rest of their escape team. He picked up his backpack and others their suitcases and bags.

Oma watched them leave. She looked so small, her lips moving as she marked the sign of the cross over her heart. Opa stood beside her, his head bowed. He didn't look up.

Franz wanted to run back and drag them along, but squared his shoulders and followed his mother.

He hoped Jani was still in the same camp, only a mile or so away from them. Mama led the way to fulfil her promise to get Jani if they escaped and take him with them.

They trekked without a word through the Hungarian area. Franz and his mother would do any talking needed. In the distance they saw long, wooden barracks by the huge barn. Jani had to be here, not sent off to another camp. How close they'd been when little, getting in and out of trouble. That had been a war away, and another life. They'd be together soon. Franz saw every movement in the wind, every person around the camp.

The group hid in tall, dead weeds. Mama motioned Franz to stay with the others.

"Better I go." Franz tipped his head to Kati, who stared at Mama, blinking her eyes as if her mother would disappear if not watched. After a brief hesitation, Franz weaved his way through the brush.

Every minute he stopped and gradually raised his head to scout around. He saw one man by himself, leaning on the fence, staring off at the sky. A huge tree stump jutted above a pile of trash. If he could get over there before the man left, he could talk to him. Move slowly, he reminded himself. What seemed a half hour, he finally got close, peeked over and caught the man's attention. He looked like a skeleton with a covering of skin and hair.

No reaction, so he wasn't likely to sound an alarm. Perfect. Which language should he use? He pointed to himself and said his name. "Franz."

"German, right?" the prisoner asked without moving his lips.

"Yes," Franz exhaled in relief. "I'm looking for my cousin, Jani Merkel. Know him?"

"He died." One weak arm rose up and slowly rubbed his head. "He died of *seele Selenkrankheit* when he heard his mother perished in a camp in Sombor. His father was in the army and no one knew where or if he were alive."

"We're talking about Jani Merkel, aren't we?" Maybe there was a mistake, and Jani was here after all. "He played the accordion."

"He talked about that." A fleeting smile formed on the man's lips. "Always tapped his fingers on flat surfaces." Another silence. "His last words were a prayer for his sister. Don't remember her name."

"Dori," Franz said. Sinking back on the grass, he cried freely, without sound. He turned, then stopped and said thank you. It felt like a knife pressed through his heart as he returned to the group.

When he told his mother Jani died of soul sickness and why, she bowed low on the ground and rocked back and forth in grief. Lissi tapped her arm.

"We've got to get to the meeting place."

Mama nodded, wiped her cheeks and gathered Kati in her arms. Standing, she began to walk. They had to get to the railroad car.

41

March 15, 1946 – 13-1/2 years old
Going to the Hungarian border

FRANZ WAS THANKFUL the few Hungarians nearby simply ignored them. His thoughts bounced from Jani to the risky hours ahead. Dead. Jani was dead. The word was final. Franz wanted to scream or sit in a dark room alone. He'd never see him again.

Jani had agreed to escape with them, but now he couldn't. He must stop thinking of his cousin. This was no time to be careless.

This is only the first step, Franz thought. *Getting north to the contact place.* He studied the immediate neighborhood and saw nothing alarming. Maybe they should have stayed with Oma and Opa close to home. Which did he fear the most? Staying in Stanisic or trying to escape Yugoslavia and the Communists? None of them knew this man who promised to take them out.

Looking around, identical expressions showed on the faces around him. Eyes darted side to side, lips pressed together, their steps precise. They'd made the decision, no turning back now.

So many things could go wrong. What if the guide tricked them out of their money? Mama felt sure he could do it and what other choice did they have? Would they make it?

Franz saw the abandoned, weather-beaten boxcar, partially obscured by tall weeds. Looking around, he was relieved that the nearest house was at least a half-block away. They slid the heavy door open, and winced as it squeaked. Franz and Tony threw backpacks inside, hopped up and stretched their hands down to help the women.

The youngest and oldest, Kati and Eva, came first since they had no suitcases to carry. Inside their pockets and hung around their necks were small items, including cigarette papers, tobacco and razor blades. Things they'd taken from Lissi's store to barter for help and food.

Mama and Lissi grabbed the boys' hands and hopped up. Last came Berbl.

It took a minute for Franz' eyes to adjust to the gloom inside. Sep was not here yet and probably wouldn't be for hours. A large bucket sat in the corner. *All the comforts of home,* he thought, *a privy.* Did their guide leave it for them? Tired, they settled to wait.

Mama curled in a corner and a few tears rolled down her cheeks and onto Kati's dull blonde hair. Franz sat beside them, knowing why Mama cried. He sat close, holding her hand.

"I keep thinking of Jani," he said. "And what it would be like to lose you and Kati." Franz didn't mention his father and felt the absence.

"Manci and I will never again sit over a cup of coffee and share in laughter." Mama leaned her head back and closed her eyes. "One of the most wonderful gifts I got when I married your father was to get Manci for a sister." She hesitated, cleared her throat and whispered. "Did you ask about Dori?"

"No," Franz answered. "I was too upset. He said Jani's last thoughts and prayers were for his sister, so that sounds like she survived."

They fell into separate silences.

The afternoon dragged on. People slept, carried on low conversations and occasionally someone squatted over the bucket. Sunlight between the cracks around the doors softened.

Franz jerked out of a light doze at the rattle of the sliding door. His heart beat triple time and he moved close to Mama and Kati, ready to jump up. All eyes faced the same direction.

A small, wiry man hopped inside, reached down to take two suitcases and helped a woman up. She stumbled and by the time she righted herself, the door was closed.

"I'm Sep." He said in a deep tone, and looked around. "Elisabeth?"

"That's me," Mama said. She stood and stepped closer to him.

Sep had a hawk-like nose and his ears stood out on the sides of his head. He looked at each person, one by one.

"This is Frau Maier," he jerked his thumb toward the lady and gave time to greet her. Sep handed a bag to the nearest woman, who happened to be Eva. "Each of you take one." Tony's aunt reached inside and lifted out a sausage and passed the bag to Berbl. Everyone took one. How good it was! Franz savored the flavor. It was real sausage, complete with grease and spices. Very much like the ones they cured on the farm. He wiped the drippings off his chin and sucked his finger for every bit of taste.

Franz stared at the new woman. She looked so healthy, with a soft layer of skin on her face. She moved rapidly toward her suitcases. Gazing at the others in his group, the difference was huge. For so long they'd survived on rations only. Frau Maier clearly had been better fed.

"How old are you boys?" Sep asked Franz and Tony.

"Thirteen," Franz said. *You can rely on us, but can we trust you?* He stopped himself from saying it aloud.

"Eleven," Tony's voice wobbled.

"You're the men of the group, huh?"

Franz squared his shoulders and nodded. Tony did the same.

"You'll do." Sep sat down and everyone returned to their resting spots.

"Just a few rules. When we leave, don't talk. Sound carries a long way here. We'll stop as needed. It's going to be a difficult night and we have to push through to the border, so rests will be short." He looked around at them again. "I've made it clear that I won't take anyone who smokes, haven't I? It's too easy for someone to see the lighting of it, and the glowing end."

"One other thing. You do as I say and do it quickly. There will be no voting. I've been hired to get you over the border, and you must follow me completely. If you're careless or draw attention, we'll all pay the price. Anyone want to turn back?"

No one said a word.

Franz wiggled under Sep's penetrating gaze at each of them. Had they passed the test? Sep hesitated at Kati, the only little one. His eyes flicked up to Mama. Franz blew out tension when the man nodded.

"Most of you brought only what you can carry. Good. It will be a tough journey." He leaned back on the side of the box car. "Any questions?" Nobody spoke and Sep pulled his hat down over his eyes. "Dark is coming fast. Sleep if you can."

Maybe Franz' muscles could rest, if nothing else. He closed his eyes most of the half-hour, but couldn't stop his mind running in circles, trying to imagine the night ahead. Light faded around the doors until it grew dark.

"Let's go," Sep growled as he stood and flexed his arms and legs.

Everyone grabbed his own things and jumped to the ground below.

Alert to everything, Franz heard the squeaking of the suitcases, shuffling of feet, and heavy breathing. Frau Maier carried one suitcase in each hand and stopped frequently to rest the weight by her feet. Then she had to hurry faster. It was hard to feel sorry for her when they'd been instructed to take only what they could carry the distance.

Sep moved very fast for a small man, and they had to hurry to leave the edge of town. Franz breathed easier when they reached peaceful farm lands. How would Sep have explained nine people, most with suitcases?

The wind blew into their faces, freezing the air they breathed. Franz closed his eyes to slits.

Wet and freshly plowed, the familiar smell of soil comforted Franz. Memories of working with Opa out in the fields flittered through his mind. Would he do that again someday?

Kati stumbled, interrupting his thoughts, and Franz pulled her up. Kati couldn't fall and sprain something. They must all be careful on this rough ground. Franz promised himself to do a better job watching out for her. From time to time, she had to run, holding Mama's coat and one of Franz' hands. Kati bit her lips and moaned any time she had to raise her arms. Franz tried to lift his suitcase higher with one hand and leaned toward Kati with the other.

The group as a whole stopped taking big steps, their shoulders hunched over and their feet moved with greater effort through clinging mud.

He was tired and wondered if they would ever stop when Sep swept his hand toward three lonely looking trees in a line ahead. Finally, they all sank on a small patch of dead grass between them.

Kati put her hands on her elbows as if they ached and hugged them to herself, and then burrowed into Mama's coat for warmth.

Frau Maier opened one suitcase and took out a frying pan. "It was my mother's," she whispered and laid it aside. "But it's too heavy."

With a shrug, she opened a bottle of apricot brandy, sipped from it and passed it around.

Kati poked her head out and sniffed. Mama gave her a swallow.

"Here," Frau Maier said to Kati. "You wear this. It'll keep your head cozy." Removing the soft red derby hat off her own head, she placed it on Kati's.

"Thank you." In the light of a half-moon, Franz enjoyed Kati's smile as she put her hands up to feel. "It's warm."

"Time's to go." Sep whispered as he stood and waited for them to get up, grab their belongings, and continue north.

He knows we don't need to be reminded to be quiet, Franz thought. *We're too tired and weak and scared to talk.*

The night felt unreal. One step, then another, always watching the plowed fields for smoother areas. Clouds drifted over the partial moon, casting them in total dark frequently.

"Over here." Sep's guttural words were greeted with thankful sighs.

The moon peeked out and Franz watched Frau Maier open one piece of luggage again. She pawed through things and pulled out a pair of what looked like brass candlesticks. She laid them aside and closed the case.

"Shove those in the dirt or behind weeds," Sep snarled. "You want to leave a trail to us?"

"No!" With a gasp, she dug a hole using one of the items and worked it back and forth until they were out of sight. "Sorry."

The break seemed too short. Franz tried to walk on a different part of his right foot. A painful blister had popped and each step rubbed it. How could he focus on something so unimportant when they might be killed or captured before morning?

The stops came more often as their energy diminished. Each time, Frau Maier dumped more of her things, until she was down to one suitcase.

"Cattle tank ahead," Franz whispered to his mother. Oh, he was so thirsty. There had to be water.

Sep used a sweeping motion forward.

Franz pushed up his sleeves and leaned over, glancing up to see Sep's smile. Shards of ice hovered on the surface, freezing his hands as he used them for a cup. It didn't matter, Franz was so thankful to have something washing down his throat and satisfying his stomach. He stopped frequently to put his clasped fists over his mouth and warmed breath. All around him, he heard sounds of water being slurped by the others.

"Don't drink too much," Sep said. "It'll make you sick."

After a ten-minute rest, they picked up their things and began to move again. They'd been walking for hours and Franz felt they'd never stop. He was so tired. Mama mirrored Sep's movements and inhaled through her nose and out her mouth. Her jaws clenched and she looked ahead as though she could see a better future. Tony held his aunt's mother by her arm to steady her. Franz admired how tough Kati had become, keeping up with the others without a whimper. He'd push himself forward, as they all did.

Clouds continued to float below the moon, first to hide it, and then allow it to shine below. Once an airplane flew above, but Franz couldn't see if it were a bomber or what country it belonged to. Stumbling occasionally, they forged ahead.

Sep stopped for them to huddle around him.

"You wait in here," Sep tipped his head toward a ramshackle barn with no doors. Like a ghost, he was gone.

What will we do if he doesn't come back? Franz thought of no answer to the question. He joined the others inside, out of the wind. He might as well sit on moldy straw and worry instead of pacing like a caged animal.

They waited about fifteen minutes, not daring to speak their thoughts, before he returned.

"I have sympathizers around here who share food with my people." Sep handed out dried bread and thin ham from his pockets and a bucket of berries.

Franz enjoyed every crumb and his whispered thanks joined the others.

"It's not far to the border. We'll search the horizon for high stands where Partisans sit." He picked up a screwdriver and drew a sketch in the dirt. "They'll be about a mile apart with guards on the top platform, and also on the ground. One walks towards the west and another towards the east, so two guards cover this area at all times. They'll meet in the middle, talk for a short time, then continue on their round. After they chat is our safest time to try crossing. All guards have machine guns."

Franz studied the scratched lines, and shook his head. "What about the guards up in the towers?"

"I just gave you the simple version." Sep saluted Franz and bent to the dirt again. "This is the border," he pressed in a heavy stroke to his markings. "We'll go closer several times and lay flat on the ground and hope we aren't seen." The clouds moved over the moon, hiding Sep's face. "Once we start over the border, we have to continue. If anything goes wrong, don't stop to have a meeting, just run to the other side. Kati, do you understand? If you hear shouts or guns, run like lightening to the other side. Your mother and brother will find you over there." He cleared his throat. "Trust each other enough to get yourselves over, and meet up there if trouble comes."

A chill ran up Franz' back.

"You had courage to start, and you have enough to finish. Remember why you're here."

Franz felt more determined.

"Watch me and immediately do exactly what I do." Sep adjusted his hat and motioned them to follow. "If all goes well, we'll reach Hungary and freedom..."

Icy wind turned to sleet and whipped their faces. Nothing looked different, but Franz felt more alert, glancing at Sep frequently.

The soft hooting of an owl caused Franz' heart to race. *Don't get jumpy over every little thing,* he scolded himself, *stay calm and pay attention.* Another glance at Sep and he took Kati's hand, to reassure her.

Sep squatted and scrutinized the sky from left to right and back to left. Everyone did the same. They walked very slowly along the edge of the plowed area. Five minutes later, they got low to the ground and studied the sky line again. Then it became a routine, searching for signs of the border guards.

Franz' breath caught when he saw a slight shadowing ahead. He looked at Sep, who used his hands like wings to motion stay down. He duck walked forward. Franz and others dropped into the same position, some crawled on hands and knees.

The quiet was eerie. Sep stopped and lay, face down, in the moist soil. They all did the same. Franz tipped his head up to look around and kept Sep in his peripheral vision. After a few minutes with nothing happening, Sep popped up in his squat and moved forward with all the speed of a turtle. Slow and steady. It was awkward moving in a squat or crawl. Down they went again, and lay still for what seemed an eternity.

Five more times they repeated these actions, each one more tense than the last. Franz could see border stations standing tall in the distance. Sep brought them midway between the two. *He's done this before, he knows the best way.* But still, tension was high.

One more time and they were close enough to see a Partisan marching from each of the two stands. Step by step, they moved toward their center.

The sound and feelings of thunder filled his chest. Franz watched the guards, but never took his eyes from Sep for more than three or four seconds. He shivered, from both cold and fear, and every sound was magnified.

The men greeted one another in Yugoslavian when close enough. One offered a cigarette to the other and lit them both.

Franz heard routine conversation complaining about the temperature and being hungry. With a wave, they each continued their way.

After they parted, Sep didn't move.

Why were they still here? Franz wanted to get up and run, but also turn around and go back. No, they were so close, they had to go forward.

Sep rose to his knees and scanned the area. Very quietly, he stood and motioned them to do the same. The moon peeked through clouds again and Franz didn't know if that was good or bad.

This is it, Franz thought, we *have one chance, life or death with no other outcome.*

42

End of March, 1946 – 13 years old
Yugoslavian and Hungarian borders.

L IKE DUCKLINGS, ALL eight of them followed their leader in a wobbly line as they went past Legin. Behind Sep, they carried their bags, first Lissi and Eva, then Tony and Berbl. Next Mama and Kati and Frau Maier. Franz took up the rear, his eyes moving from side to side, returned to Sep, and then Mama and Kati. They scurried over the hard, dry ground.

A half mile in either direction, guards were up on the stands. Maybe they watched with binoculars this very minute, machine guns trained on them. Every muscle tightened, Franz' breathing grew shallow. Could he do as Sep instructed and keep running even if things went wrong for Mama or Kati? Or Tony? With each step Franz expected to hear shouts to stop, or the sound of gunfire. Where was the actual border? Had they already crossed it? If they were seen by Partisans, the dividing line didn't matter.

They kept walking. Something darted out of the bushes nearby. Panic flooded his brain, and he stopped a moment. Another movement. It was only a dog, a wild, yellow dog. Relieved, he watched it run away.

After a while their pace slowed. Franz noticed a cold wind whipped their faces, but nothing mattered but reaching their goal of freedom. Wherever that was.

Sep led them a long distance before he dared to stop near a partially burned house. Then he grinned.

"By God's grace, we're well over the Hungarian border. We deserve a rest." He opened the front door and ushered his small group inside.

Feeling nervous, Franz dropped his backpack on the soot-covered floor and sat near his mother and sister. At first, he couldn't relax. Still alert, he listened past the racing wind and rustling of people trying to be comfortable. He glanced at Sep, who appeared to be sleeping. Sleeping? Now? Franz lay down and rolled to one side, using the pack for an uncomfortable pillow. His shoulders burned, but fatigue was greater. If Sep didn't appear worried, it must be okay. He closed his eyes.

"Up! Time to go."

Franz jerked awake. How long had he slept? A few minutes or an hour? He got up and joined the others in a tight group.

"We've got about four miles to a temporary house where you'll be safe."

Wordlessly, they shuffled along. Franz wondered what the place would be like. A work camp? An empty house? How long would they stay there?

Sep moved amongst them, asking questions. What did you do before? What do you want to do next? Mama said her children needed to continue their educations. Lissi agreed for Tony and Berbl.

"I'm hungry," Kati said.

"Me, too," Sep said, and chucked her chin with his knuckle. "We'll have food when we reach the village of Gara."

Franz marveled at how they relaxed as they thought about a better future. Choices. What a magical word. He smiled and rocked back and forth on his feet.

"I wish I could take a layer of clothes off," Franz said to Tony as they paired up in line. "But then I'd have something else to carry." The sun rose high, the wind settled to a gentle breeze. Farm houses were scattered ahead. Franz glanced at his fellow travelers. They looked as apprehensive as he felt. Knowing Hungary's history with Germany, Franz feared they would be hostile. He thought of when Hungarian forces invaded Sombor. The three days and nights they stayed below the windows, crawling around as they heard shooting both near and far. He'd been both scared and bored. Remembering, Franz bit the inside of his lower lip.

"Almost there." Sep skirted the edge of the village. He faced everyone and spread his arms. "A beautiful day to enjoy freedom, don't you think?"

Wanting to believe his words, Franz felt relief drift over his body. A little house sat off by itself on a large lot. As soon as they got close, Franz realized this must be their destination. Neither a grand house nor a prison either.

Sep knocked on the worn green door and opened it immediately. A couple, probably younger than Franz' parents, greeted them and invited them inside. The glowing heat of a wood stove at the back of the room drew everyone close.

Franz lowered the satchel. He flexed his arms, and pain shot through his shoulders as if they were being branded.

"Take off your coats," said a lady with curly brown hair and a thin face. She appeared to have excess energy as she bustled around taking clothes to hang on hooks in a row on the wall.

"Like at school," Franz and Berbl said at the same time, and chuckled.

"Put your belongings in there." The woman pointed to a small bedroom. Franz sniffed at a wonderful aroma, but waited politely. Soup in the kettle! He smelled meat, vegetables, and tomatoes. Heaven.

"This is Frau Barta," Sep nodded to the woman, then turned to the man, "and Herr Barta."

Both nodded slowly and moved their hands, palms up, to gesture to the bubbling pot in invitation. Sep helped himself to a bowlful and everyone else copied him.

Franz relaxed, scooped up his portion and picked up a generous piece of real bread. Right at this moment nothing mattered but the welcome in this house.

"Tony," Franz said. "It looks good here!" He set his bowl on the floor and sat down. Pulling off one layer of clothes, he threw them into the air.

"When we got close to the border, I knew we'd be killed." Tony shook his head. "If anyone had run back, I would have joined them."

"I'll have to confess." Mama cleared her throat. "I kept reminding myself why we decided to do this. I was terrified!"

"Crossing over the border," Sep's lip turned up on one corner, "has made many a tough, brave man sweat profusely no matter the temperature."

"I was scared something bad might happen," Kati said. "I prayed and prayed." She put her hands in her lap, straightened her elbows and beamed at them.

"You've had a traumatic time," Frau Barta said. "For the next few days, your job is to eat, sleep and regain strength." Her husband took cots from a closet and began to set them up.

"Please try to nap, even if you think you can't." Herr Barta's eyes held a twinkle.

They've done this before. Franz found the thought comforting. He couldn't rest, but it would be nice to lie down. He took off two more layers of shirts and dropped them on the floor.

Franz gasped and whimpered. He looked at the front of his shoulders where the final shirt stuck to him. His skin had been shaved off by the narrow leather straps of his backpack, leaving his shirt glued to seeped blood.

"Peel your shirt off." Mama walked over to him and pulled the shirt free in short jerks. "Let the sores air dry." She got close and studied it, pulling a bit to see how deep it went.

"We managed to get soap as a treat." Frau Barta took the role of nurse. "Being clean will help. Wash your open sores first, Franz, and then each of you will have a turn bathing with washcloths."

***

Franz woke the next morning to the sound of people talking. Slipping his shoes on, he went to the kitchen. Those sitting around the table looked up as he entered the room. He felt heat spread over his face, embarrassed at slumbering like a little kid.

"Good morning," Sep waved Franz into the room. "You haven't missed anything. Whenever I bring in a group from Yugoslavia, they always sleep hard at first." He waved a piece of toast. "Come, eat."

Only Kati, Eva, and Frau Maier weren't there. Franz got a bowl of oatmeal and sat by Tony.

"I'll leave in a few minutes," Sep's distinctive deep voice announced. "Someday, when all this is over, I hope to hear good news from you. My advice is not to get comfortable here where politics are unstable. If you get to Germany, go to the American sector. They're kinder and will be more helpful." With that, he pushed his chair back.

"What happens now?" Lissi asked, her brow furrowed and her eyes worried.

Franz wished Sep would stay. They were strangers here. Who could they trust? The Bartas seemed nice, but they'd just met last night.

"You go find work, or barter what you have. Most in this village are sympathetic." Sep looked around at all of them with his small, alert dark eyes. "You'll be fine. I've got to return to Yugoslavia."

After three days of resting and eating healthy meals, they felt stronger. Franz' shoulders healed. Without chores, he grew fidgety. Taking walks around the village became a favorite thing to do. Each day, Franz worried less and studied the people, nodding at them as they passed. As Sep had said, most of the locals were friendly to German Yugoslavians.

"A lady at the store mentioned a farmer nearby needs help," his mother said a few days later. "Our Hungarian will help, and I'm going talk to him." Mama looked off in the distance. "We won't barter our few valuables until we have to. You stay with Kati."

With that, she brushed her hair and left.

Franz and Tony spent the morning with their sisters. Although Berbl was Franz' age, she played with Kati for a while, until the boys joined them in a game of hide and seek.

Feeling increasingly anxious about Mama, Franz pretended interest in Kati's game. He kept looking toward the gate. If only she hadn't gone alone.

Kati just finished counting to ten to search for them when Mama strolled in the yard. Franz glanced at Kati's back and waved at his mother. She joined him, out of sight, behind a stack of fire wood.

"Oh, Franz, it's good," Mama whispered. "The Kelemens really do need help from both of us! Best of all, we'll live in a separate little house." Her eyes sparkled. "You, Kati and I will be together!"

"I found you!" Kati shouted and pointed at them. Mama picked her up and twirled around.

"We're moving!" she said, but at Kati's frown, she laughed. "It's a good thing." She took her by the hand, and with Franz beside her, went to find Frau Barta.

It took but a moment for Franz to fill his backpack and find his mother.

Mama stood very still, her back to Franz, and her shoulders slumped, her face tipped down. Curious, Franz walked closer. She held her wedding portrait. Vati looked handsome, his hair combed perfectly and dressed fancier than Franz had ever seen. Mama was beautiful with her jeweled veil. Startled, she jerked, and then her lips turned up slightly when she saw him.

"I'm so glad you got these photos out of our house. I haven't looked at his picture in a long time." Her chin trembled and she traced Vati's face with her finger. "How will he find us?" After a deep breath, she straightened up and wiped her eyes with the palms of her hands and hugged Franz. Gently, she returned the image of younger, innocent days to her suitcase. "That's for later. Today we earn food and shelter. Let's go."

"We'll try to see you Sundays," Mama said when she told the others about the farm. A beautiful day, they sat outside in the grass.

"I found rooms at a boarding house in the village," Lissi said. "We'll use things Franz and Tony got from my store. For one cigarette, or razor blade, I'll get a day's worth of food for my family." She leaned against a tree and locked her fingers behind her head. Her eyes were soft as she looked at Tony and Berbl.

Frau Maier had managed to bring plenty despite abandoning items along the way.

It was a hopeful group that left and ventured out to begin new lives here.

"Frau Kelemen isn't strong. I'm not sure what the problem is," Mama explained as she led Franz and Kati on their way. "I'll do all the cooking and housekeeping. Franz, you'll get the fields ready for planting and anything else Herr Kelemen needs."

Twenty minutes later, Franz met their new landlords. The man had muscular arms and wide shoulders. His wife, a tiny woman, moved about with a cane, one leg looked six inches shorter than the other, throwing her spine in an odd position. Both had gray hair, though Herr Kelemen had very little around the side of his head and nothing on top. Their smiles warmed Franz.

"Come, children," she said. "You'll live in the house across the yard. Take your things there and join us for a noon meal."

Franz smiled as they walked to the cottage. She had to tip her head up to see him, yet thought he was a little boy.

"I've had to share you with so many people for so long!" Mama giggled the way she used to as she opened the door. "It'll take about five minutes to get settled." She laughed again.

Mama and Kati put their things in the bedroom, and Franz placed his backpack and extra clothes on the divan in the parlor. Then they opened doors and cabinets to explore

"This is cozy, but not permanent," Mama pulled Franz and Kati into her arms. "Let's be thankful we're together for whatever time we're here."

Franz studied Kati. She looked around with curiosity and didn't seem to hear Mama's warning. His heart ached as he nodded. He wanted to stay here, feeling safe. From the time they were rounded up and taken to Market Square, each of the next three moves had been worse. Until now. It would be hard to leave this farm.

The next few days Franz and his mother established a routine, working from early in the morning until late, but having time at night for the three of them together made the hours worthwhile. When the Kelemens found out Franz liked to read, they showed him their books. Unfortunately, they were in Hungarian. He quickly realized speaking the language and reading it weren't equally as easy.

Each evening they ate their meal with the Kelemens and talked about the day, a lot like when they were at Oma and Opa's. Sitting and eating around a table, with little mention of war. He studied his mother. Beyond her smiles and cheerful words there were still many shadows in her eyes.

Katie bumped his arm to get his attention.

"I'm sewing buttons on for Frau Kelemen," Kati said with a satisfied smile. "Doesn't it look nice?" She held up a yellow shirt that looked about Kati's size.

"Just like a regular seamstress does." Franz leaned over and admired her work. He winked at the woman.

"We never had children." Frau Kelemen stroked the top of Kati's blond hair. "She's like a bit of sunshine."

Franz and his mother glanced at each other, thankful their little girl and this frail lady needed each other.

Feeling more useful each day, Franz welcomed exercise and being outside. H helped Herr Kelemen till the spring ground for a kitchen vegetable garden. Now Franz worked the main fifteen acres while Herr Kelemen did repairs on his wagon. After a week, the rhythm of plowing here felt the same as in Stanišić.

"You sure are a pitiful old horse," Franz muttered to the bony animal pulling the plow. He gazed off in the distance. No Gakova and its camp of death. Today felt like spring, with a blue sky and no wind. The smell of fresh dirt made him long for home.

"Opa, you should have come with us," he said as he shook the reins to remind the horse to move along. "Last time we plowed the Legin acres we used shovels. You told stories from your youth as we worked." Pain twisted in his gut as he spoke. "See what I'm doing, Opa? Talking to myself. I chat with this old nag because you aren't here." He wiped his sleeve across his nose and turned the horse and plow to the barn. He had to stop thinking of the people who weren't here. God had answered so many prayers. After a horrible nine months, they had enough food and rest.

Franz woke up the next morning, eager to see their friends in the village. He, Mama and Kati admired trees budding out, timid green grass poking up, and plants sprouting from the ground.

At last they arrived at the place where Tony's family lived. Mama and Lissi went inside, and Berbl took Kati to a nearby store.

"I hate it here, but it's better than starving in Stanišić," Tony grumbled as he and Franz sat outside on the steps of the boarding house. "Most people are nice, but they're curious and stare at us. I don't speak their language well, so I mainly talk to my family. All females." He groaned and rolled his eyes, then smirked. "You ought to see Berbl, Aunt Lissi, and Eva clean and cook on Saturdays because you're coming. Then they watch out the window Sunday mornings." Tony laughed and punched Franz on his shoulder. "I stay out of the fuss."

"No, you never miss an opportunity to hassle them." Franz grinned, and then raised his eyebrows. "Have you learned any more Hungarian this week?"

"Yes, from the witch across the hall. She spits on the floor when we pass. Yesterday she shouted "German" at me, and drew her finger across her throat. She muttered a word that sounded like *jelez*. What could that mean?"

"If I heard it in a sentence, I probably could guess." Franz frowned. What was going on? A chill went up his spine at hearing of the death sign. "What does your Aunt Lissi say?"

"To ignore her as much as possible and remember all people aren't the same."

The boys fell silent.

The afternoon sped by, eating lunch and visiting. Mama stood up, handed Kati and Franz their jackets, and they returned to the farm. It was a silent walk as Franz thought about what Tony said.

"I left our supper cooking on the stove." A tense note in Mama's voice brought him to the present. "It's horse meat and should be done about now. Adding salt will make it taste less sweet."

What was wrong? From her voice and expression, he knew there was something. The street was not the place to ask, but he felt uneasy. Franz couldn't concentrate as Herr Kelemen prayed before they ate. He wished the man would make his petitions shorter, so they could quickly eat and leave. Finally, after what seemed a long time, they walked to their private little house. Kati spent the night with the Kelemens.

"Lissi saw a notice posted at the courthouse," Mama said as soon as she shut the door. "All people who came from Yugoslavia must register. They'll know exactly where we are."

"Tony asked what '*jelez*' meant." Franz slumped against the wall, feeling as if he'd been punched in the stomach. "His neighbor taunted him with needing to be registered," Franz spoke slowly. He looked straight in the eyes of his mother. "What does that mean? Will we have to return?" Had Opa been right to stay? Franz expelled a deep breath, trying to blow out his fear. He looked down at the floor.

"Probably. And it will be worse." Mama didn't elaborate.

Pictures flashed in his mind. They could be beaten or in a death camp or shot or hanged. Franz's hands trembled. They couldn't go. But staying meant waiting day to day, hoping nothing happened. He wanted to scream, or pound the walls. Would this never end?

"Last week Frau Kelemen said there's a German prisoner of war on the next farm," Mama continued. "His name is Hans. Lissi and I are talking about escaping to Austria, but would prefer to have an adult man along. Kati and Berbl would be safer, I think."

"What if we don't register?" he asked. "No," he answered his own question, "too many people know about us." A busy roaring rolled in his head. "How soon do we need to go?"

"We'll talk to this man tomorrow. You work especially hard and stay busy. Kati will have fun with Frau Kelemen." Mama fell silent, thinking, as she bit her thumb nail. "Let's try to get some sleep."

The next morning, Mama got up well before dawn. After waving at Franz, she slipped out the door to meet Lissi.

Doing as Mama instructed, Franz took care of the horse and cow, and plowed another field. All the while, he pictured the maps in his head. It was a long day. By the time he returned to the Kelemens, Mama was busily cooking the evening meal as always.

She looked over her shoulder and gave a brief nod. Just like any other day, they visited around the table and when the kitchen was cleaned, the three of them returned to the house.

"How did it go?" Franz asked.

Kati sat and looked from one to the other, her eyes wide.

"Han's from Pfaffenhofen and I like him. He seems trustworthy and eager to leave but doesn't have means to escape on his own. Lissi and Frau Maier have enough goods to bribe officials. We'll leave two hours after the village is quiet and dark," Mama continued. "I hate not telling the Kelemens. It's better for them and us if they don't know our plans."

"How will this stranger help us?" Franz heard the skepticism in his own voice.

"Hans knows this area very well. We'll go north through Hungary and then west to cross the border to Austria."

Franz felt like vomiting. Another border crossing.

43

Late April 1946 – 13 years old
Escaping through Hungary from Gara to western border

S HOULD HE SAY something? Franz' mother turned her head and
wiped away tears as she packed food she'd hoarded, making their bags bulge. One of his father's sayings, "It is what it is,"
came to mind. Things were what they were. With heavy heart, he
finished stuffing his backpack.

"We can't stay at the Kelemen's farm," Mama said. "I'm just
feeling weepy. My hips hurt. My feet hurt. Don't worry. I'm fine."
She put her work-roughened hand on Franz' cheek for a moment.
"I just hate this for you and Kati. And myself, too." Hugging Kati,
she pulled the child out of bed. "Time to go."

"No!" Katie cried and burrowed under the blanket. "I don't
have to hide here! I get to play outside!" At that, she burst into tears.

Mama held her daughter's shoulders and looked straight in
her eyes. "Catharina Elmer! We have no choice." Mama helped
get her shoes on. "We can't be put on the registry. Things are
changing."

Clenching his teeth, Franz wanted to scream, but at who? Or
what? Would this ever end? Quietly, they filed out the front door
and left.

Franz looked back at the little house. They'd enjoyed being
together, just the three of them with adequate eating. He gazed

ahead and wondered what their landlords would think to find them gone, without a farewell. It was safer for them as well, to know nothing.

He told himself to concentrate on surviving.

"Watch for a big tree split about six feet up." Mama whispered as she led them along the creek which flowed from the village of Gara toward the meeting place.

Light rain fell. Franz pulled his coat closer, and watched Kati tug the red hat over her ears. She remained silent and stayed close to Mama. With each step they got farther from familiar territory. There were too many puddles to avoid, and his old shoes quickly filled. He heard sloshing sounds from Mama and Kati with every step.

"Listen." Franz cocked his head a half hour later. In the dim light of the moon, he imitated the whistle of a Cardinal, and then heard an answer. "Tony's just ahead."

A stranger stepped around the split tree and faced them.

Franz' heart beating faster, he held Kati's hand and moved closer to his mother. He pushed Kati behind him.

"Hello, Hans." When Mama introduced them, Franz expelled a great breath.

"Now we're all here." Something about the soft way the man spoke reminded Franz of his father. Both Franz' and Tony's families gathered around.

"We'll go to Baja and catch a train across the Danube," Hans said. "For months I've listened to their whistling. Every chance I got I asked about them, because so many tracks have been bombed and destroyed." He glanced directly at each person listening to him. "I've been eager to leave ever since I was brought here."

Wispy clouds parted, and Franz finally imagined they would escape. It felt as though weight had fallen from his shoulders. With great relief, Franz squinted to get a better look at the man. He had a fair complexion and they were about the same height. The two studied each other. Then, as if planned, they nodded.

So the walk began.

Thankful for flat land, they trudged forward against the north wind. Just as he was about to join Kati in asking when they would stop, Hans found an abandoned hut and ushered them inside. Franz noticed Hans didn't join them, but he was too tired to be curious.

Kati shook raindrops off her treasured hat and laid it beside her.

Sagging to the floor, Franz leaned on a wall, feeling the lack of sleep in the last thirty-six hours. At Mama's nudging, he took a piece of bread and ham from their bag. He ate with closed eyes until the front door opened.

"The well is good," Hans announced as he joined them. He held a weathered wooden bucket filled with water and a ladle. He walked from person to person, letting each get a refreshing drink.

"Thank you," Franz said after his turn. "We've gone about four miles, haven't we?"

"That's what I'd guess," Hans said. "Close to six more to Baja, mostly through farming land, where few bombs were dropped."

It was still dark, but the scattered rain ceased, and clouds drifted away as both families got their things and followed the man.

Two more times they stopped at streams to drink, wash and rest. Supplies they'd brought with them dwindled each time, until they pooled all the rest of their stock. At the last stop, they ran out. They worked harder at watching for things to eat along the way— bugs that weren't colorful, dandelions, anything they knew was safe.

"I wish I hadn't come," Lissi's mother, Eva, said at the last break. "I'm too old and can't keep up," she whispered, tears rolling down her wrinkled cheeks.

Franz looked at her closely, then to Mama and Lissi. They did have a long way to go.

"Mother." Lissi hugged her. "You've made it this far, and we'll help you. When we ride trains, you can rest. There's no choice."

"Maybe I could find my way back." Eva chewed her lip.

"Back where?" Lissi waved her arms around, her voice raised. "To the last camp?"

There was a long silence before Eva wiped her cheeks and stood. "I'm sorry."

Feeling tense, Franz got in line. Within an hour or so, soft light gradually climbed up the eastern sky. After trudging several miles on an old dirt road, Franz saw signs of a city ahead. Farmhouses became closer to each other, and the road grew wider. With a rush of excitement, he hurried to Hans.

"Is that Baja?" he asked, pointing toward buildings dotting the horizon.

"Yes," the older man said. "Pray for success."

Franz looked at their group. How would eight of them manage to get on a train?

A dog barked as they followed a line of trees. Hiding in tall weeds, they crept to the tracks. After an hour, a train appeared.

"It's going east," Hans mumbled. "Only speak Hungarian."

Franz and Tony looked at each other, rolling their eyes. Did Hans really think they needed to be reminded?

"Not a lot of security, is there?" Franz asked as he and Tony looked for guards. Everything remained quiet. Two more trains came by in the morning, going southeast. Franz struggled to be patient. They couldn't move away, they couldn't sleep. Two hours later, a train of coal cars came from the east and lined up for the bridge over the Danube.

"Just walk out like it's a daily thing," Hans said. "We'll watch for places between the cars."

That simple? Franz was thankful for so few men working around the train. Though he hardly dared breathe, they acted like a family heading home. After he and Tony hopped up, each turned to reach for the women's hands to help them. Within a couple of minutes they crowded on platforms between coal cars. The black locomotive started slowly, gradually gaining speed.

Franz' face and neck stung from cinders flowing back and coal dust in his eyes. Kati clutched Mama and hid in her coat. After a while the train's rumble felt like music.

Eagerly Franz looked ahead. The beauty of the Danube was awesome, even now. Trees were budding, welcoming spring. Smiling, he noticed that all of them enjoyed this as if this were a true vacation for a moment. He marveled at the turquoise blue of the water. The sun decorated the surface with dancing sparkles.

Franz turned his head to see Eva behind him. Her eyes were closed, her head swaying with the movement, but she continued to hold on to a steel support beam.

Small towns appeared along the shorelines. They were too far away to see people, or if they had farm animals. It was peaceful and beautiful. He and Mama smiled. The whistle of the train broke the spell of feeling free. Frowning when they approached the rail yard on the other side of the river, Franz wished the Danube were much wider.

Acting like citizens, they got off and moved away from the crowd. Hans blended into a group of people to find out which train would be going north next. Franz looked around and relaxed until he saw a man looking closely at them. Why? Just curious? Was he looking for people escaping? As the man came their way, Franz noticed Mama watched from the corner of her eye. Forcing smiles, he and his mother used Hungarian as they talked about a family reunion they were going to. He laughed and teased Tony they would win the game this year and the rest of the group nodded and mimicked Franz's expressions. Even Kati. The man slowed down, but continued past. Franz dared not look over his shoulder.

Leaving the rail yard, they found a small park with concrete tables and benches. Listening to everything around them, they lowered their heads and closed their eyes.

"We're in luck," Hans said when he sat down between Franz and Tony. "In a few hours we can hop on a scarce boxcar and, I hope, go north as far as Lake Balanton before we need to walk a long way."

"We have to find something to sustain us better." Mama's voice wobbled. "We can't live on the occasional bug, tubers, mushrooms and early potatoes. We're all too weak."

"Franz and I will get some and the rest of you stay." He turned to Tony and put his hand on the boy's shoulder. "They need you here."

Mama bit her lower lip and frowned. "I'll pray for you both."

"We'll hurry," Franz said. Eager to do something, he joined Hans in slipping into a dense field of weeds. "Steal, borrow or beg?"

"Had any practice begging?" The older man raised an eyebrow.

"A little," with a shrug, Franz didn't elaborate. "Farmers are more likely to have food stored away. People in town just get rations."

"When I checked on train schedules, a man answered my questions and pointed out where he lives. Let's try him first."

They walked a block down the sidewalk to a small, brown house. Franz had been thinking of how they would ask. Hans knocked, and then stepped behind Franz, leaving him in charge.

"Hello." The door opened too quickly for Franz to ask Hans what to do. "Can I help you?" The gray haired man seemed neither friendly nor hostile.

"I'm . . . we're passing through with our family. We've been walking for days and are really hungry." His words came out choppy and he stammered. Heat moved up his face.

"How many?" The man's eyes squinted.

Franz looked at Hans. What should they answer? If they say eight, will they get more? Is there danger in letting him know too much about them?

Silence stretched out before Hans spoke. "A couple of small families, actually. The youngest is seven years old."

"Where are you from? Russia?" The man cocked his head to one side, studying.

"We are escaping them, and Tito," Hans said.

Folding his shaking hands under his arms, Franz' heartbeat raced. He sure hoped Hans knew what he was doing.

"Yes, wait here." The farmer gestured to chairs on the porch. "The Soviets are the meanest people on earth. They destroy and loot wherever they go." He narrowed his eyes and Franz had the feeling he was looking for signs that they were, indeed, Russian. The man stepped inside his doorway.

Whew! Franz and Hans looked at each other in wonder. It occurred to Franz that they didn't have anything yet, and weren't safely with the others.

In about five minutes, a heavy basket was given to them, along with a pledge to pray for them. Back with their group, they all gave thanks for the bacon, bread and canned beans they feasted on. They were ready to catch the train north.

The next three days they rode when they could, and walked many miles when tracks had been bombed out. Always, before they entered a town of any size, they cleaned up, washed their hair and clothes. Mama and Lissi were ready to trade the treasures Franz and Tony had sneaked from their old homes, to feed all of them.

Turning west in one town, they heard someone playing an accordion. Franz stopped and listened. Suddenly realizing he was crying, he wiped his cheeks with his shirt sleeve. An arrow of grief hit him hard. He looked at his mother. She blinked at him in their shared mourning for Jani. Oh, how he missed his best friend and cousin. He bowed his head and got his emotions under control.

Always, the rule was to never draw attention to themselves. Bartering was handled as a business transaction. One man complained about being paid by their factory in food, not money before he said they had a little surplus and gave them something to eat.

Getting closer to the northwest border, they moved mostly at night, and needed more frequent stops to rest.

When they got close to a farm, Franz was glad Hans approached the house with him to beg for help. Most of them willingly shared. Once in a while they were answered with swearing. Humiliation forced them to hurry away.

They were being watched. Franz felt it from his back and to his left side. The streets and sidewalk were still wet from an early afternoon rain, though sunshine had pushed away clouds. He looked around. The feeling was still there, but he didn't notice anything different. They entered this city only because they desperately needed food. Franz rubbed his stomach. Even his grandmother's liver and onions would be heavenly.

Mama, Lissi and Hans walked together ahead. Eva stayed with Kati and Berbl. That left Franz free to wander off the paths from time to time with Tony. They wondered how close they were to crossing to safety.

Franz noticed a large policeman edging closer to his mother.

Maintaining a casual appearance, the boys got near enough to listen.

"Where are you going?" The large man had thick blonde hair and bushy eyebrows. His voice sounded as though he had gravel in his throat.

"We're looking for work," Mama quickly improvised.

"It's funny that you're looking for work right here at the Austrian border!" His upturned lips didn't show friendliness. He motioned to another officer and they took all eight of them to the railway waiting room and were told to sit.

They were close to the border! Franz tried to keep his face calm, the others showed no emotion either.

Why were they here? Where would they be taken? Hans seemed thoughtful more than anything as he studied the situation. Franz felt his mother put her hand on his jiggling knee. He stopped. But inside, there was no rest. Every sound from the few people working there was magnified.

"You three," the same man pointed to Hans, Lissi and Mama. "Come with us." He turned and marched off to a nearby office. Lissi picked up her suitcase and followed.

Tony, Berbl and Eva huddled together on another bench, holding hands.

"Come on, Kati." Franz took her, and their baggage to sit with them.

"What should we do if they don't come back?" Tony whispered into Franz's ear.

It was too scary to think of being separated from his mother. Franz shrugged. In silence, he sat with his arm over Kati's shoulders. They waited for a long time. Looking around the station, Franz tried to see if there were a possible direction they could go. It didn't matter. They were guarded by three officers carrying guns, who fiddled with whistles hung around their necks. Franz bowed his head and sent a short prayer to God.

What's happening in there? Franz kept glancing at the door Mama and the others had gone through. He strained his ears, hoping to hear words, or at least sounds to indicate levels of anger. He heard nothing beyond occasional murmurings.

None of them said a word. Tony, Berbl and Eva leaned on the wall behind their bench. They looked like statutes.

Franz battled worries. Kati rested on him, complaining from time to time about her arms hurting.

The door opened. Alert, Franz kept his gaze on Mama as she stepped forward, her head high, fists tight. She headed straight for her children.

Next came Hans. His eyes darted around the room before he looked at the floor. Lissi pursed her lips, hollowing her cheeks. She collapsed on the seat with her family.

"Stay here." The man with bushy eyebrows left. Minutes later, he returned. "Only coal cars run now and none are scheduled for several days. If you're here and ready at eight this evening, someone with a horse and wagon will pick you up and take you to the border."

The officers stepped outside, leaving Franz' group alone.

"What happened?" he asked the three adults.

"I'm not sure," Mama stood up and paced to the window and back to Hans and Lissi. "Did we make a bargain we'll regret?"

"We didn't have any choice but to tell the truth." Hans stated and turned to face Lissi. "Your cigarettes and cigarette papers and razor blades may have saved us all."

"After they asked a lot of questions, they mumbled amongst themselves." Lissi put her hands on her cheeks while she explained to the boys. "They were nice," her eyebrows went up, "especially after I bribed them. So you heard their plan."

"Can we trust them?" Franz asked.

"They all have rifles and we have none." Mama held her hands facing up as if she were holding a wobbling tray in front of herself.

"I'm hungry," Kati whispered. "I smell meat cooking."

Despite the serious situation, Franz' face relaxed a second. Trust Kati to her soften the mood.

The brief moment didn't last. Were they walking into a trap? Would the horse and wagon even come?

PART THREE

HEALING AND REBUILDING

44

April/May 1946 – 13 years old
Leaving Hungary and entering Austria

F RANZ LISTENED TO crickets chirping and glanced at the others. A single yellow light cast shadows, making their faces look old and ill. They'd used some of Mamma's silver to buy food, and then strolled around seeing the layout of the town before returning in the station. The promised wagon might come in less than an hour. No one truly rested, or said a word. It was like being frozen in time, waiting.

Should they have gone in the right general direction and hoped to get across on their own? Franz made a face, knowing there would be no signs announcing the Austrian border. Was there a price on their heads for being Germans or from Yugoslavia? He had to stop thinking. It wasn't as if they had a lot of choices.

A sliver of moonlight barely penetrated the darkness.

The crickets abruptly stopped singing. Franz's heart stalled then beat double time at the sudden silence. Eventually, in the distance he barely heard the clopping of a horse, the creaking of a wagon. Franz turned his ear in that direction and the rest of the group did the same.

One by one, they took each other's hands and leaned forward.

The station clock said eight o'clock when the man arrived at the train depot. He stopped, cocked his head thoughtfully, and motioned them to come closer.

"I'm on my way to the border if you want to come along."

It was hard to see his face in the dim light, but Franz thought he looked much like the farmers in Stanisic, except he kept his hand on the rifle beside him. Along with the others, Franz climbed on the wagon with a lot of apprehension.

Franz watched as the man took them across a meadow, then along plowed ground. Each landmark must be memorized. The wagon jostled them along for half an hour before he pulled his horse to a stop.

"Aim for that tree," the man said as he pointed to a lone pine beside a small creek. "Go another yard and you'll be over the Austrian border. No guards there."

One by one, they slipped to the ground, carrying their belongings. Franz walked stiffly, very conscious of the stranger behind them. They were targets, and all could be killed without a single witness. Franz' legs pumped faster as he pulled Kati along. Each moment, he expected to hear a shout or shot. Finally, with creaking of wheels and shaking of harness, the wagon pulled away when they reached the solitary tree. The man was an honest farmer after all. There wasn't time to feel relieved for too long. Which way should they go?

After walking through Austrian meadows for an hour, small pine trees began to dot the area. Soon they became thicker. A steady drizzle settled in. Everyone was hungry, tired and getting wet.

"I wish we could turn up the moonlight," Kati said after she stumbled several times.

"Someone is standing over there!" Eva whispered loudly, pointing up the path over the horizon.

Franz looked the way she indicated, then all around, not daring to move.

Lissi put her arm over her mother's shoulders and they squatted. Everyone did the same.

Had they walked into a trap? Franz felt a heavy weight on his chest. The man didn't move at all. Odd. Franz duck waddled nearer. Nothing happened. Feeling safer, he moved closer more quickly. He grinned and stood up. "Come see our company!"

Quiet giggles broke out as they saw a six foot pine tree grown in the shape of a man.

Franz' steps were lighter and he found himself smiling, until they heard shooting in the distance again, bringing a renewed sense of danger.

Staying under tree limbs, they travelled west, stopping briefly to rest a few times. In the morning, Hans found a sagging, gray barn. Within minutes their wet, outer layers of clothes were removed and draped over stalls and old hay bales. Only then did they collapse to the sound of rain falling softly, in big drops and small. The melodic patter on the tin roof made falling asleep on the old straw easy. Hans disappeared to scout the area as soon as the rain gradually stopped.

Franz and Tony found potatoes and carrots overlooked from last year. No one complained about their toughness or lack of flavor. It was food. Others found dandelion leaves, and mushrooms. A small creek nearby was stagnant, but did slake their thirst.

"These bites are getting infected," Tony grumbled as he scratched. Franz didn't respond. He was busy trying to pull a tick from his head, while Mama mumbled about Kati's lice. Everyone tended to their own problems.

From time to time, a barrage of shots rang out.

"Sounds north, maybe east a long way," Mama said. Her eyebrows lowered as she uttered the words. "We're going away from it."

"It reminds me of Leipzig before the bombs started raining." Franz whispered, not wanting the others to hear. Better they feel safe. Franz' breathing deepened and he pushed down his nervousness. This wasn't Leipzig, but Austria.

"No luck," Hans said when he returned. "There's got to be a cluster of farms ahead."

Franz and the others grabbed their damp clothes and each fell in line to follow Hans.

After many hours of walking, Franz wondered when they could find out where they were. Hans rejected two houses. The first because it had a very aggressive dog chained beside the door, the other because it had no signs of life. After several more miles, the third had a few chickens scratching in the yard and clothing on the clothes line.

"Everyone get in there and lay low," Hans said, pointing to a long, deep ditch beside the path. Weeds made a nice wall of protection. "Franz and I'll see if we can get help."

Franz hated going up to a house to ask for food and shelter. He always knew it could be a disaster. The embarrassment and shame wasn't the problem now. They simply couldn't keep walking without nourishment. No, he was nervous about who would be on the other side of the door.

After knocking, they immediately stepped back some distance in case they had to run. A man answered the door. He didn't look mean, merely thoughtful and alert.

"Are we really in Austria?" Franz cleared his throat after his voice squeaked.

"Yes, in the Russian Sector." He looked from Franz to Hans and sighed. "You know we've been split into different Allied occupied areas, don't you?" He looked sad when they shook their heads. "United Kingdom, United States, and Russia."

Feeling as if they'd walked in circles, Franz felt a punch to his belly. He turned to Hans, hoping for an explanation. Anything that distanced them from Russians.

"You're German, right?" the Austrian asked. "You'll need to be with the Brits, they're much closer than the Americans."

At their nods, he told them to wait and he'd bring them some food.

What if he returned with a gun? Or didn't return at all? Franz chewed his lower lip. Hans clenched his fists.

The door opened and the man handed Franz a bag filled with food. Franz wanted to open it right then, but stopped himself at the smell of fresh bread. Fresh bread! Eager to hurry back to the others, he knew he had to wait so they could share. He met the man's eyes, and both of them smiled. The man shuffled his feet, cleared his throat and bent to draw a map in the dirt, showing the way to safety.

From that point on they walked a slower night speed and hid in the forest during the day. Gun and canon fire drew closer. Franz tried not to worry about being captured, sent back and probably put to death.

"Look," he said to Hans early the next morning. "Someone lives down this dirt road. Maybe we can ask how close we are."

"You're going the right direction," a woman hanging out her laundry said. "You've got several nights of walking yet to get there." She set her basket down and told them to wait. She returned with a sack of potatoes and surprised them with a small portion of bacon. Meat! Oh, how good this would taste!

Continuing their schedule of resting by day, curling up in the woods in beds of dried leaves when they could, and walking at night, they checked with a farm house each day.

"How long has it been since we escaped?" Franz scratched his dirty waist. He sat on a large, flat rock.

"Seven weeks, I think," Mama said. "We're getting there. Oh, to have a real bath, with soap and warm water! We'll wash lice, fleas and ticks off, as well as our stench. After eating, I want a long and safe slumber!"

Sounds of a few dogs barking and more homes on acreages announced a city ahead. Farmers had been mostly helpful, so they stopped at the next one. A bow-legged man used his hat to fan himself as they approached. His eyes darted rom Hans to Lissi, who held hands with her mother and Berbl, Tony beside them. Mama stood tall, Kati peeking around her. Finally, the man's gaze went back to Franz and Hans.

"Which part of Austria are we in?" Hans said, pushing his shoulders back.

"The British are at the other side of the city." The man, his voice a monotone, nodded toward the back. "We have a clean shed where you can rest today. It'll be safer for you to move about during the night." He looked over group once more.

Franz looked to Mama to see if she was comfortable with this plan. A weary smile hovered on her lips. She thanked the man, and everyone else said *danke sehr* as well.

Franz slept the few hours until sunrise. Then his mind jumped from one possibility to another. He was too tired to do anything but drift in and out of wakefulness. Later in the day, Franz and Tony found an old patch of dandelions behind the outbuilding. They had to force themselves to eat even though it caused nausea. Before sunset, the man brought a basket of fruits, vegetables and a great delicacy—milk.

That night they carefully made their way through the slumbering city, praying that they not be seen by the wrong people. Relief filled Franz when they finally got past houses and businesses, and back to scattered farms. Had they entered the British sector? Passing an abandoned train station, Franz saw a clock. It was about two in the morning.

Tired, they'd all slowed down when they saw a small house with a light shining in one window.

"Let's stop and ask." Mama knocked on the door this time.

"I'll be there as soon as I'm dressed!" a man shouted.

Franz reminded himself that loud words often sounded angry when they were trying to be understood. Nervously rocking from one foot to the other, he was ready to run.

When a tall, thin man came outside, he saw all eight of them standing in his yard. His eyes scanned the group.

"It's pretty safe here in the British division."

A tiny woman peeked around her husband. "You're obviously past tired. You can stay in the barn and come in for breakfast in the morning. If you're agreeable, your little girl can bed down in here with us." She smiled at Katie. "Would you like a quick bath before you lay in a comfortable bed?"

"Yes," Kati said after she looked at Mama for guidance. At her mother's nod, she took a timid step forward.

Making his feet move, Franz thought only of collapsing in a safe place. As he closed his eyes, he gave thanks for not being out in the open. Inside the sturdy barn, the ground wasn't as cold and hard and they slept, not having to listen so intently for animals or soldiers coming their way.

"Come with me," Mama said the next morning. Without explanation, she walked to the side of the small barn and knelt. She motioned Franz to come close. Knee-high plants had pushed through the dirt with distinctive tiny buds. Mama held one gently, tears rolling down her cheeks. "Sunflowers! I found them when I came out to the privy," she said. "No matter how bad the winter, they've always promised summer and harvests." Her smile wobbled before it turned genuine. "I needed to see them."

"The lady said something about breakfast, didn't she?" Franz asked, too impatient to talk about flowers. "The others are already inside."

"Oh, Franz," Mama chuckled and swatted at him. "I guess you learned from Opa that sunflowers are a crop, and missed my love of them!" She stood and stretched her back. "Come, let's eat whatever food we can."

They went to the well and used a bar of soap left there to wash their faces and hands. Speeding up, they joined their group in the kitchen.

Franz stopped abruptly, his mind a whirl of doubting what he saw. He must be dreaming, because he thought eggs, bacon, milk, bread and fruit were spread on a large table. Fragrances of bacon and bread mingled, making it real. Mama's eyes were open wide, her mouth gaping. Tony grinned and waved a piece of bread at him. Kati bent over her plate, seriously eating eggs. She held her fork awkwardly, due to the pain in her arms. Lissi and Eva wore silly smiles and scooted over for Franz and his mother to join them.

He swallowed the lump in his throat, but couldn't manage to speak. After weeks of so little food, tears flooded his eyes and rolled down his cheeks.

"Let's take a moment to join hands and pray," Mama said. "Thank you, Father God, for this food and for kind people. You must have a special place in Heaven for them. Guide us the rest of our journey. Amen." They all did the sign of the cross and began eating slowly, savoring each bite.

The farmer hitched two of his horses to the flat bed wagon and Mama and Lissi hugged his wife and thanked her again.

"I'm taking you to the British military compound in the city. They'll get you sorted out."

Sorted out?? Franz glanced at Mama and then Tony. They were turning themselves over to others. Once there, soldiers would decide for them. Again.

Fear flooded his insides. What had they done?

45

May/June 1946, 13 years old
From British Military Compound in Austria to Germany

FRANZ BOWED HIS head and trudged forward, continuing to wrestle between fear of entering the huge gate of the Military compound and the fear of running away. He raised his hand to shield his eyes from the hot sun, and listened to people speaking familiar German and Hungarian. The British spoke in unfamiliar rhythms and words, frustrating Franz by his inability to guess what they said.

Sweating, Franz shed his coat, top shirt and pants.

Two men in brown uniforms, wearing curved canteens on their waists, came toward them. Franz stared at the British flasks. He was so thirsty.

"Line up!" Weird echoes rolled around Franz as guards interpreted the words into German, then Yugoslavian, and another man spoke Hungarian. The gate squealed as it was pushed aside. Franz saw a bombed out building, bricks stacked in piles nearby. Two other buildings appeared to have escaped great destruction. Franz watched as soldiers visited with one another in small groups.

Staying close to his family and Tony's, Franz stretched to look over and around those ahead.

Three British soldiers sat at a desk inside the gate, each one with a stack of materials in front of him. The middle man held a kerchief to his nose. Franz shrugged, assuming they stunk after the last few months.

"Your name?" Franz heard one soldier, a brown-eyed blond, ask the first emigrant. After writing that, he asked date of birth, where they were born and where they came from. Each person was handed two things, but Franz couldn't see what they were. The line moved swiftly as three stepped forward, answered questions and three more moved into place. Franz worked his way to the table.

He answered the same questions, and then looked at his cards. One had his basic information and a lot of empty squares. The second tag simply had his name.

"Come on, go through this chute and get deloused." The soldier with the kerchief led them to another area. Franz expected him to carry a cattle prod, but his voice had the same effect. "Loosen your belts and the top button of your shirts or dresses," he shouted.

Holding their pants with one hand, and a bag or suitcase with the other, they shuffled along. They looked like penguins, going from side to side until they stopped. Franz was amused, remembering when they studied the funny little animals in school.

The first five people in line stood their arms out and feet spread.

Franz and Tony looked at each other and raised their eyebrows. Five men dressed in green camouflage stepped up, a white patch covered with a red cross on their left shoulders. They held tools over two feet long, with four inch needles on one end, and a handle with a plunger on the other. The narrow end was pushed into the evacuees' pants from the back, then from the front. Puff! Puff! White powder shot out the bottoms of pants, then up from loose fitting waists. The plungers were reloaded and inserted in shirt backs, where powder went up through hair and out puffed sleeves.

Studying faces, Franz could see it wasn't painful, which was a relief.

"What is that?" Franz asked two guards speaking to one another in Hungarian.

"DDT," a young, blond officer answered. "I guarantee it'll get rid of any bloodsuckers."

"Oh," Franz blinked in surprise. No more fleas, mites or ticks? "We'd like that."

Franz waited until his turn and stepped forward to stand as the others had. When finished, he saw his mother and they all strolled to one of the tables and benches scattered in the area.

Franz leaned back and watched the process of people moving through the delousing line. He hoped it really worked. Several hours later they were taken to showers, separated by men and women.

"I wish I could stay here for an hour," Franz said to Tony and Hans over the noise of the water. He hummed as he started soaping his head and worked his way down. Then he washed all over again, especially the infected places he'd scratched too much.

"Time's up!" a voice ordered. Reluctantly, Franz stepped out and was handed a towel and underwear along with clean khaki clothes and shoes with wooden soles. His old things were dropped into a nearby trash bin.

All the ladies received khaki slacks, blouse and sturdy shoes, making them look alike.

"Franz!" He turned to find his mother and sister.

"Kati, your hair is blond again," Franz grinned. "I guess you clogged up the drain."

"Your dimples show," Kati laughed and twirled around, flipping her thin, lank hair.

"Mama," Kati put one hand on her hip. "Is the war over now?"

"That's what they say, Liebling." Mama hugged her. "It doesn't feel like it, does it? But it will."

"Attention!" The enthusiastic motion of the officer's arm drew attention. "Follow me for food." He led them to a line along the black, three-story brick wall.

Remembering the breakfast the farmer gave them hours ago, Franz was surprised he was hungry now. But he was.

"It's hotter each minute and there are so many people ahead of us!" Tony groaned after a few minutes. He shook his head.

"We can't stand for long," Franz said. "Or get up and down to move with the line."

As soon as the words were out of his mouth, a woman ahead gently slumped, then fell to the ground. He was thankful it wasn't Mama or Kati and relieved when two soldiers came and took the woman by her shoulders and pulled her out of the way, into shade for a drink.

By the time he reached food, Franz was disappointed to be handed only one canteen lid of boiled beet soup, which held about a half cup, and one slice of white bread.

"This isn't enough food," a man griped.

"Look at the Brits," Mama mumbled. "We're lucky they're sharing. They have so little."

The man opened and closed his mouth like a fish before turning around.

Eating, Franz glanced around. Not one of the British soldiers had much flesh on his bones. Mama was right. He looked at his soup and bread and felt a stirring of thankfulness.

Suddenly one of the British medics jumped on a table with a bang. He cleared his throat and with thickly accented German, began to speak. "With all of Europe on the move, we have to stop outbreaks of contagious diseases. You'll be given a series of vaccinations today and tomorrow. This will protect against typhoid, tetanus, smallpox, cholera, and diphtheria, to name a few." He hesitated and looked around. "They'll be recorded on the Immunization Register you got this morning."

Getting in line, Franz saw four nurses on each side, wearing white hats, gray dresses and white aprons with a large red cross on each bib.

As he moved forward, he received injections on his left arm, and then another from the right. The nurses told him to pull up one sleeve or the other, drop their pants when needed. By evening, it hurt to move, or sit in any position.

"I feel like one of your pincushions," Franz said to his mother. He hated that he sounded like a whining little kid.

"Men, grab your things and go there." A completely bald soldier spoke through a megaphone and pointed to the building to their left. "Women, to your right."

"No," Franz whispered. He studied Mama, her eyebrows drawn together. "We can't be separated."

"Lissi and I will be sure our girls and Eva stay with us," Mama said. "Stick with Hans and Tony. Maybe it's just for tonight," she glanced over her shoulder. "Put your important papers inside your shirt first chance you get," Mama whispered as they moved away from each other. "Protect them from getting lost or stolen."

Scanning, Franz noticed the men's building had dull red bricks, the women tan ones. Then he lost sight of Mama and Kati. He kept Tony in his peripheral vision as he followed the men into a large room laid out like a dormitory. Army cots were lined up in double rows, a number on the end of each bed. It was like one picture over and over again. Cot, space, cot, space. Windows above every other cot. Busy looking around, Franz bumped into Tony, Hans stumbled into him. Franz chuckled and the others did too.

A soldier held up a clip board and began to read names, pointing out assigned places. He told them to attach the tag with their name on it to their bags and shove them under their beds.

"Tony," Franz leaned closer and mouthed. "Get your documentation."

Franz was relieved when he and Tony had beds right next to each other. Darting like a fly, Franz opened his backpack, took out his packet with birth certificate, school records and new passes and stuffed them into his shirt.

Tony did the same before they went back outside to rest and quietly visit.

"More beet soup?" Franz bit his lower lip when they returned to the courtyard that evening. He shook his head to Tony. "When we get through this, I'll never eat any of it again!"

That night Franz fell asleep within minutes of putting his head on a pillow. Waking later, he had to get to the bathroom in the hall. Walking to the light dangling from the ceiling in the lavatory, he used the toilet, and then turned to retrace his steps. The room was really dark. He stood uncertainly, waiting for his eyes to adjust and be able to see. It didn't help much and he was so tired. With his hand on the left he started up the row. How many beds had he passed? He should have counted! When he thought he might be almost there, he felt the end of the mattress, hoping to find his empty bed. Fortunately, everyone slept soundly and no one raised an alarm when he touched feet. An empty bed finally! He reached underneath and felt his backpack. Sighing with relief, he stretched out and dozed until morning.

Oh, how he ached from all the shots. Slowly, he sat. He couldn't push himself up with his arms; it hurt to sit on his backside. He was thirsty and hungry. It helped when others did the same.

He groaned as he thought about more vaccinations scheduled. Then he scolded himself and thought about being able to move out of here and find a place to be home. No, home was Stanisic. Arguing with himself, he tried to picture a place in Germany, where they would be safe and provide food for themselves.

He patted his shirt, and felt the papers still where they belonged. Now to find food. Somewhere.

Again, they were served a watery soup with a few vegetables, but this time, two pieces of bread. How to eat? Franz joined his friends and family and stood beside one of the tables.

"How many shots will we have today?" He held his card up for Hans to see, hoping for an answer. "There are a lot of squares empty. Do you think we'll have them all filled in?"

"Probably. It's what we have to do, I guess." Hans squeezed the table as he lowered himself to the bench, only to be ordered to go back to the wall.

After this, freedom. Franz chanted to himself as he waited in line for more shots. His card was almost filled with little scribbles when he heard screams from the people ahead of him.

"This is bad." Franz felt nauseated. Tony blinked rapidly. Mama closed her eyes and took a calming breath and pulled Kati closer to her.

Beyond sharp intakes of breath and whimpers, there hadn't been strong reactions to the previous inoculations. He looked down at Kati and wished that whatever it was, he could take it for her.

"Open your shirt," the nurse said when it was Franz's turn. Biting his lip, he handed his papers to his mother. The needle was very long. He crawled up on the table, his shirt open and laid still. The nurse jabbed it into his chest bone and kept pushing. Not using skin or muscle, but pure bone. He held the edge of the table and bit his lip. Blood trickled over his chin to his neck.

Finally it was done! Franz hated to move but had to get off the table for the next person. The screams and moans continued until the last person was through. During the night, Franz woke with pain every time he moved.

The next week Franz napped while the rumbling of the train carried them to a camp rumored to be near Graz, Austria. As soon as they stopped, he dropped to the ground and narrowed his eyes and surveyed the area. Barbed wire was stretched all around and a guard walked inside the perimeter. He saw four buildings. Tomorrow he'd find a way out in case they needed to leave.

He was hungry. They were always hungry. On the way to the barracks, they passed a building with a sign identifying it as the Cantina.

"I smell cauliflower. Probably soup again," Franz said to Tony.

"Maybe we'll get more to eat." Tony stumbled when they stepped up to the barrack door. He leaned his head to the wall and sighed.

Every day in the late afternoon a truck delivered bread and Franz and Tony joined the fights and pushed to get the job of unloading. There were always crumbs and the pieces falling off the bread from the blisters on the crust. Franz really wanted to grab some whole loaves, but he'd get caught with all the guards watching.

"Behind the shack for yard tools," Franz nudged his mother one morning. "There's a place in the fence I think I can crawl under. I might find or barter for food in town."

They strolled along the barbed wires, as if chatting about the gentle breeze and cloudy sky.

"The budding trees provide some protection, and you don't have far to go." Mama frowned, looking to the town off in the distance and back to Franz. "I don't want you to go, but we're so hungry and quarreling amongst ourselves." She stretched her arm over his shoulders. "Let's think and pray about it first."

The next morning, his mother gave him some money she'd had hidden away.

"Be very careful," she said.

Staying in the trees lining an unused field, he tried to look like a local boy in town. With a relaxed expression on his face, he bought some dry bacon. Pleased, he turned back to the camp.

He kept alert, but no one seemed to pay attention to him. The next week Franz snuck out and traded goods for food, and feeling comfortable, began to go every other day.

One day as he went past the city hall, he saw a notice about Yugoslavia. Curious, and feeling invisible, he got closer to read. His heart beat faster. *German people who have come from Yugoslavia and have birth certificates to prove it, can register for a quicker transport out to Germany. Applications inside.*

Eager to get home, he hurried to tell his mother.

"Oh, Franz, I'm so tired and they already plan to take us to Germany." Brows furrowed, she sighed. "Maybe we should wait."

"But Mama, we can get there sooner!"

"We have to fill out some forms?" Her soft voice was aimed to the ground.

"Yes," Franz said. "I'll go tomorrow and try to get eight of them." He clamped his mouth shut, determined not to argue.

"Get what we need and we'll see what they look like." Mama's shoulders sagged against the doorway to their dormitory. She turned away and joined Lissi and Kati.

"I can't sleep," Franz said to Tony that night. "Maybe we'll be in Germany soon. I keep having dreams and nightmares."

"Me, too," Tony said.

Franz snuck out in the morning along with Tony. Clouds rolled in, giving cover of darkness to get under the fence and to the trees. Without a hitch, they were given applications, though the clerk who handed them over studied them more than the boys would have liked. Rolling them into two tubes, each slipped one in his shirt, under his arm where they would be safer.

They found a pen and put down information requested, plus their birth certificates. Eva's hand shook, so Lissi wrote hers. All the while, they talked about how thankful they were to have the identifications they needed and how it was due to Franz and Tony getting into their old homes and slipping them out. After taking them to town, the next week was filled with anticipation. Franz thought of little else.

"The waiting is making us crazy," Tony said.

"Every time I see a truck come in the gate, I think it's time." Franz replied.

They sat on thick, green grass and leaned on the dormitory wall, drifting into a light doze.

"All members of the Elmer and Baumgartner group report to the Cantina immediately," a rough voice shouted over the loud speakers. Crackling of the microphone heightened tension.

"It's got to be good!" Franz shook his head, pushing away thoughts of a failure.

Coming together, Franz and Kati held their mother's hands. Franz was afraid to breathe as they entered the building.

"The following names have been qualified to leave for Germany," a man shouted. "Tony Baumgartner, Berbl Baumgartner, Lissi Baumgartner, Eva Baumgartner." The man counted the four, and then looked at his list. "Elisabeth Elmer and her children Franz and Kati." He checked them off. "Hans Becker."

Hans stepped up to join them. More names were being read, but their group moved off to the side and celebrated with hugs and laughter.

"Attention!" the man by the microphone said. "In one hour, be back here to walk to the railroad station in Graz for transport."

"This feels odd," Mama said. "We don't have to hide and sneak across borders!"

Their guide opened the gate and the walk began.

As soon as they arrived in Graz, Franz asked the leader if they had time to trade something for food.

"Listen for the whistle and get back quick." He winked. "You have time to go to your usual store for something." Then his lips turned up and he looked away.

His sneaking out hadn't been so clever. The guards looked the other way!

"Well, what did he say that made you look surprised?" Hans asked.

He chuckled when Franz told him.

"Let's go," Hans moved his hands forward inviting Franz to lead.

They traded some of Lissi's cigarettes for wheat bread bulked up with straw and carrots.

Heading back, they heard the urgent call of the train. Mama stood by a boxcar, her hand over her narrowed eyes, until she saw them and waved. Running, they hopped inside and collapsed on their backs. Franz closed his eyes, far too tired to look around. He had a horrible, sharp pain in his side. With time, he felt better. Then gradually, he became aware of murmured voices and the car's sliding door slammed shut.

"Mama," he whispered as he noticed about twenty-five people sitting around. There was a little straw on the floor and the boards were so hard. "Any food left?"

"I put some in your pocket. Eat slowly. You have nothing to drink."

As the train weaved its way across Austria, at each stop a handful of people took what they had to barter and came back with food. The stations provided water and filthy privies.

The next day Franz and Hans decided to get something to lay on besides the wooden floor with thinly scattered straw. During a late afternoon stop, they took Lissi's tobacco products and razor blades for bargaining power. After hopping off the train it took them a few minutes to venture several blocks to a store to trade for a blanket and six loaves of bread. The train started to move.

"They're only switching to a different track," Hans said.

"No," Franz shouted over his shoulder as he sprinted. "It's going too fast!"

They pushed themselves to get to the last car. People reached their hands down to pull them, and their blanket full of bread, aboard.

Franz rubbed the back of his neck, and then noticed Hans was breathing heavily. Reaching into the blanket, Franz pulled out a chunk of bread and handed half to the older man.

"Not now," Hans mumbled and turned on his side.

"Eat," Franz put a small piece to his older friend's mouth. Little by little, Franz got him to eat, restoring his strength somewhat. The afternoon dragged on and temperatures dropped. The cushioning of the blanket made their bones rest more easily.

"My mother's worrying about me," Franz mumbled. "I wish I could let her know we're in a boxcar behind her."

At the next stop they rewrapped the bread into the new blanket and found their box car. Mama cried and hugged him. Kati hung on to his arm and sniffled. Hans handed out bread and gradually everyone relaxed by the light of a beautiful sunset.

"How close are we?" Franz asked everyone.

"Maybe tonight or tomorrow," Mama said. "I'm dreaming of Augsburg, where I'll see dear Anna. We'll start over again when we get our money from working in Leipzig. She's kept it safe for us."

"Elisabeth!" Lissi hissed. "Look through the crack!"

Franz followed his mother and peeked through the spaces between the wooden slats.

"The sign said Rosenheim is ahead!" Mama hugged Kati and Franz at the same time. "We're in Germany!"

The train slowed. Excitement and fear bubbled in Franz. What would happen next? More camps? Better food? The train came to a full stop. An official stood below with a clipboard, squinting in the sunshine.

Franz handed Kati down to their mother and watched Mama show the man their documents for entry. Franz hopped down and got his papers from his shirt. One by one they all gathered together. As soon as the boxcars were emptied, they heard a simple announcement.

"Welcome to Germany!"

Mama, Lissi and Eva quietly allowed tears to fall. Suddenly Mama chuckled and pointed to their right.

Franz tuned to gaze in the same direction and saw a field of beautiful, young sunflowers, bowing toward them. It was the very best of greetings, the flowers announcing the nightmare winter was over.

Franz shoved his hands in his pockets and gave a wobbly grin to Mama. Then he wondered if she thought of Opa and his sunflower acres. Later, Opa, Oma and Vati would come. They had to.

EPILOGUE

Before Franz and his family left the camp in Austria, Kati's old clothes were peeled from her arms by the Brits, to reveal oozing red rashes and boils. They swathed the little girl's arms, in gauze strips up past her elbows. Medicine (likely a sulfa of some kind) was poured in often and the wrapping left in place. Their mother, Elisabeth, cried when the doctors suggested Kati could lose her arms.

When Kati was deemed well enough to travel, the family was put on a train headed towards Augsburg which is about 28 miles west of Munich. Being on German soil after the war was a mixed blessing. Gone were Opa's home and the acres of farm land in Yugoslavia. Tito had taken it away. That life would never return. Needing refuge, they were housed in several places on their way to Augsburg.

Gradually, bit by bit, the violence of war tiptoed away from them.

As they were relocated, they stopped along the way and were placed into barracks for a couple of weeks. The walls had been white-washed but red stains showed through on many spots. They didn't know until later that they were in Dachau, and had no knowledge of what had happened there, or that it had been a Jewish detention camp. They grieved at learning this and over the useless deaths, though such anguish was not new, for

THE PROMISE OF THE SUNFLOWERS

they also mourned members of their families and friends in Yugoslavia.

Later, they stopped near Hochzoll, where trees were loaded with fruit. Quickly, they hopped over fences and gathered as much as possible. They'd eaten nothing but bread for several days. Never had fresh fruit tasted so good! Then the train took them east and stopped once more. Franz' family was among the group taken off and they said goodbye to close friends they'd been with for months. Tony and his family continued to Bavaria.

Always hungry, everyone suffered malnourishment. Once in a while someone would collapse and pass out. Elisabeth gave most of what food they had to Katie and Franz, which often left her faint.

They disembarked at Griesbeckerzell, a small village of about three-hundred-fifty people. Strangers lined up along the street and yelled horrible names at them. Before, they had been blessed from time to time by people helping them with food and shelter as they traveled, but now they seemed to be hated by all. More people came there, and they were surprised to see old neighbors from Stanisic, Mrs. Behr and her daughter, Eva, who was Franz's age.

The authorities assigned refuges to stay in people's homes that had empty rooms. Franz's family was fortunate to be sent to Mrs. Schmuttermeier's house. Her husband and grown sons were in the war and their fate unknown at that time. Her youngest son, Hans, went to school with Franz.

On August 31, 1946, Franz turned fourteen. He went to school, mornings in seventh grade and afternoons eighth grade, to catch up with where he would have been had there not been a war. Others had to do the same.

Franz' ID photo for school 1947

While in Griesbeckerzell, Franz and his mother went to the Red Cross. They learned that Franz' Uncle Adam died in Copenhagen. Elisabeth mourned the loss of her younger brother. Also, they learned Opa and Oma had been in two camps, escaped, sent back to Yugoslavia, and taken to Austria and were working in a vineyard.

They also learned Franz' father, Stefan, and Uncle Pischti had been prisoners in Russia during the war. Afterward, the Russians released them to Yugoslavia, who in turn sent them to Hungary, under Communist rule. Uncle Pischti married a Hungarian woman and didn't have to register. Stefan attempted escape a few times, but was captured and beaten. There, the trail stopped. With time, he was presumed dead.

Each morning and evening, Elisabeth walked fifty minutes to the train and rode to Augsburg to work for a textile company making fabric for export. In the evenings she returned to her children by the same long process. The Marshall Plan from America came to help rebuild Germany and workers at those export companies received a box every month. The first night Elisabeth brought her package home and opened it, what a sight it was. Things they hadn't seen in years — Chesterfield cigarettes, one lemon, a quarter pound of coffee beans, one big bar of Cadbury chocolate and one bar of coconut oil for cooking, as well as other items. Franz could trade coffee beans for flour and his mother made bread. Soon, it was all about looking for opportunities to bargain for things they needed the most.

Germany had rules about not cutting down trees that were healthy or of a certain size, so he climbed larger pine trees, carrying a small hatchet. He could chop dead branches down for heat and cooking.

The next year they moved to Augsburg, closer to his mother's job and Franz worked at the textile plant as well.

In the earlier days of the war, Elisabeth and Stefan, had worked two long years in Leipzig and saved for a better future. When they escaped back to Yugoslavia with Franz in 1943, they left their wages with Elisabeth's sister, Anna. But when Elisabeth went to Anna's, she received bad news. The money was gone. Anna's husband found the bundle and pocketed it for himself. What a very harsh blow that was!

Looking around at the previously beautiful city of Augsburg, Franz was sickened. The city was ruined. Everywhere bricks had cascaded down. An old man about eighty to ninety years old spent months cleaning them up and putting them in neat stacks to be reused in the renovations the next five or six years. Neighbors worked together to rebuild and take away signs of war. Franz started his apprenticeship at the textile company on September 9, 1947. He also received the same Marshall Plan package as his mother did, providing more food for their small family

The company had openings for three new apprentices every year, so there were always nine in the program. Three boys in first year training, and another group for the second and third sessions. The first year was the roughest. They had to make a part per blueprint that went to inspection. If it was not to specifications, he had to start over. If it passed inspection, it got thrown in the trash.

In Trade School he learned the theoretical part of what he worked on in the shop. As the work became more difficult, so was the Trade School. After three years as an apprentice (which seemed an eternity to a teenage boy!), the Company told the final year students to show up at 7:30 one Monday at a new company, M.A.N., (Maschinen Fabrick Augsburg/ Nurnberg).

About twenty-five nervous students from different companies gathered together. Each was given a small box with the steel cut in different pieces and a blueprint. Within sixteen hours they had to build a small assembly using lathes, mills, welders, drill press, surface grinder and bench work filing and bending.

They were told they would not have their names on the work, only an assigned number so there would be no bias by the instructor. When he finished the part, he had to stamp the number on it immediately.

Franz was nervous. He gave it all he had and on the second day, he finished a little over one hour early. The third day he completed an eight-hour theoretical examination. Then he finished tests in different categories of math, and made a blueprint and answered many questions in an oral examination.

Standing in front of the judges, he felt like a small mouse in front of three lions. They fired questions in quick succession and he was able to answer all of them. After this rigorous testing, he returned to the Textile Company and back to regular work.

It was a long six week wait to learn if he'd passed.

If the test was a fail, he'd have to work one more year as an apprentice with little pay. It could be taken the next year, but failing again would be the end of his chosen trade and he could only work as a machinist helper.

He passed!

With the pressure of apprenticeship finished, Franz joined friends Konrad Eberhard (a year older) and Ervin Wagner (a year younger) in bicycle trips over Germany.

A few years later, he married Gerda Hartman and they immigrated to Canada in 1956, with eighty dollars in his pocket and about 10 English words. Canadian Immigration department sent them to Toronto and, in a few days he got a job as a lathe hand in a large toy manufacturing company, making plastic injection molds for many different toys. After three years he became the Group Lead Man. Toronto was home for five years.

At that time it took seven years of waiting time to get into the US legally, with the limit for German immigrants only about 50,000 per year.

When Russia sent Sputnik into space, it started a race. America needed special trades. Franz, being a tool and die maker, was pushed to the top of the list. His visa came in six weeks, along with a permanent resident green card, allowing him to take a job in Santa Monica, California.

At Winter Engineering, he made parts for aerospace companies and personally made parts for the Surveyor Soft Landing on the moon in '67 or '68. There were seven attempts to land them on the moon. Only three or four were successful. The others crashed. Franz also did additional projects for space shuttles. After a few years with Winter Engineering, he became night foreman with twelve to fifteen people on his crew.

In 1965 he and Gerda were divorced.

In 1966, he was invited to a New Year's Eve party thrown by one of the men on his crew, Alvin Perkins, and his wife, Marcia. With no other plans, Franz decided he would go at the last minute.

Within the hour, he met Janet Rae Swain Campbell, Marcia's sister. He was quickly interested in this classy, southern California woman who was so easy to talk to. She was hesitant to date because her divorce was yet to be finalized, and she had a young son, Jason.

Franz, ever the gentleman, treated her with respect and bought her gifts and invited her to go visit Germany with him.

She wasn't sure about having a relationship at this time. With his sweet, dimpled smile, he said "If you want a fight, you are going to get a fight." She gave up and stopped worrying about taking advantage of him. They were married November 22, 1967, when Jason was four-years-old. They moved to Valencia because it was north of Los Angeles and sort of in the country. Erich Nikolaus was born in 1969. Smog and congestion grew worse and they talked about moving away. Franz had two amazing sons who would grow into successful men. He's very proud of them.

In 1972, on a long July fourth weekend, Franz and Janet drove to Springfield, Missouri and purchased nearby property in Hartville. They loved the land of beautiful meadows, rolling hills and trees.

In 1974 they moved all their material possessions, along with two boys, two cats and one dog — all packed into two trucks. They put a shell on the back of the pickup and made beds from plywood for sleeping along the way. They couldn't find a motel that would take the menagerie of pets! Franz finally had his own 167 acre farm. The California family soon adapted to their remote spot in Missouri.

For a few years Franz worked for Manufacturing Innovations, in Tulsa, as a Master Tool and Die Maker. He worked there during the week and drove home to the farm on weekends. Before long, he started his own business, Elmco Engineering, making parts for a nearby boat manufacturer and branched out to other customers. Janet, his wife, became his number one helper in the shop.

They became involved with their church, made many friends and Hartville became home for their family. Every year, Franz meets a group of men in Canada for a few days of fishing and swapping of tales.

At this writing, Franz continues to raise cows and enjoy their country home.

Life is good.

Kati about 1960

Elisabeth with grandchild
about 1962

WHATEVER HAPPENED TO . . . . . the people in Franz' life and adventures.

Nikolaus Hoger and Theresia Hoger (Opa and Oma): After the war, Franz and his mother were informed by the Red Cross that Opa and Oma had been in several camps, one was Gakova. The grandparents escaped the extermination camp, got to the border and were caught. Badly beaten, they were returned to camp. Opa knew they would die, so they escaped again and succeeded, this time making it to Austria. They worked on a vineyard, and lived in the farmer's cottage. Finally, Oma and Opa were able to join Elisabeth, Franz and Kati in Augsburg, Germany. Opa died in 1965 at age 87. Oma stayed with Elisabeth and died in 1975 at age 83.

Stefan Elmer (Franz' father): Stefan and his brother, Pischti, were in a Russian POW camp. They escaped, but were turned away from Yugoslavia because they were German. Next they were traced to a Hungarian prison, where they escaped again. Franz and his mother had no word for years. Stefan was presumed dead. Later, a woman who had nursed Stefan contacted them. Very likely, Stefan had what we call Post Traumatic Stress Disorder today, shell-shock back then. He died when about 65 years old and was buried in Szged, Hungary.

Elisabeth Hoger Elmer, (Franz'mother): She remarried and lived a happy life with her second husband. She came to Missouri twice to visit with her family and died in 1999 at the age of 87.

Katherina (Kati): traveled to Missouri once with her husband, Helmut Eisenreich, and resides in Augsburg, Germany. She lost her daughter in 2011. She is seventy-five years old and though she continues to have problems with her arms, lives a good life.

Uncle Adam Hoger: After the war, Franz and his mother went to the Red Cross with Adam's name, birthdate and birthplace, only to learn Adam died at the age of twenty-six in Copenhagen, Holland in 1945. He was buried there.

Toni (spelled Tony in the book) Baumgartner: Two years younger than Franz, Toni was his partner in sneaking out of camp at night to get food and supplies. Toni was in the escape group. He later became a bookkeeper for a large grocery chain, after being an apprentice in a bakery. He lives near Augsburg, has two daughters and owns a grocery store. His sister, **Berbl,** never married and lives near Augsburg. After their mother was released from the Russian coal mines, Berbl lived with and cared for her. **Aunt Lissi,** about ninety-three years old, is still alive.

Anton Haut: This mischievous childhood friend ended up in Vienna, Austria with his mother and two sisters. He worked for the Goodyear Rubber Co. In 1967 and 1969 his bad health was attributed to working in the rubber fumes and heavy smoking. He is presumed deceased.

Jani Merkle (cousin in Sombor): He wound up in a labor camp north of Stanisic, in Legin. He died there after learning his mother (Aunt Manci) had perished in the camp in Sombor. Jani died of *seele Selenkrankheit* (soul sickness). His sister, **Dori**, was placed in a convent for her protection and safety. She became a nun but later left the convent and became a teacher.

Stefan Baier: Grew up with his grandparents, and had a way with horses. After the war, he worked in coal mines in south Yugoslavia and wasn't allowed out until 1954 because he was 'sentenced in court'. While there, he learned

Yugoslavian language. Later, he worked as an officer in a Munich bank.

Adam Sujer: Later, he became an Architect and resides in northern Germany.

Hans Schacherl: Years after the war, he became a Master Tool and Die Maker over 250 people at Messerschmitt. He raised a wonderful family and managed soccer teams in Griesbeckerzell for many years. He died in1995 of prostate cancer at 62 years of age.

Koni Eberhard and Erwin Wagner: These friends stayed in Augsburg. Koni died in 2006. Erwin still lives.

Hans (the German P.O.W) and Sep: Both guides leading the escape group to safety in Germany at war's end are presumed dead.

Acknowledgements

I T IS WITH my sincere and heartfelt thanks that I commend Mrs. Diane Gray for all the hard work and many, many hours she has spent in bringing my story to life. I appreciate all her patience with me in the four years we have been working on this project, though some unfortunate circumstances popped up along the way.

I gave Diane the facts of my life and she did all the research into history and descriptions of people, places and things to make it interesting reading. I do so love and appreciate Diane and her husband, Stan, and the love and consideration they have shared with me.

I also want to thank my wife, Janet, for insisting and encouraging me to write my story and share it with my friends, family and especially my grandsons, Adam and Alex Elmer.

69976382R00296

Made in the USA
Columbia, SC
18 August 2019